A SHORT HISTORY OF
CHRISTIAN THOUGHT

A *Short History* of
CHRISTIAN
THOUGHT

Revised and Expanded Edition

Linwood Urban

New York   Oxford
OXFORD UNIVERSITY PRESS
1995

Oxford University Press

Oxford   New York
Athens   Auckland   Bangkok   Bombay
Calcutta   Cape Town   Dar es Salaam   Delhi
Florence   Hong Kong   Istanbul   Karachi
Kuala Lumpur   Madras   Madrid   Melbourne
Mexico City   Nairobi   Paris   Singapore
Taipei   Tokyo   Toronto

and associated companies in
Berlin   Ibadan

Copyright © 1995 by Linwood Urban
Copyright © 1986 by Oxford University Press, Inc.

Published by Oxford University Press, Inc.,
200 Madison Avenue, New York, New York 10016

Oxford is a registered trademark of Oxford University Press

Library of Congress Cataloging-in-Publication Data
Urban, Linwood.
A short history of Christian thought / Linwood Urban.
Rev. and expanded ed.
p. cm.   "The new edition has been enlarged
by the addition of chapters on the Sacraments and on the Church
and the ministry"—Pref.
Includes bibliographical references and index.
ISBN 0–19–509347–X
ISBN 0–19–509348–8 (pbk.)
1. Theology, Doctrinal—History.   I. Title.
BT21.2.U72   1995
230'.09—dc20   94-25731

1 3 5 7 9 8 6 4 2

Printed in the United States of America
on acid-free paper

To Nancy
Companion, guide, and friend

Preface

This new edition has been enlarged by the addition of chapters on the sacraments and on the Church and the ministry. In both chapters I use the same general procedure as in the rest of the book: Beginning with Scripture, the development of thought is traced through the twentieth century. Other changes include alteration of two sections on the Principle of Sufficient Reason in Chapter Six and rewriting the entire Epilogue. In the Epilogue the discussion of feminist theology has been expanded, with a section on the ordination of women and a more extensive examination of the use of gender-inclusive language about God. The treatment of Liberation Theology contained in the original Epilogue has been absorbed into the new chapter on the Church and the ministry, and the discussion of the relationship between Christianity and other religions has been significantly altered.

In preparing this edition, I am especially grateful to Daniel B. Stevick, Professor Emeritus at the Episcopal Divinity School in Cambridge, Massachusetts, who gave welcome and thoughtful advice on the two new chapters, and to my friends in the Conference of Anglican Theologians with whom I discussed the matters treated in the Epilogue. I also wish to express my thanks to Cynthia Read of Oxford University Press, whose help and encouragement are gratefully acknowledged.

Swarthmore College   L.U.
June 1994

Preface to the First Edition

I wrote this book to help my students grasp and be grasped by the power of Christianity. Not only has this venerable religious tradition been the foundation and driving force of Western culture, but it has now become a worldwide phenomenon. Many people who think of themselves as avant-garde look on Christianity as a relic of the past. That it is not is amply demonstrated by its present vitality and continuing growth, particularly in Third World countries. Part of this vitality is the result of Christianity's ability to unfold and develop in the face of new intellectual challenges, while still remaining true to its original perception and conviction that God was present in the life of Jesus of Nazareth. A short account of this intellectual pilgrimage will be presented here.

An intellectual pilgrimage ought to be a journey toward the truth. This should especially characterize Christianity's journey since its seminal vision contains a dedication to truth: "If you continue in my words, . . . you will know the truth, and the truth will make you free," said Jesus in the Gospel of John (John 8:31–32). I hope that this book makes a contribution to freedom founded on truth.

I want to take this opportunity to extend my thanks to my colleagues at Swarthmore College—J. William Frost, Laurence J. Silberstein, and Demaris Wehr—with whom I have discussed many of the issues treated in this book, and in particular to Patrick Henry and Donald Swearer who read parts of the manuscript and made valuable suggestions for its improvement. I also want to thank Oxford University Press, especially Cynthia Read and Joan Bossert; and Ann Blackburn, Patricia Carrera, Christina Devlin, and

Eileen McElrone of Swarthmore College, who helped in the preparation of the manuscript.

Swarthmore College   L.U.
June 1985

Contents

A SHORT HISTORY OF
CHRISTIAN THOUGHT

Introduction

"What do Christians believe and why do they believe it?" This question is constantly raised by students, which is puzzling because Christianity is all around us. Although students experience Christianity firsthand, they often report that, in contrast, after only a brief study they have a better understanding of Buddhism, Hinduism, Judaism, or Islam than of Christianity. Much of the reason for their puzzlement is that their own experience is limited and fragmentary. Denominational differences obscure the unity of Christian belief. Students have difficulty in seeing the whole because, paradoxically, they know the parts too well.

In this study we address this basic question. But how shall we begin? Every great movement is a developing phenomenon. It has an inception or beginning that springs from events in the past, and it has subsequent periods of change and evolution. In short, it has a complex history, and this fact itself is enough to commend a historical approach.

However, an even more fundamental reason for a historical presentation of Christian thought is the particular logic of Christian belief, a logic not found in many world views. In *Religion in the Making*, Alfred North Whitehead remarked that "Christianity . . . has always been a religion seeking a metaphysic, in contrast to Buddhism which is a metaphysic generating a religion."[1] By "metaphysic" Whitehead meant "an account of the fundamental causes and processes of reality" and by "religion" he meant "spiritual transformation" or "blessedness." Although the procedure followed by Christianity might seem to be backward, Whitehead saw it as advantageous.

It is difficult to develop Buddhism, because Buddhism starts with a clear metaphysical notion and with the doctrines which flow from it. Christianity has retained the easy power of development. It starts with a tremendous notion about the world. But this notion is not derived from a metaphysical doctrine, but from our comprehension of the sayings and actions of certain supreme lives. It is the genius of the religion to point at the facts and ask for their systematic interpretation. In the Sermon on the Mount, in the Parables, and in their accounts of Christ, the Gospels exhibit a tremendous fact. The doctrine may, or may not, lie on the surface. But what is primary is the religious fact. The Buddha left a tremendous doctrine. The historical facts about him are subsidiary to the doctrine.[2]

Although Whitehead's contrast is something of an exaggeration, it is in the main true. Christianity drew from its Jewish past an awesome, tremendous conception of God, but its origin as a distinct religion rested in the historical facts of the life, death, and teaching of Jesus of Nazareth and the faith response of the earliest Christian communities. Just as Jews believed that God revealed his righteous will in the historical events surrounding the escape from Egypt, so Christians believed that God was uniquely present in Jesus, that in him the eternal God entered and became part of time in order to bring new life to his creatures.

Let us expand on Whitehead's observation that Christianity has developed systematically. The surrounding culture of the ancient world shaped the development of Christian thought to a considerable extent, in somewhat the same way that the wind at the top of the mountain bends the trees as they grow. However, Christianity also grew by extension of principles that are internal to it, just as an organism's pattern of growth is already contained in its genes. That is, as Christians worked to draw out the meaning of the Good News that "God has visited his people!" (Luke 7:16), the growth was sometimes a matter of deduction, of drawing out the logical implications of a doctrine already held. Jewish expectations of the coming of God's Messiah, or anointed agent, were largely based on the prior conviction that God would save his people in spite of their moral lapses and unfaithfulness. Likewise, belief in creation from nothing arose because of a prior belief in God's almighty power. Any unformed matter present before the creation would be outside of God's complete control and, therefore, inconsistent with unsurpassable power. Moreover, questions concerning predestination were debated largely in terms of whether or not human freedom is inconsistent with the omniscience and omnipotence of God, whether the almighty power of God absorbs and obliterates every other center of power in the universe. These and other implications of central doctrines will be discussed in the body of this study.

A further important path in the development of Christian thought has been the gradual clarification of the presuppositions of Christian faith. Because Christian thinkers have embraced as the central affirmation of the Gospel Paul's claim that "God was in Christ reconciling the world to himself" (2 Cor. 5:19), they have sought to explicate their understanding of the nature of God, God's presence in Christ, and the nature of God's reconciling work. How is it possible for God, the ultimate source of all things, the creator of the universe, to remain God and yet be present in a human being? The doctrines of the Trinity and the Incarnation are the traditional explanations of these ideas. The doctrine of the Incarnation is also the traditional account of the way in which God and humanity are joined in Jesus, and the several theories of the Atonement have provided accounts of God's activity to restore persons to their proper relationship to him. These theories and their presuppositions were only gradually solidified and perfected over several centuries.

In the process of formulating these doctrines, their interrelationships also became clear. Some very early Christians believed that Jesus came only to teach a moral code that could be followed by all people of good will. Their redeemer needed to be only an inspired teacher and not a God made flesh. With no logical reason for an Incarnation, they had no logical reason for a Trinity to explain how an Incarnation was possible.

From this one example, we can see some of the reasoning behind several developments in Christian thought. Variations within Christianity have arisen as believers strove to understand the basis for their central affirmations and as the logical interrelationships between various doctrines became clear. This book will endeavor to explicate these conceptual relationships and explain why Christians came to the conclusions they did.

The best way to chart the historical developments while also making clear the logical relationships between doctrines is to discuss the doctrines in the temporal order in which they were formulated or extensively explored by Christian thinkers. Hence the discussion of the Trinity will precede the treatment of the Incarnation and the Atonement, and all three will precede discussion of arguments for the existence of God and of the nature of Scriptural revelation. While the Trinity and the Incarnation were debated extensively in the third and fourth centuries, arguments for the existence of God did not begin to receive similar exposition until the Middle Ages, and the issues concerning Scripture as well as miracles, not until the eighteenth and nineteenth centuries. Likewise, because inter-faith and feminist issues have been addressed systematically only in our own time, treatment of them will be postponed until the Epilogue. In keeping with this decision, no attempt will be made to adapt quotations from classical sources to sex-neutral language, nor to explore until the Epilogue the use of feminist language in classical doctrine.

An issue-oriented approach allows us to trace the history of each doctrine from its classical formulation to the present, thus avoiding the repetition that is inevitable when the reader must plod through even a select list of topics century by century. Focus on great individual thinkers rather than on central themes or doctrines fosters the same kind of repetition. Furthermore, the idiosyncrasies of each thinker tend to dominate. Augustine's Platonism and Thomas Aquinas' Aristotelianism crowd their Christianity into a corner of the stage. These problems can be avoided by adhering to a thematic approach.

Perhaps some readers will be distressed that there is no discussion of present-day ecologic concerns nor a systematic treatment of Christian ethics and life after death. All of these topics merit extended discussion, but to do them justice a good deal of specialized background would be required. Hence, to include them in this book would vastly expand its scope and length.

Finally, it is worth noting the continuing relevance of the ancient controversies. The issues concerning the nature of Christ still haunt Christian thought, as the controversy over the recent *The Myth of God Incarnate* indicates. The debate between Docetists (those who believed that Jesus was so fully God that he only appeared to be a man) and the Adoptionists (those who believed that Jesus was a man who was adopted as God's Son) are as alive today as they were in the second century, as any serious discussion with college students will reveal. This fact leads us back to consideration of the nature of Christian dialectic. These issues are perennial because Christianity is not preeminently a theory about the relationship between God and his creation, but rather a claim about the saving role of a person whose nature must be understood if his mission is to be grasped. Christianity is not a philosophy that is trying to elucidate its religious implications but, as Whitehead noted, a religion that is continually clarifying its philosophical foundations.

CHAPTER I

Scriptural Sources

Almost 2000 years ago in an obscure part of the Roman Empire, Jesus of Nazareth began to teach and preach of the coming of the Kingdom of God. He gathered a group of disciples who came to believe that he was the promised Savior. They called him "anointed one"—"Messiah" in Hebrew and "Christ" in Greek. Throngs followed him. He was put to death as a political agitator by the Roman Governor of Judea, Pontius Pilate, but his disciples claimed that God raised him from the dead, that he appeared to many persons, and that he continues to be present among his followers when they gather together for prayer and worship. Such are the bare bones of the religious faith that soon spread beyond Judea and Samaria, and that now has the allegiance of about one-fourth the world's population and continues to show a remarkable vitality and capacity for growth.

The advent of Christianity is a historical event, and as such it is shaped by its past. Jesus was born and brought up a Jew. He seems to have been well educated for his time. He used language grounded in the faith of his people and in their sacred literature, which Christians would later call the "Old Testament." The disciples continued to use many of these same ideas and appealed to the same Scriptures to vindicate their developing convictions. From the Jews, then, Christians inherited a book and a set of ideas, the most important of which was the conception of God. The God of Christians, the God whom Jesus of Nazareth called "Father," was and remains the God of the Jews, the God whom they call "Holy One" and "Almighty."

Within a fundamental unity there was considerable diversity.

Certainly not all Jews at the time of Jesus held absolutely the same view of the nature of God, and Jews and Christians then, as today, did not hold identical views. Some of these differences are directly related to disagreements over the contents of the Scriptures. A common misconception is that all Jews in the time of Jesus recognized as sacred all of the books now included in the Old Testament (called by Jews "Tanak"), and that the major difference between Jews and Christians is the Christian addition of a New Testament or New Covenant to the Old. This understanding is incomplete on two grounds. First, the Jews also have supplemented the Tanak. The Talmud has for Jews a status somewhat similar to that of the New Testament for Christians. It was compiled from the teachings of the Rabbis during the first six hundred years of the Christian Era, now often called the Common Era (C.E.). Second, from very early times Jews and Christians have differed substantially in their interpretations of their common Scriptures. These differences of doctrine are partly traceable to the fluid state of beliefs held during the time of Jesus about what constituted Scripture.

The controversy between the two dominant Jewish parties, the Pharisees and the Sadducees, concerning resurrection demonstrates the way that differences in doctrine are related to differing beliefs about the content of Scripture. The Pharisees believed in resurrection but the Sadducees did not; hence, it is not surprising that the Pharisees, and not the Sadducees, accepted as Scripture the books of Daniel and Job, in which especially clear affirmations of life after death are to be found. The debate within Judaism over the list of books that would constitute the Scriptures was not resolved until after the beginning of the Common Era. By 250 B.C.E. the Torah, or the five books of Moses, was considered by all to be a sacred text. By 100 B.C.E. the second traditional division, the Prophets, had acquired a similar status for most Jews. The third division, the Writings, Job and Daniel among them, were still being debated. The present list of Old Testament books includes Daniel and Job and was finally ratified at a meeting of Rabbis at Jamnia in 90 C.E., a time when there was no Sadducaic party left. The Sadducees were centered in the Temple Priesthood; their name was derived from Zadok, High Priest at the time of David. In the 68–70 C.E. war with Rome the Temple was destroyed, and the priestly party disintegrated. It fell to the Pharisees to provide the leadership for continuing Judaism.

Besides the Pharisees and the Sadducees, there were other groups with special understandings of Jewish faith: the Zealots (political revolutionaries), the Essenes (for example, the Qumran community, which produced the Dead Sea Scrolls), the Apocalyptists (teachers of a Last Judgment in which the enemies of God would be destroyed), and the Hellenists (admirers of Greek culture, of whom Philo of Alexandria is a noteworthy example). These groups had sharp differences. Developing Christianity and continuing Judaism both had their roots in this mix of ideas, although in separate lines of descent.

More fundamental than the differences was the conceptual unity that underlay the Jewish parties and also formed the foundation for the development of Christianity as a distinctive religious force. Certainly the Torah (the Law) and the Prophets were revered by all; even more basic, however, is the concept of God and his relationship with the Jewish nation. This unique Jewish concept will be discussed under five headings:

1. God is Lord of all things
2. God made a covenant with Israel
3. God gave Israel the Law
4. God holds Israel to account
5. God has a future for Israel

God Is Lord of All Things

By the year 200 B.C. it had become customary never to pronounce what is God's proper name in Scripture, *Yahweh,* but always to say *Adonai* or *Lord* instead. That this custom was fixed by the year 200 B.C.E. is shown by the Septuagint, the Greek translation of the Hebrew Scriptures, which did not transliterate *Yahweh,* but substituted the Greek word for *Lord, Kyrios,* instead. It is characteristic of Hebrew piety that it came to regard even the mention of God's name as a possible violation of the commandment not to take his name in vain. And it is fitting that *Lord* should have been chosen to stand in place of that name, for "lord" can be taken as the preeminent description of God in the Scriptures. He is God the Lord, Lord of all that is, Lord of heaven and earth, Lord of all supernatural beings, the Lord of all peoples and nations. He is unsurpassed and unsurpassable. The Bible does not proceed deductively from claims about God's lordship to an enumeration of all the kinds of things of which he is Lord. Instead, Scripture develops its claims contextually. Whenever God is compared to any being or power, natural or supernatural, God is invariably said to surpass that being or power. By the time the Old Testament reached its fixed form, monotheism was so thoroughly established that it is hard to find in Scripture the traces of what may well have been an earlier Jewish polytheism. There are a few scattered hints of a belief in many gods. One of the words for *God* is the plural *Elohim*. And Psalm 82 asserts that "God has taken his place in the divine council; in the midst of the gods he holds judgment" (Ps. 82:1), seemingly recognizing the existence of other gods. Even when other gods are mentioned, however, the God of Israel is preeminent. "For the Lord is a great God, and a great King above all gods" (Ps. 95:3). But such passages that allude to other gods are few and far between. More characteristic is Psalm 18:31: "Who is God, but the Lord?"

The Old Testament as a whole and also the Torah are so consistent in the assertion that there is but one God that they misrepresent the religions of other peoples. Since there is no God but God, the idols that other peoples worship are not seen to be images of divine beings, because no such beings could possibly exist. The gods whom other nations worship are equated with the idols of wood and stone carved by the artisans, or else with the hosts of heaven, the stars and planets in their courses. If one's knowledge of "primitive" religions was drawn solely from the Old Testament, one would never realize that for other peoples the idols were but the images of the gods and not the gods themselves—so fixed is monotheism in the religious consciousness of the Torah. So although some have speculated about an earlier Hebrew polytheism, the few passages that might reflect traces of earlier views are so fragmentary that no real picture of premonotheistic Hebrew religion emerges.

By the time the Torah took its fixed form, the uniqueness of God was emphasized as much as his unity and lordship. Unlike the gods of near eastern pantheons, God has no father or mother. He is underived and explicitly proclaimed as eternal. He is one and his glory is unique. "Hear, O Israel: the Lord is our God, the Lord alone" (Deut. 6:4).

That there is nothing that has power over God is also central in biblical accounts of the creation. This conviction is apparent in the usual interpretation of the first chapter of Genesis, that God created the world out of nothing. Before God created the world there was only a void, an emptiness. Here, God's power over all things is clearly affirmed, but it is also affirmed in an alternative interpretation in which creation out of nothing is denied. A different reading of the first verse of Genesis suggests the possibility of matter that exists before the creation. "When God began to create the heavens and the earth, the earth was without form and void" is just as faithful to the Hebrew as the familiar "In the beginning God created the heavens and the earth" (Gen. 1:1). Evidence that Hebrew religious sensibilities did not find objectionable the notion of God forming the universe from preexistent stuff is the fact that in at least two places the God of Israel is said to have slain the monster Rahab (Ps. 89:10; Isa. 51:9). Rahab is one of the names of the great serpent of the deep, also called Tiamat or Leviathan, whose slain body figures in the Babylonian creation myth as the foundation for the creation of the natural world. The Babylonian chronicle differs in that there a great battle takes place between the god and Rahab; in the Hebrew Scriptures, there is no battle. Rahab exhibits no power to engage in a cosmic struggle. In chapter 1 of Genesis, there is only "the deep," a formless existent.

God transcends the universe in other ways. The universe is not a part of God as it is in pantheism. The universe is his creation, his artifact. The earth is his footstool (Isa. 66:1) and not his body. The wind and storm are not the energy or power of God as they are in some ancient traditions, but the works of his hands. "The heavens are telling the glory of God" (Ps. 19:1), but they are not his glory. The whole of the natural order is desacralized and made God's instrument.

Furthermore, God is not under the power of any impersonal or natural necessity. There is no external necessity, no fate, no providence to which he is subject. He is the ruler as well as the maker of all things. Within his being, his mind or consciousness is supreme. His wisdom and will are not controlled, but controlling. "It is he who made the earth by his power, who established the world by his wisdom, and by his understanding stretched out the heavens" (Jer. 51:15). Even the Law has no power over his will and wisdom. He is the giver of the Law and not the servant of a Law that is independent of the divine maker, as in the ancient Greek tradition reflected in Plato's *Timaeus*. To be sure, "the ordinances of the Lord are true, and righteous altogether" (Ps. 19:9), but that righteousness is God's righteousness and not the righteousness of an external standard.

Thus God is utterly unique. "Great is the Lord, and greatly to be praised, and his greatness is unsearchable" (Ps. 145:3). The heaven and earth cannot contain him. He is "majestic in holiness, terrible in glorious deeds, doing wonders" (Exod. 15:11). Isaiah's vision in the Temple convinced him not only of the glory of God but also of his own unworthiness (Isa. 6:1–8). "God's holiness is the absolute glory of His Being which is so completely different that man cannot stand before it."[1] The New Testament emphasizes this aspect of the biblical conception when it speaks of "the unapproachable light" in which God dwells (1 Tim. 6:16).

God Made a Covenant with Israel

Next to the "sovereignty of God," the most important concept in the Hebrew Scriptures is that of covenant. A covenant is a solemn binding compact initiated by God, in which God promises aid and protection to an individual or nation and the individual or nation undertakes to serve God in return. The Torah is filled with covenants. God made covenants with Noah, Abraham, and Jacob, and preeminently with the Children of Israel at Mount Sinai. Although these covenants impose obligations on God as well as on individuals and nations, they never take the form of pacts between equals. It is Almighty God who initiates the relationship. "Behold, to the Lord your God belong heaven and the heaven of heavens, the earth with all that is in it; yet the Lord set his heart in love upon your fathers and chose their descendants after them, you above all peoples, as at this day" (Deut. 10:14–15). "You are the sons of the Lord your God . . . For . . . the Lord has chosen you to be a people for his own possession, out of all the peoples that are on the face of the earth" (Deut. 14:1–2).

The offering of a covenant is, then, an act of sheer graciousness and love on the part of the Lord of lords and God of gods. The covenant relationship that God establishes is most clearly fixed in Israel's religious consciousness by the Exodus from Egypt and by the giving of the Law. Each of these two events is crucial for Hebrew religion and Jewish self-identity.

From very early times, and certainly in the Torah as we have it, the Exodus is taken as the conclusive evidence of God's action and God's favor. Modern historical scholarship has raised many questions about the details of the biblical account, and some interpreters doubt that such an event occurred at all; but the escape from Egypt is historically plausible, although perhaps not on the scale of the biblical story as it stands. We are dealing with what in literary and cultural terms is called saga and, as Martin Buber has said, "even if it is impossible to reconstitute the course of events themselves, it is nevertheless possible to recover much of the manner in which the participating people experienced those events. . . . The meeting of a people with events so enormous that it cannot ascribe them to its own plans and their realisation, but must perceive in them deeds performed by heavenly powers, is of the genuine substance of history. In so far as the saga begins near the event, it is the outcome and record of this meeting."[2]

The Exodus event and its meaning constitute the foundation of the Jewish nation. It is often cited as the decisive revelation of God's power and intention to intervene in history, and of God's righteousness and goodness. It is also described as the bringing of the Jewish people to full consciousness of their obligation to respond in gratitude and loving service to God's beneficence. In short, it is the paradigm covenant event.

If Genesis were our only source for understanding God's relationship with human beings, we would conclude that God appears to individuals in dreams as he did to Jacob, that he sometimes appears in visions as to Abraham at the oaks at Mamre, and that very occasionally he intervenes in human affairs by exercising control over the natural world, as in the Flood, and the destruction of Sodom and Gomorrah. These interventions seem the exception rather than the rule. God specifically promises not to use a flood again to punish the unrighteous, and the destruction of Sodom is a single manifestation of power in a story whose main focus is the life of Abraham. In the Book of Exodus, God's active power in history moves to center stage. The number and catastrophic character of the plagues visited on the Egyptians, and the recalcitrance of the Pharaoh, dramatize the conviction that God will go to any lengths to win his purpose. The Exodus focuses and makes central, rather than originates, the conviction that subsequently dominates the prophetic literature—that God acts in history.

In rescuing the Children of Israel from Egypt, God acts on behalf of those who are oppressed and in bondage. "We were Pharaoh's slaves in Egypt; and the Lord brought us out of Egypt with a mighty hand . . . that he might bring us in and give us the land which he swore to give to our fathers" (Deut. 6:21, 23). Nowhere in the Hebrew Scriptures is there a more vivid affirmation of God's active righteousness.

Because God has shown his love to Israel, Israel is obligated to reciprocate by keeping the commandments.

> Then take heed lest you forget the Lord, who brought you out of the land of Egypt, out of the house of bondage. You shall fear the Lord your God; you shall serve him, and swear by his name . . . And it will be righteousness for us, if we are careful to do all this commandment before the Lord our God, as he has commanded us. [Deut. 6:12–13, 25]

Out of love and mercy God has saved Israel and made it a Holy nation. Out of gratitude and loving thanksgiving springs Israel's special duty to the almighty Creator and Redeemer.

God Gave Israel the Law

The gift of the Law to Moses at Mount Sinai is an integral part of the Exodus story. Pious Jews have always understood the Law to be a manifestation of God's love for Israel. That the Law is not a burden, but a means of liberation and a source of joy is expressed in Psalm 119.

> I will keep thy law continually,
>   for ever and ever;
> and I shall walk at liberty,
>   for I have sought thy precepts.
> I will also speak of thy testimonies before kings,
>   and shall not be put to shame;

> for I find my delight in thy commandments,
>   which I love. [44–47]

The Law provides the boundaries and signposts on the way to redemption. The spirit of thanksgiving and rejoicing in the gift of the Law is caught in Psalm 19.

> The law of the Lord is perfect,
>   reviving the soul;
> the testimony of the Lord is sure,
>   making wise the simple;
> the precepts of the Lord are right,
>   rejoicing the heart;
> the commandment of the Lord is pure,
>   enlightening the eyes. [7–8]

Paul's attitude to the Law is very different, and we discuss his views below. For the moment, however, we note the gratitude of the faithful Jew for God's generosity as shown in the rescue from Egypt and the gift of the Law. "Know therefore that the Lord your God is God, the faithful God who keeps covenant and steadfast love with those who love him and keep his commandments" (Deut. 7:9).

The Law is God's gift, but it is not a product of God's will alone. His wisdom and justice also play a part. "The ordinances of the Lord are true, and righteous altogether," continues Psalm 19. There are indeed a few passages in which God's will seems the absolute and unbridled authority, especially Exodus 33:19: "I will be gracious to whom I will be gracious, and will show mercy on whom I will show mercy." Here God seems to be arbitrary and capricious. Yet, in the end, Hebrew religion refused to raise God's will above his justice. One of the last books to be accepted into the canon (i.e., formally approved list) of the Old Testament, the Book of Job, makes this a major theme in its exploration of the problem of evil. Job is quoted only once in the New Testament and then only in the Epistles of Paul (Job 41:11; Rom. 11:35). Paul quotes Job because, like Job, he explains God's apparent injustice by affirming that God's wisdom and righteousness are past human understanding. Paul's "O the depths of the riches and wisdom and knowledge of God! How unsearchable are his judgments and how inscrutable his ways!" (Rom. 11:33) echoes Job's "Can you find out the deep things of God? Can you find out the limit of the Almighty?" (Job 11:7). The fact that both Job and Paul defend God's righteousness by asserting our human inability to plumb the depths of his wisdom, is but one indication of the congruence between first century Christianity and Judaism, although in other areas profound differences also developed.

God Holds Israel to Account

God has chosen Israel to be his special people, but that fact does not exempt them from his justice. Nowhere is this more clearly expressed than in the oracles of the prophets. Time and time again they speak of God's judgment on Israel for its failure to fulfill the Covenant. This day of judgment is called the "Day of the Lord" and is described as a day when God will "destroy them with double destruction" (Jer. 17:18).

The prophetic denunciations are often bitter. An example is the prophet Amos (eighth century B.C.E.). He sets a context for his denunciation of Israel by first castigating some of Israel's neighbors for their terrible cruelty and brutality in war. "For three transgressions of the Ammonites, and for four, I will not revoke the punishment; because they have ripped up women with child in Gilead, that they might enlarge their border" (Amos 1:13). "For three transgressions of Gaza, and for four, I will not revoke the punishment; because they carried into exile a whole people to deliver them up to Edom" (Amos 1:6). There has seldom been a more forceful and compelling condemnation of the brutality and excesses of war. When Amos turns to Israel, however, it is crimes of social injustice that are singled out. "They sell the righteous for silver, and the needy for a pair of shoes—they that trample the head of the poor into the dust of the earth, and turn aside the way of the afflicted" (Amos 2:6–7). They "deal deceitfully with false balances . . . and sell the refuse of the wheat" (Amos 8:5–6). These sins of greed and avarice are so heinous that Amos adds: "The Lord has sworn by the pride of Jacob: 'Surely I will never forget any of their deeds'" (Amos 8:7).

Besides crimes of war and of social injustice, the prophets also condemn idolatry—worship of physical objects as gods, and sacrilege—profanation of the places dedicated to the worship of God (Jer. 19:4, 32:34; Amos 2:7–8). Philosophers of later times have drawn a sharp distinction between religious and moral duties—duties toward God and duties to human beings. But Scripture does not. The Law in its totality is a gift from God; failure to fulfill its moral injunctions is failure in the religious duty to obey the precepts of the Torah with a loving and thankful heart. The Torah is a web. To break one strand is to break the whole.

God's day of judgment, the "Day of the Lord," is variously conceived. Amos speaks of a day in which the Lord will "make the sun go down at noon, and darken the earth in broad daylight," a day in which "the land [will] tremble on this account, and everyone mourn who dwells in it" (Amos 8:9, 8). His near contemporary Isaiah sees it as a military defeat. "Your choicest valleys were full of chariots, and the horsemen took their stand at the gates" (Isa. 22:7). But whatever the specific means of judgment, it will be a terrible destruction and one from which there will be no escape.

Clearly, God's judgment is seen to be in tension with his love for Israel. Over and over again the prophets preface their condemnations with expressions of God's love for his people. Hosea expresses this theme with special poignancy. "When Israel was a child, I loved him, and out of Egypt I called my son" (Hos. 11:1). Amos similarly stresses God's love for his people. "Hear this word that the Lord has spoken against you, O people of Israel, against the whole family which I brought up out of the land of Egypt: 'You only have I known of all the families of the earth; therefore, I will punish you for all your iniquities'" (Amos 3:1–2).

Moreover, the prophets never tire of teaching God's willingness to forgive the penitent. "Though your sins are like scarlet, they shall be as white as snow" (Isa. 1:18). A penitent and reformed Israel can look forward to a renewal of its relationship with God. "The Lord will have compassion on Jacob and will again choose Israel" (Isa. 14:1). The analogy between God's punishment of Israel and a loving parent's punishment of a wayward child never left Hebrew religious consciousness, but it finally seemed not to express fully God's love for the human race.

Reconciling God's justice with his love will continue to occupy the theological and pastoral attention of Judaism and Christianity. We shall return to this theme often. It runs like a thread through our entire story and provides both the springboard for Jewish hope for the Messiah and a starting point for Christian theories of the person and work of Jesus Christ.

God Has a Future for Israel

In the Hebrew Scriptures there is a strong theme of hope for the future. This hope is based not only on faith in God's love, which will never be extinguished in spite of human backsliding, but also on faith in God's almighty power, so clearly expressed in the Book of Isaiah's teaching about God's control over nature and history (Isa. 40:9–17). This theme is carried further in the apocalyptic literature, works that claim to be visionary revelations of future events and that comprise some of the latest Jewish writing before the New Testament period. These writings of unknown authorship recount visions of a supernatural being called "Son of Man," who is variously described. In the Book of Enoch, he is pictured as standing before the throne of God and judging the nations.[3] In 2 Esdras (also known as 4 Ezra), he is described as the leader of the forces of righteousness against the forces of darkness in a final battle at the end of the world (2 Esd. 13). Why did this literature arise? What challenges was it attempting to meet? These questions are difficult to answer because we do not have as much data as we would like. Although we know that this literature traveled widely, the only full-scale apocalypses included in the Bible are the Book of Daniel in the Old Testament and the Book of the Revelation in the New Testament.

To begin to answer these questions we need to remember the dynamics of doctrinal development already discussed. The Bible does not present a definition of "God" from which conclusions are then drawn. Instead, theological reflection proceeds dialectically. Confronted with a power that might rival God's power, the Prophets sought to show that God is the more powerful. The apocalyptic hopes seem to have sprung up in a similar way. Israel's military defeat and subsequent vassal status challenged Israel's faith in the power of God to fulfill his purposes. King David's kingdom, triumphantly established about 1000 B.C.E., had been divided into two kingdoms after the death of his son Solomon. Israel, the northern kingdom, was subjugated by the powerful state of Assyria in 722 B.C.E. Judah, the southern kingdom, was defeated by Babylon in 597 and many Israelites were carried into exile in 586 B.C.E. The defeat and exile in Babylon were followed by a return of some from exile and partial restoration of the Jewish state under the leadership of Ezra and Nehemiah (c. 450 B.C.E.). There followed a period of subjugation to Alexander the Great's successors, the Ptolemys of Egypt and the Seleucids of Syria (323–168 B.C.E.). Under the Seleucids the Jews' freedom to practice their religion did not go unchallenged. The brief period of the Maccabean Kings (168–63 B.C.E.) rekindled hopes that the Kingdom of David had been reestablished, that the bond of unity between a faithful people and God had been restored, and that the people of God would continue to be free. But the Roman general, Pompey, conquered Jerusalem in 63 B.C.E., and Rome took effective control of the country.

In this time of crisis, when powerful and opposing forces faced each other, many Jews gave up their faith in God's rule over history and deserted the religion of their fathers. But others developed creative new concepts. Confronted by their faith in God as the all-powerful creator and ruler of history who had set his love on Israel, and the empirical fact of Israel's subjugation, faithful Jews concluded that God could not allow the forces of injustice and oppression to have the last word. They became convinced that he would vindicate his justice by sending an Anointed One, a Messiah, who would both bring Israel back into the way of the Lord and reestablish the kingdom.

The messianic hope took two principal forms in the period before the birth of Jesus. Some looked for an earthly king, a second David, a king who would also have some of the qualities of Moses—an impartial judge as well as military leader. Others looked for the coming of a supernatural person to establish the reign of peace and justice. The symbol of this hope was the concept Son of Man.

The Son of David

The prophet Jeremiah clearly expects a second David.

> Behold, the days are coming, says the Lord, when I will raise up for David a righteous Branch, and he shall reign as king and deal wisely, and shall execute justice and righteousness in the land. In his days Judah will be saved, and Israel will dwell securely. And

this is the name by which he will be called: "The Lord is our righteousness." [Jer. 23:5–6]

This vision exercised a powerful influence during the first century C.E. The party of the Zealots, whose settled policy was the expulsion of Rome from the land of Israel, certainly looked for this type of Messiah, and indeed more than one individual declared himself to be the messianic King. The Acts of the Apostles in the New Testament speaks of four such messiahs, one of whom is also mentioned by Josephus, a Jewish historian of the first century C.E. Herod Agrippa II, great grandson of the Herod who is mentioned in the birth stories of Jesus, claimed a messianic role for himself, as did Bar Kochba, the leader of the Jewish revolt against Rome in 135 C.E. It is clear that this concept of the Messiah, which has had the greatest appeal to continuing Judaism, had considerable currency at the time of Jesus.

There is a very strong New Testament tradition that Jesus repudiated this role for himself. The Gospel of John, after telling the story of the feeding of the five thousand, says, "Perceiving then that they were about to come and take him by force to make him king, Jesus withdrew again to the mountain by himself" (John 6:15). And in the trial scene in the same Gospel, Jesus denies that he is the kind of Messiah the Zealots expected: "My kingship is not of this world" (John 18:36). This tradition could underlie the decision of the Christian community at Jerusalem not to join their fellow Jews in the war against Rome in 68 C.E., a decision which provoked the Christians' expulsion from Jerusalem and resulted in their move to the gentile city of Pella, whose ruins lie close to modern Amman in Jordan. The separation of Christianity from Judaism resulted from many factors, but primarily from the rapid increase in the number of gentile converts after the Jewish war with Rome. In this, a fundamental difference in the conceptions of the messianic kingdom played a critical role.

The Heavenly Son of Man

The heavenly Son of Man is portrayed in the Book of Daniel:

> I saw in the night visions,
> and behold, with the clouds of heaven
> there came one like a Son of Man,

and he came to the Ancient of Days
and was presented before him.
And to him was given dominion
and glory and kingdom,
that all peoples, nations, and languages
should serve him;
his dominion is an everlasting dominion,
which shall not pass away,
and his kingdom one
that shall not be destroyed. [7:13-14]

This powerful image captured human imagination, although "Son of Man" seems not to have been a unified concept, but rather a picture variously interpreted and variously fleshed out. We have already seen that in Enoch, Son of Man is the arbiter at the last judgment and in 2 Esdras, a military leader in the final conquest of evil by good. This same looseness seems to have intensified in New Testament times. By the time the Gospels were written, the phrase Son of Man had become merely a general messianic title, one not necessarily referring to a supernatural being. Matthew, Mark, and Luke all use it as a synonym for "Christ." In Mark (8:27-33), for example, after Peter acknowledges Jesus as the Christ, Jesus implicitly approves Peter's confession by immediately using Son of Man with reference to himself in such a way that there can be little doubt that Mark sees the two terms as interchangeable. There are, to be sure, passages in which Jesus seems to some interpreters of the New Testament to speak of the coming Son of Man as a person distinct from himself. "For whoever is ashamed of me and of my words in this adulterous and sinful generation, of him will the Son of man also be ashamed, when he comes in the glory of his Father with the holy angels" (Mark 8:38; Luke 12:9). Later we shall return to the issue of Jesus' conception of himself; for now, we note that early Christianity as expressed in the Synoptic Gospels clearly draws on the Son of Man imagery, which can be traced back to the Book of Daniel, while Rabbinic writings show that such notions had little impact on continuing Judaism. The canonical status of Daniel was not yet secure at the time of the writing of the Gospels, for Daniel is not cited in discussions between Pharisees and Sadducees concerning the resurrection; and Christian Bibles place Daniel among the Prophets whereas Jewish Bibles place it among the Writings. Because of their differing views of Scripture, the Christians took Son of Man to be a messianic title while the Pharisees did not.

One might conclude that in Judaism the Messiah is always seen as a man to be chosen by God and anointed as a political leader. Even when the Messiah is compared to Moses, perhaps on the basis of God's statement to Moses, "I will raise up for them a prophet like you" (Deut. 18:18), it is Moses' qualities as a leader in battle and as a judge that are singled out. However, there is yet another tradition about the Messiah. The Jewish commentary Genesis Rabbah speaks of three things as having been created before the creation of the world. One of them is "the name of the Messiah," which in the context does not refer to a concept or idea of Messiah but to a real, though incorporeal, being.[4] Likewise, the Book of Enoch contains almost the same words about "the name of the Son of Man."[5] Hence, in addition to the heavenly Son of Man tradition, there are indications of pre-Christian Jewish speculation about a Messiah who exists with God before he enters the world as a savior. However, these notions had a far more lasting influence on Christians than on Jews.

Into this ferment of ideas came Jesus preaching the Good News (Gospel) of the Messianic Age—the Good News that the Kingdom of God was not just near at hand but already here. Something had happened—a major event had taken place—the promises of God were now made real and actual.

The Gospel of Thomas

Until recent decades all discussions of the life of Jesus of Nazareth began with the New Testament. However, the discovery in 1945 of the Gospel of Thomas in the Gnostic library at Nag Hamadi in Egypt, raised questions about this reliance on the New Testament as the premier source for the origins of Christianity. The Gospel of Thomas purports to contain the secret teachings of Jesus as preserved by one of the Apostles, Judas Thomas, who, it was also claimed, was the twin brother of Jesus. Some scholars propose that some of the sayings attributed to Jesus in this Gospel are more authentic than many of those attributed to Jesus in the New Testament. If this is true, the Gospel of Thomas must be at least on a par with, if not

superior to, the New Testament as a source for the teachings of
Jesus.

The status of the Gospel of Thomas continues to be hotly debated. Scholars are almost universally agreed, however, that there
was a document, or an oral tradition, of the sayings of Jesus which
was known to Matthew and Luke but unknown to Mark. There is
a considerable amount of material that is common to Matthew,
Mark, and Luke; hence, the term "synoptic," meaning "like-view" or
"similar-perspective," is used to designate these three Gospels. The
usual explanation for this overlap is that Matthew and Luke both
relied on Mark as their primary source. But there is other material,
common to Matthew and Luke, which is not found in Mark. This
body of material has been designated "Q" (from the German *Quelle*,
meaning "source"). Passages in the Gospel of Thomas are close to Q
in both content and style, and some analysts suggest that Thomas
may reflect a more primitive form of Q than that which has been
extracted from Matthew and Luke.

This thesis, that the Gospel of Thomas is a witness to the life and
ministry of Jesus as venerable as the New Testament itself, is challenging, but we must distinguish between a modest and a robust
form of it. The claim that some of the material in the Gospel of
Thomas is at least as old as Q is a modest one, but one which adds
nothing to the picture of Jesus found in the canonical Gospels. This
modest claim implies no negative judgment on material not found
in Q. But the Gospel of Thomas itself contains a much more robust
claim—namely, that it records a secret tradition of Jesus' teachings,
teachings not found in the public tradition of the Synoptic Gospels.
This claim to a secret tradition is the distinguishing characteristic of
Gnosticism (from the Greek word for "knowledge" or "enlightenment"). Gnostics taught that salvation came only through the knowledge that they alone possessed. The Gospel of Thomas makes the
full Gnostic assertion that Jesus entrusted a secret Gospel to only a
few of his disciples, and that this, his real message, concerned the
progress of the soul to a mystical enlightenment and a liberation
available to only a few. According to the Gnostics, the purpose of
the public ministry was only preliminary—to attract the multitude so
that the few could be extracted from it.

Do we have reason to suppose that this is the true picture of Jesus?
The intellectual leaders of the early Church did not think so. They

expressly rejected Gnostic claims. Irenaeus, Bishop of Lyons in Gaul, writing about 185 c.e., proposed the view that came to be generally accepted. He argued that the bishops, as disciples and successors of the Apostles, were in the best position to validate the teaching of the Apostles. That teaching, he argued, is best represented in the four New Testament Gospels. The bishops did not know and the Gospels did not say anything about the secret teachings of this Gnostic Jesus; and so, Irenaeus argued, the public tradition about Jesus, which the Gnostics considered a trap, is the guarantee of the truth.

The Gnostic claim cannot be directly verified or falsified from the public tradition, since by the Gnostics' definition the public tradition is defective. However, Gnostic claims can be called into question from the inside. Gnostics claimed to a knowledge of Jesus and his mission which no one else possessed. Yet Gnostics radically disagreed among themselves, particularly over the extent of Jesus' knowledge and his mission. Was Jesus omniscient? Was he a heavenly being who appeared to be a man, or was he only a man, but one possessing special religious talents? One would expect the Gnostics to have special knowledge on these issues, yet they debated them as much as other Christians did.

These are complex problems and a fuller discussion of them is reserved for Chapter III, "The Mystery of the Incarnation." The argument thus far, however, serves to justify the traditional starting point for a discussion of the life and ministry of Jesus, namely, the New Testament Gospels of Matthew, Mark, and Luke.

The New Testament is a complex document in that it is composed of many different types of writing. It contains four versions of the life of Jesus (the four Gospels), an account of the expansion of Christianity in its very early period (The Acts of the Apostles), a group of letters (Epistles), and finally an account of a disciple's visions (The Revelation to John). Although these works have much in common, they also have differences that sometimes reflect patterns of thought drawn from different intellectual heritages. To separate the central from the peripheral, and to bring out the inner coherence of this material, has always been one of the central tasks of Christian thought.

The Picture of Jesus in the Synoptic Gospels

There is a good deal of common material in the Gospels of Matthew, Mark, and Luke, but the pictures they present of Jesus are by no means identical. The central theme of all three Gospels is that Jesus came to proclaim the coming of a new age in which God's rule over all things would be reestablished, and moreover, that he was the agent by which this new Kingdom of God (Kingdom of Heaven in Matthew) would become a reality. In this the Gospels echo the words of Paul, "God was in Christ reconciling the world to himself" (2 Cor. 5:19). However, each of the three Gospels describes the kingdom and Jesus' agency in a particular way.

The Picture in Q

To begin with Q is not to assign it a special priority. It seems incontestable that Q was a real source. The contents of Q can be decided with reasonable probability, though their order is more problematic. Still more uncertain is whether all, or even a substantial part, of Q has been preserved, and whether it predates Mark significantly. Q preserves a sayings tradition not found in Mark, but its assessment of the person and work of Jesus is not strikingly different from that found in Mark.[6]

In Q Jesus proclaims not only the nearness of the kingdom—"The Kingdom of God has come near to you" (Luke 10:9; Matt. 10:7)—but also that the Kingdom of God is present in Christ's power and work. Q sees as evidence for this claim Jesus' power over demons and the forces of darkness of this world. Scribes and Pharisees, when confronted with Jesus' ability to cast out demons, accuse him of being in league with Beelzebub, the prince of the devils. Jesus denies that he works by the power of evil. "Every kingdom divided against itself is laid waste, and a divided household falls. And if Satan also is divided against himself, how will his kingdom stand? . . . But if it is by the finger of God that I cast out demons, then the kingdom of God has come upon you" (Luke 11:17–21).

Q identifies Jesus as the agent of the kingdom, but does it explicitly identify Jesus as the Son of Man as described in Daniel? In Q Jesus speaks of himself in his ministry as Son of Man. "Foxes have holes, and the birds of the air have nests; but the Son of man has nowhere to lay his head" (Luke 9:58; Matt. 8:20). Jesus also speaks of the Son of Man as one who is to come in the future.

> The days are coming when you will desire to see one of the days of the Son of man, and you will not see it. . . . For as the lightning flashes and lights up the sky from one side to the other, so will the Son of man be in his day. [Luke 17:22, 24; Matt. 24:27]

These passages are confusing because the second suggests that the Son of Man is a different person from Jesus. However, there is another passage in Q in which Jesus implicitly identifies himself with the Son of Man. Speaking to James and John, he says:

> You are those who have continued with me in my trials; and I assign to you, as my Father assigned to me, a kingdom, that you may eat and drink at my table in my kingdom, and sit on thrones judging the twelve tribes of Israel. [Luke 22:28–30; Matt. 19:28]

The background for this statement is the image of the Son of Man in the apocalyptic literature, in particular the Book of Daniel, where the Son of Man is given "dominion and glory and kingdom, that all peoples, nations, and languages should serve him; his dominion is an everlasting dominion, which shall not pass away, and his kingdom one that shall not be destroyed" (Dan. 7:14). Daniel goes on to suggest that this dominion will be shared with "the saints of the Most High" (7:27). In Q Jesus claims explicitly that he will rule in heaven, thus implicitly identifying himself with the Son of Man of the apocalyptic tradition. However, if the Son of Man is as fluid an image as it seems to be, then we cannot, on the basis of this passage alone, conclude that Jesus also claimed that he was a preexistent being, chosen and hidden with God before the creation of the world, as is said of the Son of Man in the Book of Enoch.[7] As we shall see, Paul and John make this claim about Jesus, but it is not clearly substantiated by Q.

Q also contains moral and ethical instruction, including some of the most familiar parts of the Sermon on the Mount (Matt., chaps. 5–7). This famous passage is a collection of Jesus' teachings which is said to have been delivered on a mountainside. Many people have regarded it as the core of his teachings. Here Jesus makes the standards of discipleship high, demanding personal sacrifice and exemplary behavior towards others. "Love your enemies, and do good, and lend, expecting nothing in return; and your reward will be great, and you will be sons of the Most High; for he is kind to the ungrateful and the selfish. Be merciful, even as your Father is merciful" (Luke 6:35–36; Matt. 5:44–48).

Q contains prayers of Jesus, which use a form of address also present in the non-Q material of all four Gospels. Jesus, like the contemporary synagogue prayers preserved for us in Jewish sources, addresses God as "our Father." Some of the prayers of Jesus, however, address God as "my Father" (Matt. 26:39) and others, very strikingly, by the familiar form of address "Abba" (Mark 14:36). This linguistic clue provides a glimpse into the intimacy of Jesus' relationship with God.[8] Indeed all four Gospels present Jesus as being dominated by this sense of the presence of God.

Thus we find in Q the outline of the New Testament thinking about Jesus. He is the agent of the kingdom, which is both a present and a future reality. The kingdom is also both an external and an internal reality, defeating the powers of darkness which lie outside the human soul, and freeing individual souls from demonic possession and from excessive preoccupation with the self in egoism and narcissism.

The Picture in Mark

The central message of Mark is that Jesus is both Son of God with power and Son of Man, so the picture of Jesus in this Gospel is not strikingly different from the one in Q. However, Mark makes explicit what remains implicit in Q. Mark heightens the urgency of Jesus' mission by placing his proclamation "The time is fulfilled, and the kingdom of God is at hand" at the very beginning of Jesus' ministry (Mark 1:15). Although both Q and Mark draw the same conclusions from Jesus' ability to cast out demons, Mark highlights Jesus' power by reporting many incidents in which Jesus confronts demonic possession, and adds other striking miracles like the Calming of the Sea (Mark 4:35–41). Q is made up of teachings, with few narrative sections; Mark has much narrative, as well as substantial teaching sections. Although Mark draws on different teaching traditions from Q, they are congruent with the central thrust of the

Q teachings. There is the same call to sacrifice and high standards, the same command to turn our concerns outward toward others. Both these elements are exemplified in the story of the rich young man whom Jesus counsels to "go, sell what you have, and give to the poor" (Mark 10:17–22).

Although Mark explicitly identifies Jesus with the Son of Man, his supernatural status is revealed progressively. At first only the demons recognize him (Mark 5:7). Then the disciples do so on the road to Caesarea Philippi when Peter confesses that Jesus is the Christ. Immediately afterwards, Jesus speaks of himself as the Son of Man, cautions his disciples not to reveal his identity, and predicts his passion and death (Mark 8:27–9:1). At his trial before the High Priest, Jesus makes his divine status known to the people of Israel. In answer to the question, "Are you the Christ, the Son of the Blessed?" he replies: "I am; and you will see the Son of Man sitting at the right hand of Power, and coming with the clouds of heaven" (Mark 14:61–62). Finally, at the Crucifixion even the Gentiles are seen to recognize his status when the centurion declares: "Truly this man was the Son of God" (Mark 15:39).

In summary, Mark affirms more definitely than Q that Jesus is the agent of the kingdom as the Son of Man of the apocalyptic tradition. As in Q, Jesus defeats the dark and alien powers that possess the human soul. But, in contrast with expectations for a second David, Jesus does not seek a military victory or a political kingdom.

The Picture in Luke

Luke does not contradict anything that appears in Q or Mark but enlarges on both. The teaching sections are substantially longer. Here alone in the Gospels appear the parables of the Prodigal Son and the Good Samaritan. The birth narrative is added and there is an extensive version of the Resurrection, which does not appear at all in what we have of Q and is brief in Mark. But the most striking difference separating Luke from Mark and Q is Luke's emphasis on the presence of the Spirit.

It is important to remember that the Acts of the Apostles is the second volume of a two-volume work of which Luke's Gospel is the first. Together, these two books by one author form a short history of the beginnings of the Christian movement, from the birth of Jesus through the imprisonment of Paul in Rome. In both parts of this history the power of the Spirit is the unifying and dominant theme. Early in Acts, the disciples are overcome by the power of the Spirit at Pentecost and are then empowered by the Spirit to carry the Gospel to all nations (Acts 2). Luke stresses the fulfillment in the person and work of Jesus of the prophecies of the Old Testament, especially those prophecies that have to do with the Spirit. Words of Isaiah summarize the Gospel that Jesus proclaimed and manifested:

> "The Spirit of the Lord is upon me,
> because he has anointed me to preach good news to the poor.
> He has sent me to proclaim release to the captives
> and recovering of sight to the blind,
> to set at liberty those who are oppressed,
> to proclaim the acceptable year of the Lord."
> [Luke 4:18–19, quoting from Isa. 61:1–2]

Early in his ministry Jesus read this passage publicly in the synagogue. When he finished reading, he added, "Today this scripture has been fulfilled in your hearing" (Luke 4:21).

This incident, which appears only in Luke, highlights Luke's special stress on the Spirit. Matthew as well as Luke write that Jesus is born of a virgin and conceived by the Holy Spirit, but Luke adds the story of the Annunciation, in which the activity of the Spirit is again expressed (Luke 1:26–35). In all three Synoptic Gospels the Spirit is said to descend on Jesus like a dove at his Baptism, but only in Luke is the Spirit said to descend "in bodily form, as a dove" (Luke 3:22); and while all three Gospels speak of Jesus then being led by the Spirit into the wilderness to be tempted by the devil, only Luke adds that Jesus was "full of the Holy Spirit" (Luke 4:1).

Luke echoes Paul's "God was in Christ reconciling the world to himself" in Zachariah's Song predicting the birth of Jesus: "Blessed be the Lord God of Israel, for he has visited and redeemed his people" (Luke 1:68). According to Luke, it is because Jesus manifests the power of the Spirit that he could do what Mark and Q as well as Luke claimed that he did. The presence of the Spirit enables Jesus to preach and to teach the conditions necessary for entrance into the kingdom, and also to defeat the forces of darkness in the guise of demons. By combining Q and Mark with some other sources of his own, Luke places Jesus as the Christ in a context extending back into the past, before the beginning of Jesus' earthly ministry, and forward into the future to the life of the early Church and its conviction of his Resurrection.

Luke develops an additional theme, the identification of Jesus with the Suffering Servant. The Suffering Servant is depicted in a poem found in Isaiah (52:13–53:12). Although he is described as despised, rejected, tortured, and finally killed, he seems to be a person of great significance, for he is also said to be "exalted and lifted up" (Isa. 52:13). There is no evidence that before the time of Christ Jews saw the Suffering Servant as a Savior, but Christians soon noticed the similarity between this poem and the passion, death, and resurrection of Jesus. The Book of the Acts tells the story of the Apostle Philip's encounter with an Ethiopian, a minister of Queen Candace, who is puzzled by a passage from Isaiah.

> "As a sheep led to the slaughter
> or a lamb before its shearer is dumb,
> so he opens not his mouth.
> In his humiliation justice was denied him.
> Who can describe his generation?
> For his life is taken up from the earth."
> [Acts 8:32–33, quoting from the Greek of Isa. 53:7–8]

Philip goes on to identify this Suffering Servant directly with Jesus and by implication with Jesus in his passion. Luke also includes a saying found only in his Gospel where Jesus himself makes the identification: "For I tell you that this scripture must be fulfilled in me, 'And he was reckoned with the transgressors'" (Luke 22:37, quoting from Isa. 53:12). The notion that unearned suffering is redemptive and that such suffering is an essential part of the saving work of Jesus as the Christ has been explored many times in Christian thought. These themes will be at the center of our discussion in Chapter IV, "The Atonement."

The Picture in Matthew

The Gospel of Matthew incorporates themes already presented in the discussion of Mark, Luke, and Q, but has, in addition, a distinctive perspective on Jesus and the kingdom. This Gospel extends the notion of the kingdom to encompass God's rule of human hearts and minds. In Matthew, the Lord's Prayer includes the petition, "Thy will be done, on earth as it is in heaven" (Matt. 6:10), to bring home the point that the kingdom is present when God's will, God's purpose, is fulfilled; and God's purpose extends into hearts and minds as well as to the public world of human relationships and the world of nature, for God is not only the omnipotent creator of all, the Lord and ruler of history, the universal Lord of all human beings—he is also the ruler of the heart. Jesus commands his followers to "Go therefore and make disciples of all nations, baptizing them in the name of the Father and of the Son and of the Holy Spirit (Matt. 28:19); he also commands them to "love the Lord your God with all your heart, and with all your soul, and with all your mind" (Matt. 22:37).

God's rule in hearts and minds is depicted strikingly in the Sermon on the Mount (chaps. 5–7). The kingdom is presented as the highest good, the pearl of great price for which the householder will sacrifice all in order to possess it, and the purest blessedness (the blessedness of fulfillment of spiritual hunger and the blessedness of tranquility of mind). The kingdom is also a self-involving way of being in the world, which prepares human beings for a life beyond the grave.

> Do not lay up for yourselves treasures on earth, where moth and rust consume and where thieves break in and steal, but lay up for yourselves treasures in heaven, where neither moth nor rust consumes and where thieves do not break in and steal. For where your treasure is, there will your heart be also. [Matt. 6:19–21]

The kingdom thus is not primarily something physical, but something spiritual. The opening verses of the Sermon on the Mount, commonly called the Beatitudes because they promise blessedness to the virtuous, make this point clearly. The first six of the Beatitudes deal with inner dispositions: meekness, purity of heart, hunger for righteousness, and the like. Requirements for entrance into the kingdom include the virtues of hope and faith. "Therefore do not be anxious about tomorrow, for tomorrow will be anxious for itself" (Matt. 6:34). Trust in God's righteous will, repentance for past misdeeds, and obedience to his will not only in word and deed but also in thought and desire, are all necessary. Words are not enough.

"Not every one who says to me, 'Lord, Lord,' shall enter the kingdom of heaven, but he who does the will of my Father who is in heaven" (Matt. 7:21). Deeds are also not enough. Not only must one not kill, one must also root out the emotions of anger and jealousy which lead to murder. One must not commit adultery, but the ideal is also to be free even of adulterous desires. Alms are to be given, but in secret so the desire for human approval will be thwarted. Promises must be kept, and guaranteed by a simple affirmation and without the public display of taking an oath upon a holy object. Grudges are not to be held; indeed, one ought to love one's enemies even when they are abusive; turn the other cheek so that a kind word might turn away wrath.

Matthew stresses the virtue of sincerity as essential to duty. The Summary of the Law, to love God wholly and the neighbor as the self (Matt. 22:37–40) is the heart of the law; and in the words of Rabbi Hillel, a near contemporary of Jesus, "all else is commentary." But this simplicity does not make the law less demanding. The Sermon on the Mount is a call to the highest morality, a morality which exceeds the righteousness of even the most respected members of society in any age. "You, therefore, must be perfect, as your heavenly Father is perfect" (Matt. 5:48).

The teachings of Jesus in Matthew do not, of course, explicitly address all significant ethical issues. "Is an act just and good solely because it is commanded by God, or is it commanded by God because it is right and good?" "Does love make unnecessary the obligations of the law, or is the keeping of the law one of the duties of love?" "Does love include equity or justice, or are equity and love opposed or at least diverse notions?" These questions have claimed a great deal of attention in Christian thinking, and we shall return to some of them in later chapters. For now we note that the Gospel teaches an unqualified love toward God and others, a love which does not count costs or calculate personal gains. Insofar as the self is regarded, it is to be regarded in the context of God's universal plan.

The most distinctive feature of the Gospel of Matthew is its portrayal of Jesus as an interpreter of the Law, the second Moses—a portrayal perhaps inspired by the text from Deuteronomy, "I will raise up for them a prophet like you [Moses]" (Deut. 18:18). Like Moses, Jesus preaches a sermon from a mount. Like the Torah or Pentateuch, Jesus' Sermon and Matthew's Gospel are divided into five major sections. Moreover, the Gospel is presented as a New Covenant; at the Last Supper, Jesus speaks of "my blood of the new covenant" (Matt. 26:26). This Gospel's stress on keeping the law inwardly, echoes the words of Jeremiah: "I will make a new covenant with the house of Israel . . . I will put my law within them, and I will write it upon their hearts; and I will be their God, and they shall be my people" (Jer. 31:31, 33).

To summarize, Jesus is called Messiah in the Synoptic Gospels. However, he is not portrayed as a military or political leader, a second David. He is pictured as the *new Moses*, the *teacher and interpreter* of the Law, the *prophet* of the kingdom and also its *agent*, both in defeating the demons of personal life and in ruling the natural forces of the world through healings and other miracles. After Jesus' death on the cross, his role in God's plan of salvation is vindicated at the Resurrection. As Paul proclaims in Romans 1:4, Jesus is "designated Son of God in power . . . by his resurrection from the dead." This is the message common to all the Synoptic Gospels.

But how are these wonders possible? By the power or Spirit of God, to be sure, but by what power, what Spirit exactly? Is it the power or Spirit by which God created the world, or the power or Spirit by which he inspired the Prophets? These are questions which dominate the Epistles of Paul and the Gospel of John.

The Gospel of John and the Epistles of Paul

We really know very little about the authors of Matthew, Mark, and Luke. Matthew has traditionally been identified with one of the group of disciples closest to Jesus, known as the Twelve Apostles. Mark and Luke have been identified with two of Paul's associates. We know a bit more about John and a great deal more about Paul. From evidence internal to the Gospel of John, we know that the author was a companion of Jesus, although he may not have been the John listed among the Twelve. The tradition that the author was the John who was Bishop of Ephesus (c. 100 C.E.) has much to commend it. As for Paul, we not only have his Epistles or Letters, but about half of the Acts of the Apostles describes his missionary journeys. Although the Letters and Acts differ in detail, there is a large measure of agreement. Paul was not one of Jesus' disciples, but was converted from Judaism to Christianity in the early days of the movement. He was its most successful missionary. He was executed by the authorities in Rome (c. 63 C.E.).

The Pauline and Johannine writings, in spite of some important differences, have much in common. Both authors emphasize spiritual transformation. This theme is certainly present in the Synoptics, where much attention is given to repentance and conversion; but in their vivid descriptions of spiritual transformation as death and rebirth, Paul and John put this theme at the center of their concerns. Paul proclaims, "Do you not know that all of us who have been baptized into Christ Jesus were baptized into his death? We were buried therefore with him by baptism into death, so that as Christ was raised from the dead by the glory of the Father, so we too might walk in newness of life" (Rom. 6:3–4). "If the Spirit of him who raised Jesus from the dead dwells in you, he who raised Christ Jesus from the dead will give life to your mortal bodies also through his Spirit which dwells in you" (Rom. 8:11). Similarly, the Gospel of John speaks of a spiritual rebirth. "Unless one is born anew, he cannot see the kingdom of God" (John 3:3). And "unless one is born of water and the Spirit, he cannot enter the kingdom of God" (John 3:5).

Both Paul and John emphasize the power of God present in the historic Jesus, the power that constitutes his divinity and by which he does God's work in the world. While Luke speaks of that power as the Spirit of God, Paul and John have a more complex conception. Both conceive of a preexistent Son of God, called Son and Word (*Logos*) in John, and Christ, Son, Spirit, and Wisdom in Paul. This preexistent Son is the agent of the creation of the world as well as the source of light and life of human beings. Both of these writers ground the very possibility of spiritual transformation for us in the power of God at work in Christ. The activity by which God raised Jesus from the dead is the same as that by which he raises us from a dead to a new and fuller life. In both Paul and John the primary emphasis is on Christ as savior of the world through God's presence in him.

Classical Judaism has always held that *the turning to God* and *the will to keep his laws* are human works. Each one of us must make the decision to act justly and to serve God. To be sure, Judaism has spoken of God's grace; but continual insistence upon the necessity of God's grace characterizes Paul's writings. Furthermore, Paul's conviction that grace determines right attitudes, dispositions, and intentions explains why he insists on the "spirit" rather than the "letter" of the law, or on the inner attitude of "faith" rather than external deeds, "works of law" (Rom. 3:28). When Paul says, quoting Habakkuk, "The righteous shall live by faith" (Rom. 1:17), he does not mean, as some of the sixteenth century Reformers held, that for the Christian faith takes the place that Torah or Law had for the Jew. Paul insists that faith does not *overthrow*, but rather *upholds* the Law (Rom. 3:31). Paul does not juxtapose Law and Gospel, or even, as some recent interpreters have suggested, Law and love.[9] For Paul the goal of God's work of salvation in Christ is this, "that the just requirements of the law might be fulfilled in us, who walk not according to the flesh but according to the Spirit" (Rom. 8:4). Salvation is first a matter of the inner life—faith, hope, and love; but deeds which conform to the law are a close second.

Paul did believe that those portions of the Old Testament law which have come to be called "ceremonial" have been cancelled; for example, he considered circumcision and the dietary rules to have been abrogated in the New Covenant. But he believed the moral commandments and the religious duties contained in the Ten Commandments to be still binding. Like Jesus, he makes love the supreme command and cites love of neighbor as the epitome of the second group of the commandments, not a substitute for it.

> The commandments, "You shall not commit adultery, You shall not kill, You shall not steal, You shall not covet," and any other commandment, are summed up in this sentence, "You shall love your neighbor as yourself." [Rom. 13:9]

There is not even the contrast between love and justice which some purport to find. Paul continues this passage by saying that love and justice are united; "Love does no wrong to a neighbor; therefore love is the fulfilling of the law" (Rom. 13:10).

Paul's attitude toward Judaism is misunderstood when he is credited with (or accused of) rejecting the tradition of Pharisaic interpretation in which he had been brought up. While he rejects the ceremonial precepts of the Torah, he retains the conclusions of much Rabbinic commentary. Jesus, Paul, and Hillel, one of the most famous rabbis of New Testament times, all agree on the centrality of love of neighbor. A more striking example of Paul's dependence on Rabbinic commentary, however, is the advice Paul gives to his gentile flock at Corinth on the conjugal rights of husband and wife. Here he takes the same stand as the very early Rabbinic commentary called the "Mishna." The husband may not refuse the wife nor the wife the husband, except for the sake of religious observances, and this only for a limited time.[10] In the Mishna, the permissible religious observance is the study of the law; and in Corinthians, it is prayer.[11] Paul here summarizes Rabbinic conclusions rather than reciting their disputations, but this is hardly surprising since he is writing for a gentile audience. The thesis that he is thinking out afresh everything in his newfound faith is implausible. What would be more natural than for him to draw on his heritage, except in those areas where a revolution had taken place?[12]

Paul's Problem with the Law

Paul had been an especially committed Jew before his conversion to Christianity and so needed to define the relationship between his new faith and the central Jewish reality, the Torah or Law. In spite of his acknowledged debt to his religious past, Paul's Epistles give many indications that instead of finding the keeping of the Law a joy, as classical Judaism conceived it to be, he found it a burden. What was Paul's problem with the law? It is that he could not by his own effort bring his mental life into conformity with the law's demands. After many struggles, he concluded that this conformity had to be brought about by the grace of God. In Romans 7, Paul makes it clear that his inner life, not the external deeds required by the law, was the problem for him. He tells us that "the very commandment which promised life proved to be death to me" (Rom. 7:10). It is significant that out of all the ten, he selects the command "Thou shalt not covet" to comment upon. "Yet, if it had not been for the law, I should not have known sin. I should not have known what it is to covet if the law had not said, 'You shall not covet'" (Rom. 7:7). This is the one commandment that deals with internal states, dispositions, or attitudes. Paul continues, "sin, finding opportunity in the commandment, wrought in me all kinds of covetousness. . . . For sin, finding opportunity in the commandment, deceived me and by it killed me" (Rom. 7:8–11). "I do not understand my own actions. For I do not do what I want, but I do the very thing I hate. Now if I do what I do not want, I agree that the law is good. . . . Now if I do what I do not want, it is no longer I that do it, but sin which dwells within me. . . . Wretched man that I am! Who will deliver me from this body of death?" (Rom. 7:15–24).[13]

Paul is telling us that he is torn asunder. Half of him longs to keep the law, but the other half rebels against it. He has what has come to be called "a divided will." But why is he divided? He does not say specifically why, but one need not search far for an answer. The attempt to rule the inner life by sheer will power cannot succeed. Nothing produces more quickly the state of internal strife and warfare, of which Paul speaks so movingly, than the attempt to beat back unwanted drives and impulses by an act of sheer will power. One cannot just decide to have faith or to have a united will. As so many of the saints and sages have known, that takes not just a decision, but a healing. And Paul found this gift of healing, this gift of power, in the one whom he had once persecuted. "I can," said he, "do all things in him who strengthens me" (Phil. 4:13). The war that Paul sometimes calls the war between the spirit and flesh is over. A new integrity is born and the future can now be met with new possibilities of victory. "For God has done what the law, weakened by the flesh, could not do: sending his own Son in the likeness of sinful flesh and for sin, he condemned sin in the flesh, in order that the just requirement of the law might be fulfilled in us, who walk not according to the flesh but according to the Spirit" (Rom. 8:3–4). To keep the Law, says Paul, we need more than a decision; we need the Divine Incarnate Son to dwell in our hearts by faith so that we may live in the fullness of God. No wonder Paul thought of this transformation as a new birth unto righteousness.

Our understanding of Paul's thinking can be further clarified by comparing what he says here to the teachings of the Rabbis. The Rabbis recognized a good impulse (*yetzer tov*) and an evil impulse (*yetzer hara*) in human beings. Paul speaks of a "delight in the law of God, in my inmost self" but sees "in my members another law . . . making me captive to the law of sin which dwells in my members" (Rom. 7:22–23). While the Rabbis held that the *yetzer hara* is dissipated by study of the Torah, Paul holds that the evil impulse can only be nullified by grace, and, in particular, the grace of Christ.

Johannine Literature

Spiritual transformation is also prominent in the Gospel of John. John speaks of being born again. This rebirth is not just a change of status, or the healing of "a divided will" as in Paul, but a change of being. The climax of the rebirth is the interpenetration of God in human life and of human life in God, in knowing and loving God, and in being known and loved by God. These themes have made the Gospel of John a favorite of Neo-Platonists, of Mystics, and of Idealists, who in their varying ways have asserted that knowing is a kind of being. The phrase "Kingdom of God," so central in the Synoptic Gospels, hardly figures in John's account of the preaching of Jesus. It is used a few times, notably in the dialogue with Nicodemus where Jesus says that one must be born again if one is to enter the Kingdom of God (John 3:3, 5), and also when Jesus says, "My kingship is not of this world" (John 18:36). The characteristic Johannine phrase, however, is "eternal life." Instead of saying, as Jesus does in Luke, "If it is by the finger of God that I cast out demons, then the kingdom of God has come upon you" (11:20), in John Jesus says, "I came that they may have life, and have it abundantly" (John 10:10). "Whoever drinks of the water that I shall give him will never thrist; the water that I shall give him will become in him a spring of water welling up to eternal life" (John 4:14). In this Gospel eternal life, like the kingdom of God in the Synoptics, is not only a future hope, but also a present reality. "This is eternal life, that they know thee the only true God" (John 17:3), and this knowledge is available to human beings on earth. The thesis that in John there is "a realized eschatology," that the kingdom is already here, is correct, but this fact does not differentiate John from the Synoptics.

What does differentiate John from the other Gospels and from Paul is his emphasis on the union between God and human beings, a union which amounts to an interpenetration of being. The three metaphors of incorporation—eating, drinking, and grafting—while present in the Synoptics and Paul, are uniquely central in John. "I am the living bread which came down from heaven; if any one eats of this bread, he will live for ever" (John 6:51). "He who eats my flesh and drinks my blood has eternal life" (John 6:54). "I am the vine, you are the branches. He who abides in me, and I in him, he it is that bears much fruit, for apart from me you can do nothing" (John 15:5). These are metaphors of union, but what is the deeper reality of which they are images? That deeper unity is the divine love by which God makes human life a part of himself and the human love by which persons make God a part of their lives. When in John Jesus explains the perfect unity of the believer with God, he does so in terms of love. "As the Father has loved me, so have I loved you; abide in my love. If you keep my commandments, you will abide in my love, just as I have kept my Father's commandments and abide in his love" (John 15:9–10; cf. 17:22–26). John's understanding of Jesus as mediator in the union between God and man would be the sheerest idolatry if it were not for the fact that John also believes that Jesus is God.

The Deity of Christ

Like the Synoptics, the Gospel of John identifies Jesus as God's Son. But in this Gospel, to be the Son of God is to be not just a human being, or even the heavenly Son of Man, but the Word of God, who was "in the beginning with God" and "was God" (John 1:1–2). This same Word of God is also said to be the agent of creation. "All things were made through him, and without him was not anything made that was made" (John 1:3). This set of ideas is so extraordinary coming from Jewish monotheism that it needs careful explanation, particularly so because it had such influence on the development of the doctrine of the Trinity. Similar ideas about the agent of creation are to be found elsewhere in the New Testament, in addition to the Gospel of John. For example, much the same claims regarding the Son of God appear in the Letter to the Hebrews, "through whom also he created the world" (Heb. 1:2), and in Colossians, "in him all things were created . . . all things were created through him and for him" (Col. 1:16); and regarding God's Son, the preexistent Christ or Messiah, 1 Corinthians says, "through whom are all things and through whom we exist" (1 Cor. 8:6). There is a common thread running through all these passages, that God created the world through the agency of his Son, and therefore, that the Son existed before the world came into being.

The ancestry of these ideas is to be found in Jewish speculation about the creation of the world. Psalm 33:9 speaks of God's creation by his word, "For he spoke, and it came to be; he commanded, and it stood forth;" and Psalm 136:5 says that God "by understanding made the heavens." Over time, these two notions begin to coalesce into a single idea. The uniting of the two is made possible by the fact that "word" can mean not only an oral utterance, but also the concept or idea that the sound of the word conveys to a hearer. Thus "God creates by his word" is taken to mean "God creates by the ideas or the plans that he has in his mind." Another development is that wisdom or word is personified, as in the Book of Proverbs in the Old Testament. "The Lord created me at the beginning of his work, the first of his acts of old. Ages ago I was set up, at the first, before the beginning of the earth. . . . When he marked out the foundations of the earth, then I was beside him, like a master workman" (Prov. 8:22–23, 29–30).

The same concepts are to be found in a work called the Wisdom of Solomon, but written too late to be of his authorship (c. 100–50 B.C.E.). The Wisdom of Solomon is one of the Books of the Apocrypha, a collection of Jewish writings that was highly respected but not included when the present list of books in the Old Testament was first proposed by the Rabbis meeting at Jamnia, in Palestine (c. 90 C.E.).[14] This work was influential because it combined both Jewish and Hellenistic thinking. It describes God as creating the universe by his word and by his wisdom. Indeed, it seems to equate the two in the manner of Hebrew poetry, which repeats the same idea in different words in the two halves of a verse, "who has made all things with thy word, and ordained man through thy wisdom" (Wisd. of Sol. 9:1–2 KJV). Wisdom is described as "worker of all things," "holy," "only begotten" (in the Greek), "the breath of the power of God," "the brightness of the everlasting light, the unspotted mirror of the power of God, and the image of his goodness." It is also said to be "more beautiful than the sun . . . being compared with the light, she is found before it" (Wisd. of Sol. 7:22–29 KJV passim).

The similarity of conception and image to Hebrews, Colossians, John, and 1 Corinthians is striking. In the opening verses of Hebrews, the Son is identified not only as the agent of creation but also as the reflection of "the glory of God" and the bearer of "the very stamp of his nature" (Heb. 1:3). The creator Son is called "first-born," and "the image of the invisible God" in Colossians (1:15); and in John, "only begotten Son," "life and . . . the light of men," "the glory . . . of the Father," and revealer of the invisible deity; "No man hath seen God at any time; the only begotten Son, which is in the bosom of the Father, he hath declared him" (John 1:1–18 KJV). The correspondence between these New Testament documents and the Wisdom of Solomon is clear. There also appears to be kinship between the Wisdom of Solomon and the undisputed letters of Paul.

The Preexistent Son and Wisdom in the Epistles of Paul

Few scholars now think that Paul wrote Hebrews. Many think he did not write Colossians. But themes of the preexistence of the Son and of Wisdom are embedded in undisputed Pauline letters: Romans, Galatians, and 1 Corinthians.

As in the prologue of the Gospel of John, Paul asserts that God sent his Son into the world. "God sent forth his Son, born of a woman" (Gal. 4:4); God sent "his own Son in the likeness of sinful flesh" (Rom. 8:3). When Paul speaks of Christ as the Son of God, he is thinking of a preexistent being. This conception is in accord with Jewish thinking. The Rabbinic literature asserts the preexistence of the Messiah as well as of the Torah.[15] The Rabbis also often spoke of the preexistent Messiah as God's Son on the basis of Psalm 2:7, "You are my son, today I have begotten you," which they regularly took as a messianic passage. But Paul also draws from the Hellenistic Wisdom tradition. When Paul affirms that there is "one Lord, Jesus Christ, through whom are all things and through whom we exist" (1 Cor. 8:6), he is uniting two streams of thought; he is identifying the preexistent Creative Wisdom of the Hellenistic Wisdom tradition with the preexistent Messiah of the Rabbinic tradition. He makes this point explicit by identifying Christ and Wisdom: "We preach Christ . . . Christ the power of God and the wisdom of God" (1 Cor. 1:23–24).

But Paul also speaks of the Spirit of God as that which makes Jesus God's Son, although the Spirit of God is the divine power in both Jesus and human beings. Paul seems not to make the same distinction between the Spirit and the preexistent Messiah or Son as does the Gospel of John, where the Spirit is said to come after Jesus the Christ has ascended into heaven. Paul appears to identify the preexistent Christ not only with the preexistent Wisdom but also with the Spirit; or, if he does not precisely identify them, he uses the terms interchangeably. There are two arguments that are sufficient to support this position.

First, Paul seems to be drawing on the Wisdom of Solomon and the work of Philo of Alexandria (20 B.C.E.–42 C.E.), in both of which Spirit and Wisdom are equated (cf. Wisd. of Sol. 1:6). Philo was a prolific writer of commentaries on the Books of the Torah from a point of view heavily influenced by Greek thought. Indeed his account in *The Creation of the World* is drawn from Plato's *Timaeus* as well as Genesis. Philo seems to be part of the same tradition as the Wisdom of Solomon. This tradition had extensive impact on Christian thinking in the next centuries, and we shall explore some of this in the next chapter. How much influence Philo had upon the New Testament, and on Paul and John in particular, is a subject of extensive controversy. However, Paul does at times have ideas very similar to Philo, particularly when Paul is looking for ways to express the Divine status of Christ. For example, Paul seems to draw upon a Philo-like idea in 1 Corinthians 10:4 where, in a puzzling allegorical passage, he speaks of Christ as the Rock that gave water to the Children of Israel in the wilderness. In the Hebrew Scriptures there are two stories in which Moses, by the power of God, draws water from rocks to preserve the wandering Israelites. One explanation was that there were two rocks, but some of the Rabbis proposed that there was but one rock, which physically followed the Israelites to supply their needs. Philo, accepting the interpretation that there was but one rock that followed them, understood that Rock allegorically to be the divine "Wisdom."[16] Paul uses the same unusual image in 1 Corinthians (10:4) but equates the Rock with Christ, that is, the preexistent Messiah. This equivalency is not surprising, since he has already identified Christ with the Wisdom of God in

Chapter 1 of this same Epistle. Paul then goes on to call not only the water that the Children of Israel drank, but the Rock itself "spiritual." It appears that Paul is echoing Philo, and that the pre-existent Christ is understood by Paul to be not only the Wisdom of God but also the Spirit of God.

Second, in Romans (8:9–11), Paul uses "Spirit of God," "Spirit of Christ," and "Christ in you" interchangeably. Paul advises Christians that they can be freed from the bondage of the flesh and spiritual death "if in fact the Spirit of God dwells in you." But then in the next sentence he deplores anyone who "does not have the Spirit of Christ" and affirms that "if Christ is in you . . . your spirits are alive because of righteousness." And then finally he asserts that "he who raised Christ Jesus from the dead will give life . . . through his Spirit which dwells in you."

As we mentioned earlier, these considerations are important for the doctrine of the Trinity. If our description of Paul's views is correct, he has not made a clear Trinitarian statement. Instead of Father, Son, and Holy Spirit, Paul seems to think in terms of a duality, of a Father and a Son-Spirit. In this Paul seems to differ from the Gospel of John, where the Son and Spirit are more clearly differentiated; the Spirit is said to come after the Son has ascended into heaven.

This type of difference will in one form or another occupy Christian theologians in the next centuries as they begin to sort out the issues which result in the doctrine of the Trinity. The earliest formulations of the Christian doctrine of the Trinity followed John, Paul, and the other Epistles just discussed, in affirming that the power of God present in Christ was the same power by which God created the world. Athanasius (c. 319 C.E.) reflected this tradition when he said, "The renewal of creation has been wrought by the Self-same Word Who made it in the beginning."[17] But when Athanasius wrote this, he was not quietly meditating in his study. He was engaged in a momentous debate within the Christian community over the nature of God and the proper interpretation of Scripture. Jewish speculations about God's creative power had become central to the Christian understanding of God at work in Christ.

CHAPTER II

The Mystery of the Trinity

At the Council of Nicea (325 C.E.), the bishops approved a Trinitarian formula in which it is said that God is three persons, Father, Son, and Holy Spirit, united in one substance. Although this doctrine has had a venerable history, it has always been difficult to understand. In our own time an increasing number of Christians have come to consider it so much excess theological baggage and have urged its retirement. These contemporary thinkers believe it quite unproblematic that the one God should act in diverse ways and that this single Divinity should do the work often distributed among the three persons—creation, redemption, and sanctification. Bishop James Pike, for example, asks why Christians cannot simply acknowledge God as the one and only "Ultimate Ground . . . Source, Evolver, Energizer, Savior, Sustainer, and Inspirer of all that is."[1]

However, we fail to grasp the point of the Trinitarian discussions if we think that God's relationship with the world was unproblematic to the Fathers of the early Church. The doctrine of the Trinity is primarily concerned with how the one eternal God could create and sustain in time our world of multiplicity, and, in addition, inspire and save human beings involved in history. Does a relationship to many things inevitably demand complexity in God? Such issues began to be discussed more often by both Jews and pagans as their ideas of God increasingly emphasized his transcendence. God seemed too exalted to have anything to do with our world. The problem of God's relationship with the creation was particularly insistent for Christians, whose fundamental claim was "God was in Christ reconciling the world to himself" (2 Cor. 5:19). Here God is intimately related to a finite temporal creature.

45

Many modern critics of the doctrine of the Trinity fail to address the questions that arise from this central Christian claim. "To what extent is God present in the historic Jesus?" "Is it a part, an aspect, or a power of God that is present?" Questions like these were central concerns of the formulators of the doctrine of the Trinity. However, the classic statement of the doctrine, that God is three persons in one substance, raises problems of its own. "What is meant by 'substance' and 'person'?" "How are the persons related to each other, and what is the role and function of each?" "Are there sources of the doctrine in pre-Christian thinking that will help to understand it, and has there been significant theological development of the doctrine since Nicea?" All of these issues must be addressed if we are to understand this doctrine.

The doctrine of the Trinity is not the irrational and contradictory enigma that many interpreters of Christianity would like to make it. It is a reasoned answer to an important set of questions. In answering these questions, the Fathers proposed a unique conception of God. Monotheists have generally assumed not only that there is but one God, but that God is simple—that is, undifferentiated or not complex. However, by asserting that God is triune, the Fathers were proposing that God possessed distinctions within himself, that he was complex rather than undifferentiated. This new conception of God so captured human imagination that it came to have a life of its own, and in some of its later manifestations it tended to lose its moorings in the issues from which the doctrine was generated.

The Beginning of Trinitarian Thinking

No one thought that the whole of God was present in Jesus of Nazareth. But the question was, how can one distinguish God present in Jesus from the rest of God? From the inception of the Christian movement, there was almost universal agreement that the "aspect" of God in Jesus was that by which God created the world, rather than that by which God inspired the prophets. As we have already seen, John and Paul, and also the authors of Hebrews and Colossians, identified the Divine in Jesus with God as agent of creation. This claim was often reiterated, as for example by St. Athanasius, a pivotal figure. In his early work, *The Incarnation of the Word of*

God, Athanasius summarizes the majority view, "The renewal of creation has been wrought by the Self-same Word Who made it in the beginning."[2]

Athanasius asserts that the Redeemer must recreate the cosmos, and must do so fundamentally, because the condition of the world is so disastrous. With the fall of Adam and Eve, the whole of creation fell. Not only did individuals and society show moral degeneration, but even nature itself suffered debilitating effects. Human beings no longer lived as long as they once did. Disease was rampant, the ground was no longer as fertile. Everything was running downhill! The situation was so catastrophic that only radical recreation could rectify the devastation.[3]

Athanasius' view seems extreme to us today and indeed may have seemed so in his own time. Certainly there was scriptural foundation for his dismal account of the state of the world. Genesis states that the early descendants of Adam lived for centuries but, later in the Bible, three-score years and ten became the projected life span. The flood was only a partial remedy for the failings of human beings, and the prophets inveighed against sins of all kinds, seen in all places. Much was needed to bring the world back to the idyllic garden of Eden. The New Testament portrays Jesus Christ as the needed Savior, but how could he accomplish the needed redemption? In addition to bringing light and wisdom, and in addition to leading others to share in his sense of the presence of God, Jesus is also recorded as stilling storms, restoring people to health, defeating demons, raising from the dead—in other words, controlling the elemental forces of the universe. In Athanasius' time no Christian doubted the truth of these stories; and because Jesus is said to have vast powers over the creation, it seemed probable to Athanasius that the God in him was the divine agency that created nature in the first place.[4]

But what is the relationship of this divine creative aspect to the rest of God? Here the early Church Fathers drew upon the vision of pre-Christian Jewish thinkers. The doctrine of the Trinity was not invented by Christians in its entirety. Its origin is to be found in the speculation of a Jew, Philo of Alexandria, and in the book known as the Wisdom of Solomon. As already discussed in the previous chapter, both held a similar conception—that to understand God's creative activity one must recognize that he projected from himself a Son, his Word and Wisdom, to act as the agent of creation.

Philo of Alexandria

There were two major groups of Jewish thinkers during New Testament times—Hellenists and Palestinians. Hellenists are so called because they were greatly influenced by Greek culture and philosophy. Those who rejected Greek culture and ideas are called Palestinians, since most of them came from that geographic area.

For the first third of the twentieth century, it was generally believed that the Hellenistic thinking of Philo of Alexandria had contributed much to New Testament conceptions of the deity of Jesus of Nazareth. Later it became popular to claim only Palestinian rather than Hellenistic Jewish origins for these conceptions. Recently Rudolph Bultmann (1884–1976) directed attention away from both Palestinian and Hellenistic Jewish antecedents by proposing that the background for the Johannine and Pauline conceptions was an early form of another Hellenism, the Gnostic Redeemer Myth. The two more recent views are precarious, Bultmann's especially so. No one has been able to provide any examples of the Gnostic myth before the year 200 c.e.; Philo, on the other hand, could have influenced John and Paul because he lived and wrote before them. Moreover, Gnostic myths characteristically divorce the Redeemer from the Creator, and so differ in a fundamental way from John and Paul. As to the suggestion of an exclusively Palestinian origin for these conceptions, Samuel Sandmel passed the following judgment in 1979:

> While the student needs to be aware of the viewpoints here cited, he can be reasonably assured that to search Palestinian Judaism for backgrounds to John, rather than in Hellenistic writings, is to prefer the remote and marginal rather than the omnipresent and explicit.[5]

Philo was but one example of Hellenistic thinking. The Wisdom of Solomon was another. The claim that it was Philo's Hellenism that influenced John and Paul is controversial, in spite of the good reasons for maintaining it. But since a judgment on this issue is not essential to our story, we will not pursue the matter further, but will turn to Philo's influence on the writings of the early Fathers, where his imprint is easily found.

Philo does not deserve his reputation as an unashamed Hellenizer. To be sure, his *The Creation of the World* draws nearly as heavily on Plato's *Timaeus* as it does on Genesis, but his loyalty to Judaism comes first. Philo claims that Moses is the supreme philosopher, and that his teachings appear in a garbled version in Plato. At the same time, Philo appropriates Greek ideas in order to express more clearly the biblical conception of God.

The preeminence of God, not merely his existence, is the single most fundamental premise of Philo's thinking. Like the Greeks, he occasionally gives arguments for the existence of God; but more often, like the Torah, he takes God's existence and uniqueness as given. Commenting on the verse from Genesis 2:18, "It is not good that man should be alone" (which he believes to imply that "it is good for the Alone [i.e., God] to be alone"), Philo continues, "God, being one, is alone and unique, and like God, there is nothing."[6] Philo further emphasizes God's transcendence when, speaking of Moses' teachings on monotheism, he says, "This lesson he continually repeats, sometimes saying that God is one and the Father and Maker of all things, sometimes that He is the Lord of created beings, because stability and fixity and lordship are by nature invested in Him alone."[7] From the unity and uniqueness of God, Philo derives God's eternity ("the one, who alone is eternal"), his self sufficiency ("for there is absolutely nothing which he needs"), and finally his simplicity ("God is alone and one alone; not composite; a simple nature; whereas each one of us and also all other created beings is made up of many things").[8]

The preeminence, uniqueness, eternity, self-sufficiency, and simplicity of God inform Philo's interpretation of the words spoken to Moses at the burning bush, "I am who I am" (Exod. 3:14). Following the Greek translation of the Torah, "I am the one who is," Philo believes this text affirms that God is "Being" or "The One."[9] Philo thus stands at the beginning of a long tradition of exegesis which passed through the Church Fathers, Augustine, and St. Thomas Aquinas, and began to be seriously challenged only in this century. The naming of the ultimate metaphysical principle or reality as the

"One" or "Being" is Greek; but Philo sees this conception and its implications of "immutability," as well as of "simplicity" and "eternity," as firmly grounded in biblical revelation.[10]

Another corollary of this conception is God's unknowability and incomprehensibility. Commenting further on the Exodus story, Philo concludes that by saying "I am who I am," God proclaimed that he is nameless. To this Philo adds, "If He is unnamable, he is also inconceivable and incomprehensible."[11] This thoroughgoing affirmation of the divine transcendence, together with the affirmation of the extratemporal nature of God, would imply that the One could not be involved with or enter time without losing his immutability, or become directly known without losing his incomprehensibility and inconceivability. So far there is no connection between God and the world. To explain God's relationship with the world, Philo follows the tradition we have already found in the Wisdom of Solomon. The Wisdom or Word (Logos) of God is the agent of creation and of revelation, and mediates all of the One's relationships with the created order.

Philo gives several nearly identical accounts of the Logos and the relationship of the Logos to the One.[12] The most convenient for our purposes is one in which he recounts a revelation that he describes as spoken by "a voice in my own soul."

> While God exists ontologically after the analogy of the One he is yet two with respect to his highest and first Powers, Goodness and Authority; by Goodness he begat the universe and by Authority he rules what he has begotten. And there is a third thing which, being between them, brings the two together, his Logos, for by Logos God is both ruler and good. . . . The Logos was conceived in God's mind before all things and is manifested in connection with all things.[13]

Philo thus has the conception both of God (the One or Being), whom he also calls Father, and of the Logos, whom he also calls Son.[14] Philo makes it clear that this Logos is the source of the creative and ruling agency. Philo occasionally speaks of the Logos as God, and sometimes as one who stands in the place of God. However, the exact relationship between the Logos-Son and God the Father is not clear; nor is it clear what relationship Father and Son bear to the Holy Spirit, of whom Philo also speaks. On these issues the two foremost interpreters of Philo in this century have taken different stands.

Harry A. Wolfson has suggested that there are for Philo three temporal stages of the Logos. In the first stage the Logos is God's Wisdom present with God from all eternity. In the second stage another Logos is created in time as an independent being. This Logos, made in the image of God, is the agent of creation. In the third stage another Logos is projected into the world as rational order or world soul. In addition, according to Wolfson, Philo believed that there is a Holy Spirit of God, distinct from the Logos, who inspired and enlightened the prophets.[15]

Erwin Goodenough, however, believes that Philo thinks of the Logos as an emanation from the Father, and not a creation.[16] As the passage from *The Cherubim* implies, the Logos is not made, but begotten by an act of thinking by the One. Goodenough proposes a one stage theory of the Logos—the Logos as agent of creation is identical with the Wisdom of the Father.

The reason for such divergence in scholarly judgments is Philo's method of exegesis. Philo often proposes several different interpretations of the same biblical passage. When Wolfson says that Philo really believed that the Logos as creative agent was himself a creation, and Goodenough that he is "begotten not made," we can agree with Sandmel that such disagreement is possible not only because there are passages which support either interpretation, but also because Philo himself did not think it important to decide among the various explications.[17]

There are passages in Philo which contradict Wolfson's view. Philo says that the Logos "is neither uncreated as God, nor created as you, but midway between the two extremes."[18] Philo felt no need to resolve this ambiguity such as the Christian Fathers felt when they sought to interpret the divine presence in Christ as the presence of the creative Logos or Wisdom. For them it was important to know whether the Logos was begotten of God, and thus God, or just a creation of God, like an angel. This is the issue which precipitated the convening of the Council of Nicea in 325 C.E., when Arius (d.c. 336 C.E.) shocked many by proposing a kind of "Wolfson version" of Philo's understanding of the relationship of Father to Son.[19] Before we can appreciate Nicene and Post-Nicene Trinities, however, we must consider Pre-Nicene Trinities.

Pre-Nicene Trinities

Early in the second century, soon after the completion of the major New Testament writings, the Fathers began to try to bring the various New Testament proposals into a conceptual unity. This project begins with the work of Ignatius of Antioch (c. 110–117 C.E.), the Shepherd of Hermas (c. 115–140 C.E.) and Justin Martyr (c. 150 C.E.). They all follow the main outline of the views already sketched. The Father generated his creative Logos. This Logos is present in the historic Jesus. The Holy Spirit, the inspirer and enlightener, was present before Christ among the Prophets and after Christ in the Christian community. All of this sounds like Philo, with Goodness (the creative power) and Authority (the ruling power) no longer differentiated from the Logos. But there is some terminological confusion. In the Wisdom of Solomon, the Word of God, or Logos, is identified not only with Wisdom but with the Holy Spirit as well, as it also seemed to be in Paul. One might conclude that, although in these very early days of Christian thinking there was much talk of Father, Son, and Holy Spirit, there was not a real Trinity but rather a Duality—since the second and third members were not clearly distinguished. Justin Martyr might be understood in this way when he says that the Spirit of God moving over the face of the waters (Gen. 1:2) is the Logos, and also when he says that the Holy Spirit who conceives Jesus (Matt. 1:20) is really the Logos incarnating himself.[20] At times, however, Justin Martyr seems to follow the Gospel of John in its differentiation of Logos and Spirit, and so he, like Philo, has been declared inconsistent by some modern scholars.

But inconsistency in terms is not synonymous with incoherence in thought. A creedal formula found in the writings of Irenaeus of Lyons (d.c. 200 C.E.) gives an account of Christian conviction that is much like the Creed of Nicea and reveals the real coherence of Pre-Nicene Trinities, and yet is sufficiently different in detail that it is possible to see the lacunae that opened the way for Arius' challenge.

Irenaeus' Creedal Statement

The creedal statement found in Irenaeus focuses several issues and presents the emerging orthodox consensus on the Trinity.

> This, then, is the order of the rule of our faith. . . . God the Father, not made, not material, invisible; one God, the creator of all things: this is the first point of our faith. The second point is this: the Word of God, Son of God, Christ Jesus our Lord, Who was manifested to the prophets according to the form of their prophesying and according to the method of the Father's dispensation; through Whom (i.e. the Word) all things were made; Who also, at the end of the age, to complete and gather up all things, was made man among men, visible and tangible, in order to abolish death and show forth life and produce perfect reconciliation between God and man. And the third point is: the Holy Spirit, through Whom the prophets prophesied, and the fathers learned the things of God, and the righteous were led into the way of righteousness; Who at the end of the age was poured out in a new way upon mankind in all the earth, renewing man to God.[21]

This statement summarizes a good deal of what has already been discussed in this chapter, but it does not really address the issues which were to demand so much attention during the Arian controversy. It does not prefigure the Nicene formula, "three persons in one substance," nor does it prefigure the Arian position that the Son and, by implication, the Spirit are not of "the same" but merely of "like substance" with the Father. But this is to anticipate. A more immediate issue raised by this creed is the apparent overlapping of the attributes of the various members of the Trinity. Both the Father and the Son are said to be creators. Both the Son and the Spirit are mentioned in connection with the "prophesying" of the prophets. The Spirit is identified as the inspirer and illuminator of the prophets. About the Son's relationship to the prophets, the creed seems intentionally vague. He "was manifested to the prophets according to the form of their prophesying and according to the method of the Father's dispensation." Does this verbal difference between what is said of the Son and the Spirit reflect a substantial distinction? Several of the Fathers, such as Justin Martyr, seem not to distinguish between Son and Spirit in other contexts. Typically, "Spirit" at the creation and at the conception of Jesus refers not to a separate being but to the Logos in one of his activities.[22]

There are two ways to dissipate the apparent incoherence of the various statements in Irenaeus' creed. One is the solution adopted by other Pre-Nicene Fathers: some members of the Trinity are subordinated to others. The other, that of Augustine and other Post-Nicene Fathers: the three members of the Trinity interpenetrate each other. This second solution will be discussed in its proper historical context, but our present concern is with the Pre-Nicene solution.

In Pre-Nicene Trinities, the Father is the Godhead. He is eternal, immutable, unbegotten, the ultimate source of everything. God the Son, who is begotten of the Father, is *God in relationship to the world.* He is thus creator and is also the redeemer and sanctifier. God the Spirit is God in the hearts and minds of human beings, the inspirer and the illuminator. Thus, God the Father is God in all of his attributes. Everything that can be said of God can be said of him. To use a mathematical analogy, the Son's attributes are a subset of the Father's. Moreover, since he is *God in relationship with the world,* he in turn includes as a subset the attributes of the Spirit. It is readily apparent why this model of the Trinity is often called hierarchical. The members of it are not coequal, in that more is attributed to the Father than to the Son, and more to the Son than to the Spirit.

But then how, using this model, can one deal with the scriptural assertions that the "Spirit of God" is active in creation, or that Jesus was conceived by the Holy Spirit? We have already noted the suggestions made by early Christian thinkers. When it is said that the Spirit moved on the face of the waters or that it conceived Jesus, it is really the Son or Logos that is referred to, not the inspirer of the prophets. This figure of speech can be understood if we suppose that the Fathers employed the following language rule: it is permissible to call the whole by the name of its part, as when Homer said the Greeks launched their keels, meaning that they launched their ships. In this usage, the Logos can be called "Spirit" when he is in the act of creation or conception. But the Logos as creator is thus referred to and not, strictly speaking, the Spirit, whose special role is inspiration.

The Fathers also seem to employ a second language rule: it is permissible not only to substitute the name of the part for the whole, but also to substitute the name of the whole for the part. This second figure of speech is also in common use. "Al Capone felt the strong arm of the law" means not that the law put its hand upon Capone, but rather that a policeman, an agent of the law, arrested him. Likewise, God the Father can be said to be the inspirer of the prophets because the Father is the ultimate source and cause of the Spirit and its activity. Application of these linguistic rules makes the Pre-Nicene solution rational. In addition, there is no passage in Scripture which is inconsistent with this Pre-Nicene scheme.

But the analysis thus far still leaves untouched the question of the Deity of the Son and the Spirit. Origen (c. 182–251 C.E.), who was the speculative genius of the early Church, answered this question in a manner adopted by many of the early Fathers. First, the Son and the Spirit are God because what is born of God is God.[23] Second, the Son and Spirit do not come into existence in time because Son and Spirit are eternally generated from the Father.[24] Origen's solution to this problem might seem to raise another even more serious. By concluding that what is born or generated from God is God, he seems to erode the difference between God and the world. What difference is there between a created world and a generated Son or Spirit? If the Son and Spirit are God, then it seems that the world must also be God; but this conclusion would severely diminish God's transcendence.

This problem did not arise for some early Christians who took the first chapter of Genesis to affirm that the universe was created much as in Plato's *Timaeus,* out of preexistent, unformed matter. As we have already seen, Genesis is open to this interpretation, which is supported by Isaiah 51 and the Wisdom of Solomon. Justin Martyr is among the early Christians who read Genesis this way.[25] The Shepherd of Hermas, on the other hand, affirmed creation out of nothing. In such a view, the world is clearly not God.

By the time of Origen's teacher, Clement of Alexandria (d.c. 215 C.E.), the Fathers were firmly convinced, as Philo had been before them,[26] that God's omnipotence demands that nothing have power against him, even the meager resistant power that unformed matter would have.

How great is the power of God! His bare volition was the creator of the universe. For God alone made it because he alone is truly God. By the bare exercise of his volition he creates; his mere willing was followed by the springing into being of what he willed.[27]

With this conception, the problem of differentiating the world from the Son becomes acute. If God created the world by willing it, how can this process of creation be distinguished from the process of generating the Son and the Spirit? Are Son and world really the same kind of reality? To be able to distinguish the Son from the creation became increasingly important as the Arian controversy developed, for it was one of Arius' distinctive theses that the Son was no different from the creation.

The Fathers met this challenge by explaining the difference between generation and creation as follows: Generation is a process in which the matter or stuff of the source passes to the effect. Thus, the heat of summer is the same stuff or matter as the heat of the sun from which it came; or, to use a more modern analogy, the electricity which lights a lamp has not changed its nature since it left the generator. Creation out of nothing is a very different process. In creation from nothing there is no stuff or matter out of which something is made. It is not made out of the substance of God or of any other substance. For the Fathers, then, the stark assertion that the universe came into existence from nothing by the activity of the creative Word of God seemed sufficient to differentiate the universe from the Son, because he was generated from the Father. When Arius asserted that the Son, like the world, was created out of nothing, he radically called into question the deity of the Son.

Monarchianism

As we shall see, Arius kept the preexistence of the Son but made him into a creature. A quite different challenge to the deity of the Son came from those who, following the terminology of Tertullian, have come to be called Monarchians.[28] They were given this title because in one way or another they insisted on the unity and simplicity of the deity. Traditionally they have been classified into Dynamic and Modalistic Monarchians. While there has been some debate about the usefulness of these titles (the views grouped under each title either have only a loose connection with each other, or shade into each other), there is advantage in sticking with the traditional names.

One way to safeguard the unity and simplicity of God is to insist as did Arius that the element of the Divine in Jesus was a creation. Another way, chosen by the Monarchians, is to insist that the element of Divinity is some sort of activity or appearance of the one simple God. The Dynamic Monarchians took this aspect to be an activity or energy of God. Thus their name derived from the Greek word for energy, *dynamis*. The Modalists took this aspect to be not an energy but a mode of God's being. Both groups of Monarchians were attempting to account for the element of the divine in Jesus without sacrificing their unitarianism.

Dynamic Monarchianism

Which power did Dynamic Monarchians choose to explain what made Jesus divine? Theodotus of Byzantium (c. 190 c.e.), who is often regarded as the founder of Dynamic Monarchianism, proposed that it was the Spirit.[29] He thought of Jesus as primarily a teacher of spiritual truth, and perhaps also as an exemplary human being in communion with God. Thus he saw no reason to affirm more of God's presence in Jesus than what the orthodox Irenaeus had attributed to the Spirit. This view, which has recently been reasserted, for example, by G. W. H. Lampe,[30] was rejected by the growing tradition. It is difficult to recover the full context of the early debate because of the lack of documentary evidence. However, in light of what has already been discussed we can see that this view does not describe the work of Christ in broad enough terms. In the earliest tradition, Jesus is not just a teacher and exemplary person, but a worker of miracles and Lord of the created world. Hence the presence of the Spirit in him is not sufficient to explain his deeds. To explain Christ's control over nature, the power of God as creator as well as his power as inspirer and illuminator must be present. Dynamic Monarchianism saw the work of Jesus as the Christ in too restricted a fashion to satisfy the collective wisdom. It preserved the simplicity of God, but at the price of unfaithfulness to the tradition.[31]

Modalistic Monarchianism

Modalistic Monarchianism also insisted upon the unity, indivisibility, and simplicity of the Deity. One of its earliest proponents, Praxeas (c. 210 C.E.), asserted that it was the whole God who was present in Jesus. The names Father, Son, and Holy Spirit were merely different titles applied to the one, simple being. This insistence that the whole of the Deity is present in Jesus is very different from the Dynamic Monarchian view that only a restricted aspect of the Deity was incarnate. Modalistic Monarchianism meant that it is the Father himself who entered the Virgin's womb. It is the Father— that is, the full Godhead—who suffered and died and rose again. In order to preserve the indivisibility of Deity, Praxeas was willing to say that God suffered like us. Of this kind of unitarianism, Tertullian (c. 155–225) wittily remarked, "Praxeas did two works of the devil in Rome . . . He put to flight the Holy Spirit and crucified the Father."[32]

Tertullian was appalled by this conception of God and found fault with Praxeas for supposing that the Godhead in its deepest nature could suffer and thus undergo change. Tertullian's view has been called into question by many, including Jürgen Moltmann, who has recently insisted that the God of the Bible is capable of sharing human suffering.[33] Tertullian's stress on God's inability to suffer must not, however, distract us from the main issue, which is transcendence. If the whole of God is present in the historic Jesus, the *transcendence* of God is nullified. The Pre-Nicene solution asserts that there is part of God which is not incarnate, and so allows for God to transcend his presence in Jesus. It says that the whole of God was not present in a single human being who lived 2,000 years ago. The Father is not incarnate, only the Son.

Sabellius (c. 215 C.E.) is traditionally said to be the last of the Modalistic Monarchians. His views are somewhat ambiguous, but at least it is clear that he tried to find a version of Monarchianism that would maintain the unity and simplicity of the Deity. He appears to have proposed that the *modes* of God the Father (Son and Holy Spirit) were temporal "dilations"; God the creator at one time projected himself as Son, at another time as Holy Spirit.[34] Sabellius seemed ready to allow God to change radically in order to preserve his incomplexity. His proposal, however, was in direct conflict with Origen's view that the Son and Spirit were eternally generated from the Father.

Sabellius' ideas seem not to have attracted a wide following. Given a choice between preserving the simplicity of God or the eternal generation of the Son and Spirit, they chose the latter. To make God subject to the radical change envisioned by Sabellius seemed to compromise God's transcendence by reducing him to the level of unstable things. In order to preserve God's stability, Trinitarians were ready to give up the divine simplicity. Trinitarians assert that, although God is one and simple in most respects, there are some in which he is Triune. Hence, in different ways, Modalistic and Dynamic Monarchians challenged the orthodox to clarify their conception of the divine unity.

The Unity of God

Having rejected Monarchianism, the Fathers proposed a different relative unity in God. He is not to be thought of as absolutely one in all respects; rather, he is one in some respects and three in others. But how did they describe the unity? The solution adopted at Nicea was that the Word was "begotten not made" and "of the substance of the father." But what was meant by "substance" (ousia) in this context? At least some of this divisive controversy was over the meaning of terms. Several of the terms used in the discussions had more than one meaning, and ousia or "substance" was one of these.

Of the three possible meanings of ousia or "substance," two were not of primary significance. We will dispose of these two before we discuss the third and primary use. "Substance" was sometimes used to mean "individual thing," such as "this horse" or "this person." Aristotle called this "First Substance." "Substance" could also mean the "kind" or "class" to which an individual thing belongs. Thus "substance" could mean "horseness" or "humanity." Aristotle called this "Second Substance."[35] However, none of the Fathers used "of one substance" to mean "one individual thing." This could not express the kind of complex unity for which they sought. Athanasius, the champion of the Nicene solution, and his predecessor Origen, sometimes spoke of "unity of substance" as the unity of "type or kind" in the sense of Aristotle's Second Substance.[36] Another staunch defender of Nicea, Basil (330–379 C.E.), similarly used the analogy of three men, each of whom shares the common nature of manhood, as an analogy for the unity and difference between Father, Son, and Holy Spirit.[37]

This almost tritheistic interpretation "of the substance of the Father" was not the primary one, although it sometimes existed side by side or was identified with another more common use of the term "substance," which refers not to Aristotle's First or Second substance, but to a common material substratum, the Stoic *"hypokeimenon."* "Material" here does not mean "physical" or "corporeal," but "that out of which something is made." For example, H_2O is the material substratum of water, ice, and steam. It is that out of which water, ice, and steam are made and which underlies the various changes of state. Of course, God is not a material being in the sense of a physical being, but the Fathers thought of the substance of God as the spiritual stuff of deity. This conception is found in Basil, where "unity of substance" is said to be the common material, bronze, from which coins are made;[38] and in Augustine, who compares the Father, Son, and Holy Spirit to three statues made from the same gold.[39]

The examples of the three statues and the three coins for the unity of substance in the Trinity suggests as tritheistic a conception as Basil's analogy of the three men. We must not, however, be misled. The material substratum of God was not understood to be discontinuous, as the gold appears to be in the three statues. If we are to understand the analogy we must imagine that the gold is continuous when present in the three icons.[40] A common symbol for the Trinity, the triangle, will help to explain this conception. Picture a triangle made of gold with each angle taken as one of the three persons. The material out of which the triangle is made is the common substratum and provides the unity of substance. The three angles provide the triad since they are identical neither with each other nor with the gold out of which the figure is made. This analogy of course is better suited to later conceptions of the Trinity, for in Pre-Nicene Trinities the Father is the Godhead. In Pre-Nicene Trinities, the Father is the underlying material substratum that remains a continuous unity in spite of the fact that it also expresses itself in Son and Spirit.

Before considering how the three persons are to be distinguished, we should ask why father, rather than mother, is used as the analogy for material source. The choice represents a shift in the understanding of reproduction. In very early times, the material source symbol was the mother. Hence there were mother goddesses, closely associated with birth and fertility. The baby coming out of the mother was an apt example of "material causation," with the mother "that from which something is made." But later, when more about reproduction became known and the indispensable role of the father became clear, the analogy shifted to plant reproduction. The father was thought to plant a seed as in the ground. This shift had already taken place in the Hebrew Scriptures, where the male secretion is called "seed." In this view, the women did not provide the substance of the child. That came with the seed. The mother provided only the food for the seed to grow and the womb in which it was housed. Although this theory of biological reproduction is now obsolete, it was so much a part of the culture of early Christian times that it was simply impossible for the Fathers to express the notion of a material derived from the parent as "of the substance of the mother." To be sure, material source considerations were not the only influences upon the choice of "Father" as a description of Godhead, but they were not insignificant either. Taken together with scriptural custom, they made the use of "Father" for Godhead inevitable.

Multiplicity in God

The Fathers had begun to use the Latin term "persona" and its Greek equivalent "prosopon" and also the additional Greek term "hypostasis" to identify the threeness of the Trinity. The English translation of "persona" is "person." Father, Son, and Holy Spirit are said to be three hypostases or persons in one substance or *ousia*. What is an hypostasis or person? In modern usage, "person" means "human being." This is clearly not the meaning of "person" in the doctrine of the Trinity. A second modern meaning of "person" is "self" or "center of consciousness." While these senses are permitted by the ancient usage, they are not the primary meaning of the term. The tritheistic conception of the Trinity, which is implied by using "persons" to mean "centers of consciousness," is not demanded by the original meanings of the words "persona," "prosopon," or "hypostasis," but it is not ruled out either. There was a wide range of possible meanings for the two key terms and it became necessary for the Fathers to clarify their own usage. Since in discussions of the Trinity and also the Incarnation the word "persona" or "person" is used in a technical sense different from the modern usage of person, in what follows the technical usage will be indicated by quotation marks.

"Persona" and "prosopon" originally were names for the masks worn by actors in dramas.[41] By transference they came to refer to the role or character to be played. In this usage they also meant "distinguishing characteristic." But they also had a second meaning, "real individual beings."[42] "Hypostasis" has an equally broad range of meanings, all the way from Basil's "mode of existence" (similar to "distinguishing characteristic") to Origen's "real individual existent" (similar to the modern meaning of person).[43] Later theologians, looking back to the early Fathers, could find support both for the tritheistic views which see all three "persons" as centers of consciousness and for views which see the three "persons" as only modes or aspects of Godhead.

Arianism

With this understanding of the terms used in the orthodox statement of the nature of the Trinity, which was enunciated at Nicea, we are in a position to grasp the issues which precipitated the council. When a radical interpretation of the "person" and work of Christ was presented by Arius, his Bishop, Alexander of Alexandria, convened a local synod (320 C.E.) which condemned Arius. Arius appealed for help from other bishops. The controversy became so extensive that it threatened to divide the Church. This prospect did not suit the plans of the Roman Emperor, Constantine, who had begun to look to Christianity as a force to unify the empire now that the old gods had lost much of their following. Constantine therefore called a general council to meet in Nicea.

The best way to understand the Arian position is to see that it had two interrelated parts: a theory of Christ's saving work (salva-

tion), coupled with a theory about the nature of Christ. Let us begin
with the theory of his saving work.

For Arius and his party, the Savior's primary work was to serve as
an example for us. He was made perfect through suffering and
through spiritual development. He was a Son of God, but a Son by
adoption. Arians liked to quote the first verse of Hebrews, "a Son,
whom he appointed the heir of all things," which, when coupled
with Luke's "Jesus increased in wisdom and in stature and in favor
with God and man" (2:52), seemed to suggest that Christ had
become the Son of God through gradually perfecting his wisdom
and godliness. For Jesus Christ to be this kind of model for us, however, carried certain implications about his nature. He would have
to be capable of change, since without change there could be no
improvement. Hence, he could not share in the perfection of the
Father. He could not be God, who does not change. He must be a
creature like us, for only the created order is mutable.[44]

We might suppose, then, that Arius views the Christ as a man
who achieves adoption as God's son through perfecting his obedience and spiritual life. But for Arius the Christ is not just a human
being. Along with John, Hebrews, Corinthians, and Colossians,
Arius believes that the Son was the preexistent creator of the world.[45]
Hence, Christ must be like an angel. He is a creature, the agent of
creation, a demi-God. He is a being who is neither God nor man.

In summary, for Arius the Christ is both preexistent creator and
creature. Arius insists that he came into existence in time, "there was
a time when the word was not," and so he was changeable like us.[46]
Were he not changeable, he could not be a spiritual example. The
passages of Scripture that speak of Christ as "suffering," "increasing
in wisdom," and "eating," "sleeping," and "drinking" show that he
is mutable and thus not God, but a creature like us.[47] On the other
hand, the passages that speak of him as "maker of all things" show
that he is not a mere man. The Arians, therefore, seem to see him
as a kind of demi-god or angel. Apparently, they do not see him as a
unity of two natures, the divine and human, but as a composite nature, a human body with an angel's soul.

The notion that Jesus Christ is an example to be followed was
extremely attractive and would have its place in orthodoxy, as we
shall see in the next chapter. However, the kind of status accorded

to him by Arius was deeply troubling to Athanasius and, as it turned out, to the Church as expressed through it councils. At its deepest level, Arianism denied two fundamentals of New Testament thought as enunciated in the Pauline Epistles: "God was in Christ reconciling the world to himself" (2 Cor. 5:19), and "But when the time had fully come, God sent forth his Son, born of a woman" (Gal. 4:4). The Pauline conception is that it is God who saves, it is God whose action is primary in salvation (Rom. 5:6), but equally important is the claim that Jesus is a human being.

The Nicene Reaction to Arianism

Arian views on salvation and the person of Christ were not the main topics of concern at Nicea. These issues were addressed at later councils and will be discussed in the next chapter. The Council of Nicea focused on the Arian claim that the Logos was not fully God. The council formulated its insistence on the full Deity of the Son by inserting into an earlier creed the words "of one substance with the Father." The full creed (with additions italicized) now reads as follows.

> We believe in one God, the Father almighty, maker of all things, visible and invisible;
> And in one Lord Jesus Christ, the Son of God, *begotten from the Father*, only-begotten, *that is, from the substance of the Father*, God from God, light from light, *true God from true God, begotten not made, of one substance with the Father*, through Whom all things came into being, things in heaven and things on earth, Who because of us men and because of our salvation came down and became incarnate, *becoming man*, suffered and rose again on the third day, ascended to the heavens, and will come to judge the living and dead;
> And in the Holy Spirit.

To this creed was appended the following anathema:

> But as for those who say, There was when He was not, and, Before being born He was not, and that He came into existence out of nothing, or who assert that the Son of God is from a different hypostasis or substance, or is created, or is subject to alteration or change—these the Catholic Church anathematizes.[48]

In the years immediately following Nicea, the Arians tried to convince the Church that the council was in error; they argued that the Nicene position had been formulated with a faulty understanding of the nature of God and God's power. The bishops at the council had accepted and the Arians rejected a dual principle enunciated by Origen in the third century: first, "what is begotten of God is God," so the Son must share the divine substance; second, the Son has been begotten eternally, for if the Son had been generated in time, a change would have taken place in the Father, and the Father's own completeness and perfection would have been compromised.

Arians were unwilling to concede that the Son was eternal, but they concentrated their attack on the first part of Origen's claim, that "what is begotten of God is God." The Arians understood this notion of begetting to be one of the passing on of properties. "Man begets man," said Aristotle, and "dog begets dog" added Augustine, in agreement with the Arians.[49] Just as a human father passes on traits to his son, so also God the Father gives divine traits to his Son.

The Arians argued that this analogy was inappropriate to the relationship between God and the Logos. They gave three reasons for this conclusion. An essential property of God is that he is self-existent (unoriginated). God the Father cannot give this property to the Son since he is produced by the Father.[50] Secondly, if the Father is unbegotten and unbegettable, then following Origen's principle, the Son whom he begot must also be unbegotten and unbegettable, but this makes no sense at all. Finally, if the Son has all the same properties as the Father, he must likewise generate a Son, and that Son another and so on ad infinitum.[51]

Athanasius' reply to these charges was to amplify the orthodox understanding. The orthodox were not thinking of generation as a passing on of traits, but as a sharing of something more basic—the material substratum that we have already discussed. The Son, like the Father, is "made out of" godness. Thus the Arians had missed the point of the analogy. However, Athanasius did agree that self-existence is an essential property of the divine substratum. He explained that both the Son and Father shared the self-existent substratum in the following way. The whole of God, i.e., the whole of the Trinity, including all its aspects, is underived and unbegotten. It does not derive its being from anything else, whereas the world

is derived. But within the Trinity there are relationships of derivation. We can speak of the Father as the begetter of the Son and the
Son as begotten of the Father. On this second level, the terms Father
and Son describe not God but the "persons" of the Trinity. In one
context unbegotten describes the Trinity as a whole; in the other, it
describes the Father when contrasted with the Son.[52] Hence the Son
is both unbegotten and begotten—unbegotten as part of the whole
of Deity, begotten of the Father as a relationship inside the Trinity.

Augustine and the Coequal Trinity

A further reaction to the Arians denies any grounds for considering
the Son and Spirit to be less than God by affirming that all members of the Trinity are coequal—that is, all have the same properties
except for their relations of origin. This view is clearly articulated by
Augustine (354–430 c.e.) in his *The Trinity* and is enshrined in
the Athanasian Creed, a creed that could not have been written by
Athanasius himself since it so clearly shows the influence of Augustine's *The Trinity*, written half a century after Athanasius' death.

The Fathers at Nicea understood "of the substance of the Father"
to affirm that Father and Son shared the same material substratum.
Augustine acknowledges this, but in addition he also argues that to
be of one substance with the Father is to possess all the essential
properties of Deity,[53] that is, to be equal with the Father except for
the properties of origin. The Father differs from the Son and Spirit
only in that the Father generates the Son, and the Spirit proceeds
from him as well. Thus the Athanasian Creed states:

> But the Godhead of the Father, of the Son, and of the Holy Ghost
> is all one, the Glory equal, the Majesty co-eternal. Such as the
> Father is, such is the Son, and such is the Holy Ghost.

Equality of the members of the Trinity was a way of insisting on
the full deity of the Son, but it brought about a different understanding of the roles of the members of the Trinity. If all divine
properties are to be predicated of each member of the Trinity, then
it must be said that the Father is creator, the Son creator, and the
Holy Ghost creator. It must be affirmed that the Father is the re-

deemer, the son redeemer, and the Holy Spirit redeemer; and Father, Son, and Holy Spirit are all sanctifiers. Yet this conclusion does not accord with the earlier tradition of Pre-Nicene Trinities that differentiated the members of the Trinity in accordance with their distinct functions in relation to the creation. In this tradition, the Holy Spirit properly is the inspirer and enlightener, the Son properly the agent of creation, and only the Father properly the source of all. The coequal doctrine seems to eradicate all this.

The need for a coequal Trinity was intensified as the scriptural passages about the Spirit that moved on the face of the waters in creation and that conceived Jesus of Nazareth came to refer not, as earlier, to the second "person" of the Trinity, but to the third. The Spirit as third "person" was accorded a role in creation which Pre-Nicene Trinities had reserved for the Son. These developments are reflected in additions made to the third paragraph of the Creed of Nicea at the Council of Constantinople (381 C.E.). To the single phrase, "And in the Holy Spirit," of Nicea was added "the Lord and the Life-giver," and the remainder of the paragraph, "who proceeds from the Father, who with the Father and the Son is worshipped together and glorified together, who spoke through the prophets."

The move toward the coequal Trinity is further indicated in the division of function between the "persons" of the Trinity that was gaining popularity. The primary work of creation was now disassociated from the Son. Creation was increasingly associated with the Father, redemption with the Son, and sanctification with the Spirit. Augustine maintained that this is not an essential, but an accidental or contingent division of labor, which we know about only through revelation. However, since Scripture seemed also to say that the Son was the creator, and the Spirit likewise the creator, it seemed necessary to affirm that all three "persons" of the Trinity were involved in every act of God,[54] that indeed they acted inseparably, and further that they interpenetrated or coinhered in each other.[55]

Now this is a tremendous shift. Earlier Trinities distinguished the members by their relationships to the world. Given equality and coinherence, however, this is no longer possible. The belief in a Trinity cannot then be based on a consideration of the various functions by which God is related to his creation, but only on the fact that Scripture speaks of a Father, and a Son, and a Holy Spirit. This outcome has been a source of concern to some contemporary theologians, who have concluded that unless the members of the Trinity are distinguished one from another by differences of economy and differences of work, there is no reason to have a Trinity at all. If each member of the Trinity is coequal with every other member, and if each acts inseparably with and interpenetrates every other member, then there does not seem to be any reason to posit three eternal persons within the Godhead.[56]

The Social Trinity

In this situation, apologists for the doctrine of the Trinity have turned in two directions. Some have been concerned to preserve Christian monotheism. Fearing tritheism, they would rather conceive the three "persons" to be aspects or modes of the one Deity than to consider them separate "centers of consciousness." Others, fearing Modalism, have been willing to accept an apparent tritheism; among this latter group are proponents of Social Trinities. Social Trinities take as primary the New Testament affirmation that "God is love" (1 John 4:16). Love, it is claimed, is possible only between separate centers of consciousness. The love that is God must then be a love between persons, the three "persons" of the Trinity.

This view has a long history. In *The Trinity,* St. Augustine spoke of the Holy Spirit as the love that binds the Father and the Son to each other.[57] This suggestion does not imply that the Spirit is a "person" in the way that the Father and the Son are "persons," but it does assume that Father and Son are centers of consciousness. It was Richard of St. Victor (d. 1173 C.E.) who first wrote of all three "persons" as bound together by love.[58] From time to time this conception has been championed—for example, by the Anglicans, F. D. Maurice in the nineteenth century and Leonard Hodgson early in this century,[59] and most recently by the Lutheran theologian, Jürgen Moltmann.

Social Trinities reinforce the social teachings of the Gospel. The titles of F. D. Maurice's *The Kingdom of Christ* and Jürgen Moltmann's *The Trinity and the Kingdom* reflect this emphasis. If the internal life of God is a community of love, if community is the essence of the divine life, then Christians have added incentive to strive for such a kingdom on earth. To be a part of a loving fellowship is to share the life divine. One can see why Maurice and Moltmann, both Socialists, should be drawn to this view of God.

Critics of Social Trinities fear that it compromises Christian Monotheism. Karl Rahner prefers "Sabellian modalism" to what he calls the "vulgar tritheism" of Social Trinities.[60] Social Trinities have no problem in maintaining distinctions between the "persons," but they need to attend to the divine unity. In order to avoid the tritheistic implications of older Social Trinities, Leonard Hodgson proposed what he called an "internal constitutive unity." What he had in mind was the unity of a cell with the larger organism of which it is a part. He thought this was a better analogy for the Trinity than a pure mathematical unity.[61] This is an attractive suggestion, but it has a serious flaw. Societies are not really organisms. It is only in a very extended sense that we can speak of an anthill as itself an animal, or the "persons" of the Trinity as cells that constitute another living being. Hodgson's analogy thus only masks his tritheism rather than removing it. Furthermore, the New Testament gives very little support to an organic view of the divine unity. Our earlier discussion did not uncover any biblical reference to such a view.

An alternative is to regard the unity of the Social Trinity on two or perhaps three levels. On the first level is the "unity of the one substance." The Father generates the Son and both generate the Holy Spirit. At the second level, the three "persons" are bound together in love. Here the inner unity of the divine life is expressed through community and fellowship.[62] To these two levels of unity, Moltmann adds a third level which he describes as a unity of "mutual transfiguration and illumination."[63] This unity is one of glory. "The Persons of the Trinity make one another shine through that glory, mutually and together. They glow into perfect form through one another and awake to perfected beauty in one another."[64] Moltmann thus does not propose an organic unity but a three-tier model of unity, which he believes is appropriate to a Trinity because each level is specific to a particular member of the Trinity. Illumination is especially associated with the Spirit, love with the Son, and the unity of origin with the Father.[65]

In spite of many attractive features, Moltmann's view seems to have two defects. First, it still seems tritheistic, and inevitably so since the three separated centers of consciousness cannot be dispensed with if there is to be a divine society. Second, it seems strained for him to regard the Holy Spirit as a separate center of consciousness. If Augustine's suggestion that the Holy Spirit is the love which binds Father and Son together is adopted, the divine society could be better described as consisting of two rather than three "persons."

Moltmann is hard put to justify his view of the Spirit as a center of consciousness. He tries to find such justification in the New Testament, particularly in the writings of Paul. While he notes that Paul nowhere personalizes the Spirit, he thinks that in Paul the Spirit is a "subject." The "subject" is the "center of an act,"[66] but this implies only an unconscious agency, an agency which falls far short of that necessary for the full Social Trinity that Moltmann is advocating.

Augustine and the champions of Social Trinities have relied heavily upon Scripture for support. However, their own study of the scriptural witness has shown how problematic their interpretations are and that the Pre-Nicene Trinities are much closer to the New Testament than is the Social Trinity. It is noteworthy that an influential contemporary Roman Catholic theologian, Karl Rahner, after reexamining Augustinian and Social Trinitarian thinking, has concluded that the main lines of a defensible doctrine of the Trinity have been obscured.

Karl Rahner's Distinctions Between the Persons

Moltmann has had hard things to say of Rahner: "Is there really any greater 'danger' than this 'modalism'?"[67] Moltmann accepts and Rahner rejects the interpretation of "persons" as "centers of consciousness." We noted earlier that the modern notion of *person* was not required by either "persona" or its alternative, "hypostasis." Those who fear tritheism have generally interpreted "person" in its weakest sense, meaning not a conscious center but a distinguishing or individuating characteristic, be it aspect, property, or structural principle. An historically important expression of this view is found in the writings of St. Thomas Aquinas (1225–1274 C.E.), who to the unwary seems to have adopted without alteration Boethius' definition that a "person is an individual substance with a rational nature."[68] St. Thomas, however, modifies the use of "person" with respect to the Trinity and proposes that it here means "something subsisting in an intellectual nature."[69] This change is crucial because it implies a distinguishable *something in an intellect,* but not an *intellect.* This redefinition enabled interpreters of the Trinity to employ a whole set of analogies of "threeness in one" derived from intellectual natures.

One of the most popular of these analogies of Father, Son, and Holy Spirit is "memory, understanding, and will." In a somewhat similiar way, Karl Barth suggests a Trinity of revelation. The Father is the Speaker, the Son is the spoken Word, and the Holy Spirit is the Response in the hearts of human beings. They are all one in that they are all parts of the act of revelation itself. They can be distinguished as constitutive elements of the act, but are indispensable and inseparable parts of a real act of revelation.[70] In somewhat the same fashion, Dorothy Sayers suggests a Trinity of artistic creativity: Book as Thought, Book as Written, and Book as Read.[71] While these analogies have the virtue of providing trinities in aspects of things intellectual or mental, they are very distant from Johannine, Pauline, and Nicene conceptions of the activities of the Father and Son, if not of the Spirit. Sayers wisely insists that there is only an analogous relationship between the Nicene Trinity and the three elements of artistic creativity that she identified. Although in many discussions of the Trinity, the memory, understanding, and will are taken to be analogous to the Father, Son, and Holy Ghost, Sayers suggests that Father, Son, and Holy Spirit are themselves only analogies of a more basic understanding of the nature of God. Thus the Trinity moves from the center of Christian thinking to its periphery. God the Revealer, God the Creative Artist, God the Knower are seen as basic, and the traditional Trinity becomes a sort of complicated image to be prized for its ability to shock the intellect and jog the memory.

Alternative to all of these—the Augustinian failure to differentiate the "persons," tritheism, the Social Trinities, the Modalism of Barth and Sayers—stands the Nicene Trinity with its clear distinction between the "persons" and its solution to the problem of unity. This is essentially the view upheld by Karl Rahner. The members of the Trinity are to be distinguished in terms of their economies, their activities in relation to the world, yet they share a unity of substratum. This Nicene Trinity is thoroughly in accord with the witness of Scripture. In the eyes of some, it is suspect because it abandons what has become so important in the West, the doctrine of the equality of the "persons." Rahner seems to accept this consequence. If the doctrine of equality means that the same essential properties are predicated equally of all three members of the Trinity, then Rahner admits that this is not possible. In his view "person" is predicated differently of the Father, Son, and Holy Spirit.[72] More significant than the use of "person" is the fact that the Son, not the Spirit, is properly creator of the world, and the Father is the creator of the world through the Son.

But is this lack of equality a significant problem? As St. Augustine indicates, the coequal doctrine was adopted in reaction to Arianism and its subordination of Christ.[73] Augustine feared that unless the second "person" of the Trinity was fully God, there would still be the possibility of his being a lesser god. Yet if the Son and Father have the same substance, that is, material substratum, and the Son is a "person" in St. Thomas' usage as "something subsisting in a rational nature," then in what sense is he not fully God? Only in the sense that God the Father is God in all of his attributes, and God the Son is God in relationship with the world. The Son is all there is of God that could be in the world or in Jesus of Nazareth. What more could anyone ask of the Word made flesh?[74]

CHAPTER III

The Mystery of the Incarnation

The Doctrine of the Incarnation gauges the extent of God in Jesus of Nazareth and the relationship between God and man in him. In the Gospels two quite disparate estimates of Jesus are made. In the Gospel of Luke, just after Jesus died, the centurion in charge of the Crucifixion is reported to have said: "Certainly this man was innocent!" (Luke 23:47). However, the Gospels of Matthew and Mark record the words as: "Truly this was the Son of God" (Matt. 27:54; Mark 15:39).

These two appraisals of Jesus, as a righteous and holy man or as a divine being who appeared here on earth, have arisen in various forms in every century. As we shall see, groups loyal to these opposing ideas of Christ began to arise by the end of New Testament times. Although neither of these assessments of Jesus taken by itself received the endorsement of the leaders of the Church, they are still found in pure form today. A typical class of students was asked whether Christianity teaches that Jesus is God or human, and the vast majority chose one or the other alternative; only a minority answered with the classic Christian doctrine that Jesus Christ is both God and man.

But to affirm that Jesus is both human and divine—that in the words of the traditional formula he is "two natures in one 'person'"— seems absurd on the face of it. Søren Kierkegaard (1813–1855) gave a particularly clear statement that this idea is inherently paradoxical: "The absurd is—that the eternal truth has come into being in time, that God has come into being, has been born, has grown up, and so forth, precisely like any other individual human being, quite indis-

73

tinguishable from other individuals."[1] How could God the creator
of the heavens and the heaven of heavens squeeze himself into one
creature? Yet for Kierkegaard absurdity is not a reason for rejection,
but rather a reason for admiration and agreement. For Kierkegaard,
the mysteries of God are beyond all human understanding. Nothing
so petty and weak as human reason could ever comprehend anything
so fraught with significance as the being and activity of God.

Tertullian, father of the terminology of much of Latin theology,
is often cited as one of the most outspoken proponents of this view.

> The Son of God was crucified; I am not ashamed because men
> needs be ashamed. And the Son of God died; it is by all means to
> be believed, because it is absurd. And He was buried, and rose
> again; the fact is certain, because it is impossible.[2]

Yet this statement by itself is misleading; Tertullian expends a great
deal of effort expounding and explaining what he takes to be Christian teaching on the relationship between God and man in Christ.
And his discussion is rational, in that it is thoughtful; reasons are
produced and arguments are given. He looks for analogies from
ordinary human experience that will illuminate this God-man relationship. For Tertullian, Christian belief is not irrational in the sense
that it is based on whim or feeling. It is, however, nonrational in the
sense that it demands acceptance of beliefs which cannot be justified
by the evidence of the senses and the processes of deduction and in-
duction alone. Like ancient Judaism, Christianity is ultimately based
on revelation, but a revelation that uses reason in its service.

Tertullian's theological analysis is but one of many which formed
the traditional doctrine concerning the person and nature of Christ.
After preliminary decisions at three councils, it was not until the
Fourth Ecumenical Council at Chalcedon (451 C.E.) that the classic
settlement was reached. There the Bishops assembled accepted the
formula that there are in Christ two natures, God and man, united
in such a way that they are

> without confusion, without change, without division, without sepa-
> ration; the difference of the natures being in no wise taken away
> by reason of the union, but rather the properties of each being pre-
> served and coming together into one person and one *hypostasis*—not
> parted into two persons, but are one and the same Son and Only-
> begotten, the divine Logos, the Lord Jesus Christ.[3]

The road to this statement was a gradual sifting out of major issues from minor ones, and a gradual focusing on the central claims of Christianity and on suitable analogies for the God-man relationship. This is not to say that every Christian has been satisfied with the Definition of Chalcedon or with subsequent attempts to make it more precise, but Chalcedon represents such a milestone in the clarification of Christian commitment that later thinkers have had to define their own positions with reference to it. For the Definition of Chalcedon is a reasoned statement, and one which ought to command respect from all, even from its critics.

Early Heresies

The fundamental question of Christology is, then, the extent and character of the relationship between God and man in Christ. The New Testament attributes to Jesus both divine and human qualities. As Tertullian reminds us, he is said to be the Son of God, and yet he died on the cross. He is the creator of the world; and yet he was hungry and thirsty, grew weary and slept. From very early times those who called Jesus "Lord" disagreed about whether the divine or the human characterization was the more fundamental. On the one hand, there were those who emphasized the Deity to such an extent that they denied he had even a human body, much less a human mind. These were called Docetists, from a Greek word meaning "appearance." Justin Martyr said of them, "There are some who declare that Jesus Christ did not come in the flesh, but only as spirit, and exhibited an appearance as flesh."[4] On the other hand, some stressed Jesus' human characteristics, looking on him as primarily a good man, who was adopted by God as his special son because of his well-doing. These were called Adoptionists.

Among Docetists of the second century C.E., Saturninus can be regarded as typical. He is reported to have said that "the Saviour was without birth and without body and without figure and in appearance only was he seen as a man." Another, Basilides, is said to have stated that Jesus "appeared on earth as a man" and that "accordingly he did not himself suffer death"; Simon of Cyrene died in Jesus' place "while Jesus himself took the form of Simon and, standing by, laughed at them."[5]

Adoptionists of the second century, like Cerinthus and Carpocrates, said that "Jesus was the son of Joseph, and was just like other men."[6] Later, Paul of Samosata (260) explains their view: "Mary did not bear the Word, for Mary did not exist before the ages. Mary is not older than the Word; what she bore was a man equal to us, but superior in all things as a result of holy spirit."[7] Some Adoptionists held that because Jesus perfectly kept the Law of Moses, at his Baptism he was adopted by God with the words: "This is my beloved Son in whom I am well pleased." Justinus (second century) asserted that at age twelve Jesus was given the gift of prophecy by an angel named Baruch.[8] Others seem to have regarded either the Resurrection or the Ascension as the moment of adoption. But all Adoptionists held in common the view that Jesus was born like others and that he held his sonship as recognition of his obedience and purity of soul.

Both Adoptionism and Docetism came very early to be regarded as heresies. These views simply do not accord with the witness of Scripture. In opposition to Docetism, it has often been pointed out that the Gospel of John seems to go out of its way to stress the bodily characteristics of Jesus. In this Gospel alone appears the incident of the spear being plunged into his side, with the blood and fluid pouring out. This incident seems intended to stress the notion that Jesus is really dead and that a dead body is truly hanging there. Likewise, in this Gospel, Jesus is said to be hungry and asks for food; he weeps, and he lies down to sleep. Other New Testament writings make similar statements. Luke portrays Jesus as having a birth and childhood and "increasing in wisdom and stature." In this Luke directly contradicts Saturninus, who seems to have thought that Jesus had no birth, but just appeared, either at his Baptism or in the Synagogue at Capernaum.

Paul contradicts Adoptionist as well as Docetic claims when he speaks of the preexistent Son-Messiah as "born of woman, born under the law" (Gal. 4:4). Matthew and Luke seem to give concrete expression to Paul's theology when they speak of Jesus as begotten by the Holy Spirit, for Paul interchangeably uses "Spirit" and "Christ" (who is preexistent). In Matthew this divine-human birth is described by saying that before Mary and Joseph, her betrothed, came together "she was found to be with child of the Holy Spirit" (Matt. 1:18). In Luke the same notion is expressed in the angel's words to Mary: "The Holy Spirit will come upon you, and the power of the Most High will overshadow you; therefore the child to be born will be called holy, the Son of God" (Luke 1:35). Indeed, the Pauline interpretation of Luke 1:35, whereby it is the Son-Spirit that incarnates itself, is almost universal among the earliest exegetes,[9] as in the Shepherd of Hermas: "God caused the holy, pre-existent spirit which created the whole of creation to dwell in the flesh which he desired."[10]

But to appeal to Scripture as a standard for what is and is not Christianity presupposes an understanding of what is and what is not a Scripture. Of course, the New Testament itself uses the word "Scripture" a number of times. In these cases the reference is most reasonably taken to be the Old Testament. For the very earliest Christians, there was as yet no New Testament. After the various books were written, it was some time before they were accorded the authority of sacred texts. It is helpful to consider, at this point, the process by which these books came to be accepted as Scripture, since views on the Incarnation cannot be evaluated without some historical details about the life and death of Jesus of Nazareth. Historical detail is far more important here than in the case of the doctrine of the Trinity, where the issues are more speculative and universal. Those issues had to do with God's relationship to the world. Here, as to the Incarnation, we are discussing claims about a particular man, Jesus of Nazareth.

Gnosticism

To understand why the canon of Scripture developed as it did, it is necessary to understand something of the Gnostic movement. Gnosticism was not an institution, either a formal school or a church, but rather a name for a somewhat diverse group, all of whom taught that salvation is to be attained by *gnosis*—that is, spiritual knowledge. We might call this *gnosis* "enlightenment." Gnostics claimed that there is a secret or hidden way of seeing the world and the place of human beings in it, and that this way is profoundly liberating.

What kind of knowledge produced this liberation? In order to gain liberation, one had to understand one's enslavement. Gnostics proposed that human beings became enslaved because they fell from a previous state of blessedness. They had fallen from a state of pure spirit into a bodily existence. Gnostic systems varied a good deal in detail. But all postulated a number of graded stages of reality, and corresponding graded stages of perfection, through which the pure spirits had fallen into the imperfections of fleshly existence. The authors of these systems seem to have exhibited considerable imagination and ingenuity in spelling out the various different kinds of beings that peopled the hierarchy, from the Supreme Deity down to the lowest levels of reality.

The way to salvation lay in reascending the ladder of existence to reunion with the Absolute. There was thus a correlation between the spiritual state of the individual and his ontological state, that is, between his level of knowing and his level of being. The progress to enlightenment involved a change of being, a progressive liberation from enslavement to the body.

A second feature of Gnostic systems was rejection of the God of creation and hence of the God of the Old Testament. This rejection follows from the notion that imprisonment in the body is the mark and cause of human enslavement. If having a body is part of human degradation, then the God who "breathed the soul in the body" is the cause of that degradation. The God of the Hebrew Bible is regarded by Marcion (c. 140) as vindictive. Various cults sprang up to praise and adore those who had challenged the authority of God the Creator—for example, the Ophites, who worshipped the serpent who tempted Eve, and the Cainites who praised Cain for his murder of Abel. All of this is quite understandable if one sees the body as a prison house and human beings as imprisoned in their bodies by God the Creator.

Gnosticism was a movement that extended beyond the limits of any one religious tradition. There were Pagan Gnostics and Jewish Gnostics as well as Christian ones. The Christian Gnostics claimed to derive their teachings from Jesus of Nazareth himself. The Gospel of Thomas claims that a select group of disciples received a secret teaching more authentic than the public preaching, which is recorded in the other Gospels. In this secret teaching Jesus gave interpretations of some of his public utterances as well as altogether new instructions.

In the face of such claims to special, private teachings, a decision had to be made as to which writings contained trustworthy accounts of the life and words of Jesus of Nazareth.

The Orthodox Reply

Men like Irenaeus, Hippolytus, Origen, and Tertullian formulated the orthodox reply (150–250). According to them, Gnosticism was a recent development and could not be traced to teachings of Jesus. For support they called upon apostolic tradition. They claimed that because they stood in the steps of the Apostles, they alone had the authority to interpret the mind of the Savior and of his first disciples. Irenaeus was in a particularly good position to advance this claim, for he had come to Lyons from Ephesus, where he had been a disciple of Polycarp, who was a disciple of John the author of the Gospel. As bishop and successor of an Apostle, he was in the strongest position possible to know what the apostolic teaching was.

The standard of apostolic lineage and authority was crucial in decisions about books of the New Testament. Books were accepted because they were thought to have been written by an Apostle. The name of an Apostle in the title was not taken as sufficient evidence of authorship. The extent to which the doctrine in the book agreed with the teaching tradition was also considered, as were the apostolic credentials of the congregation that recommended the book. Thus Hebrews, which was strongly commended by Alexandria, was one of the last books to be accepted into the Canon, in part because Paul was not remembered as having had anything to do with the Church in Alexandria. A thorough examination of the way in which the various books were finally adopted is beyond the scope of this study. For our purposes it is enough to say that the four Gospels and those Letters today regarded as genuine Epistles of Paul were generally accepted as canonical by the year 200. An Easter letter of Athanasius in 367 is the earliest surviving list of the sacred books to include all of the present Canon. Universal acceptance of the list seems to have been postponed for another 50–100 years. The books that were last to be accepted are among those whose Apostolic authorship has been most in question in the twentieth century: Hebrews, 2 Peter, 2 and 3 John, Jude and Revelation.[11]

The Bishops appealed to the public apostolic tradition as opposed to the secret Gnostic tradition. At first sight the Bishops do not seem to have the stronger argument. Gnostics always acknowledged that the public tradition was genuine, but they insisted that it was incomplete. Some Christians in the present century have been attracted to the Gnostic account of Jesus in the newly discovered Gospel of Thomas. Jesus is presented there as a teacher of enlightenment, and supernatural claims and the doctrine of the Incarnation are only in the background. Furthermore, the sayings tradition recorded in the Gospel of Thomas is in part at least as old as Q. But the problem with Gnosticism has always been—Which Gnostics are to be believed? For every Gnostic writing in which Jesus appears as a spiritual sage, there is one in which he is portrayed as a Docetic heavenly being. It is precisely this issue that the Church was facing when Gnosticism became prominent. Was Jesus a man, a holy and revered teacher of righteousness, or was he a heavenly being who appeared on earth in the guise of a human being, but who had no body and so was a pure spirit? There was considerable internal pressure for Gnostics to accept this second view. Surely a Savior who was to free human beings from bodily existence and return them to the existence of pure spirit would not himself have had a body. The point, however, is that the Gnostics were divided on this important issue. If they had possessed an oral tradition that led directly back to Jesus himself, surely they would have had the answer to this question. The fact that they simply mirrored the debate taking place in the public Church undercuts their claim to a more reliable secret tradition of teaching.

The failure of the Gnostic case of course strengthens the position of the orthodox, and that case is further strengthened when one notes the critical, even skeptical, stance taken by the Church. A great many works which claimed apostolic authorship were either expressly excluded from the Canon or were never seriously considered for inclusion.[12] Among the latter were a group of works which were grossly miraculous—for example, the Infancy Stories about Jesus and various accounts of the acts of the Apostles and of Mary. Among the former were the Didache, or "the Teaching of the Twelve Apostles," and the Epistle of Barnabas, two works that twentieth century research has shown to borrow heavily from the Manual of Discipline found in a cave at Qumran near the Dead Sea soon after World War II.[13] While contemporary scholars have questioned the apostolic authority of some of the books now included in the New Testament, those that the early Church excluded, except for the Gospel of Thomas, have had no champions.

Some look with nostalgia to a time before the formation of the Canon, to a time of open speculation and creative imagination. But imagination is held in check by the claim advanced by orthodox and Gnostic alike, that their doctrine is founded in the life of an individual who actually lived and taught. Such claims depend on authority. As St. Augustine once said, in matters of history "understanding" taken as personal discovery must give way to "belief" based upon authority. Among credible things "some there are which are always believed, and never understood; such is all history, ranging over the temporal doings of man."[14] We have more to say on the problem of the historical accuracy of the Gospels in a later chapter; the central issue involved was clearly recognized in the early Church.

Word-Flesh and Word-Man Christologies

Against Adoptionism it was concluded that Jesus was more than a mere man, and against Docetism that he was not merely God. The issue then became how the human and divine elements were combined. Was Jesus half man and half God (human flesh, and the divine Word in the role of mind and will); or was he a whole human being, with a human mind and a human soul, and united by the Word's presence and action in his mind and consciousness and his human response in love and loyalty. The Bible and the early Fathers are sometimes ambiguous and can be used to support both alternatives. For example, when John said, "The Word became flesh and dwelt among us" (1:14), did he mean that the Word was united with a whole human being, or only with a human body? When the tract, Shepherd of Hermas, states that "God caused the holy pre-existent spirit . . . to dwell in the flesh which he desired," which of these two possibilities is it affirming? Both Word-flesh and Word-man Christologies are found among the Pre-Nicene Fathers. Hippolytus (170–235) is not wholly clear and has been quoted on both sides of the issue.[15] Origen and Tertullian, however, clearly adopt a Word-man Christology. Tertullian speaks of a union of "two substances." It was the Word, the divine Spirit, who "took man to Himself" and "mingled God and man in Himself."[16] Likewise, Origen spoke of the union, not just of a human body, but of a body and soul with God. "The very Logos of the Father, the Wisdom of God Himself, was enclosed within the limits of that man who appeared in Judaea; nay more, that God's Wisdom entered a woman's womb, was born as an infant, and wailed like crying children."[17] Malchion (268), on the other hand, represents the Word-flesh position. "We recognize only one difference, admittedly a very important one, between His constitution and ours, viz. that the divine Logos is in him what the interior man is in us."[18] "Interior man" here means "mind" or "soul."

Word-flesh and Word-man Christologies have different strengths. Word-man Christologies have the advantages that Adoptionist Christologies had. As a complete human being, Jesus can be held up as a pattern for his followers. All the New Testament passages which emphasize Jesus' exemplary character can be cited. His patient endurance of suffering, his calm fearlessness before Pilate, and his dedication to the will of the Father can, in Word-man Christologies, be commended for people to emulate. The passage from Hebrews, "Who in every respect has been tempted as we are, yet without sin" (Heb. 4:15), summarizes this position.

Yet the Word-man Christologies had to struggle to explain the unity of God and man in Jesus. Unity was not a problem for Word-flesh Christologies; the Logos took the place of the human mind or soul. But unity *was* a problem for Word-man Christologies. Some explanations were self-defeating in that they undermined the integrity of the humanity that Word-man Christologies sought to protect. When called upon to explain the unity, both Origen and Tertullian spoke of the predominance of the divine over the human in the Incarnation.[19] While neither believed, as did the later Monophysites, that the human nature or substance was absorbed into the Godhead, they seemed to come dangerously close to that view, as seen in Origen's analogy of Incarnation—a lump of iron placed in a bed of hot coals. The more powerful fire so predominates over the iron that it seems to absorb it. Origen goes even further when he says that in the Incarnation Jesus' bodily parts "by their union and mixing up receive the highest powers, and after participating in his Divinity, were changed into God."[20] This sounds much like later Monophysite doctrine and could indeed be quoted by the Monophycites in support of their position. Clearly, there was a good deal of fluidity and ambiguity in Christology before the four General Councils made pronouncements.

Apollinarianism

Christian thinkers from Alexandria, a great intellectual center of the Church, leaned toward Word-flesh Christologies. This was true of both protagonists in the Trinitarian controversy, Arius and Athanasius, although Athanasius does not seem to be wholly clear on the issue. In the early work, *The Incarnation of the Word of God,* Athanasius seems to vacillate between the Word-man and the Word-flesh conceptions. However, Apollinarius (d.c. 390) presented such a well-developed and consistent Word-flesh Christology that both its negative implications and its strengths are highlighted. In a straightforward way Apollinarius held that the Logos was the principle of movement and of consciousness in the body of Jesus. He affirmed that "the divine energy fulfils the role of the animating spirit and of the human mind."[21] This is a strong statement, implying that the Word was the sole life of Christ on all physical and biological as well as intellectual levels.

For Apollinarius this position held at least two advantages. On the one hand, it guaranteed the Savior an undoubted unity. As Apollinarius stated, "He is one nature since He is a simple, undivided Person."[22] On the other hand, it guaranteed the truth of Jesus' teachings. Whereas a human mind is "fallible and enslaved to filthy thoughts,"[23] the Logos is immune from fleshly passions. Moreover, Christ, having the Logos as his only mind, must be omniscient. In addition, Apollinarius concluded that the flesh of Christ was divinized and, therefore, that partakers of his body and blood in the Eucharist were also divinized.

The Bishops were quick to react to this thorough and consistent position. It was condemned at the First Council of Constantinople in 381. The similarity to Docetism was not missed; the Savior only "appeared as a man."[24] Gregory of Nyssa (330–379) made much the same point in asserting that even Jesus' body could not in the strict sense be called a human body since it was not the body of a human soul. Some of the Fathers proposed that if Apollinarius were correct, then only the human body and not the Soul would be saved. "What has not been assumed cannot be restored."[25] This was especially effective against Apollinarius, since, as noted above, it was his own theory that it is union with God that saves.

Although the latter argument was important historically, the most weighty objection to the Apollinarian position is that it is not scriptural. The rejection of normal human psychology for Jesus is contradicted by the evidence of the Synoptic Gospels where on occasion Jesus' lack of omniscience is affirmed. Luke twice states that "Jesus increased in wisdom and in stature, and in favor with God and man" (Luke 2:52, 40). Mark also relates that Jesus did not know the date of the final judgment. "But of that day or that hour no one knows, not even the angels in heaven, nor the Son, but only the Father" (Mark 13:22). Furthermore, in the garden before he was betrayed, Jesus prayed: "Abba, Father, all things are possible to thee; remove this cup from me; yet not what I will, but what thou wilt" (Mark 14:36). And in Matthew he utters from the cross the cry of abandonment: "My God, my God, why hast thou forsaken me?" (Matt. 27:46). All these references strongly suggest that Jesus did not know what the future might bring. Apollinarius seems to have no way of accommodating these passages within his Christology.

Nestorianism

It is not surprising that after the condemnation of Apollinarius at the First Council of Constantinople, Word-man Christologies should have become predominant. This Christology had long held the ascendancy at Antioch—another of the major centers of Christianity—and it now received a thorough and perceptive exposition from Theodore of Mopsuestia (d. 428). The strength of the Antiochean understanding lay in its emphasis on the full humanity as well as the full deity of the Savior. Theodore describes the Incarnation as analogous to a king clothing himself with "royal apparel" and speaks of the Logos inhabiting the manhood as "a temple." He also spoke of the union as a "conjunction"[26] of God and man, and concluded that the proximity of God and man in Christ justified adoration of the man in the same way that the presence of the royal person made veneration of his vesture proper.

From these analogies and from other remarks, it is evident that the Incarnation was seen as resulting from the "good pleasure" of God.[27] Although the manhood might respond in obedient dedication, it seems clear that God takes the initiative; the Incarnation depends on the action of the Logos. Theodore is, therefore, not really an Adoptionist, as he is sometimes accused of being, because the continuance of the Incarnation is primarily the work of God and not the response of the human nature.

Nestorius, the Patriarch of Constantinople (428–431), was greatly influenced by Theodore, and in his writings one can trace each of the points made above.[28] Had he reaffirmed only these teachings of Theodore, he might have escaped notice.[29] However, in his Easter Sermon of 428, Nestorius took exception to the word *Theotokos*, "God bearer" or "Mother of God," as applied to Mary, on the grounds that Mary was not the mother of the Logos, but only of the human nature. He was willing to accept the designation of Mary as *Christotokos*, "Mother of Christ," Christ being the name of the Logos and man as conjoined.[30]

Whether or not to call Mary *"Theotokos"* continued as part of the controversy; but the central issue, the nature of the union between God and man in Christ, soon came to the fore. Following Theodore, Nestorius affirmed that God dwelt in Christ as in a temple, and that this in-dwelling was a result of the divine good pleasure: "The union of God the Word with them (i.e. the body and human soul) is neither 'hypostatic' nor 'natural', but voluntary."[31] Also like Theodore, Nestorius went on to affirm that there were in Christ three "persons" or *prosopa*: a *prosopon* of the Logos, a *prosopon* of the human nature or substance, and a *prosopon* of union. What Nestorius believed was that if Jesus was fully God and fully man, there must be a *prosopon* of each nature and also a *prosopon* of the union.[32]

It was primarily this third *prosopon* of which opponents were rightly wary. For what kind of a thing was it supposed to be? Certainly it does not seem to be a "center of consciousness."[33] Perhaps it was intended to be only a way of designating the unity produced by the conjunction of God and man. But then it does seem to be some sort of "third thing." Nestorius used the word "conjunction" to describe the kind of union between God and man that he had in mind.[34] However, this kind of union is called by Aristotle "juxtaposition," as an example of which he cites "a bundle made one by a band."[35] There should be concern about the nature of the third *prosopon,* since the unifying band seems to be neither God nor man.

The Council of Ephesus (431) in its Formula of Reunion strongly asserted the two natures doctrine.[36] It also asserted the doctrine of the union between God and man in one "person" (*prosopon*). However, the council did not affirm Nestorius' favorite word "conjunction"; nor did it affirm the favorite notion of Nestorius' chief opponent, Cyril of Alexandria (412–444)—"union in one hypostasis," the hypostasis being the hypostasis of the Word. It remained for Chalcedon to finally settle the matter by ruling that "person" and "hypostasis" would have the same meaning in the discussion. It is not at all clear why Nestorius, hearing of the Formula of Reunion just before his death, refused to accept it. The emphasis on the two natures doctrine was his own and so was the use of "person." However, he left his own views on the nature of the union so obscure that they were open to a variety of interpretations.

Monophysitism

After Ephesus the Alexandrine concern for the unity of the Savior asserted itself in Monophysitism, the doctrine that there is one nature in Christ rather than two. Cyril of Alexandria, the most vocal of Nestorius' opponents, had come very close to a one nature doctrine. He later affirmed what became Chalcedonian Orthodoxy—that there are two natures in Christ united in one hypostasis—but since he sometimes used "hypostasis" and "nature" interchangeably,[37] it is possible to interpret him as saying that, while Jesus Christ inherited a human nature from Mary that was combined with the divine nature of the Word, after the moment of Incarnation the human nature was obliterated in the divine.

The spokesman for this view was Eutyches (c. 448), who is quoted as saying: "I confess that before the union our Lord was of two natures, but after the union I confess one nature."[38] Behind this statement lies an analogy drawn from the Aristotelian discussion of mixtures, in which the stronger element is said to predominate over the weaker. The use of this analogy is clear in Theodoret of Cyrrhus' (c. 443) dialogue, in which a Monophysite is asked, "Explain to us, however, in what sense do you assert one nature after the union.

Do you mean one nature derived from both or that one nature remains after the destruction of the other?" The Monophysite then answers, "I maintain that the Godhead remains and that the manhood was absorbed by it." He adds, by way of explanation, that it is "like the sea receiving a drop of honey, for straightway the drop, as it mixes with the sea's water, vanishes."[39] Thus, Eutyches and the other Monophysites were persuaded by Aristotelian images of predominance—that is, of "a drop of wine" mixed "in ten thousand gallons of water," or the light of a candle lost in the brilliance of the sun; no thing could maintain its individual existence when brought into the proximity of the power and presence of God.

Such was the Monophysite's logic, but this position had serious defects. First, absorption of the weaker element is not a necessary consequence of "predominance." In the same dialogue, the defender of orthodoxy replies that there are examples of predominance, like iron in fire, in which the weaker is not absorbed into the stronger although it takes on some of the properties of the stronger. The orthodox continues, "If then in natural bodies, instances may be found of an unconfounded mixture, it is sheer folly in the case of the nature which knows neither corruption nor change to entertain the idea of confusion and destruction of the assumed nature."[40] Second, although formally different from Docetism and Apollinarianism, Monophysitism ran afoul of Scripture in the same way they did. The Monophysite position could not accommodate, any more than could the Docetist, the references to Christ's suffering and death. The letter sent by Pope Leo to the council forcefully stated: "Plainly it is a human thing to hunger and thirst and get tired and sleep."[41] It is also a human thing to grow in wisdom as well as in stature and to be ignorant of the time and the seasons of the Last Days. Although Leo does not touch upon this second point, perhaps he hints at the possibility of these human limitations when he refers to Christ as "the one whom the Devil's cunning tempted as a human being."[42] The character of the scriptural witness is more consonant with the two natures view where "the characteristic properties of both natures and substances are kept intact and come together in one person."[43]

The Achievement of Chalcedon

Pope Leo's letter, the *Tome of Leo*, seems to have made a strong impression at Chalcedon and was approved by it in its final decree.[44] The Definition of Chalcedon echoes the *Tome of Leo* in its support of the Word-man Christology and in its rejection of Docetism, Apollinarianism, and Monophysitism. It describes the Lord Christ as "at once complete in Godhead and complete in manhood, truly God and truly man, consisting also of a reasonable soul and body; of one substance with the Father as regards his Godhead, and at the same time of one substance with us as regards his manhood; like us in all respects, apart from sin." At the same time Chalcedon adopted the "hypostatic union" terminology of Cyril of Alexandria: "the distinction of natures being in no way annulled by the union, but rather the characteristics of each nature being preserved and coming together to form one person and subsistence [hypostasis] and, not as parted or separated into two persons, but one and the same Son and Only-begotten God the Word."[45]

It is important to note that the key terms "hypostasis" and "person" are left undefined, though the context gives us some clues. First, they are used interchangeably; second, at a minimum they must mean "principle of unity" or "principle of individuality," the one meaning gleaned from the Nestorian and the other from the Trinitarian discussions. The Definition is a reaffirmation of the decision against Nestorius; it is denying that the *prosopon* of union is something other than the Logos or Son. The Definition of Chalcedon clearly holds that the "principle of union" is the second "Person" of the Trinity. It is God, not man or something "neither God nor man." The Definition is in this way thoroughly biblical. In Scripture God is depicted as the primary actor in the Incarnation; the human response is derivative. For example, John states: "In this is love, not that we loved God but that he loved us and sent his Son to be the expiation for our sins" (1 John 4:10). Likewise, Paul affirms that "while we were still weak . . . Christ died for the ungodly" (Rom. 5:6). In the context of the Nestorian use of *prosopon*, Chalcedon makes it clear that it is God in Jesus that is the source and cause of the unity.

But does the Definition mean more than that? Certainly "person" cannot mean "empirical ego" or "self-consciousness," for then Jesus would not have had a complete human nature. The Bishops at Chalcedon were not speculative theologians. It was left for subsequent thinkers to determine just what might be meant in addition to an anti-Nestorian and anti-Monophysite declaration.

Since Chalcedon

Chalcedon did not provide a definition of "person" or "hypostasis" or explain the kind of union between the natures. It has become popular to criticize the attempts of subsequent theologians to deal with these questions. First, they are accused of failing to protect the integrity and distinctiveness of each of the two natures from the encroachments of the other. Maurice Wiles has recently complained: "Most commonly it has been the humanity of Christ that has suffered; the picture presented has been of a figure who cannot by our standards of judgment (and what others can we apply?) be regarded as recognizably human."[46]

A second recent criticism is that Christian theologians have failed to explain how one "person" can have two natures. "Indeed," says John Hick, "the long history of the christological debates is the story of the church's failure to achieve a clear and agreed spelling out of the broad imaginative conception that God was incarnate in Jesus the Jewish Messiah. . . . We have the officially adopted metaphysical hypothesis of the two natures, but no accepted account of what it means for an individual to have two natures, one human and the other divine."[47]

A third criticism has been voiced by Paul Tillich (1886–1965). "The doctrine of the two natures in the Christ," he says, "raises the right question but uses wrong conceptual tools." For Tillich, the traditional formula is bound to the inadequate Greek concept of "static essence," whereas what is needed is a set of concepts which can express "dynamic relation."[48]

These three issues were recognized and debated by thinkers following Chalcedon. It was first necessary to achieve some clarity about how the integrity of each nature could be protected, before the second issue concerning the nature of the union could be adequately addressed. And the third criticism concerning the adequacy of the conceptual tools could only be clearly posed and discussed in the light of attempts to solve the other two issues.

The Integrity of the Natures

In trying to reach a clearer understanding of the integrity of each nature, the first problem to demand attention involved Christ's will. Was there in Christ a human will and a divine will, or just one will? The issue was not whether there was agreement between the two wills, that is, whether the human nature willed the will of God; but whether, as John of Damascus (c. 700–c. 753) held, there were "two natural wills and two natural operations."[49] The controversy was finally resolved in favor of the two will doctrine at the Sixth Ecumenical Council at Constantinople in 681. This solution simply drew out the logical conclusions of Chalcedon. For if the "character of each nature" is preserved in the union, there is every reason to insist on the preservation in each nature of the agency or power of decision. Certainly ample scriptural support for the two wills doctrine can be drawn from such verses as: "I seek not my own will but the will of him who sent me" (John 5:30), and "I have come down from heaven, not to do my own will, but the will of him who sent me" (John 6:38). To assert that there is but one willer or decider in Christ is to vitiate one of the natures.

A second closely related, but more complex, question concerns the kind of knowledge possessed by the Christ. One of the supposed advantages of the Apollinarian position was that it guaranteed the truth of the sayings of Christ because they were uttered by the divine Logos. After the Apollinarian position was declared heretical, it became necessary for those who thought the teachings of Christ a prime instrument of salvation to find some other guarantee for their truth. If the mind of Christ was not just the divine Logos, if he had a human as well as a divine mind, could he be held to be inerrant? At least two major solutions were proposed.

One solution was to attribute to the human mind the sayings that showed human limitations, while assigning to the Logos those that bore upon issues of salvation. Thus, the *Tome of Leo* asserts: "It is not an act of one and the same nature to say: 'I and the Father are one' (John 10:30) and to say: 'The Father is greater than I' (John

14:28)."[50] A venerable tradition of exegesis developed from this single example. It was suggested that when on the cross Jesus said, "Today you will be with me in Paradise" (Luke 23:43), it was his divine nature speaking; but when he said, "My God, my God, why hast thou forsaken me?" (Matt. 27:46), it was his human nature. When he foresaw his Passion, and when he affirmed his existence before Abraham, he spoke through his divine knowledge; but when Scripture says that "he increased in wisdom" (Luke 2:52), and says about the date of the Judgement, "no one knows, not even the angels in heaven, nor the Son, but only the Father" (Mark 13:32), Jesus' human mind is characterized.

Although many respected theologians have adopted this position, it does not seem to be the most reasonable solution. It seems to yield a schizophrenic Jesus the Christ—now speaking from one mind, and now from another—and it also compromises the integrity of his human nature. It thus violates the Definition of Chalcedon, which asserted that "the character of each nature" was preserved in the union. Instead, the human nature seems to have been invaded by the divine nature in such a way that the Christ can no longer be said to be a union of two complete natures, but is a hybrid of the two. Fortunately for those who desired to preserve the possibility of divine sanction for the words of Jesus, there was another alternative.

According to St. Thomas Aquinas, it is always the human nature in Christ that speaks to us, but a perfected human nature.[51] As perfected, it has the beatific vision.[52] It also has infused knowledge such that it knows past, present, and future.[53] But it is not omniscient[54] and it increases in wisdom as well as in stature.[55] The mind of Christ as it is turned toward us is human, a human mind that, although in union with God, may have ignorance but not error. A sinless human mind in union with God may not know all, but it is incapable of error. This same view is expressed by the nineteenth century Presbyterian B. B. Warfield: "the human nature remains truly human while yet it can never fall into sin or error because it can never act out of relation with the Divine nature into conjunction with which it has been brought."[56]

Fallibility and Human Nature

Many modern commentators believe the account of Christ's knowledge given by St. Thomas Aquinas and by B. B. Warfield violates the human nature because fallibility seems to be an essential property of human nature. For example, the seventeenth century Anglican, John Hales, held that "infallibility either in judgement, or interpretation, or whatsover, is annext neither to the See of any Bishop, nor to the Councils, nor to the Church, nor to any created power whatsoever."[57] It is important to remember that St. Thomas Aquinas and Warfield are not claiming that Jesus was *infallible* in the sense that he knew everything from birth, and thus did not grow in knowledge, but *infallible* in the sense of being *inerrant*. *Being mistaken*, they held, is not an essential human property.

To show that a particular property is an essential property one must show that to remove it destroys the unity of structure of that of which it is a property. For example, being small in size is an essential property of being a spider, for a spider as large as a house would collapse of its own weight. Identifying the essential properties of human nature is extraordinarily difficult. It might be possible to show that susceptibility to disease and death are essential properties of animal organisms. It might even be possible to demonstrate the more controversial thesis that the ability to grow in knowledge is an essential human property. It seems impossible, however, to establish that being mistaken is such a property. What other human property would be jeopardized if an individual, though he or she grew in scope of knowledge, did not as a matter of fact ever make a mistake in judgment? This would certainly be unusual, but not in the strict sense superhuman. Being mistaken about what is most important is certainly not in the Bible or in Christian tradition regarded as an essential human trait. The blessed in paradise are said to have achieved a knowledge surpassing anything they have achieved on earth. There they know even as they also are known (1 Cor. 13:12). One who objects to the doctrine that Christ is inerrant will have to object to it on some other grounds—for instance, that he could not be an example for us, or that there is contradictory historical evidence.

The Unity of the Person

Chalcedon sought to protect the integrity of the two natures in the Incarnation while explaining the unity of the natures as a union in one "person." The meaning of "person" is quite as problematic in the doctrine of the Incarnation as it is in the doctrine of the Trinity. Added to this fact is the complication that "person" is not used in precisely the same way in both doctrines. It is clear that in both contexts it means "the principle that gives something its individuality," but there are two different ways in which this individuation is accomplished. In the doctrine of the Trinity, the "Persons" are the three eternal distinctions within God. In the doctrine of the Incarnation, however, the "Person" of Christ is the principle that forms the union of the two natures. In the Trinity, "Person" individuates in the sense of distinguishing or differentiating, whereas in the Incarnation, "Person" individuates by uniting or integrating the two natures. However, there need be no confusion as to the use of the same term for somewhat different functions. Indeed, there is a certain economy in so doing because, according to the Definition of Chalcedon, it is the second "Person" (or Distinction) of the Trinity which is the "Person" (or integrating principle) of the God-man. That is, it is God, and not man, that is the source of the union.

Since Chalcedon many theologians have sought to make the nature of the unity in Christ even more explicit. Some have attempted a psychological interpretation. Paul Tillich praises Jesus for "the undisrupted unity of the center of his being with God,"[58] meaning that the integrating principle of his conscious life was his awareness of and dedication to the Father. As one might say that a project, end, or goal is the integrating principle in one's own life, so dedication to God is said to be that principle in the life of Jesus of Nazareth.

However well-grounded this kind of unity may be in the New Testament picture of Jesus, and however inspiring the image of Jesus' selfless dedication to God's truth and to God's larger purposes for mankind, this cannot have been the unity the Fathers at Chalcedon had in mind when they spoke of the second "Person" of the Trinity as the "Person" of Christ. As noted in the discussion of Christ's knowledge, they insisted on two minds or consciousnesses

in Christ. It follows that in Christ there will also be two awarenesses of God, the one in his divine consciousness and the other in
his human consciousness. Awareness of God cannot alone constitute
the union.

However, theologians like Tillich may be proposing something a
little different. They may mean not that the awareness of God in
the human mind of Jesus *constitutes* the union between God and
man, but that it is the *source* of it. It is that awareness of God which
Jesus maintained "against all the threats of alienated existence"[59]
that made him one with God. If this is what is meant, then the
other aspect of the Definition of Chalcedon is violated, the statement
that God, and not the human nature, is the source of the union.

If Tillich seems to see the human nature as the source of the
union, there are others who have stressed the being and action of
God. Some propose that "person" or "hypostasis" be conceived as the
basic reality that holds an object together—that in which properties
or qualities of any object inhere. This is Thomas Aquinas' usage.
Although in his discussion of the Trinity he took "hypostasis" to
mean "individuating aspect" or "distinguishing characteristic," here
he employs the other meaning, "the real individual being of a thing."
Especially in regard to rational and intelligent beings, St. Thomas
called the individual real being of something the "supposit." As
such it is identical with the deepest self.[60] This can be put another
way. The philosopher Kant proposed that there is in each human being an empirical ego, a self-consciousness. But, in addition to the self
of which we are conscious, there is another ego, a transcendental ego,
that never appears directly in our awareness but is a real entity—the
subject of every act of awareness, and the agent of every deed. It also
provides continuity, or identity, over time. To explain Kant's reasons
for asserting the existence of the transcendental ego would take us
beyond the scope of this book. However, it is worth noting that
analyses of the self very much like Kant's have been convincing to
many philosophers as diverse as Jean Paul Sartre and Roderick N.
Chisholm. This highly respected theory is for many an explication of
the meaning of the term "supposit."

One might say that the divine "Person" is the supposit, or transcendental ego in Christ. As such, it is the subject and agent of the
human nature. Jesus' conscious self remains fully human; the underlying reality, or subject, of this human self is the divine Word, the

second "Person" of the Trinity. This view differs from Apollinarianism in that in the latter the Word is not only the transcendental ego or supposit but also the human empirical ego or self-consciousness.

This solution, though not without its critics, is probably the most widely accepted interpretation of the "unity of Person."[61] Not only does it have the authority of St. Thomas Aquinas, but it can also claim to provide a unity between God and man at the deepest possible level. It is not a union of consciousness, but a deep union of being. Indeed, without this kind of union, St. Thomas believed that there could be no union at all, only juxtaposition.[62]

Some proponents assert that the chief merit of the supposit interpretation of "person" is its guarantee that God is not only the first actor of the Incarnation but also the only agent in the united natures. If the second "Person" of the Trinity is the supposit of the human nature, then it is God, and not a human being, who is the subject of the suffering that is experienced in the human nature. It is God who teaches and heals, and not a human being who does so. "The personal subject of these acts is not a man but God."[63] Meister Eckhart's (1260–1327) assertion is typical of this perspective. "In him [Christ] there is no other act of existence save the act of the divine supposit, and therefore there is absolutely no way in which he can sin."[64]

Eckhart's affirmation that the only agent in the God-man is the divine "Person," and that for this reason the God-man is incapable of sin, compromises the human nature in two important ways. First, the claim that God is the only agent in Jesus makes nonsense of the sacrificial theories of the Atonement, in which reconciliation between God and man is dependent on the initiative of the human nature. Second, if the human nature is incapable of sin because of the agency of the divine supposit, then the integrity of the human nature is no longer maintained.

One way to avoid the unsatisfactory results of Eckhart's interpretation of the supposit theory is to limit further the role of the supposit in the Incarnation by eliminating its active aspect and reducing it to being only the possessor or bearer of the properties, both human and divine. The supposit would only keep the two sets of properties in existence. It would be like Kant's "thing in itself," quite barren. There would be nothing in it to coerce the manhood.

If the full humanity is to be protected, the role of the Deity in the

Incarnation has to be restricted. Such appears to be the motivation behind *kenotic* theories, which take their name from a Greek verb meaning "to empty." Following a hint from a passage in Philippians in which Paul said of the preexistent Christ that he "emptied himself" in order to be "born in the likeness of men" (Phil. 2:7), several nineteenth century Lutheran and Anglican theologians proposed that the second "Person" of the Trinity must have laid aside some of his divine properties in order to take on some of the properties of humanity. However, *kenotic* theories seem quite ambiguous. Do their adherents propose that God in the Incarnation actually divests himself of some of his properties, or do they suggest that he merely limits his activities? If the second alternative is meant, then *kenotic* theories merely draw attention to the fact that any theory of God's activity must allow God to limit the effects of his action so as not to overwhelm his creation. The first alternative seems to have all the disadvantages of Sabellian Modalism.

An Organic Theory

There is a third option for understanding the unity of "Person" in the God-man that avoids some of the drawbacks of both the metaphysical and the psychological theories. This might be called the organic view. When a cell is part of a living plant, it has no individual existence, although it does have the potentiality for such existence in laboratory experiments. In the natural state it is part of a dynamic interacting system, in which it has its own proper functioning and is coordinated with other cells and with the whole. In a similar way, the human nature of Jesus has the potentiality for separate existence and functioning but, in fact, is part of the larger interactive reality, the God-man. It functions according to its own nature in its own special role, but it can do so because it is enlivened and nourished by the larger whole. In both the plant and the God-man there is a unifying element or force. The life force in the organism, however biologists describe it, is analogous to the divine Word or Second Person of the Trinity in its relation to the human nature of Jesus. To say, then, that the "Person" of the God-man is the Second Person of the Trinity is to say that it is God and not man that is the primary source of unity in the God-man. In the words of the contemporary theologian, Hans

Küng, "The relationship between God and Jesus . . . has its foundation in God."[65] The divine Word is present in the human nature, giving it direction and purpose, as well as holding it to itself. Like the cell, the human nature retains its separate identity or distinctiveness, and responds in love and loyalty.

Two Types of Christologies

In New Testament times two differing judgments were made about the man Jesus of Nazareth. He was said to be a manifestation of God, "the Word of God" (John 1), and the one in whom "all the fulness of God was pleased to dwell" (Col. 1:19). He is also said to be a man of God, a servant of the Father. "We have not a high priest who is unable to sympathize with our weaknesses, but one who in every respect has been tempted as we are, yet without sin" (Heb. 4:15). In the subsequent history of Christian thought these different emphases have persisted. Docetism and Adoptionism were followed by various versions of the Word-flesh and Word-man Christologies until Chalcedon attempted to resolve the tension inherent in its two natures doctrine by giving equal weight to both emphases. Chalcedon did not, however, wholly resolve the tension. Since Chalcedon, accounts of the unity of the "person" of Christ have tended to lean now toward Deity, now toward humanity. In the modern period a new consideration has been introduced into the discussion. Before the advent of the historical-critical study of the Scripture, the New Testament accounts of the life of Jesus were taken to substantiate the two natures doctrine. "Some facts about Jesus showed him to be fully human. Other facts about Jesus (his supernatural power, etc.) showed him to be fully divine."[66] However, since the beginning of the nineteenth century, when the miracle stories began to be severely questioned, doubts began to arise about the historical accuracy of the Gospel accounts. This issue will be discussed more fully in Chapter VII, "Authority and Revelation."

It is nevertheless important to realize that the most substantial Christological issues have not been settled by historical-critical study of the Gospels. Among those committed to that study, the same two Christological emphases reappear. In our own time, some see the Christ as the Word or Revelation of God (Barth and Bultmann) or as the Liberator through his manifestation of the divine Love (Ogden). This type of view shows surprising affinities with Docetism in that it is often coupled with a radical skepticism concerning our ability to know anything about the historical Jesus beyond the fact that he lived and died under Pontius Pilate. According to views like this, it is not what Jesus said and did that is important, but rather that God was in him and that he was the vehicle of the power of the Spirit in bringing new life to humanity. Salvation is thus still entirely God's work, although it is mediated to us by the Gospel witness to and evaluation of Jesus as the inaugurator of the New Age.

If these critical thinkers believe that their task is to present for our age the message of the early Church that Jesus is "the decisive representation of the meaning of God for us,"[67] and thus to propose a Christology which moves from God to humanity, a second group of thinkers moves in the opposite direction from humanity to Deity. "The critical historian," said Don Cupitt recently, "no longer sees both natures displayed in Jesus' life. He sees a purely human Jesus, a first-century man of God in the Jewish tradition."[68] It is the human experience of Jesus' relationship with God as Abba, Father (Küng), his consciousness of "an undisrupted unity with God" (Tillich), his sense of companionship with the Father in whatever he did or in whatever he endured—in short, Jesus as the pattern for human life, that holds a great attraction for many in our time. Whereas the members of the first group despair of finding the historic Jesus and insist that Christian thought begins with the New Testament witness, the second group of modern critics believes that we can find the historical Jesus behind the New Testament judgments.

Chalcedon Again

Since these two Christological perspectives persist and are left unresolved by critical-historical methods, one might suppose that the two natures doctrine of Chalcedon would be especially attractive, since it provides a foundation for both perspectives. For Chalcedon, Jesus the Christ is both God facing humanity and humanity turned toward God. The fact that Chalcedon continues to be criticized reveals that objections to Chalcedon lie, not simply in the critical approach to history, but more importantly in the three criticisms of the two natures doctrine cited earlier.

The most recent of the three criticisms has been voiced by Tillich. As noted above, in his judgment the traditional formula is bound up with the inadequate Greek conception of "unchanging essences" or "static essences." The immutability of the divine nature was a common belief among the Fathers, as was the belief that human nature was permanently fixed at the creation. To be sure, the idea of God's immutability is out of favor today (see Chapter V₁, "The Age of Natural Theology"); and in view of the dramatic changes which have taken place in animal species over time, many contemporary thinkers are ready to abandon any fixity of animal species. But what have these changes of belief to do with Chalcedon? Very little. The Definition of Chalcedon did not commit itself to either a static or a dynamic concept of the divine or human nature. That the Bishops at the Council believed in static essences has no bearing on the two natures doctrine. In order to make good Tillich's criticism, one must demonstrate that a static concept of natures renders the two natures doctrine incoherent. This has not yet been done.

A charge of incoherence of a different sort is leveled against the postulate that one individual can "have two natures, one human and the other divine."[69] We have already noted several points relevant to the rebuttal of this charge.

1. Chalcedon did not define "person" or "hypostasis," but left that task to later thinkers.

2. In the doctrine of the Trinity and in the doctrine of the Incarnation, "person" and "hypostasis" have broadly the same meaning: "that which individuates," that is, in the Trinity by distinguishing Father, Son, and Holy Spirit, and in the Incarnation by uniting the human and divine natures. Several later thinkers tried to give "person" precisely the same meaning in both contexts by adopting Boethius' definition, "a person is an individual substance with a rational nature." In the doctrine of the Trinity, this led to tritheism and in the Incarnation to the theory that the second Person of the Trinity is the supposit or transcendental ego of the human nature of the Incarnate. We have noted that this view has been attacked from two sides, as denying the integrity both of the human nature and of

the divine nature. On the one hand, it has compromised the full humanity of Jesus and on the other hand, the full Deity.

3. The unfortunate consequences of this interpretation of "person" can be avoided if the "unity of person" (that which makes the two natures into one individual) is regarded as analogous to organic unions of cells. The separateness of the human individual disappears where it is united with the divine Person, just as a cell loses its distinctiveness as an entity when it becomes part of a larger unity. In spite of the historical popularity of the supposit theory, the organic theory is the most reasonable.

Discussion of the Incarnation leads directly into theories of the Atonement. Like theories of the Incarnation, theories of the Atonement tend to stress either the work of humanity or the work of Deity in reconciling us to God. The two natures doctrine allows genuine roles for both God and human agency in Christ's saving work. This added reason for respecting the Definition of Chalcedon can be adequately appreciated only in the examination to be undertaken in the next chapter.

CHAPTER IV

The Atonement

In the Lord's Prayer, Christians pray that God will "deliver us from evil" (Matt. 6:13). It is the Christian conviction that since the creation God has acted to overcome evil and to bring the creation's potentiality for good to fulfillment and fruition. To complete this work, "God sent the Son into the world, not to condemn the world, but that the world might be saved through him" (John 3:17).

The New Testament variously describes the mission of the Son as one of salvation or protection (Luke 2:11), deliverance or rescue (Gal. 1:4), redemption or freeing from enslavement (Rom. 3:24), reconciliation or the reunion of the estranged (2 Cor. 5:18), and rebirth or the giving of new life (John 10:10). The general term for all of these activities is "Atonement." "Atonement" (at-one-ment) was coined from the English word elements to express the overcoming of separation or estrangement of the world and of human beings in it from God's purpose for his creation, from each other, and from God himself.

The doctrine of the Atonement has been called the primary response of God to the problem of evil.[1] It states that the unification of the world with God's plan for it will bring about the eventual conquest of suffering and evil, if not in this world, at least in the world to come. Skeptics tend to abandon even the hope of total conquest of evil, so vast is the evidence of disorder, suffering, disease, moral degradation, and perversion. They conclude that, if there is a God at all, he is too weak, or perhaps too evil, to be served and adored. Underlying this chasm between skeptics and Christians lie differing assessments of the way to overcome evil. The ideal God of the skeptics is the watchmaker who adjusts the balance of good and evil in the world with the precision of an engineer. Christian sensibilities, however, have never been won over to this view. Christians seem more impressed by a loving God who has shown over time his power over evil by seeking to rescue and save through example and persuasion.

All the great religions have theories about the overcoming of evil. They all speak of the uniting of what is separated. Yet in spite of this similarity, Christianity stands alone in its strong emphasis on suffering and death in its account of the divine reconciliation. A major part of that understanding is based on the Savior's death on Calvary. Where other faiths have peaceful and serene images, like the reclining Buddha, Christianity has an image of suffering and pain, the body of Jesus on the cross.

This fact is so extraordinary that both defenders and critics have remarked on it. For some of St. Paul's listeners the cross was an "offence" (Gal. 5:11 KJV), although for Paul himself it was otherwise. "For the word of the cross is folly to those who are perishing, but to us who are being saved it is the power of God" (1 Cor. 1:18). It is still an offense for many today. For how could a horrible death like this one be an answer to the problem of evil? The event itself seems to deny this possibility. The Crucifixion exemplifies the evil it is said to overcome. It is a horrifying example of suffering and not a diminution of its presence. Moreover, the death on the cross seems to exalt only secondary virtues. It seems to glorify stoic endurance and subservient acquiescence. Neither the ability to endure pain, nor the obsequious acceptance of fate, it is said, will undermine the causes of war and lead to a better world. Yet from earliest times, Christians have called the Friday on which Jesus hung on the cross "Good Friday" and have thought of his death as part of God's plan for the conquest of evil. In order to understand this paradox better, we need to explore Christian concepts of evil.

Types of Evil

The evils of hunger, suffering, and disease are recognized by all. Christianity, however, has also been concerned with other types of evil. It has identified evil with sin and guilt; alienation and the breach of personal relationships; failure of will (sometimes linked to a corruption of nature); bondage to Satan and demonic possession (sometimes understood as a form of idolatry); and death, destruction, and annihilation. All five types are discussed in the New Testament as well as in subsequent Christian literature. It is useful to review what has been said in these sources before we examine the proposals about how these evils are to be overcome.

Sin and Guilt

The fact that the New Testament focuses so much upon forgiveness reveals how deep was its concern over sin and guilt. At the opening of his ministry, John the Baptist preached "a baptism of repentance for the forgiveness of sins" (Mark 1:4). The call to repentance and the promise of forgiveness are prominent also in Jesus' teaching. Luke's version of the Lord's Prayer specifically petitions God to "forgive us our sins" (Luke 11:4), and Jesus is accused of arrogating divine powers to himself when he forgives the sins of a paralytic (Mark 2:5–12). Likewise, in Acts, Paul is reported to have said: "Let it be known to you therefore, brethren, that through this man forgiveness of sins is proclaimed to you" (Acts 13:38). So central is this concern in the presentation of the gospel that we need not linger further over it.

Alienation and the Breach of Personal Relationships

Closely related to guilt and sin is the sense of separation and alienation, since the sense of guilt drives human beings apart and separates them from God. The desperation of those separated from human companionship is glimpsed in the words of Cain to God when exiled for the murder of his brother, Abel. "My punishment is greater than I can bear. Behold, thou has driven me this day away from the ground; and from thy face I shall be hidden; and I shall be a fugitive and a wanderer on the earth, and whoever finds me will slay me" (Gen. 4:13–14). Restoration of personal relationships is a prominent theme in the teachings of Jesus. When asked, " 'How often shall my brother sin against me, and I forgive him? As many as seven times?' Jesus said to him, 'I do not say to you seven times, but seventy times seven'" (Matt. 18:21–22). Jesus advises those who come to the altar with a gift that, if they remember that their neighbor has something against them, "first be reconciled to your brother, and then come and offer your gift" (Matt. 5:24). Over and over again, Jesus stresses love and forgiveness of others as necessary conditions for human fellowship and for entrance into the Kingdom of God.

Failure of Will

"Failure of will" usefully groups together a large assortment of ills having to do with defects in human desires and motivations. These range all the way from simple failure of perseverance to the inability to mediate between two equally strong impulses, and to more radical disorientations of the will—perverse desires and depraved affections.

The failure to persevere is such an obvious moral evil that it needs no further comment. More striking is the New Testament emphasis upon the conflict of inclinations and intentions. A classic expression of this failure of the will is found in the writings of Paul when he speaks of "a war" in his members (Rom. 7:23), which he further explains as a conflict between his "sinful passions . . . at work in our members to bear fruit for death" (Rom. 7:5) and "the law of my mind" (Rom. 7:23). The depths of his despair over his inability to bring about an integration between his inclinations and intentions, which is also described as a captivity (Rom. 7:23), is poignantly expressed in the words: "Wretched man that I am! Who will deliver me from this body of death?" (Rom. 7:24).

Paul sees a similar captivity among some of his fellow human beings. "They were filled with all manner of wickedness, evil, covetousness, malice. Full of envy, murder, strife, deceit, malignity, they are gossips, slanderers, haters of God, insolent, haughty, boastful, inventors of evil, disobedient to parents, foolish, faithless, heartless, ruthless" (Rom. 1:29–31). Often this sorry state of affairs is explained as a corruption of human nature. Athanasius cites these passages from Paul in connection with a more general spoilage of nature brought about by the fall,[2] and Paul himself saw it, at least in part, as a consequence of idolatry (Rom. 1:21–23). Regardless of cause, both Athanasius and Paul take this class of affections to be fundamental evils that must be eliminated.

Demonic Possession and Bondage to Satan

For most people today, the existence of a personal Devil is not a possibility. Still, the phrase "demonic possession" was used in ancient times for states of being that could be readily recognized. Today we would describe some of these states as mental and emotional disease, but at the time of Jesus they were regularly regarded as the work of demons. That Jesus had the ability to heal many who had such disorders is frequently reported in Scripture (cf. Mark 1:34). Although most of us today would not use the phrase "demonic possession" to refer to mental illnesses, except metaphorically, still, the illnesses are real enough and are among the types of evil vividly depicted in the Gospels.

The concept of "demonic possession" has also been applied to a different kind of enslavement. It might be called the bondage to "spiritual wickedness in high places," to borrow a phrase from the King James translation of Ephesians (6:12). Frequently cited examples of this kind of demonic possession are the corrupting power that Nazism had upon the German people and Jim Jones had upon Jonestown. Sometimes we allow ourselves to be enslaved. When that happens we are guilty of a form of idolatry. Such was apparently Paul's meaning when he spoke of idolatry as bringing in its wake enslavement of will (Rom. 1:28).

Death, Destruction, and Annihilation

In the Scripture, "death" refers to physical death and, through it, to all forms of physical annihilation, and also to spiritual death. Not only does Paul speak of physical death as "the last enemy to be destroyed" (1 Cor. 15:26), but he also speaks of death as an inner state in the being of the believer. "We were buried therefore with him by baptism into death, so that as Christ was raised from the dead by the glory of the Father, we too might walk in newness of life" (Rom. 6:4). John echoes these same themes. "Truly, truly, I say to you, he who hears my word and believes him who sent me, has eternal life; he does not come into judgment, but has passed from death to life" (John 5:24). The Existentialists have made real to many in our time the annihilating power of meaninglessness, guilt, weakness of will, the hopelessness that can bring us to despair and self-destruction. Thus, Paul Tillich saw death or annihilation as a sub-class of the fundamental evil, non-being, which he believed recapitulated all the rest.[3] Still, Christians have not always seen it this way, as is evidenced in the evils singled out by various theories of the Atonement.

Early Accounts of the Atonement

Three theories of reconciliation are found in Scripture and in the early Fathers. Reconciliation or atonement is said to be accomplished by the Incarnation itself, by the sacrificial death of Christ on Calvary, and by the conquest and defeat of the Devil. It is helpful to prepare for discussions of these theories in their classic expressions by indicating the respective historical antecedents.

The Incarnation as the Atoning Act

In interpreting the Pauline declaration "God was in Christ reconciling the world to himself," all agreed that God and humanity had met in Jesus of Nazareth. To amplify, God acted and humanity responded in such a way that the death on the cross was the culmination of that action and response. However, different theories of the Atonement place different emphases on the various phases of Christ's life and work. In one view the primary locus of atonement is God's entering human life in the Incarnation. In Scripture the Gospel of John displays this view prominently. "And the Word became flesh and dwelt among us, full of grace and truth; we have beheld his glory, glory as of the only Son from the Father" (John 1:14). "No one has ever seen God; the only Son, who is in the bosom of the Father, he has made him known" (John 1:18). "I have come as light into the world, that whoever believes in me may not remain in darkness" (John 12:46). Writing in about the year 185, Irenaeus carried on this theme: "Because of his measureless love, He became what we are in order to enable us to become what He is."[4] Just by the Logos' becoming human, Irenaeus believed, human nature is mystically restored, because Christ "recapitulated" the whole human race. A similar view is found in other Fathers, most notably in Athanasius.[5] One account of this mystical recapitulation is called "the physical theory" and seems to rely on the Platonic notion that all human beings are connected through their common nature or *physis*. Thus it is held that the Logos, by restoring the human nature of one human being to perfection, that is, by enabling one human being to live a sinless, fully God-centered life, automatically restores the human nature of all persons. However, this Platonic interpretation appears to be contradicted by continuing human sinfulness. Later we shall see how the atoning significance of the Incarnation can be more adequately expressed when stripped of Platonic ideas. In any case, neither Irenaeus nor Athanasius limits himself to one theory. Both employ sacrificial terminology when speaking of the work of Christ and both speak of Christ's defeat of Satan and the consequent liberation of the human race from Satan's enslaving power.[6] Neither author coordinated these themes perfectly, nor did other writers of the period.

The Sacrificial Death

In the New Testament, the sacrificial theme is most fully developed in the Epistle to the Hebrews. Prominent is its comparison of the Temple purification rites of animal sacrifice and the death of Christ on the cross. In explanation, Hebrews speaks of Christ as "having been offered once to bear the sins of many" (Heb. 9:28) by his death, and of Christ's death as more efficacious than the sacrifices of the old covenant. "If the sprinkling of defiled persons with the blood of goats and bulls and with the ashes of a heifer sanctifies for the purification of the flesh, how much more shall the blood of Christ, who through the eternal Spirit offered himself without blemish to God, purify your conscience from dead works to serve the living God" (Heb. 9:13–14). Sacrificial concepts are also found in the Epistles of Paul when he declares, "Christ, our paschal lamb, has been sacrificed" (1 Cor. 5:7), and when he speaks of Christ as "an expiation by his blood" (Rom. 3:25). The first Epistle of John likewise describes Christ as an "expiation for our sins" (1 John 2:2).

The early Church Fathers frequently express the same themes. The Epistle of Barnabas (c. 130) speaks of Christ as dying "so that we might be cleansed by the remission of our sins, which cleansing is through the blood of His sprinkling."[7] Tertullian also stresses sacrifice: "It was necessary for Him to be made a sacrifice for all nations," and "He delivered Himself up for our sins."[8] Likewise, Basil asserts: "He offered Himself as a sacrifice and oblation to God on account of our sins."[9] Clearly the idea that Christ's death has an efficacy analogous to that of ritual sacrifice is well represented in early Christian thinking.

The Conquest of Satan

Equally well-established was the theme of the conquest and defeat of the devil. In the New Testament, the Epistle to the Colossians clearly expresses this idea. Colossians affirms that God "has delivered us from the dominion of darkness and transferred us to the kingdom of his beloved Son" (Col. 1:13). God does so by defeating the dark powers. "He disarmed the principalities and powers and made a public example of them, triumphing over them in [the cross]" (Col. 2:15). These statements are thoroughly congruent with other Pauline writings. First Corinthians affirms that Christ will deliver up the kingdom to the Father at the last day "after destroying every rule and every authority and power" and "put all his enemies under his feet" (1 Cor. 15:24–25). And in Romans Paul asserts Christ's sovereignty over all heavenly powers. "I am sure that neither death, nor life, nor angels, nor principalities, nor things present, nor things to come, nor powers, nor height, nor depth, nor anything else in all creation, will be able to separate us from the love of God in Christ Jesus our Lord" (Rom. 8:38–39).

Among the early Fathers, Justin Martyr speaks of Christ as "Lord of the powers"[10] and further states that the purpose of the Incarnation is the conquest of Satan. This victory is accomplished at the Crucifixion, which "shattered the might of the serpent, who instigated Adam's transgression."[11] In a similar vein, Origen states that Christ's death "not only has been set forth as an example of dying for religion, but effected a beginning and an advance in the overthrow of the evil one, the Devil, who dominated the whole earth."[12] The imagery of the defeat of the devil was so popular and pervasive in early times that it is convenient for us to begin with this idea in our systematic examination of the doctrine of the Atonement.[13]

The Classic Theory

This theory was given its name by Gustav Aulén (1879–1977) in his famous book, *Christus Victor*. Some commentators have seen this idea as a family of similar perspectives rather than a unified concept. However, whether the Classic Theory is regarded as variations on a theme or a family of views, there is one continuous thread. This is a common identification of the source of evil in the universe and a common concept of human redemption. Human beings are held captive by an alien power or powers. These powers enslave, thereby making union with God impossible. They also pervert the human will, making it impossible for human beings to do good. Irenaeus, whom Aulén selects as an exemplar of this view, describes redemption in part as a defeat of the dark powers and the release of human beings from bondage. "Mankind, that had fallen into captivity, is now by God's mercy delivered out of the power of them that held them in bondage."[14] In another place, Irenaeus adds: "The Word of God was made flesh in order that He might destroy death and bring men to life; for we were tied and bound in sin, we were born in sin and live under the dominion of death."[15] The context makes clear that Irenaeus uses "sin" and "death" to refer to the demons, sin and death. There is also some, though not conclusive, evidence that Paul used these terms similarly,[16] as the Fathers commonly did.[17]

Belief in the existence of personal demons was widespread in ancient and medieval times. The two most famous medieval writers on the Atonement, Anselm of Canterbury (1033–1109) and Peter Abelard (1079–1142), criticized the Classic Theory, not for its belief in Satan and his minions, but because God need not defeat these evil beings by so drastic a remedy as an Incarnation. If God is omnipotent, they argued, surely he need only destroy them outright. If Anselm and Abelard found much to criticize in the Classic Theory, one would expect that twentieth century theologians who do not believe in the existence of real devils would be even more critical. However, this has not universally been the case. Aulén's enthusiasm for the Classic Theory has been infectious. Perhaps the fact that this theory reached the height of its recent popularity during the Second World War is significant. While a belief in a personal devil had waned, belief in the objective presence of demonic forces like Nazism became pervasive. It is a demythologized version of the Classic Theory that has attracted contemporary theologians like Leonard Hodgson, H. A. Hodges, John Macquarrie, and Paul Tillich,[18] and that finds expression in the writings of Martin Luther King, Jr. To explain and assess this view, examination of both ancient and demythologized versions will be necessary.

The Devil Is Defeated

An early explanation of the Atonement was that on the cross the forces of darkness tried to put Jesus to death, and they could not. God raised Jesus from the dead, thereby showing that life is stronger than death, good wins out over evil, love over hatred. Sometimes this concept is expressed in a battle metaphor. "Life and death have contended in that combat stupendous. The Prince of Life reigns immortal." So runs the medieval hymn *Victimae Paschali*, echoing Colossians: "He disarmed the principalities and powers and made a public example of them, triumphing over them in [the cross]" (Col. 2:15).

In addition to the battle metaphor, it was also believed that the devil lost his power over human beings because he overstepped his rights. In one version, Satan believes that Jesus is a blasphemer because he claims to be the Son of God. Because of Jesus' apparent sin, the devil claims Christ's soul as rightfully his. But in reality Jesus is sinless. Because of this error, the devil forfeits his rights to the souls of all sinners, and so they are rescued from his domination. This view is often expressed in terms of a snare, a mousetrap, or a fishhook. In this vein, Gregory the Great (540–604) proclaimed that God deceived Satan by baiting the hook of Christ's Deity with the worm of his humanity. Satan is caught when he makes his hideous mistake.[19]

The metaphor of ransom was also employed. Paul's "you were bought with a price" (1 Cor. 6:20) is understood as a price paid to the devil. Underlying this concept is the notion that the devil must be given his due. He has legal and moral rights which must be satisfied. Gregory the Great uses an analogy from slavery and emancipation. "We of our own free will had sold ourselves" to the devil by taking up his service. "God in His goodness would restore us again to freedom. There was a kind of necessity for Him not to proceed by way of force, but to accomplish our deliverance in a lawful way. It consists in this, that the owner is offered all that he asks as the redemption-price of His property."[20] Underlying this idea is Origen's notion that God is so good that he is always ready to forgive and so no payment is required by God. If any price is to be paid, it must be paid to the devil. "But to whom did He give His soul as a ransom for many? Surely not to God. Could it, then, be to the Evil One? For he had us in his power, until the ransom for us should be given to him, even the life (or soul) of Jesus."[21]

All of these pictures of the frustration of demons seem so crude that one wonders how they could have been seriously entertained. Yet they were the accepted explanations until Anselm and Abelard took issue with them. In addition to insisting that the omnipotent creator did not need an Incarnation and a cross in order to defeat the devil, Anselm and Abelard could not understand how the devil could have any rights to forfeit or that could be satisfied by the payment of a price. Furthermore, the notion that God would defeat the devil by trickery seemed to betray God's righteousness.[22]

Arguments such as these seem conclusive condemnations of these ancient proposals. However, certain modifications have made the ideas somewhat more appealing. It has been suggested that deception need not be invoked to explain why the devil might have mistaken Christ for a blasphemer. When Paul said: "None of the rulers of this age [the demons] understood this; for if they had, they would not have crucified the Lord of glory" (1 Cor. 2:8), he could have had in mind the fact that evil hearts have difficulty in recognizing goodness when they see it. Evil minds deceive themselves by projecting their own evil intentions onto the well-intentioned. In answer to a different objection, a sensible meaning may be given to the idea of the devil's rights in some contexts. If to sin is to take up the devil's service, to enlist in his army, to swear an oath of allegiance, then the devil has the rights of contract. But however much this explanation aids in deciding what kind of rights the devil might have, there is still a logical gap. To rebel against God is not precisely the same thing as swearing allegiance to Satan, any more than a vote against a bill in Congress implies a permanent pact with others who vote against the bill. Since these explications of the ancient theory provide only a modest amelioration of its difficulties, the unreconstructed Classic Theory has long been out of favor. However, demythologized versions have been developed and have proved more satisfactory.

Modern Restatements of the Classic Theory

The basis for modern restatements of the Classic Theory can be found in a passage from Augustine: "Christ is never conquered. . . . He has conquered in your behalf, and he has conquered for you, and he has conquered in you."[23] In the original theory, the demons are powers that exist in the external world. For example, Athanasius suggests that it is fitting for Christ to be crucified so that the Prince of the Air might be defeated in his own territory.[24] But Augustine asserts that the battleground is both overhead and in human hearts and souls. The demons are within, as the dark part of the individual psyche. This shift to an interior focus is further developed in modern restatements of the Classic Theory and brings it into closer relationship with Abelard's view, as we shall soon see. However, there is an important difference between Abelard and these modern restatements. To anticipate, Abelard does not see a need to free human beings from the control of alien powers. He focuses on the question "How can I love God?" and not "How can I escape foreign control?"

George Fox (1624–1691), the founder of the Society of Friends, provides a good example of the Classic Theory. He fears alien domination by external as well as internal forces. In his journal he writes:

> So I was brought to call to mind all my time that I had spent, and to consider whether I had wronged any: but temptations grew more and more, and I was tempted almost to despair; and when Satan could not effect his design upon me that way, he laid snares and baits to draw me to commit some sin, whereby he might take advantage to bring me to despair.[25]

But Fox puts more stress than Augustine on evil as threatening from without. He fears seduction by evil companions.

> I durst not stay long in a place, being afraid of both professor and profane, lest I should be hurt by conversing much with either. For

Fox is an unusual example!

which reason I kept myself much as a stranger, seeking heavenly wisdom, and getting knowledge from the Lord; and was brought off from outward things, to rely on the Lord alone.[26]

Similarly, many in later generations have feared seduction by wicked politicians, by economic structures, and by the false promises of manipulators. To keep pure and untainted one must be constantly on guard.

Fox found his answer in the example of Christ.

When I was in the deep, I could not believe that I should ever overcome; my troubles, my sorrows, and my temptations were so great, that I often thought I should have despaired, I was so tempted. But when Christ opened to me how He was tempted by the same devil, and had overcome him, and had bruised his head; and that through Him and His power, light, grace, and Spirit, I should overcome also, I had confidence in Him. Christ, who had enlightened me, gave me His light to believe in, and gave me hope, which is Himself revealed in me, and gave me His Spirit and grace, which I found sufficient in the deeps and in weakness.[27]

What is it about the life of Jesus of Nazareth that gives people like Fox their answer? In *Christian Discourses*, Søren Kierkegaard (1813–1855) saw Jesus' maintenance of the unity of himself with God as the key to his triumph over external evil and failure of the will. In the mystery of the Incarnation, the human mind, heart, and will of Jesus responded totally in commitment to the God present in him.

How did He manage to live without anxiety for the next day—He who from the first instant of His public life when He stepped forward as a teacher knew how His life would end, that the next day was His crucifixion, knew this while the people exultantly hailed Him as King . . . knew when they were crying, 'Hosanna!', at His entry into Jerusalem that they would cry, 'Crucify him!' . . . He who bore every day the prodigious weight of this superhuman knowledge—how did He manage to live without anxiety for the next day? . . . He had eternity with Him in the day that is called today, just for this reason He turned His back on the next day. . . . He had Eternity with Him in the day that is called today, hence the next day had no power over Him, it had no existence for Him.

It had no power over Him before it came, and when it came and was the day that is called today it had no other power over Him than that which was the Father's will, to which He had consented with eternal freedom, and to which He obediently bowed.[28]

There are several modern expressions of the conviction shared by Fox and Kierkegaard that the key to overcoming evil is found in the example of Jesus' personal relationship with God. Schleiermacher called it "God-consciousness,"[29] Moltmann and Schillebeeckx "the Abba experience,"[30] and Paul Tillich an "undisrupted unity."[31] Tillich calls the threat from without and its consequent sapping of the will "the threat of non-being." Non-being encompasses every negativity—death, meaninglessness, despair, estrangement, and alienation from others—anything that deprives human beings of their courage to be and the power to resist destruction. Tillich saw in the New Testament picture of Christ, especially in his passion, the same overcoming of separation as did Kierkegaard. Christ manifested for all the possibility of a New Life and a New Being—

first and decisively, as the undisrupted unity of the center of his being with God; second, as the serenity and majesty of him who preserves this unity against all the attacks coming from estranged existence.[32]

Fox, Kierkegaard, and Tillich see that Christ's personal victory over the dark forces is based in his unity with God. They present union with God as the ideal for human life. These ideas echo the words of union from the Gospel of John, "Abide in me, and I in you" (15:4) . . . "As the Father has loved me, so have I loved you; abide in my love" (John 15:9). Words like "participation," "faith-union," and "indwelling of the Spirit" have been used for this same notion. "Faith," concludes Tillich, "is based on the experience of being grasped by the power of the New Being through which the destructive consequences of estrangement are conquered."[33]

Another Modern Reformulation

Whereas Fox and Kierkegaard talk of withstanding threats to the person, another reformulation of the Classic Theory focuses on disarming and converting external forces of evil. The Epistle to the

Colossians says of Jesus, "He disarmed the principalities and powers and made a public example of them, triumphing over them" in [the cross]" (Col. 2:15). Martin Luther King, Jr. (1929–1968) saw in Christ's innocent suffering the key to understanding not only the saving power of the Crucifixion, but also the conquest of evil in society. King saw the principalities and powers as the entrenched and prejudiced political rulers rather than as supernatural demons. In a well-known passage, King speaks of his own experience of the transforming power of unmerited suffering.

> I have lived these last few years with the conviction that unearned suffering is redemptive. There are some who still find the Cross a stumbling block, others consider it foolishness, but I am more convinced than ever before that it is the power of God unto social and individual salvation.[34]

Unlike sacrificial theories where gratuitous suffering pays the debt to God's justice, Martin Luther King saw it as a force able to neutralize the dark powers by forcing them to act openly. Unmerited suffering brings "to light the things now hidden in darkness and will disclose the purposes of the heart" (1 Cor. 4:5). It brings sin out into the open, where it can be dealt with.

> Like a boil that can never be cured so long as it is covered up but must be opened with all its ugliness to the natural medicines of air and light, injustice must be exposed, with all the tension its exposure creates, to the light of human conscience and the air of national opinion before it can be cured.[35]

Here was King's application of the Atonement to the struggle for civil rights. King is sometimes mistakenly described as teaching nonresistance, but in fact what he advocated was nonviolent resistance to evil. Like Jesus in his passion, King and his followers walked fearlessly into the valley of the shadow of death, all the while making their innocence seen. The fact that much prejudice remains should not blind us to the fact that great social changes brought about by their actions do provide some empirical proof of the validity of this theory of Atonement.

> Nonviolent resistance paralyzed and confused the power structure against which it was directed. The brutality with which officials would have quelled the black individual became impotent when it

could not be pursued with stealth and remain unobserved. It was caught . . . in gigantic circling spotlights. It was imprisoned in a luminous glare revealing the naked truth to the whole world.[36]

In addition to robbing oppressors of their weapons, unearned suffering can also bring about the oppressor's collapse from within. It can change the heart of the oppressor by teaching him about himself, showing him the evil in himself and its effect on others, and so bringing him to a sense of his guilt. It can transform "the face of the enemy." It can "free [the] oppressor from his sins."[37] Some of the dynamics of this process are described by the late Archbishop of Canterbury, William Temple (1881–1944):

> In Christ's agony we see what our sin costs God; and in His bearing before His enemies we see how God regards us as we inflict the blow. . . . We cannot go on wounding One who accepts our wounds like that; we are filled with fear, not the old craven fear of punishment, but the fear of wounding the tenderest of hearts.[38]

Modern restatements of the Classic Theory have captured contemporary imagination. However, two reservations are sometimes noted. It is argued that the six million Jews who died in the Holocaust, and also the followers of Ghandi and Martin Luther King, present more extreme instances of unmerited suffering than Christ on the Cross. Furthermore, the victory over dark forces is not always assured. Many Nazis remained unmoved by the sufferings of their Jewish victims. Yet the vision of the Suffering Servant who by his unmerited pain overcomes evil touches on some of the deepest stirrings of the human heart. The Classic Theory does reflect many of the dynamics of the conquest of evil by good. However, in most versions of the theory, the conquest is presented as a continuing process, with the outcome not final until the end of the world. Other theories express more definitely the claim that the death of Jesus is the unique vehicle of salvation, and once and for all removes sin as a barrier to salvation. Both of these ideas are prominent in Anselm's version of the Atonement where, in the words of the Book of Common Prayer, the death of the Savior is seen as an "oblation of himself once offered, a full, perfect and sufficient sacrifice, oblation and satisfaction, for the sins of the whole world."

The Perfect Sacrifice

Anselm's *Why God Became Man* is without doubt the most brilliant exposition of the sacrificial theory of the Atonement. The fact that it has flaws should not blind us to its power and depth. After discounting the ideas that the omnipotent God needed to come down from heaven in order to defeat the devil and that the devil had any rights over human beings,[39] Anselm launches into his positive doctrine, which can be outlined as follows:

1. God is faced with a dilemma. He is merciful and wants to forgive human beings for their sins, yet his justice will not allow his mercy to operate unrestrained. The moral order of the universe and God's honor would be debased if reparation were not made for the sins of humankind.[40] "Without satisfaction, that is, without the voluntary payment of debt, God can neither pass by the sin unpunished, nor can the sinner attain happiness like that which he had before he sinned."[41]

2. A sufficient payment cannot be made by ordinary human beings. Since all their good deeds are already owed in total obedience to God, they have nothing to give voluntarily. Furthermore, it would take great resources to make satisfaction for all the present and past sins of human beings.[42]

3. An offering of incalculable worth freely given could make reparation for the innumerable human sins.[43]

4. The voluntary sacrifice of his life by a sinless person would be such an offering, because a sinless human being would not otherwise have to die.[44] According to Anselm, and according to a long tradition of understanding that we shall explore in the next chapter, death is a punishment for Adam's sin.[45]

5. Since the God-man is born without original sin inherited from Adam and has not sinned himself, he does not deserve death. He does not have to die, so his sacrifice of his own life is purely voluntary.[46] Hence, the free offering of his life by the sinless man, Jesus of Nazareth, is of infinite value. As Anselm's interlocutor puts it in the dialogue, the life of Christ is worth more than all the sins of the world, since the slightest injury to the God-man is more to be hated than all other evils.

I would far rather bear all other sins, not only those of this world, past and future, but also all others that can be conceived of, than this alone. And I think I ought to say this, not only with regard to killing him, but even as to the slightest injury which could be inflicted on him.[47]

6. With the full oblation of himself once offered, Jesus satisfied God's justice, so that God's loving and merciful forgiveness were restrained no longer.

Anselm's theory addresses directly the evils of sin and guilt and the need for forgiveness. It also addresses estrangement in personal relationships, at least in respect to God. Anselm leaves it to other aspects of God's grace to correct the human will. The conquest of death he leaves to the final resurrection of the dead.

The strength of Anselm's conception is that it emphasizes God's justice rather than simply his wrath, as it might at first appear. Guilt is taken away and the breach with God is removed because God's justice is really satisfied. Anselm has often been criticized for basing his theory on a system of justice that demands reparations for harm done. But such criticism is not telling because human justice *does* demand that restitution be made where possible. This part of the ordinary legal code is perhaps a reflection of a theme deeply enshrined in the books of the Bible. One of Anselm's strengths is that he calls upon this traditional understanding. The difficulty with Anselm's proposal lies rather in his calculation that the voluntary offering of Christ's life is of incalculable worth and thus capable of making just reparation. Abelard was troubled over just this point. If the life of Christ was of infinite value, surely his execution was of infinite disvalue. "What expiation will avail for that act of murder committed against Christ?"[48] It is certainly reasonable to question Anselm's account of how the values of obedience and rebellion, murder and self-oblation are to be calculated and balanced.

The infinite value of Christ's self-oblation is further called into question if death is viewed as natural to human beings and not a punishment for Adam's sin. It is the voluntary nature of Christ's sacrifice that gives it transcending worth. But if he, like all human beings, must die, then his dying is robbed of its special value. Only the time or manner of his death could be voluntary, but not death itself. Could it be that the kind of death, rather than the fact of Christ's death, is the source of its extraordinary value?

This question is addressed by St. Thomas Aquinas, who modifies Anselm by proposing a different satisfaction or payment. Where Anselm spoke of the life of Christ, St. Thomas speaks of his suffering. It is the suffering of Christ that takes away the sin of the world.[49] While this proposal grounds the voluntary nature of Christ's offering without arguing that as sinless he did not have to die, calculations designed to support the inestimable worth of Christ's suffering become even more difficult. For example, Christ's sufferings do not seem more acute than those of many others who have been tortured and killed. St. Thomas argues that since Christ is perfect in manhood, his sensitivities were more acute than those of ordinary human beings. Hence "Christ suffered the maximum of pain."[50] But how great will the maximum have to be in order to pay the price of sin? St. Thomas gives up and affirms that it will have to be at least enough to satisfy God's justice.[51]

Others have also been troubled by these problems. In the view of the philosopher and theologian, John Duns Scotus (1265–1308), the death and suffering of Christ did not really satisfy God's justice, but God in his mercy accepted them as a full payment even though they fell short.[52] The Protestant Reformer, John Calvin (1509–1564), proposed that Christ satisfies God's justice by being punished in our place,[53] but this only seems to make matters worse. How can God's justice be satisfied when the wrong person is punished?[54] This shift in metaphors, then, does not materially change the facts. It seems but an act of God's mercy to accept the death of Christ or his suffering in lieu of something owed by human beings. If it is after all really a matter of mercy, why cannot God simply forgive us without any reparation?

Further Reflections

Anselm's view, which started out so bravely, seems to have collapsed. Yet its themes have such a hold on Christian consciousness that we ought to wonder whether we have really got to the heart of it. Many commentators have tried to locate the power of this view in its emphasis on the cost to God of forgiveness. Tillich speaks of love and justice as producing "a tension in God."[55] This tension is expressed in more personal terms by Paul: "He who did not spare his own

Son but gave him up for us all, will he not also give us all things with him?" (Rom. 8:32). Indeed, Paul emphasizes the cost to God by adding that if God's love for us is willing to undergo this, it must be boundless. However, although in sacrificial theories God's forgiveness is certainly costly, it is costly in other theories as well. So costliness does not seem to get to the heart of this theory's appeal.

The power of Anselm's conception seems to lie not in the effect of the reparations on God, as Anselm thought, but in their effect on the wrong-doer. Reparations cannot assure God's forgiveness but are necessary to enable that forgiveness to take effect in the human heart. A child breaks a treasured vase. He fears not only that he will be punished but also that he has destroyed the loving relationship with his parents. Although he knows that the pennies from his bank will never be enough, he offers them to his parents. It is the best he has to offer. Because it is the best, the child believes that it can be accepted, and that belief enables the child to accept the forgiveness and love which the parents offer.

R. C. Moberly (1845–1903) in his influential *Atonement and Personality* comes close to expressing this view in his suggestion that the sacrifice of Christ is a Vicarious Penitence, and not a vicarious death or suffering. "The perfect sacrifice of penitence in the sinless Christ is the true atoning sacrifice for sin."[56] But Moberly narrows the offering too much. Not merely the oblation of a sinless being (Anselm), the maximum suffering of the perfect man (St. Thomas Aquinas), and perfect penitence (Moberly), but the offering of the whole life from birth to death of a sinless person is the central focus of the tradition. "All Christ's life was a cross and a martyrdom," said Thomas à Kempis (1380–1471).[57] It is an offering that can be accepted by God because it is the best that human beings could offer.

But the traditional Christian thinking is even more complex. All must share in that offering if they are to share in God's forgiveness. This will involve not only their offering of themselves, but seeing Christ's offering of himself as their offering too. Thomas à Kempis continues: "In likewise thou oughtest to offer . . . willingly thyself in pure oblation daily in the mass with all thine affections and strengths."[58] Christ is the best that we have to offer God. He offers himself freely on our behalf. We offer ourselves in him and through him. We offer him in ourselves—and through ourselves—he in us and we in him. We are hanging there along with Christ on the cross.

Abelard's Moral Influence Theory

The third great theory of the Atonement is Peter Abelard's. We have already mentioned Abelard's criticism of the Classic Theory and of Anselm's Sacrificial Theory.[59] Abelard's positive doctrine can be put simply. Incredible as it may seem, God loves us by sending his son into the world. When we fully recognize this love of God for us, our stony hearts are changed and we find a new freedom and a new ability to fulfill the best that is in us. Abelard wrote:

> Now it seems to us that we have been justified by the blood of Christ and reconciled to God in this way: through this unique act of grace manifested to us—in that his Son has taken upon himself our nature and persevered therein in teaching us by word and example even unto death—he has more fully bound us to himself by love; with the result that our hearts should be enkindled by such a gift of divine grace, and true charity should not now shrink from enduring anything for him.[60]

It is in the Incarnation itself—God's gift of himself in the total life of Jesus, in his teaching as well as in his obedience to death—that God's incredible love for his creatures is manifested. In the words of the Epistle of John: "In this is love, not that we loved God but that he loved us and sent his Son . . ." (1 John 4:10), and in the words of the Gospel of John: "God so loved the world that he gave his only Son, that whoever believes in him should not perish but have eternal life" (John 3:16).

But the Epistle of John continues: "If God so loved us, we also ought to love one another" (1 John 4:11). Abelard also echoes John's understanding of the effects on human beings of their awareness of God's love.

> Wherefore, our redemption through Christ's suffering is that deeper affection in us which not only frees us from slavery to sin, but also wins for us the true liberty of sons of God, so that we do all things out of love rather than fear—love to him who has shown

us such grace that no greater can be found, as he himself asserts, saying, "Greater love than this no man hath, that a man lay down his life for his friends."[61]

In God's determination not to be separated from humanity, which is manifested in the Incarnation, in his forgiveness of sins, and in Jesus' willingness to endure the Crucifixion, we come to realize the high value that God gives to humanity. Because we are so prized, we are able to accept ourselves as God does, and we turn from excessive concern over our sin and guilt. Freed from self-preoccupation, we become free to love others.

Luther's Doctrine of Justification by Faith

Although the great reformer Martin Luther (1483–1546) often preached and commended a sacrificial theory of Atonement, he nonetheless gave classic expression to the essentials of Abelard's insight. In Luther's early life as a monk, he was overwhelmed with a sense of his own guilt and his inability to find peace with God. During this period of his life, he was greatly troubled about himself and about the meaning of the sentence from the Epistles of Paul, "The righteous shall live by faith" (Rom. 1:17). He wrote of his own perplexity as follows:

> I greatly longed to understand Paul's Epistle to the Romans and nothing stood in the way but that one expression, "the justice of God," because I took it to mean that justice whereby God is just and deals justly in punishing the unjust. My situation was that, although an impeccable monk, I stood before God as a sinner troubled in conscience, and I had no confidence that my merit would assuage him. Therefore I did not love a just and angry God, but rather hated and murmured against him. Yet I clung to the dear Paul and had a great yearning to know what he meant.[62]

Luther then continues:

> Night and day I pondered until I saw the connection between the justice of God and the statement that "the just shall live by his

faith." Then I grasped that the justice of God is that righteousness by which through grace and sheer mercy God justifies us through faith. Thereupon I felt myself to be reborn and to have gone through open doors into paradise. The whole of Scripture took on a new meaning, and whereas before the "justice of God" had filled me with hate, now it became to me inexpressibly sweet in greater love. This passage of Paul became to me a gate to heaven.[63]

What constituted this great enlightenment, as it is called, is the realization of God's love and mercy in the forgiveness of sins. As Luther puts it in "A Treatise on Christian Liberty," "Faith in the promises of God fulfills what the law demands."

> If you wish to fulfil the law, and not to covet, as the law demands, come, believe in Christ, in Whom grace, righteousness, peace, liberty and all things are promised you; if you believe you shall have all, if you believe not you shall lack all.[64]

Here is the heart of Abelard's intuition. Fear of punishment breeds concern for the self. Souls filled with a sense of God's forgiving love are freed not only from objective guilt but also from the paralyzing effects of the feeling of guilt. Out of love for God, they can love those whom God loves, their neighbor.

> Lo, thus from faith flow forth love and joy in the Lord, and from love a joyful, willing and free mind that serves one's neighbor willingly and takes no account of gratitude or ingratitude, of praise or blame, of gain or loss.[65]

It is no wonder that Luther concludes the passage in which he records his great enlightenment with these words:

> If you have a true faith that Christ is your Saviour, then at once you have a gracious God, for faith leads you in and opens up God's heart and will, that you should see pure grace and overflowing love. This it is to behold God in faith that you should look upon his fatherly, friendly heart, in which there is no anger nor ungraciousness. He who sees God as angry does not see him rightly but looks only on a curtain, as if a dark cloud had been drawn across his face.[66]

Atonement Is Many Faceted

Although no one theory of the Atonement is complete, each has a truth that it seeks to express. Christian thinkers have largely abandoned Anselm's idea that Christ's death on the cross could be an adequate satisfaction for human sin. Nonetheless, Anselm's concern over the destructive consequences of sin and guilt has found other expressions. Luther experienced in his own life the ruinous effects of these evils in alienating human beings from God and from each other. Abelard's theory is popular today, that is, the appreciation of God's love as a means of spiritual transformation so that the will is healed and we become free to love others. However, Abelardians often fail to see the strength of Anselm's view. The reconciliation and restructuring of the will usually requires some reparation. Before we can fully accept the gift of forgiveness, we must make an appropriate offering in recompense.

However, both Anselm and Abelard concentrate almost exclusively on individual salvation and do not address the social concerns that are so prominent in the writings of Martin Luther King and that the Classic Theory is able to address. Any complete treatment of reconciliation will have to take into account all these views. But there is another reason for doing so. The Definition of Chalcedon affirms that Jesus the Christ is both God and man. Hence, any reconciliation effected by the God-man would be expected to involve both the divine and the human natures. This, as we have noted, was one of Anselm's insights. Theories that emphasize only the divine or the human contribution will be incomplete; but taken together such theories see atonement and reconciliation as the work of both natures. Only a combination or synthesis of the theories will reflect the fullness of the original insight.

CHAPTER V

The Fall and Original Sin

*The Genesis story
Does Not say that.*

To many in this century the doctrines of the Fall and Original Sin seem bizarre. The theory that the human race had only two ancestors and that, as a result of their disobedience to God, human nature became distorted and that this defect was inherited by subsequent generations, seems but the remnant of a prescientific mode of thought too crude and primitive to be retained. This sequence of ideas is particularly vulnerable because it contradicts two of the most well-established doctrines of contemporary biology. The theory of evolution renders obsolete the view that the human race had but two ancestors; and modern genetics, the view that characteristics acquired by parents can be biologically transmitted to their offspring. Hence, it seems best to consign these doctrines to the scrap heap, along with Ptolemaic astronomy and the flat earth theory.

However, we shall not proceed so summarily. An understanding of the historical development of these two doctrines, and of the theological and empirical reasons that prompted Christians to adopt them, reveals them to be far less bizarre than they at first appear. The historical and conceptual investigation that we shall undertake illumines a fascinating chapter in the history of religious thinking, as well as providing the material on which twentieth century minds can reasonably decide whether Christianity is simply stuck with these doctrines, whether it can jettison them without destroying itself, or whether it can modify them in such a way that they remain true to central Christian affirmations while embracing the results of modern science.

A discussion of Original Sin might have preceded the treatment of theories of the Atonement. It might have done so because Atonement has often been conceived as overcoming human estrangement and alienation from God, and at least one modern proposal, to be discussed below, describes Original Sin as just this alienation. It is also the case that the doctrine of Original Sin has played an important role in theories of the Atonement. To review, Anselm of Canterbury believed that Jesus did not ever have to die because he was free of Original Sin, since mortality was one of the defects of human nature brought on by Adam's disobedience. Christ, then, could make an offering of his life as a free gift. Because totally free, the sacrifice of his life is so magnificent an outpouring of love, and of such surpassing value, that it satisfies God's justice.

But the reasons for considering the doctrines of Original Sin and the Fall before discussion of the theories of Atonement are outweighed by others. For one thing, the doctrine of Original Sin is not a necessary part of sacrificial theories of Atonement. Anselm believed in Original Sin and sought to make a place for it in his theory of the Atonement, but similar discussions could and did proceed without it.

This point is part of a larger and more general logical relationship. As we have understood it, the central Christian affirmation is "God was in Christ reconciling the world to himself." The overcoming of Original Sin is but one special task of reconciliation and is logically separable from it. Only if there *is* Original Sin will its removal be included in the work of redemption. The logical relationship is borne out historically. Theories of the Atonement had begun to take shape long before the doctrine of Original Sin was put in schematic form by Augustine. The Classic Theory was already well articulated before Augustine wrote, and the Sacrificial and Moral Influence Theories were already sketched out.

In what follows we first present the traditional view of Original Sin, then the historical development of the doctrines of the Fall and Original Sin through Augustine, and last, some modern interpretations of these doctrines.

The Traditional View

An exposition of the traditional view can be summarized under four headings. (1) God created perfect human beings in the Garden of

Eden. The reasoning behind this assertion is that if God is omnipotent and good, he will desire to create human beings who are as perfect as human beings can be. Being creatures, they cannot have all the perfections of the creator—for example, immutability. Thus, one of the weaknesses which they possess by nature is that they are capable of change. (2) Adam sinned. He not only disobeyed his creator by defying the command not to eat of the tree in the midst of the garden, but also he thought only of his own advantage rather than the good of the creation. Adam's act of disobedience and self-seeking was a free choice and not one that was necessitated. (3) The result of Adam's disobedience was the ruin of the human race. His act of sin corrupted human nature so much that human beings lost the ability to see the good clearly and to will it unselfishly. As a result they perform many good deeds, but their actions always fall short of true excellence. Hence, in sinning human beings not only imitate Adam, but also act out of an inherited, bruised, and damaged nature that has distorted and perverted their wills and desires. (4) Finally, human beings not only share in a corrupt nature, which they obtain by inheritance, but they also share in Adam's guilt. The solidarity of the human race is such that all are guilty because all were mystically present in Adam when he sinned.

Some Distinctions

Before continuing, it is important to distinguish clearly four ideas that play an important role in the traditional view: Original Sin, the Fall, Original Righteousness, and Original Guilt.

The term "Original Sin" is not found in Scripture or the literature of the next generation. An early version of this idea appears in Tertullian's treatise *On the Soul:* "The evil that exists in the soul is derived from the fault of our origin and . . . [is] in a way natural to us."[1] This statement is not very helpful except that it links evil in the soul or sin with origins. Some have taken "origin" in the sense of "first in time." For example, several dictionaries define "Original Sin" as "the first sin committed by Adam" (cf. Funk and Wagnalls). However attractive this definition might be, it is simply not the way the tradition, both Catholic and Protestant, has used this phrase. A more standard usage is to define "Original Sin" as the "basic tendency toward sin," or as the "inclination to sin."[2] Thus, Anselm locates Original Sin primarily in the "origin or beginning of each person" and not in "the origin or beginning of human nature."[3] Likewise, the reformer Calvin (1509–1564) speaks of Original Sin as "a hereditary depravity and corruption of human nature."[4]

The Fall

It is important to understand how this inclination to sin is related to but distinct from the actions of Adam and Eve in the garden in Genesis 3. As we shall see, the story of the Fall in Genesis is used to provide a historical explanation for the human tendency or inclination to sin. The philosopher Immanuel Kant (1724–1804) made this point with particular vividness. In contrast to the general optimism of his contemporaries in the Age of Reason, Kant believed in "a radical principle of evil" in human nature. However, he was unwilling to accept the traditional explanation for its origin. He commented that "of all the explanations of the spread and propagation of this evil through all members and generations of our race, the most inept is that which describes it as descending to us as an *inheritance* from our first parents."[5]

"Original Sin" an Improper Usage?

Talk of "tendencies to sin" or "inclinations to sin" and of "preconditions for sin" raises a question about the legitimacy of the use of "sin" in this context. What is called sin in the phrase "Original Sin" seems not really sin at all since, it is claimed, sin involves conscious acts of decision for which the individual could be held accountable. Hence, the use of "sin" in the phrase "Original Sin" seems improper.[6]

In evaluating this criticism, two points ought to be kept in mind. First, as we shall see, neither the Old Testament nor Jesus restricts the word "sin" to "wicked acts consciously chosen." They sometimes use "sin" to refer to states of being like "hardness of heart." Second, even if the word "sin" once meant only "wicked deeds for which one is responsible," it is not surprising that over time its meaning should have been extended and altered to include not just actions but proclivities and dispositions to perform the actions. Aristotle notes a similar extension and alteration of the meaning of the word "healthy."[7]

When we speak of a healthy animal, we are using "healthy" in its central meaning. But we also speak of a healthy diet because diet is a cause of health in the animal; and we talk of a healthy complexion, which is a result or symptom of the health of the organism. Likewise, Original Sin is a cause of sinful deeds in somewhat the same way that a healthy diet is a cause of health in the animal. Similarly, alienation or estrangement from God is called sin because it can be seen both as an effect of sinful action and a cause of it.[8] Guilt over sinful deeds stands in the way of union with God, and loss of the sense of presence of God's perfect goodness leaves a vacuum easily filled by ignoble impulses that are no longer ordered by a higher principle.

Original Righteousness and Original Guilt

These two remaining ideas can be briefly explained. "Original Righteousness" is the state of Adam and Eve before the Fall. "Righteousness" here means "rightness," and it is further specified by Anselm as "rectitude of will," by Luther as "faith or trust in God," and by St. Thomas Aquinas as "obedience to God." Thus, "original" is not used in the way it is used in "Original Sin," but in the sense of "first in time." It designates that state of rightness that Adam and Eve had before the Fall.

These observations ought not be taken to imply that the Fathers had no notion of an inherited inclination to righteousness. When they wished to express this idea, they spoke of the image of God implanted in human nature at creation (Gen. 1:27), an image that, although damaged by the Fall, was never wholly destroyed. They saw the goodness of human nature as an assured part of its original constitution. As we shall see, it was the evil in human nature that needed explanation.

"Original Guilt," however, uses "original" in the same way as does "Original Sin." It is the theory that the human race not only inherits an inclination to sin from their first parents, but also inherits or shares in their guilt as well. Hence each person is both sinful and guilty at birth. This is a view held by Augustine and most classic theologians, both Catholic and Protestant, but it is often rejected in modern times. But before considering modern evaluations of tradition, it is important to turn to the development of these ideas.

The Idea of Sin in the Old Testament

Over the centuries, the word "sin" has become so ambiguous that it is helpful to banish from consciousness everything that we have learned about it and begin at the very beginning. In the Old Testament, the words most often translated by "sin" are the Hebrew *Chattah* and *Chet*. For both words the primary meanings are "missing the mark" or "failure to meet a standard," or "fault." These words are used in the Old Testament in both moral and nonmoral contexts, such as transgression of law and an arrow missing its target.

How is it that someone is at fault or misses the mark? In the Old Testament, fault is spelled out in terms of moral failings and also in terms of impurity. The Book of Leviticus cites both types—the pollution caused by bodily emissions and menstrual blood (Lev. 15:1–32), and moral failings—lying and stealing (Lev. 19:9–17). Both these types of "fault" are seen as deviations from the divine plan. Modern anthropology has been particularly helpful in advancing our understanding of these ancient ideas. Mary Douglas in *Purity and Danger* successfully argues that fear of blood is connected with fear that the Chaos is about to break out, because blood signals the possibility of rupture or fault in the order of creation.[9] The connection between rupture and impurity explains why impurity and moral failings are treated together in much of the Holiness Code of Leviticus; it also explains why both types of "fault" were apprehended subjectively with both dread and a sense of defilement. However, when the emission of these and other bodily fluids no longer was taken as a breach in the divine creation, this fault was demoted to mere ritual impurity and lost its primitive importance. But these are only the first strata of Old Testament concepts of sin. At a deeper level sin is presented as a breach of personal relationship with God by failure to keep the Covenant.

Philosophers of religion and theologians have sometimes puzzled over the conundrum: Does the believer keep the moral law because it is right to do so, or does he keep that same law because it is the will of God or commanded by God? If believers answer that they do so because it is right to do so, then the critic answers that loyalty to God has nothing to do with morality. On the other hand, should believers reply that they keep the moral law because it is commanded by God, then the critic in turn replies that believers may in fact act rightly, but for the wrong (nonmoral) reasons. If one keeps the moral law only because God commands it, one is not acting morally, but only to please someone.

This dilemma is useful because it brings out an important element of biblical faith. The Bible implies that believers keep the moral law for both reasons—because it is right to do so and because it is commanded by God. Put another way, to fulfill the moral law because it is the moral law is also to fulfill one's religious obligations, because God wants and desires human beings to be moral beings. We can illustrate this relationship by considering the two kinds of laws. The first part of the Ten Commandments deals with duties toward God and the second part deals with duties toward others. In the biblical conception, the second group is included in the first. Loving God includes keeping the moral law as moral law. To put it even more briefly, the duty of human beings is to love God by keeping the commandments.

For the religious believer, then, sin is not just a failure to keep the moral law, although it is that, but it is also a sin before God. It is a failure to do his will, a failure to keep the Covenant, a failure in a personal relationship with the gracious creator and giver of all. Dread born of failure has added to it dread from betrayal of a benefactor. This may explain why in the Old Testament the root of another Hebrew word often translated as "sin" is "transgression" or "rebellion."[10]

A third stratum of the use of "sin" in the Old Testament is "guilt." Guilt involves not only the recognition of failure to hit the mark, or transgression against the law of God, but in addition stresses personal agency. Guilt involves the recognition not just of fault but of my fault. Many of the elements of sin are summed up in the cry for forgiveness in Psalm 51:

> Have mercy on me, O God, according to thy steadfast love;
>   according to thy abundant mercy blot out my transgressions.
> Wash me thoroughly from my iniquity,
>   and cleanse me from my sin!
> For I know my transgressions,
>   and my sin is ever before me.
> Against thee, thee only, have I sinned,
>   and done that which is evil in thy sight,

so that thou art justified in thy sentence
and blameless in thy judgment. [1–4]

Here, the sense of pollution associated with fault and the breach of
personal relationship with God have become even more devastating
with the acceptance of personal agency or responsibility.

Finally, the Old Testament speaks of "sin" as "a state of being"
that leads to or causes sinful actions in much the same way that we
spoke of Original Sin as a cause of sinful deeds. Unbelief in god's
power is faulted (Isa. 7:9), and trust in human strength is called an
iniquity (Isa. 22:8–14). Hardness of heart is similarly condemned
when it leads to a rejection of the Covenant (Deut. 9:6, 13–14; Isa.
46:12). Sin in the Old Testament is a many-faceted concept involving states of being as well as actions, moral failure, betrayal of God,
and the recognition of personal agency and responsibility.

The Story of the Fall

Like much of the material in the first eleven chapters of Genesis, the
story of the Fall (Gen., chaps. 2–3) has echoes in other early religious literature. The story of a Tree of Life guarded by monsters or
serpents is part of the heritage of the peoples of India as well as of
the Near East. Often the hero must slay the beast in order to eat
of the Tree of Life. Sometimes, as in Genesis, there are two trees and
the guardian serpent tries to trick the hero into eating of the second
tree in order to keep him from the prize. These mythic pictures are
elucidated in interesting detail by Mircea Eliade.[11]

The presence of parallels between Hebrew Scriptures and stories
found in the literature of other peoples was a fact well recognized
by the Rabbis and the Fathers of the Church. But they drew a different conclusion from these echoes than the one that is popular
with many contemporary scholars. Contemporary scholars of comparative religion sometimes conclude that the Bible and these other
literatures drew upon a common literary ancestor. However, the
Fathers and the early Rabbis concluded that the pagan literature
represented garbled versions of the truth that was found in Scripture. For example, Philo and Clement of Alexandria represent a
common exegetical tradition that regarded pagan wisdom as inaccu-

rately derived from the revelation given by Moses in the Pentateuch.[12]

Whether one shares the triumphalist views of the ancients, or the more moderate view of contemporary scholars, a central issue is the difference between Genesis and these other stories. A significant variation is God's part in the biblical story and a corresponding shift in the Serpent's role. God forbids Adam and Eve to eat of the Tree of the Knowledge of Good and Evil. In the biblical account, the Serpent no longer attempts to keep Adam and Eve from eating of the Tree of Life, but tempts them to eat the forbidden fruit of the Tree of the Knowledge of Good and Evil. The biblical account is centered in a theistic context and shifts the focus of the story from heroes who are tricked by the serpent to sinners before God who hide themselves in shame when they become aware of their disobedience. A dimension is added to the story that is not present in non-biblical versions of it.

Jewish Interpretations of the Fall

Interpretations of the Fall story are not to be found in the Old Testament. However, there is discussion of it in the Apocrypha and other books written between the Old and the New Testaments. Almost always these Jewish interpretations have two elements. Taking their cue from God's decision to drive Adam and Eve from the garden to prevent them from eating fruit of the Tree of Life, these writings regard physical death as the punishment for Adam's disobedience. They also regard the disposition or inclination to evil, *yetzer hara*, as present in Adam from the creation and thus the cause of Adam's sin. Typical of this dual understanding is 2 Esdras (also called 4 Ezra). Of the punishment for Adam's sin, the 2 Esdras says: "And unto him thou gavest thy one commandment; which he transgressed, and immediately thou appointedst death for him and in his generations."[13] As to the presence of the *yetzer hara* as an explanation for the Fall, 2 Esdras adds: The "grain of evil seed . . . was sown in the heart of Adam from the beginning."[14] The Wisdom of Solomon asserts that death is not an original part of man's nature: "For God created man to be immortal . . . nevertheless through envy of the devil, death came into the world."[15] Jesus ben Sira, who was the author of the book later called Ecclesiasticus, expresses the common

Rabbinic belief that the evil inclination explains Adam's fall: "God created man from the beginning, . . . and gave him into the hand of his inclination (*yetzer*). If thou choose, thou mayest keep the commandment."[16] This last passage is echoed by one of the most important Talmudic texts on the *yetzer hara*: "I created the evil *yetzer*; I created for you the Law as a remedy. If you are occupied with the Law you shall not be delivered into its hand."[17] This text epitomizes the Jewish understanding of the interrelationship of the Law, evil, and human responsibility.

Jesus' View of Sin

The teachings of Jesus on sin that are relevant to our present inquiry can be treated very briefly. Central to Jesus' teachings are the Old Testament concepts of sin as defilement, as guilt brought about by the transgression of God's commandments, and as the rejection of God's love. He does not discuss the Fall story at all, but he is concerned with evil states of being. "For out of the heart come evil thoughts, murder, adultery, fornication, theft, false witness, slander" (Matt. 15:19). It is in this context that Jesus is concerned about inherent biases toward evil. It is in the writings of Paul, who had such personal difficulty in keeping the commandments, that we find extended emphasis on deep-seated attitudes that lead to sin and that may possibly be inherited from Adam.

Paul on the Fall of Adam

Romans 5 has been cited as confirmation of the traditional doctrine of Original Sin, at least since the time of Augustine, who gave the doctrine its classic exposition. However, many scholars do not find the traditional view stated unequivocally there. Certainly what Paul says in Romans 5 is consistent with the traditional view but, because his references are so brief, there are at least two possible interpretations. In Romans 5, Paul mentions Adam's sin in three closely related verses:

> Sin came into the world through one man, and death through sin, and so death spread to all men because all men sinned. [12]

Death reigned from Adam to Moses, even over those whose sins were not like the transgressions of Adam. [14]

As by one man's disobedience many were made sinners, so by one man's obedience many will be made righteous. [19]

Several points ought to be made about these verses. To begin with, Paul echoes the Rabbinic conclusion that death is punishment for Adam's sin. Although Paul sometimes uses "death" for "spiritual death" as well as "death of the body," here he is not using "death" solely in a metaphorical sense. He has in mind physical death as well as death of the soul. Second, Paul affirms both that Adam is the first sinner and that later generations are made sinners through him. Paul does not, however, explain how Adam's sin has this causal efficacy. What he says is certainly consistent with the traditionalist view that a disposition to sin is biologically inherited, but this does not exhaust all the possibilities. A disposition to sin might be transmitted psychologically rather than genetically. For example, just as parents and teachers consciously shape children for good, they also sometimes unwittingly influence them to evil.

But even more important, it is not clear what Paul means by "sin" when he says that "sin came into the world through one man." Paul uses "sin" in at least two contexts. In one passage he contrasts enslavement to sin with enslavement to righteousness (Rom. 6:18). Here "sin" seems to mean "wickedness," and Paul seems to have in mind the adoption of wickedness as a settled policy, since he also speaks of "yielding" oneself "as an obedient slave" to either sin or righteousness (Rom. 6:16). If Adam brought this kind of sin into the world, he would be the first in a line of persons who accepted wickedness rather than righteousness as their norm of behavior. If this is what Paul means, then he is not asserting the traditional doctrine of Original Sin.

However, Paul sometimes speaks of sin as a kind of power that controls or influences human beings to immoral action. For example, he says in a famous passage: "Now if I do what I do not want, it is no longer I that do it, but sin which dwells within me" (Rom. 7:20). He also says that all people fail to keep the law because they "are under the power of sin" (Rom. 3:9). There are also passages that speak of the war of the flesh against the spirit and the spirit against the flesh, which might reflect the Rabbinic distinction between the *yetzer hara,* about which we have already spoken, and the *yetzer tov* (the inclination for good), also identified by the Rabbis. If it is sin as either an alien power or the impulse to sin that Adam brought into the world, then it is plausible to say that Paul did in fact hold a doctrine of Original Sin, although he did not call it by that name. However, it is impossible to settle this matter with any certainty, since Paul's remarks on the kind of sin that Adam brought into the world can also be interpreted as meaning the *choosing* of wickedness as a policy, rather than meaning an inherent impulse toward evil, or an alien power.

Primary and Secondary Sins

In a famous text in Romans, Paul singles out idolatry as the root of a variety of evil impulses and actions. Speaking of what he takes to be particularly vile activities by pagans, he says:

> Because they exchanged the truth about God for a lie and wor-shipped and served the creature rather than the Creator . . . God gave them up to dishonorable passion. . . . They were filled with all manner of wickedness, evil, covetousness, malice. Full of envy, murder, strife . . . they are . . . inventors of evil. [Rom. 1: 25–31]

What Paul is saying is that idolatry consists of having as the primary object of concern something created, rather than God, and that this disorientation of values brings with it every kind of evil behavior. To put it in secular terms, when one ceases to honor supremely one's highest good, impulse control will be severely reduced. A very similar idea is found in Ephesians.

> Alienated from the life of God . . . they have become callous and have given themselves up to licentiousness, greedy to practice every kind of uncleanness. [Eph. 4:18–19]

These passages suggest that Paul regarded alienation from God as even more fundamental than idolatry. The worship of the creature seems to be the result rather than the cause of estrangement. How-

ever, it is nearly fruitless to try to be exact. As we have already suggested, estrangement from God can be both cause and effect of sin.

Paul's point of view draws criticism from contemporary atheists,
who object to the idea that lack of belief leads directly to the forms
of gross immorality of which Paul writes. Quite rightly they point
to the many morally virtuous atheists and agnostics. However, the
soundness of the atheists' objections on this point falsifies only some
of what Paul has to say. For example, Reinhold Niebuhr (1892–
1971), the distinguished American theologian and social critic, never
tired of telling us that idolatrous individuals are those who lift "some
finite and contingent element of existence into the eminence of the
divine"[18]—that is, they falsely absolutize something of inferior worth.
Misplaced loyalties and the elevation of provisional goods to preeminence are the roots of much of the world's moral evil.

With this understanding of sin, Paul may be the originator of the
tradition that regards Adam's sin as one of self-idolatry. This interpretation of the story sees Adam and Eve as allowing themselves to
be separated from God and choosing their own private good over
the good of the whole. In acting on the words of the serpent, "When
you eat of it your eyes will be opened, and you will be like God,
knowing good and evil," they chose themselves rather than God
(Gen. 3:5).

Original Sin among the Early Fathers

There is really no explicit discussion of Original Sin among the very
early Fathers. Justin Martyr continues the Rabbinic tradition. Although he asserts that "the whole human race will be found under a
curse," the curse is not inherited depravity, but physical death. "The
human race from Adam," he explains, "had fallen under the power
of death."[19]

Justin also reflects Ben Sira and the Rabbinic *yetzer hara* tradition
in stating that there is "the universally evil and manifold appetite
which exists in each man."[20] He echoes them in asserting the "free
will" of both men and angels, and the Law as a remedy for sin.[21]
However, Justin expands the Rabbinic heritage by emphasizing
causes or sources of human evil over which the individual has no

control. He speaks of "necessity and ignorance," from both of which human beings can be freed by the grace of Baptism.[22] Ignorance he attributes to two sources: the "wicked and impious demons" who corrupt the morals of men by false teaching, and cultural inheritance or "the bad habits and wicked training" in which children are brought up.[23] He has, then, some sense of what is sometimes described as sociologically transmitted inherited tendencies to sin. He also has a sense of the effects of finitude on human wrongdoing, since "necessity" probably includes both chance and the inherent limitations of a material existence. However, Justin Martyr does not systematically address the problem of the sources of the sort of human sin for which individuals are not personally responsible. Apparently he does not think the issue very pressing. Yet this does become an urgent problem for Origen and for others after him. Why this change? The answer lies in the fact that, like the Rabbis, Justin does not think of Adam and Eve as perfect human beings; the *yetzer hara* was with them from the beginning. However, new strains of thought began to appear in other Jewish sources. Philo and the treatise Genesis Rabbah adopted the view that God created Adam and Eve perfect in the Garden of Eden, so the presence of the inherent inclination to evil needed to be explained.[24] That the *yetzer hara* should be seen as a consequence of Adam's fall seemed an obvious solution.

Irenaeus

Another early view of the Fall in which Adam and Eve were portrayed as initially far from perfect is Irenaeus', who characteristically pictures them as children. "The lord [of the earth], that is man, was but small; for it was necessary that he should grow, and so come to perfection."[25] Furthermore, because Adam and Eve were childlike and immature, they were easily tempted. "Man was a child, not yet having his understanding perfected; wherefore also he was easily led astray by the deceiver."[26] Having been made in the image of God, human beings were not yet perfectly like God.[27] Irenaeus holds that the whole purpose of the creation and of the role of the redeemer is to bring these imperfect beings to their fullness. It is not surprising that his views have been attractive to many who have had difficulties with the traditional doctrine.

*Much more
needed on Irenaeus
here.*

Origen

For Origen, God was of such power and goodness that it was inconceivable that the universe as it came from the hand of the creator should be less than perfect. Origen is well known for his view that human souls preexist their embodiment, that they come into being at the dawn of creation, and that the story of the Fall in Genesis is an allegory of a precosmic fall of the angels. Origen's ideas on the preexistence of souls were not accepted by the Church, but his emphasis on a Fall as the source of human imperfection was. He states, "Before the ages, they were all pure intelligences, whether demons or souls or angels. One of them, the Devil, since he possessed free-will, chose to resist God, and God rejected him. All the other powers fell away with him, becoming demons, angels, and archangels according as their misdeeds were more, or less, or still less, heinous. Each obtained a lot proportionate to his sin. There remained the souls; these had not sinned so grievously as to become demons . . . God therefore made the present world, binding the soul to the body as a punishment."[28]

It is evident that for Origen the prehistorical Fall explains not only the limitations of human finitude such as death and bodily material existence, but also the reality of human sinfulness: "All we men are clearly prone to sin by nature."[29] The Fall also accounts for the calamities and sorrows of life: "It is plain that the souls concerned were guilty of previous sins."[30]

Athanasius

These themes, except for the preexistence of souls, find repeated expression in the writings of other Fathers. Athanasius, writing in *The Incarnation of the Word of God,* regards the story of the Fall in Genesis as a historical, not a prehistorical, event. But otherwise he is true to the picture of Eden as a Garden of Delights. Adam and Eve were made in the image of God and, if they had kept the commandment, would have had a life "without sorrow, pain, or care, and after it the assurance of immortality in heaven." Because of their sin, their descendants "live no longer in paradise, but, dying outside of it, continue in death and corruption." Indeed, the corruption is such that not only are human beings subject to sinful affections and evil inclinations, but the whole of the cosmos is running downhill and toward "non-existence."[31] Nowhere are the effects of the Fall pictured more catastrophically.

Augustine

The doctrine of the Fall reaches classic expression in the anti-Pelagian writings of St. Augustine. Pelagius was an English (or perhaps Irish) monk who settled in Rome about 400. He held a very optimistic view of human nature, believing that human will was by nature good and could choose rightly. Pelagius therefore put a good deal of emphasis on personal responsibility. Augustine saw these views as a deep threat to Christianity. He spent much of the last twenty years of his life in controversy with the Pelagians.

Pelagius' denial of an inherited defect from Adam was the occasion for Augustine's expression of his views rather than for their formation; Augustine had written of them many years earlier in *The Free Choice of the Will*.[32] However, Augustine did shift his thinking somewhat. In *The Free Choice of the Will*, not only is Adam capable of change, and thus of sin and falling, but his wisdom is incomplete and imperfect. He has enough wisdom to know his duty, and enough to develop morally; but he does not have that perfection of wisdom that would have made the temptation unthinkable. However, toward the end of his life Augustine states that Adam had the "highest excellence of wisdom" and possessed "no imperfection whatever."[33] For Augustine, the excellence of Adam's original endowments increased the heinousness of the crime. This "unspeakable sin" caused the present disastrous human condition. That wretched condition Augustine never doubted. As with Paul, the divided will and its enslavement to the passions were all too real to him. Only an inherited disposition to sin could explain these deep-seated and universal torments.[34] The general wretchedness of the human lot could not have been the work of the all wise, loving, and powerful God. It must have been the work of human rebellion and evil, as Origen and Athanasius had claimed.

In addition to believing that a disposition to sin is inherited from Adam, Augustine believed that future generations shared Adam's guilt. Augustine makes his view here abundantly clear. It is precisely this stain or guilt that is removed in Baptism.[35] St. Augustine explains this sharing in Adam's guilt by the thesis that, since all are descendants of Adam, all shared in his decision to sin. "In the misdirected choice of that one man all sinned in him, since all were that one man, from whom on that account they all severally derive original sin."[36] The idea that somehow we are Adam, and therefore share his guilt, seems strange to modern people. No one of Augustine's theses on original sin has been more controversial than this one. F. R. Tennant found it one of the most objectionable features of the traditional doctrine, although Paul Ricoeur finds strength in its paradoxicality.[37]

Many have been the objections to St. Augustine's formulation of the doctrine of Original Sin. In what follows we shall address two of them and lay the groundwork for considering the further objection that his theory flies in the face of evolutionary and genetic science. This latter is the most serious of the criticisms, although both Catholic and Protestant contemporary thinkers have restated the doctrine of Original Sin in the light of these scientific theories.

The Paradox of the Knowledge of Good and Evil

It has seemed contradictory to many thoughtful people that Adam and Eve are said to attain the "knowledge of good and evil" only after having eaten of the forbidden fruit and yet they are held morally culpable for eating that fruit. Surely, it is suggested, if Adam and Eve did not know what was morally good or morally evil before eating of the tree in the midst of the garden, they could not be expected to know that what they were doing was wrong. Hence, it is claimed, the story is incoherent. Adam and Eve do not really sin. Therefore, the story cannot function as a satisfactory account of sin, whether interpreted mythically or historically.

One interesting attempt to solve this dilemma makes a distinction between the several ways by which one might come to know right and wrong, good and evil. Adam and Eve could certainly have known the difference between right and wrong, as well as the obligations that they owed their generous benefactor, and yet come to know moral good and evil in a new and different way after the Fall. St. Augustine writes of the new knowledge in this way: "Such, then, was 'the opening of his eyes' which the serpent had promised him in his temptation—the knowledge, in fact, of something which he had better been ignorant of. Then, indeed, did man perceive within himself what he had done; then did he distinguish evil from good,—not by avoiding it, but by enduring it."[38] The knowledge of good and evil that Adam and Eve acquired was the knowledge of evil that comes by doing it, the experience of evil and its attendant shame and guilt. The Genesis story itself bears this out. What specific knowledge is recorded there is a consciousness of shame, symbolized by the feeling of nakedness. In this sense, the Fall is a loss of innocence. Adam's and Eve's new knowledge is a guilty knowledge of evil, contrasted to an innocent knowledge that they once possessed. The story of the Fall still seems meaningful if such a distinction is made between two quite different kinds of knowing evil and, by contrast, knowing good.

However appealing this solution, it is not without its own difficulties. Later in the story, God expels Adam from the garden with these words: "Behold, the man has become like one of us, knowing good and evil" (Gen. 3:22). This passage is troublesome because, if the foregoing interpretation is correct, Adam and Eve did not acquire the kind of knowledge of good and evil that would make them like God, but a guilty knowledge such as God does not possess. Why then should the passage say "man has become like one of us?" There is a contradiction between the interpretation and this text.

However, it is important to point out that no one has found an alternative interpretation of "the knowledge of good and evil" that does not have difficulties with this same text.[39] Augustine's solution at least solves the initial problem. God justly punished Adam and Eve for disobedience because the knowledge of good and evil that they acquired was not the knowledge of right and wrong that distinguishes good deeds from bad, but rather the experience that comes from actual transgression, that is, shame and guilt.

The Perfection of Adam

Another objection to the traditional doctrine of Original Sin also alleges an incoherence, this time not so much in the Genesis story as in Augustine's treatment of it. It is argued that if Adam and Eve were perfect and without blemish, then their fall would be inconceivable. Friedrich Schleiermacher (1768–1834) put it this way: A perfect or "incorrupt nature could not have indulged appetite in express disobedience to the divine command."[40] A perfect human being would have full awareness of the presence of God, of his goodness and the righteousness of his commands, and would have been without contrary appetites and passions, and would also have had clear knowledge of the far reaching and devastating consequences of his actions, so that to disobey the divine command would be so irrational as to be unthinkable.[41]

While it must be admitted that, if anyone were in this state of mind, disobeying God would be unthinkable, it is important to note that St. Augustine's vision of an Adam without any blemish or imperfection did not become the rule. None of the Protestant or Catholic Reformation thinkers proclaim such an exaggerated view of Adam. Instead Adam is said to be possessed of Original Righteousness or Justice. Original Righteousness is described as rectitude of will or "uprightness of will kept for its own sake."[42] Adam is said to be willingly obedient before the Fall but capable of disobedience. Furthermore, in earlier writings Augustine himself did not attribute perfection of knowledge or wisdom to Adam. In Augustine's words, Adam was "rational," but not necessarily "wise." "If, therefore, a man is so created that, although he is not yet wise, he is able to understand a command which he obviously ought to obey, it is no wonder that he could be seduced." Furthermore, "It is not unjust that he should suffer punishment when he did not obey the command."[43] Hence, Schleiermacher cannot be said to be criticizing the more usual understanding of either Original Righteousness or Adam's state of mind.

The Motivelessness of the Fall

Schleiermacher also suggests a different but related criticism. The Fall is unintelligible, he claims, because no reason can be given for Adam's choice to disobey God's command. Some have suggested that Adam and Eve misused their free will. But Schleiermacher sees no solution here. "Misuse of free will by itself is no explanation, but forces us to assume something else as prompting it."[44]

What Schleiermacher seems to have in mind is the following

problem. If Adam and Eve knew that a certain course of action was in conformity with the greater good, then it is not at all clear why they would choose a lesser good. Of course they could have been so addled that they confused one good with another. But then they no longer would have known which course of action was in conformity with the greatest good. Again this objection seems at first sight to have its merits. However, it fails because it is blind to a very obvious human problem. Through failure of nerve human beings quite often choose what they fully recognize to be the lesser good. And unless one is simply rejecting free will altogether (a possibility that we shall consider in the next chapter), there is no reason to regard all failures of nerve as beyond our control. Thus, there is nothing incoherent in St. Augustine's theory that Adam and Eve had the ability and the freedom either to adhere to the greater good or to turn their backs on it for the lesser good. The latter choice may seem irrational, but it must be possible, since people do it all the time.

A Protestant–Catholic Divergence

Up to this point, Catholic and Protestant thought is in agreement concerning the nature and definition of Original Sin. However, there is an important divergence in the thinking of these two branches of Christianity, which particularly merits attention since it bears on restatements of the doctrine in light of modern science. Protestant thought tends to regard Original Sin as an "active power,"[45] or an "active *habitus*,"[46] a drive or impulse of the will. For example, one of the Anglican Thirty-nine Articles speaks of Original Sin as "concupiscence," which has a wider meaning than lust—it includes not only sexual but any inordinate desire.

Roman Catholic thinking has followed St. Thomas Aquinas. It does not regard inordinate affection as Original Sin, but rather as the effect of Original Sin.[47] Original Sin lies further back in human nature. It is a state of being,[48] perhaps something of which we are not directly aware, "a passive inheritance"[49] that requires "the conscious voluntary act of the individual" in order to become sin.[50] It is more a precondition of sin than a force or active power. Catholics think in terms of analogies like insensitivity or blindness, whereas Protestants use analogies like rage or lust. Therefore, Protestant restatements of the doctrine of Original Sin tend to focus on drives and impulses toward sin, and Roman Catholic restatements center on states of being or preconditions that make those drives possible.

Christianity without the Historical Adam

There are many who deny that a Christianity without a historical Adam and Eve is possible. One of the most astute defenders of this view is the contemporary philosopher Peter Geach. He asks us to picture a three-paneled altar piece. On the one side is a painting of Eve falling victim to the temptation in the garden. On the opposite side a picture of the Annunciation—Mary accepting the divine commission to be the Mother of Christ. The middle panel depicts Christ in glory. "Now imagine," suggests Geach, "that the Eve panel has been stolen or destroyed: the balance and artistic worth of the picture is irreparably spoiled."[51] What Geach argues by means of this analogy is that traditional Christianity presents us with a double movement of Fall and Restoration, of death and rebirth, of Adam and Christ, and that this balance is disrupted if Adam and Eve did not really exist and the Fall did not really distort human nature.

Geach's position is linked to the notion that the first eleven chapters of Genesis record science and history. The possibility that these chapters do not record actual events has been an important topic of discussion during the last two centuries, and we shall investigate this issue in the next chapter. In the meantime, we shall look at what sort of structure Christianity has when the story of Adam and Eve in the garden is taken mythologically.

To return to the tryptic, what panel would replace the picture of Adam and Eve? For surely Geach's supposition that there would be no panel is ill-founded. What would appear would be based on the theory of evolution, a picture of human beings emerging from their evolutionary past. The first human beings would be depicted not as perfect, but imperfect, in the tradition of Irenaeus and Justin Martyr. Although the central panel would remain the same, the panel depicting Mary might also be replaced. It would no longer be an Annunciation scene (Mary to balance Eve) but a picture of redeemed creation, perhaps drawing on the imagery in the Book of Revelation. Hence, the tryptic would depict the role of the Redeemer in

I once argued with Peter Geach as to whether it was possible to believe in the Incarnation without belief in the Virgin Birth.

perfecting the human species. What is changed is not the doctrine of God, or the outcome, but the picture of the beginning. God's purpose in creating the world is still to create beings who share as many of God's own perfections as possible. In the words of St. Thomas Aquinas, God "intends only to communicate his perfection, which is his goodness."[52] The difference implicit in this version of Christianity is that God did not create human beings perfect in the first place, but provides his grace so that they may achieve that perfection partly in historical time and partly at the end of time.

Original Sin as "Inherited"

It is reported that Reinhold Niebuhr liked to quote from the *London Times* to the effect that "Original Sin is the most empirical of all Christian doctrines." Certainly if it is taken as "an inclination to sin over which the individual has no control, but which comes to that individual from the past of the race," there is abundant evidence that it exists, and there are at least three plausible explanations of it.

Natural limitations of human beings predispose them to sin, for example, limitations of knowledge. Human beings simply do not know all the consequences of their actions. They often so misjudge a situation that unforeseen evils result. Had they known ahead of time what these evil and unfortunate consequences would be, they would not have embarked on certain courses of action. To put it simply, if Hitler had foreseen Germany's terrible devastation as a result of the Second World War, there is every reason to believe that he would not have begun it. Limitations of knowledge lead inevitably to sin. Other limitations of material existence, like limitations in space and time, prevent human beings from achieving many of the goods that they envision.

Some have suggested that inherited dispositions to sin as well as dispositions to good derive from our evolutionary past.[53] This is a very plausible hypothesis, since it must be presumed that instincts which contribute to the survival of the individual and the race will not always be in accord with the moral good. For example, the instinct for self-preservation will sometimes run counter to a moral obligation to give one's life for others.

According to many social thinkers too much attention has focused on a biological transmission of evil. "It has diverted our minds from the power of social transmission, from the authority of the social group in justifying, urging, and idealizing wrong," said Walter Rauschenbusch (1861–1918).[54] "Cultural Determinism" is certainly one of the forces that predispose people to sin. Insofar as it is a force for evil, it bears out the Christian insistence that dispositions to evil are deep-seated in the human psyche and sometimes come to us in such a way that the individual is not responsible for their existence and their power.

That there are dispositions to sin which come to human beings from outside the self and from the past is beyond doubt. The question becomes whether or not any more of the traditional account of Original Sin remains. Many have been troubled over the apparent immorality of St. Augustine's claim that we inherit Adam's guilt. As N. P. Williams put it: "Nor is it necessary to do more than point out the absurdity of the theory of 'original guilt,' which asserts that human beings are held responsible by an all-just Judge for an act which they did not commit."[55] Such people would agree with J. S. Whale: "We must abandon the classical doctrine of Original Sin where it is bound up with the morally insupportable doctrine of Original Guilt, but we are still left with the historical fact of universal moral imperfection, whose reality that grim doctrine attested."[56]

Reinhold Niebuhr

A popular and influential contemporary interpretation of the doctrine of Original Sin can be found in Reinhold Niebuhr's many writings. Niebuhr's views are particularly noteworthy because they were shaped largely by his political and social analysis. During the Great Depression he wrote *Moral Man and Immoral Society*, in which he traced many social ills to the self-interest of the ruling classes—that is, the economically and culturally powerful. Later, for the Gifford Lectures, Niebuhr wrote *The Nature and Destiny of Man*, in which he analyzed both collective and individual egoism. There he wrote, "The Christian doctrine of original sin with its seemingly contradictory assertions about the inevitability of sin and man's responsibility for sin is a dialectical truth which does justice to the fact that man's self-love and self-centredness is inevitable, but not in such a way as to fit into the category of natural necessity."[57] Niebuhr did not deny the truth of theories of inherited dispositions to sin accounted for by cultural influences, but faults their lack of completeness. "This idea of a cultural lag is plausible enough and partly true. But it does not represent the whole truth about the defect of our will."[58] He insists that the heart of the doctrine of Original Sin is located in the assertion of our guilt as well as of our inheritance—"responsibility despite inevitability."[59] To explain this, he insists that self-centeredness or self-love is the source of all sin, that human egoism is inevitable, and that this inevitability is what the doctrine names or refers to. In a brilliant analysis, Niebuhr traces sin to human attempts to deal with anxiety and insecurity.[60] Under the tension that finitude and responsibility place on them, human beings attempt to allay anxiety by grandiose claims for the self, by denying their finitude in prideful self-assertion, or by escaping from their responsibilities in the pursuit of pleasure. "When anxiety has conceived it brings forth both pride and sensuality. Man falls into pride, when he seeks to raise his contingent existence to unconditioned significance; he falls into sensuality, when he seeks to escape from his unlimited possibilities of freedom, from the perils and responsibilities of self-determination, by immersing himself into a 'mutable good,' by losing himself in some natural vitality."[61] According to Niebuhr both those who seek power (those who find their self-worth in being able to control or rule others through feigned or real superiority), and those who avoid responsibility through alcohol or other dissipation, are attempting to deal with their anxieties, but inauthentically. Thus Niebuhr agrees with St. Augustine that other sins are "derivative of the more primal sin of self-love."[62]

The sorry fact of human life is that egoism is inevitable. "The selfishness of men and of nations is a fixed datum of historical science."[63] Doctrines of Original Sin are correct in that human egoism taints even the best that human beings achieve. We know this not only from the observation of others, but also from our own deep introspections. Niebuhr's analysis of egoism as primary and inevitable, and as identical with Original Sin, makes clear why he liked to say that Original Sin is the most empirical of all Christian doctrines.

Responsibility Despite Inevitability

Niebuhr's assertion of human responsibility despite inevitability explains why he could remain unmoved by certain criticisms of the doctrine of Original Guilt. Indeed, he suspects that critics of this doctrine are evading or obscuring the core Christian insight.[64] Niebuhr recognized that "responsibility despite inevitability" is controversial, but he nonetheless maintained it as essential. In this Niebuhr echoes Augustine but also and more particularly a long Protestant tradition affirming that "ought" need not imply "can," and that obligation does not entail the ability to perform.

In *The Institutes of the Christian Religion,* John Calvin denies "that sin is the less criminal, because it is necessary."[65] The contemporary theologian Helmut Thielicke puts this doctrine in an equally stark form: "At the very point where [man] deludes himself in the arrogant assurance of, 'You ought and therefore you can,' he experiences the pain of 'You ought but you cannot.' "[66] Paul Ricoeur makes a similar assertion about the evil called Original Sin: "Evil is a kind of involuntariness at the heart of the voluntary . . . it is this which is the servile will."[67] Hence, when Niebuhr asserts that the inevitability of human egoism does not abolish human responsibility for egoism, he is following the path of a particular understanding of the relationship between obligation and necessity. The conclusion that human beings are inevitably burdened with a guilt that can only be lifted by God is in part responsible for the grim view of life that characterizes much Calvinism.

Adam and Eve

Niebuhr's treatment of the Fall story can now be discussed briefly. Niebuhr regards it as a statement of the human condition at all times and not a report of a past event. This is not only because modern science gives another account of human origins, but also because, like Schleiermacher, and like the ancient Jewish tradition, Niebuhr believes that no matter how far back sin is traced we find something like the *yetzer hara,* the temptation that leads to sin. "This is the meaning of Kierkegaard's assertion that sin posits itself."[68] Hence the story does not explain sin so much as it exemplifies the human condition. The story of Adam and Eve presents us with the inevitability of human wrong-doing and also of human guilt before God.

Modern Roman Catholic Perspectives

Since Vatican II legitimated abandonment of the belief that the human race is descended from a historical Adam and Eve, Roman Catholics, like Protestants, have been rethinking the traditional doctrines. As previously noted, Protestant reinterpretations tend to identify Original Sin with an active impulse, whereas the Roman Catholic tradition, following St. Thomas Aquinas, considers active impulses to sin to be the result of something more basic, a structural flaw, which in turn is equated with Original Sin. This structural limitation in all human beings is alienation from the life of God. "Original sin, then, is defined as the dynamic incapability, prior to an individual's personal choice, of entering freely into dialogue."[69] In this tradition, Original Sin continues to be described as the loss of Original Righteousness, where "Original Righteousness" is understood as "being in the right relationship with God" and thus dominated by a sense of the presence of God. Without a strong sense of the presence of God, human beings are unable to resist temptations.

Like Reinhold Niebuhr, some Roman Catholics reject the historicity of the story of the Fall and take Original Sin to express something about "man as such." "That all men are born in original sin means that all are sinners from the first moment that they are men because it happens to be an historical fact that all men sin."[70] However, Karl Rahner finds justification for the traditional account. Accepting the findings of modern biology, he presents the Thomistic view with only two modifications—there is no historic Adam and the transmission of Original Sin is only incidentally genetic.

Rahner insists first that the phrases "Original Sin" and "Original Guilt" are metaphorical, since sin and guilt in the strict sense are always the result of personal decision.[71] Next, while rejecting the notion that the human race is descended from only two parents, Rahner does believe in a historical Fall. To him, the Fall represents the fact that at some point in its history the human community became alienated from the life of God, lost its sense of the presence of the Holy Spirit, and thus was deprived of God's grace.[72] Without a lively sense of the presence of God, human beings lost the ability to rule the passions. Finally, while sociological influence is the most obvious way to explain the transmission from our ancestors of this loss of life in God,[73] one ought not to neglect the possibility that biology plays a role as well, since the goals of a human society determine to a considerable extent which traits are prized and which will be selected from the genetic pool for transmission.

Rahner's restatement of traditional Roman Catholic teaching is but an example of similar work done by numerous theologians. However, to some this type of approach does not sufficiently emphasize the internal, subjective dimension of sin. Just as Niebuhr felt that theories which stress "natural inertia" and "cultural lag" did not recognize sufficiently that sin is a matter of a corrupted will, so B. O. McDermott raises a similar complaint. Like Paul Ricoeur, he insists: "Original sin is not sin solely because it comes from sin and leads to sin (like concupiscence in Catholic theology), nor exclusively because it is the deprivation of God's sanctifying holiness prior to my choice. More than this, the sinner in confessing his guilt discovers a desire to be held captive which, if untouched by grace, would surely be effective, for it is at once a desire that effects powerlessness and the expression of powerlessness."[74]

Adam's Sin as Archetypal

Adam's sin, in addition to its role in theories of a sinful inheritance, has been taken as the archetypal sin. It has been described in various ways, as alienation from God, idolatry, or egoism.

As for the first of these alternatives, Protestants as well as Catholics identify the primary change in Adam's will as a losing of the sense of the presence of God. Luther and Kierkegaard believed that Adam's first failing was the loss of faith in God.[75] And Schleiermacher quite explicitly identifies the loss of a full God-consciousness as the precondition of Adam's sin.[76] Like Paul, the common conviction of Christians has been that if one is filled with a sense of the perfection, goodness, and power of God, disobedience to his will is unthinkable.

The second alternative, idolatry, is also emphasized by both traditions. Again following Paul, John Macquarrie explains that a turning from God is always a turning to the creature.[77] When the highest good disappears from view, some lesser or mutable good slips in to take its place in human consciousness.

Finally, Protestants and Roman Catholics have usually agreed that self-love or egoism is the form which idolatry ultimately takes. St. Thomas explains: "Every sinful act proceeds from inordinate desire of a mutable good. Now the fact that someone desires a temporal good inordinately is due to the fact that he loves himself inordinately."[78] St. Thomas seems to believe that every choice of a lesser good in place of a greater occurs from motives of self-interest. For St. Thomas the focus of temptation for Adam and Eve lay in the words of the serpent: "If you eat of the tree which is in the midst of the garden, you shall be as God." So thorough is St. Thomas in claiming that all inordinate love is self-love that he regards the inordinate love of another human being as a kind of self-indulgence,[79] as indeed does much modern psychology.

Since it is claimed that all sin is ultimately traced to egoism or narcissism, it is natural to think of their opposites as the highest virtue. What is required for that virtue is a love that, in the words of Paul in the King James translation, "seeketh not her own" (1 Cor. 13:5). For Niebuhr this means a totally "disinterested love," a love that always puts the need of the other ahead of one's own. When he quotes Jesus' advice to the rich young man, "If thou *wilt be perfect*, go and sell that thou hast and give to the poor," Niebuhr adds, "What is demanded is an action in which regard for the self is completely eliminated."[80] For him, Christian love is a love which is completely other-regarding. But since this kind of love can never be attained, everyone is always a sinner in need of forgiveness. Hence Niebuhr quotes Pascal with approval: "There are only two kinds of men, the righteous who believe themselves sinners; the rest, sinners, who believe themselves righteous."[81]

But surely this approach is radically defective. It is based on an inaccurate assessment of the varieties of sin; it is sometimes psychologically destructive; and it reflects only partially the teachings of Jesus. In the first place, to be other-regarding is not always a virtue; it may reflect the lack of a sense of self-worth, which often prompts sinful actions. Valerie Saiving Goldstein has recently argued that sin as self-assertion and self-centeredness at best reflects the experience of only half the human race.

The temptations of woman *as woman* are not the same as the temptations of man *as man,* and the specifically feminine forms of sin . . . have a quality which can never be encompassed by such terms as "pride" and "will-to-power." They are better suggested by such items as triviality, distractability, and diffuseness; lack of an organizing center or focus; dependence on others for one's own self-definition; tolerance at the expense of standards of excellence . . . In short, underdevelopment or negation of the self.[82]

While Saiving may be correct that this type of failing is often exemplified among women, it of course is also found among men. Such individuals, whether women or men, are often victimized by their own sense of guilt; and their inability to integrate their lives makes them prey to domination from without—a different kind of idolatry. They do not have enough ego–strength to assert themselves sufficiently to be guilty of any form of pride.

Second, Niebuhr's theory leads to thinking that is psychologically self-destructive because it encourages self-loathing and hatred. It tends to foster denial and manipulation rather than openness to reality.

This prescription for avoiding sin is also in disagreement with the teachings of Jesus. Jesus not only says "Thou shalt love thy neighbor as thyself," thus asserting that there is a proper or ordinate self-love, but he also continually promises rewards. To the rich young man he offers "treasure in heaven" should he sell all that he has. To those who leave house, and brothers, and sisters, and parents, he promises brothers, sisters, and parents in the new life of the beloved community (Mark 10:29–30). He also promises that "whoever loses his life for my sake and the gospel's will save it" (Mark 8:35). Indeed, making promises is the whole pattern of the Beatitudes: "Blessed are the pure in heart, for they shall see God" (Matt 5:8). Instead of urging his followers to act in such a way that "regard for the self is completely eliminated," Jesus regularly promotes self-regard.

What then can Jesus have meant when he spoke of first losing and then finding the self? St. Bernard of Clairvaux (1090–1153) spoke of the three stages of love of God.[83] First, there is the stage in which one loves God for the self's sake—for what he can do for us. Bernard thought that most people were in this stage. Second, there is the stage in which one loves God for God's sake—for what he is in himself. Bernard thought that some attained this stage in this life, but only for brief moments of sheer adoration of the beauty and majesty of God. The third stage, said Bernard, was more difficult to attain—to love the self for God's sake. This stage Bernard thought only a few could attain in this life. Many commentators have been convinced that stage three is but stage one over again. That it is not can be illustrated by an apocryphal story told about this same Bernard. Bernard was a famous preacher who when he first began to preach, it is said, felt his sermons were just terrible. Time after time he left the pulpit believing himself to have been a failure, feeling guilty that he had not done better, and punishing himself for not having worked harder. Later he felt himself to be an extraordinarily effective speaker. He became quite conceited and puffed up. He was sure he was one of the finest preachers alive and could move even the stoniest hearts. Still later he came to a more balanced view of his abilities. What is interesting for our present purpose is the evaluation of these three periods of his life. Most people, the story continues, think that the second stage is worse than the first. The self-abnegation of the first stage they hold is nearer to the Kingdom of Heaven than the conceit of the second stage. But Bernard himself would have believed otherwise. From his Letters[84] we know that Bernard believed that a just estimation of one's abilities is consistent with true humility. Thus, he would have held that the second stage was superior to the first because the conceited person at least has a faith in God, a faith that God can do something through him, that is lacking in the first stage. Although Bernard did not yet love the self for God's sake, he was nearer to that stage than when he believed that he could do nothing to please God.

By a different route, we have circled back again to Luther's thoughts on justification by faith. To see human reality as God sees it, to grasp his love for his people, his faith in them, to possess the ability to accept ourselves because God accepts us, is at the heart of Christian faith. This is an insight that keeps getting lost and must be reaffirmed in every age. In the words of Paul Tillich:

We are wont to condemn self-love; but what we really mean to condemn is contrary to self-love. It is that mixture of selfishness and self-hate that permanently pursues us, that prevents us from loving others, and that prohibits us from losing ourselves in the love with which we are loved eternally. He who is able to love himself is able to love others also; he who has learned to overcome self-contempt has overcome his contempt for others. But the depth of our separation lies in just the fact that we are not capable of a great and merciful divine love towards ourselves.[85]

We are now in a position to explain the sin of Adam as the archetypal sin. What characterizes the sin of Adam and Eve is the loss of the vision of themselves in relationship to God. In the absence of God's presence in the noon day, they were drawn in upon themselves, and they acted from within this perspective only. Perhaps their action was one of rebellion; but perhaps it was only the result of the whim of the moment. Certainly there are those who seek to make themselves God, but there are also those who just follow the line of least resistance. They make no decision, but are swept along by indecision. But in either case, Adam and Eve did not transcend the self. The heart of sin seems best described as seeing the world only from one's own perspective. Contrarywise, true right-mindedness is best described as the ability to see the world and one's place in it from God's point of view—that is, to see it as it really is.

CHAPTER VI

The Age of Natural Theology

Natural theology is typically described as the systematic attempt to provide rational demonstrations for the major tenets of the Christian faith. "Rational demonstration" in this context refers to arguments derived solely from considerations of reason and nature. Natural theology hopes to base religion on principles whose truth can be established by all, independently of any special source of religious knowledge such as revelation, mystical experience, or the like. Historically, natural theologians have concentrated most of their attention on three areas: arguments for the existence of God and considerations against the existence of God; the problem of evil; and the paradoxical relation between human freedom and responsibility on the one hand, and God's complete and absolute foreknowledge on the other. All three of these issues were treated by St. Augustine with a depth and clarity beyond anything that had been attempted earlier. For this reason, it is appropriate to date natural theology as beginning with him. In succeeding centuries, many of the West's most illustrious thinkers—St. Anselm of Canterbury, St. Thomas Aquinas, G. W. Leibniz (1646–1716), Jonathan Edwards (1703–1758)—were its champions. Although the decline of natural theology is usually credited to the skeptical writings of David Hume (1711–1776) and Immanuel Kant, it still has its defenders. Since Kant, however, philosophically minded theologians have increasingly shifted their attention elsewhere. Instead of trying to show that belief in God is securely grounded in nature and reason, they have sought to demonstrate its rationality. They have sought to show both that Christian faith is internally consistent and that considerations in its support are as strong as those against it. They have reasoned that it is as rational to affirm the basic premises of the arguments for the existence of God as to deny them. If this is so, the conclusion of many skeptics that "the balance of probabilities . . . comes out strongly against the existence of a god"[1] is an exaggeration. Kant's sober appraisal seems more accurate. "For the purely speculative reason . . . the objective reality of [a Supreme Being] . . . though it cannot be proved, can neither be disproved."[2] But as Kant also recognized, rather than leaving matters at a rational stalemate, this conclusion establishes the possibility of a supernatural being both logically and metaphysically. God's existence is a logical possibility since the idea of God contains no internal contradictions and so is not rendered impossible in the way that a square-circle is. It is metaphysically possible, or really possible, because the reasons for the existence of God are as strong as those against it. Thus, a place is provided in the scheme of things for whatever aspects of unseen reality might be revealed in moral and religious experience.

Why did an interest in natural theology take so firm a root? Several reasons might be advanced. Augustine's personal genius as well as the need to respond to critics are sometimes mentioned as causal influences. But natural theology continued to flourish long after Augustine's works had been superseded as the standard writings and long after Christianity had become the nearly exclusive religious conviction of the West. Under these circumstances one must look elsewhere to explain the hold that natural theology has had on Christian sensibilities.

The attraction of the rational search for God is connected with two elements in the Christian understanding of the life of faith. Both elements can be found in Scripture and both received expression in the writings of Augustine. First, there is the rocklike character of the faith itself. "God is our hope and strength . . . ," proclaims Psalm 46 (BCP) "therefore will we not fear, though the earth be moved, and though the hills be carried into the midst of the sea." The faith of the believer should be as secure and immobile as God himself. It seems to many that only a faith based in rational certainty could have such solidity. Only such a faith could provide the stability and security that Augustine sought, and that find expression in the words so often quoted from the beginning of his *Confessions*: "Our hearts are restless until they find rest in Thee."[3]

Second, the Scripture proclaims that God is to be loved with all one's heart, and soul, and mind, and strength. To love God wholly involves not only the affections of the heart but also the decisions of the mind in a rational and reasonable commitment. Such commitment St. Augustine and his follower, St. Anselm, regarded as superior to belief on authority. In a striking passage, Augustine claimed: "Moreover, he who by true reason arrives at an understanding of what he had only believed in is in a better state of advancement than he who still only desires to understand what he believes."[4] Faith, or the acceptance of belief on authority, is important because it promotes humility and thus "purifies the heart,"[5] but the ideal pilgrim will "at length learn how pre-eminently possessed of reason those things are which he pursued before he saw their reason."[6] But finally even reason or understanding must give way to vision. "If we continue in that which is believed we shall attain to that which may be seen."[7] For Augustine and his disciples, ideally the life of faith will mature into the life of reason, and the life of reason into insight.

The Ontological Argument

Augustine's own argument for the existence of God, the Argument from Truth, was heavily dependent on certain premises of Platonic philosophy. Although it has not been very influential, at least since the Middle Ages when Platonic Idealism largely went out of style, it has had its recent champions; Hastings Rashdall in this century and Josiah Royce in the last both offered versions of it. Far more influential has been the argument first developed 600 years later by one of St. Augustine's brilliant disciples, Anselm of Canterbury. Anselm's argument seems simple to understand and easy to dismiss, but it is as difficult to refute as it is to establish. In every age it has had distinguished champions as well as critics. In our own time, Charles Hartshorne and Alvin Plantinga have presented impressive restatements of it.

This argument has been named the Ontological Argument because it claims to demonstrate the existence of God from the definition of God. It begins with the description of God as "that being than which no greater can be conceived" and concludes that, because we can conceive of God in the mind, God must exist in reality, since to exist in reality is greater or more perfect than mere mental existence. In St. Anselm's words, the crux of the argument is:

> Assuredly that, than which nothing greater can be conceived, cannot exist in the understanding alone. For, suppose it exists in the understanding alone: then it can be conceived to exist in reality; which is greater.

> Therefore, if that, than which nothing greater can be conceived, exists in the understanding alone, the very being, than which nothing greater can be conceived, is one, than which a greater can be conceived. But obviously this is impossible. Hence, there is no doubt that there exists a being, than which nothing greater can be conceived, and it exists both in the understanding and in reality.[8]

God necessarily exists, because to deny his existence is self-contradictory. Anselm concludes that only fools can say in their hearts, "There is no God."

Gaunilo's Objection

Critics soon appeared to challenge the crucial step from *existence in the mind* to *existence in reality*. The monk, Gaunilo, undertook to write in defense of the fool. He claimed that Anselm's argument proved too much. If it could prove from the concept of God's greatness or perfection that God exists, why should it not as well follow from the concept of a perfect island that the island also exists. "You can no longer doubt that this island which is more excellent than all lands exists somewhere, since you have no doubt that it is in your understanding."[9]

In reply to Gaunilo, Anselm asserted that, although he did not believe his argument would prove the existence of a perfect island, if Gaunilo could convince him that it did then he would find that island somewhere in the universe. Why was Anselm so convinced that his argument proves the existence of God, but not the existence of a host of other entities: perfect islands, perfect horses, perfect devils, and the like? The answer to Gaunilo's challenge is to note that the concept of God is different from these other concepts, for God is described as a being of maximal excellence. "But *maximal excellence* entails *omniscience, omnipotence,* and *moral perfection,*"[10] and one should add *eternity* and *self-existence.* This is what differentiates God from all else. Only God is eternal, only God is self-existent. It is impossible to think of God as coming into existence; the idea is self-contradictory. It is part of our concepts of islands, and devils, and horses that they are contingents and they come into existence. Just imagine what an eternal island would be like—one whose shores were never eroded and never washed away by hurricanes—or a devil who was incapable of being destroyed or vanquished, or a horse who could not contract any animal diseases. These would no longer be islands, or devils or horses.[11] Perhaps they are even contradictory notions, and thus not even possible beings. Perhaps they are merely pictures in the imagination.

God as a Construct

This reply has provoked another line of criticism that is closely related to Gaunilo's original one. The idea of God, it is said, is a human creation—made up of other ideas in the same way the idea of the unicorn is made up of the idea of a horse and a narwhale's horn, and the idea of a satyr is made up of parts of the trunk and head of a man and the body and legs of a horse. Thus Hume suggested that the idea of God is concocted by collecting together the ideas of surpassing power, wisdom, and goodness, and of first cause of the universe. If the idea of God is really such a concoction, the ontological argument would be attempting to move from a figment of the imagination to reality. Anyone who attempted to do so would be a greater fool than a skeptic is.

But is the concept of God such a figment of the imagination? Anselm himself did not make up his idea of God. It is rooted in St. Augustine and also in the Scripture. Anselm's definition of God clearly echoes Augustine's words: "When the one God of Gods is thought of, even by those who recognize, invoke, and worship other gods either in heaven or earth, He is thought of in such a way that the thought seeks to attain something than which there is nothing better or more sublime."[12] Augustine's description in turn has its scriptural roots. In the Psalms God is said to be "far above all gods" (Ps. 97:9). Furthermore, there is reason to believe that even the ancient Hebrews did not invent this concept, but that something like it is found as far as back as there is any evidence of theistic beliefs. Thus, we have no direct evidence that it was ever constructed by anyone. There is a theory that it was, but that theory is no more well-grounded than one of its alternatives that regards the concept of God as an innate idea—part of the very constitution of human rationality. So far the supporters of the argument and its opponents have at least a draw.

Existence Is Not a Real Property

The ontological argument claims that *existence* in reality is implied by the concept of God in the same way that having three sides is implied by the concept of triangle or having four legs is implied by the concept of horse. Immanuel Kant proposed what has often been regarded as the most significant objection to the argument. *Existence,* he argued, is not really a property of anything, as three-sidedness and four-leggedness are, and so cannot be part of any definition; therefore, it cannot be implied by a concept.[13] To put this point in the context of the ontological argument, *existence* is not a genuine property like omnipotence, moral perfection, and omniscience, for these make a real difference to our understanding of God. *Existence,* on the other hand, does not add anything to the concept of God, but merely indicates that the concept is exemplified or instantiated. Kant made this point in a striking way: "One hundred real dollars contains not one dollar more than a hundred imaginary dollars."[14]

Recently William Alston has offered the following counter-objection to Kant's claim that existence is not really a property. Anselm did not speak of *mere existence,* but of *existence in the understanding* and *existence in reality.* Surely these are properties because they describe different states of affairs, and thus result in different concepts. Following William Alston, we might think of a whole series of different kinds of existences: existence in the mind, existence in myth, existence in the imagination, existence in novels, as well as existence in reality.[15] Clearly these are descriptive properties because statements about the existence of Ronald Reagan and David Copperfield have different meanings and describe quite different states of affairs. *Mere existence* may not be a descriptive concept, but *existence in the understanding* and *existence in reality* are.

This reply raises another objection. How can one move from one type of existence to another? *Existence in myth* does not entail *existence in poetry* (Homer might not have written about the gods), and *existence in a novel* does not entail *existence in the understanding*. For instance, there might come a time when *David Copperfield* is not read by anyone although there are copies of the book in the library. Why, then, should we take it that *existence in the understanding* entails *existence in reality* in the case of God? Even if we can conceptualize a being who is maximally excellent (which includes having existence), such a being may not have real existence. One may not move from one type of existence to another by merely logical considerations. Hence, it is said, the mental concept of God does not logically entail his existence in reality.

This particular form of the general objection to the ontological argument is open to the following counter-argument. It is quite usual to deny existence to various pseudo-entities on the grounds that they involve a contradiction. We deny that there could be square circles or triangles with three sides and four angles, or that a plane surface could be black all over and white all over at the same time, because these are contradictory states of affairs. If it is permissible to deny by logic alone that a square-circle exists, why is it not permissible to argue on the basis of logic alone that God exists? Perhaps we have good reasons to accept the first argument and other reasons to deny the second. But in either case, no good reasons are forthcoming. It seems that the critics of the ontological argument are relying only on intuition. However, to supporters of the ontological argument, it seems that their own intuitions are just as good. They think it arbitrary of the critics to argue the nonexistence of some objects by logic alone and yet refuse to accept the parallel proposition that something could be proved to exist by logic alone.

Is God a Possible Idea?

Thus far it has been argued that the traditional objections to the ontological argument are mistaken. The argument does not prove the existence of a perfect island because islands do not have perfect existence. *Mere existence* may not be a descriptive property, but *existence in the mind* and *existence in reality* certainly are. They do make a difference in the concept of the entity. Lastly, it seems arbitrary to deny that something could be demonstrated to exist *a priori* given that we deny *a priori* that some things exist. There is, however, one last objection, which is harder to remove. Is the idea of a maximally excellent being a possible idea? Does it contain within it some hidden contradiction that would make it like the square circle, impossible of instantiation? The fact that no one has yet found a contradiction will not remove all doubts. Thus, Alvin Plantinga, one of the foremost contemporary students of the ontological argument, has asserted that the only unresolved question of interest is "whether its main premise—that maximal greatness *is* possibly instantiated—is *true*. I think it *is* true." He continues, "but it must be conceded that not everyone who understands and reflects on its central premise . . . will accept it."[16] Still, Plantinga concludes "that there is nothing *contrary to reason* or *irrational* in accepting this premise." In other words, the ontological argument "establishes not the *truth* of theism, but its rational acceptability."[17]

The Cosmological Argument

The name "cosmological" was given to this type of argument by Kant, who so characterized it because it seeks to provide an explanation for the origin of the universe. The most influential version of this argument was proposed by St. Thomas Aquinas in the thirteenth century.[18] St. Thomas believed that there are five arguments, or Ways to God, as he preferred to call them. The first three of these Ways are cosmological, but of these the Third Way is the most significant. The first two Ways, the argument from motion and the argument from efficient causation, treat two different kinds of change, whereas the Third Way deals with coming-into-existence. It deals with the question: "Why is there anything at all? Why is there something rather than nothing?" Hence, the Third Way focuses on a more fundamental issue than either the First or Second Way. St. Thomas' Third Way has been championed recently by a number of distinguished thinkers, including Etienne Gilson, Jacques Maritain, F. C. Copleston, and Peter Geach.

Given the fact that the Third Way has been so popular, one is surprised to discover that St. Thomas presents it very tersely, suggesting that he expended little effort on it. Perhaps he thought it to be just obviously compelling. In any event, his economy of presentation has produced disagreement over the exact goal of the argument and the meanings of some of its terms. In order to convey fully the force of the argument, it is useful to give a free paraphrase that will provide a rough map of the terrain.

> Everything in the universe depends for its nature and existence on something else. Even the universe as a whole does not seem capable of keeping itself in existence, but depends on some other being that sustains not only the universe, but also itself. The most likely candidate for this dual role of sustaining itself and the universe is the God of religion.

Before beginning a detailed discussion of the argument, it is important to note that St. Thomas is not trying to prove a first cause in time, that is, a first cause in a temporally ordered series. He is trying to give reasons to believe that there is a first cause in a series of conserving causes, that is, causes that keep things in existence. Although St. Thomas thought that the first chapter of Genesis truly asserted that the universe had a beginning in time, he believed that reason was powerless to prove this truth. Neither could reason disprove it.[19] Since reason must remain neutral on this point, the fact of the beginning of the world could only be known by revelation.[20]

St. Thomas thought that it would be comparatively easy to prove the existence of a first cause if we were certain that the universe had a beginning and ending. But since we have only the assurance of faith for these beliefs, St. Thomas concluded that "the most efficacious way to prove that God exists is on the supposition that the world is eternal"—that is, that it has no beginning or ending in time.[21] Accordingly, the Third Way accepts the possibility of the eternity of the world and is best understood as an attempt to demonstrate, not a first cause in time, but a cause that keeps the universe in existence whether or not it is of finite duration.

The second preliminary consideration is related to this first one. St. Thomas describes the argument as based on the difference between "possible beings" and "necessary beings." Over the centuries people have debated over the meaning of these terms. Kant thought that "necessary" meant "logically necessary," and thus this argument is simply the ontological argument in disguise. But in a previous discussion, St. Thomas rejected the ontological argument, and so we have to look for a different interpretation of "necessary."

Many interpreters of St. Thomas, including F. C. Copleston,[22] have suggested that he uses "necessary" to mean "self-existent." It is argued that St. Thomas is trying to prove that there is a being who is independent of everything else for his existence and on whom everything else depends. But whatever "necessary being" means in the argument, it cannot mean "self-existent being," for then the argument would make no sense. At the beginning of the second part of the argument, St. Thomas states: "Every necessary thing has its necessity caused by another or not." Were we to understand "necessary" to mean "self-existent," then we would take the statement to read: "Every self-existent thing has its self-existence caused by another or not." Clearly *self-existence caused by another* is contradictory, and thus St. Thomas could not have had this idea in mind, despite F. C. Copleston.

There is another reading of "necessary" which has none of these problems. "Necessary" might mean "imperishable" or "eternal"— "necessary" in the sense of "cannot come into existence or go out of existence."[23] This interpretation does make sense of St. Thomas' statement. It reads: "Every necessary (eternal) being either has its necessity (eternity) caused by another or not."

The reason this proposal makes sense and is not a contradiction is that we can easily picture a situation in which an eternal being depends for its existence on another eternal being. Imagine an ordinary battery generating a current of electricity. Now imagine that the current is being generated eternally. Then the battery must be an eternal battery. Of course now it will be true to say that the electricity gets both its being and its eternity from the eternal battery. Analogously, St. Thomas is trying to prove that even though the universe may be eternal, it derives its being and eternity from a single, eternal, self-existent being, who is God.

As a final preliminary, we will state briefly the meaning of "possible" in this argument. Since "possible" and "necessary" are used as antonyms, "possible" must mean "perishable or of limited temporal duration." Indeed, St. Thomas' own words bear this out, since he explains "possible beings" as beings that "are generated and corrupted."

Part One of St. Thomas' Cosmological Argument

St. Thomas begins the first part of his argument by stating: "We find in nature things that are possible to be and not to be, since they are found to be generated and to be corrupted."[24] If our preliminary discussion is correct, we can clarify the argument by restating this first sentence as: "We find in nature things that are perishable (i.e., temporal) since they come into existence and go out of existence." St. Thomas then proceeds to try to establish that "Not all beings are merely possible, but there must exist something the existence of which is necessary." Again we paraphrase, "Not all beings are merely temporal; there must be at least one being whose existence is eternal."

The argument by which St. Thomas hopes to establish this conclusion has struck many commentators as fallacious. Rather than examine this controversy in detail, we will give another argument that establishes the conclusion directly and that is both successful and based on a principle accepted by St. Thomas. This argument employs one additional principle not known in the Middle Ages. The principle accepted by St. Thomas is: "Something cannot come out of nothing," or as expressed in another form: "Every event has a cause." No argument is given for this principle; perhaps St. Thomas thought it to be self-evident. Hume, to the contrary, thought that it was not.[25] However, J. L. Mackie's judgment represents the view of the majority of thoughtful people today. "Still," says Mackie, "this principle has some plausibility, in that it is constantly confirmed in our experience (and also used, reasonably, in interpreting our experience)."[26] While arguments using this principle can never be watertight, they can be judged rationally acceptable provided the rest of the reasoning is sound. Given the principle: "Something cannot come out of nothing," or alternatively: "Every event has a cause," it will follow that there has always existed something in time past. Take any event. There will be another event preceding it in time that is its cause. But that second event will also have a prior event-cause, and so on infinitely. At no point will we reach a stopping place in the chain of event-causes.

To this principle, modern physics has added another which holds that the chain of event-causes will continue on infinitely into the future. This principle is the law of the conservation of mass-energy; among other things it affirms that the amount of mass-energy in the universe remains constant. Hence, the amount of energy may decrease, as it is converted into mass, and vice versa; but the universe in the form of either energy or mass will continue in existence.

These considerations show that although each particular thing in the universe may be of limited duration, there is at least one thing that is eternal, namely, the causal chain stretching infinitely back into the past and infinitely forward into the future. Put another way, the universe taken as a whole might be the eternal being. In an earlier version of the argument on which St. Thomas drew, the Jewish philosopher, Moses Maimonides (1135–1204) concludes: "If there are, as we perceive, existents subject to generation and corruption, there must be a certain existent that is not subject to generation and corruption . . . [whose] existence is necessary, not possible."[27]

Part Two of St. Thomas' Cosmological Argument

In part two of the Third Way, St. Thomas hopes to show that the eternal causal chain or universe is held in being by God. Slightly paraphrased, the argument runs:

> Everything that is eternal (in the present case the infinite causal series) either has the cause of its eternal existence in itself, or is held in existence by something else.
>
> It is not possible to go to infinity in a series of eternal beings each of which gets its eternal existence from some source outside itself.
>
> Therefore, we must conclude that there is some thing that is the source of its own eternal being and that does not have a source of its being outside itself, and is the cause of the being of other beings.
>
> This all men call God.

Our earlier example of the eternal battery and the eternal current of electricity may help to explain what St. Thomas has in mind. Imagine the eternal electric current as made up of a series of short impulses each following the other in time. Thus, each impulse will be perishable, but the whole series of impulses will be eternal. Of course the battery will also have to be eternal if it is to keep this everlasting series of impulses in existence. But now let us turn to the battery. Even an eternal battery would be dependent on something else for its existence. A battery is made up of various physical elements. But these elements are made up of atoms, and the atoms of protons, neutrons, and electrons, and these of subatomic particles, and so on, perhaps ad infinitum. St. Thomas was convinced that one cannot go to infinity in a series of eternal beings each dependent on another. One must eventually reach a being who is the source and sustainer of all else. The success of the argument will depend on the ability to sustain this claim, and also the claim that this being is God.

David Hume's Response

David Hume's *Dialogues Concerning Natural Religion* contained such a clear and thorough examination and critique of the whole enterprise of natural theology that it has become a kind of text for modern atheism. Although not all of Hume's points are well taken, they are challenging and have made so lasting an impression that natural theologians continue to take them seriously. One of Hume's arguments strikes at the very heart of St. Thomas' Third Way. Hume asks why it is necessary to proceed to the second part of the argument at all. Why not be content with the results of the first part?

> In such a chain, too, or succession of objects, each part is caused by that which preceded it, and causes that which succeeds it. Where then is the difficulty? But the *whole,* you say, wants a cause. . . . Did I show you the particular causes of each individual in a collection of twenty particles of matter, I should think it very unreasonable, should you afterwards ask me, what was the cause of the whole twenty. This is sufficiently explained in explaining the cause of the parts.[28]

What Hume is arguing is that, given the temporal sequence of cause and effect, it is unreasonable to ask for a total explanation as St. Thomas and, later, Leibniz do.[29] But is it unreasonable? Our example of the electricity and the battery suggests that it is not. It might be the case that a whole chain of causes is kept in existence by something outside the chain. In that case, explaining the dependence of each element on another element in the chain would not explain the existence of the whole chain.

The Principle of Sufficient Reason

A second criticism of St. Thomas' argument alleges inconsistency. Since St. Thomas allows an infinite series of *temporal* causes in the first part of the argument, why does he now argue that an infinite series of *conserving* causes is impossible? The answer to this question is found in the Principle of Sufficient Reason, which also justifies the need for the kind of explanation that Hume thought unnecessary. Although Leibniz was the first to formulate the principle clearly and to call it by that name, St. Thomas clearly relied on it or its near relative, as William L. Rowe has shown.[30]

The Principle of Sufficient Reason states that only a complete explanation is a sufficient explanation. To some philosophers such a total explanation seems to imply an absolute determinism because every aspect of the universe would then have an explanation. They conclude from this that the principle is most likely false because it would be inconsistent with modern subatomic physics and evolutionary biology, in which chance plays an important explanatory role. However, this negative assessment is too hasty. The Principle of Sufficient Reason does not tell us what states of affairs will occur. Rather, it tells us that whatever is the case, there is an explanation for it. Thus, if quantum theory is correct and the universe is governed partly by chance, then the Principle of Sufficient Reason tells us that there is an explanation for the presence of these areas of chance; alternatively, if every aspect of the universe is determined, then the principle holds that there is an explanation for this outcome. There is therefore no reason to abandon this principle in the face of present-day physics or biology. Indeed modern physics embraces the principle in its search for an overarching explanation—a Grand Unified Theory—that will ideally explain why we have the kind of universe that we do.

To provide a sufficient account of any state of affairs, we must not only explain each part of it but we must also explain why it is the kind of totality that it is. Hence, we must provide an explanation of the infinite causal chain taken as a whole, the explanation that Hume thought it unreasonable to require. Suppose that in order to explain A, B, and C, we have to mention D, E, and F; and to explain these, we might have to mention G, H, and I; and so on, without end, because of the infinite series stretching into the past. But, asserts Leibniz, "as all this detail only involves other contingents . . . each of which needs a like analysis for its explanation, we make no advance, and the sufficient or final reason must be outside the sequence or series of this detail of contingents, however infinite it might be."[31] The explanation of the causal series of A, B, and C, etc., cannot be in the series itself because it is the series that must be explained.

An Infinite Series of Conserving Causes Is Impossible

If we picture the infinite temporal series as a horizontal series, and the series of conserving causes as a vertical series, why then cannot there be an infinite vertical series? If this were the case, we still would not, in Leibniz's words, have made any advance. If an infinite series on the horizontal does not explain itself, neither can an infinite vertical series explain itself. Given the Principle of Sufficient Reason, we cannot be satisfied with less than a complete explanation for everything. This requirement is not satisfied by any infinite regress. What we need is a substance that explains its own existence, and eternity, and the existence and nature of everything else whether perishable or imperishable. "And thus," concludes Leibniz, "it is that the final reason of things must be found in a necessary substance, in which the detail of changes exists . . . [inherently] as in their source. And this it is that we call God."[32] To use St. Thomas' concept, the final reason is only found in a being that has of itself its eternity, or is necessary through itself.

And This All Men Call God

Leibniz and St. Thomas also held that there could be only one such being. This is because only a unitary being can satisfy the Principle of Sufficient Reason. If the universe is made up of two substances, there will have to be a reason why there are two and not more or less. Only a single explanation can stop the questions. Only a single explanation can be the final reason. But is this being God?

In order to see what justifies St. Thomas and Leibniz in calling this being God, we need a distinction between the *is of identity* and the *is of synonomy*. "Car" is synonomous with "auto" because the definition of "car" is the same as the definition of "auto." By extension, to say that the God of the Third Way *is* the God of the Bible is to say that both have the same description. This is clearly not the case. If this is what St. Thomas means when he says, "And this all men call God," then he is clearly mistaken.

However, St. Thomas and Leibniz might be thinking of the *is of identity*. For example, in the sentence, "The President of the United States is the former Governor of California," "President of the United States" and "former Governor of California" do not have the same definition or description, but the two phrases pick out the same person. Thus, it can be claimed that the description of God in the Bible and the description of God in the cosmological argument pick out the same being, although the descriptions themselves differ. To put it another way, there could not be both an omnipotent, omniscient, omnibenevolent creator and sustainer of the universe, and also another being that has its necessary existence from itself and that keeps the rest of the universe in existence.

Assessment of the Argument

This is a powerful argument if the Principle of Sufficient Reason not only is an ideal or model of the kind of explanation that we try to provide, but also correlates with the deep nature of the universe. If the universe really does have a complete explanation, then St. Thomas and Leibniz have proposed a very plausible candidate for that explanation. But does the universe in fact have such an explanation? Skeptics argue that we cannot know that it has. Their reasoning can be summarized as follows: It does not seem to be a necessary or logical truth that there is a complete explanation for everything.[33] But if the principle is not a necessary or logical truth, is there observational evidence for it? The only way we can gather evidence of this kind is to observe that our many questions about what is the case have answers. To know empirically that there is a complete explanation for every state of affairs requires that we do have explanations, if not for all, at least for most states of affairs. It is argued that we finite creatures can never acquire such extensive evidence.[34] Hence, we can never get the evidence needed to know whether or not the universe conforms to the requirements of the Principle of Sufficient Reason.

Nonetheless, many believe that there is a way to achieve empirical confirmation. In the search for a Grand Unified Theory, theoretical physicists are committed to the Principle of Sufficient Reason. Of course the idea of a Grand Unified Theory is but one candidate for a complete explanation of the universe, but if such a theory were empirically confirmed, it would be strong evidence that the Principle of Sufficient Reason reflects the deep nature of the universe. However, such confirmation has not yet been achieved, and in the meantime many theoretical physicists follow the example of Albert Einstein (1878–1955). Like the principle that no logically impossible thing can exist, the Principle of Sufficient Reason seemed to Einstein to be too fundamental an explanatory principle to be capable of or to require any proof. His belief that the universe had a complete rational explanation was what motivated him in his lifetime search to express that belief in physical laws.

Although the correlation of the Principle of Sufficient Reason with reality has not been demonstrated, it nonetheless reflects the conviction of a highly respected group in the scientific community. Thus this discussion of the cosmological argument has brought us to a stronger position than we reached at the end of the ontological argument. There we concluded that speculative reason, although unable to provide a demonstrative proof of the existence of God, has given evidence of the possibility of a transcendent realm, which might make itself known by revelation or through religious experience. Here we have found not only additional evidence for this conclusion, but also a more forceful argument. The fact that the Principle of Sufficient Reason finds a place in the thinking of eminent theoretical physicists increases the credibility of the cosmological argument as a whole.

Arguments from Design

Natural theologians have developed a third type of philosophical argument attempting to prove the existence of God, the argument from design, or teleological argument. These arguments rely on the apparent adaptation of means to ends in nature as evidence of intelligent planning by a supernatural being. Elephant trunks seem so uniquely fitted for lifting food to the mouths of these large animals, and the thumb and forefinger of a human hand so wonderfully adapted for grasping, that they seem to be the works of intelligence. Speculations like these are very ancient. Moved by such wonders, the Psalmist proclaims: "The heavens declare the glory of God; and the firmament showeth his handiwork" (19:1 KJV); and in the philosophical *Fragments,* Aristotle speaks of a race of men who looked up at the stars and concluded that surely these were the works of gods. Later St. Thomas argued that the web of regular causal interaction requires for its explanation a farsighted intelligent designer.[35] Yet, in spite of the long history of the argument from design, it was not until the eighteenth century that it received classic formulation. In *The Dialogues Concerning National Religion,* David Hume gives an appealing summary of this formulation.

> Look round the world: contemplate the whole and every part of it: You will find it to be nothing but one great machine, subdivided into an infinite number of lesser machines . . . All these various machines, and even their most minute parts, are adjusted to each other with an accuracy, which ravishes into admiration all men, who have ever contemplated them. The curious adapting of means to ends, throughout all nature, resembles exactly, though it much exceeds, the productions of human contrivance; of human design, thought, wisdom, and intelligence. Since therefore the effects resemble each other, we are led to infer, by all the rules of analogy, that the causes also resemble; and that the Author of Nature is somewhat similar to the mind of man; though possessed of much large faculties, proportioned to the grandeur of the work, which he has executed. By this argument *a posteriori,* and by this argument alone, do we prove at once the existence of a Deity, and his similarity to human mind and intelligence.[36]

In his widely read exposition of this argument, William Paley (1743–1805) added a great deal of detail. He hoped to bring home the apparent analogy between objects of human contrivance and natural phenomena. The human eye he compared with the telescope, the bones, joints and muscles of the human arm with an articulated crane, the heart with a pump, and the instincts of animals, which led to the efficient use of raw materials, with the instruments of human beings. He spoke of the bees' ingenious use of wax combs to preserve their honey, although he apparently failed to notice that the hexagonal shape of the cells of the comb is the most efficient use of the wax possible.[37] To these few examples might be added scores more. With such impressive testimony to nature's efficiency, who could deny its intelligent design?

Hume's Criticisms

In spite of the initial attractiveness of his own version of the argument, David Hume developed a devastating critique of it. In order to understand his critique, it is helpful to note that the logical structure of the argument is that of an analogy of the type $A:B$ as $C:D$—the human mind is to a machine as God is to nature. This argument form has frequent application, as in the mathematical problem to find x in the equation $2/4 = x/8$. Hume did not question the argument form, but he did question the use of it in teleological arguments. Three of Hume's criticisms are as follows.

First, Hume did not think that the analogy between nature and a machine was as close as Archdeacon Paley believed. Although a close analogy may exist between machines and small-scale natural phenomena, like eyes and honeycombs, it is not nearly as close for such large scale phenomena as the propagation of species. Here there is prodigious waste. Under ordinary circumstances, hundreds of thousands of eggs are needed to produce a stable population of fish or frogs since so many fail to hatch or are eaten by predators. Thus, for every example of teleology that might be produced, it is not difficult to find another example that suggests dysteleology and lack of intelligent design.

Second, Hume argued that it is always theoretically possible to provide a naturalistic or nonpurposive explanation for every apparent adaptation of means to ends in the natural world. What appears to be designed might merely be the result of the operation of chance or natural laws.

Third, Hume argued that even if mind is necessary to explain the apparent teleology of the natural world, it need not be the mind of God. An argument from analogy is like an equation. One need put only as much mind into the equation as is necessary to explain the effect. Thus, the small scale and limited teleology of the natural world does not need for its explanation the infinity, the perfection, and the unity of mind or intelligence that classical theism posits. A committee of minor gods might better explain the combination of teleology and dysteleology that we observe in the world than does the single omniscient and omnipotent creator God of Western theism. In the tradition of Hume's *Dialogues*, Stephen Jay Gould has recently suggested that much of nature's handiwork seems more the product of a group of neighborhood handymen than the work of omniscience. Toes that have become hoofs and smell receptors that have become the layers of the brain suggest an absurd ingenuity rather than a grand design.

> Orchids manufacture their intricate devices [which ensure cross-pollination] from the common components of ordinary flowers, parts usually fitted for very different functions. If God had designed a beautiful machine to reflect his wisdom and power, surely he would not have used a collection of parts generally fashioned for other purposes. Orchids were not made by an ideal engineer; they are jury-rigged from a limited set of available components.[38]

The Theory of Evolution

Although all three of these criticisms are impressive, to many thoughtful people the second seems the most telling. While Hume himself proposed only that a naturalistic explanation is always possible, the development of the theory of evolution in the nineteenth century in fact provided such an explanation. This theory purports to explain the appearance and continued presence of just such data as eighteenth century arguments from design relied on; and it does so not by an appeal to intelligence but by positing the chance mutation of genes and natural selection. In brief, the theory states that chance produces many variations in the genetic pool of the various animal and vegetable species, but only those variants that give their possessors an advantage in the struggle for survival are preserved. Hence, although the human eye, the articulated arm, and the horse's hoof seem to be designed to fulfill certain functions, according to this understanding of evolution, they were not. Their appearance and preservation are the result of merely natural forces. So conclusive seem these considerations that many have suggested that the argument from design ought to be gracefully retired. Nonetheless, new versions of the argument have evolved.

The Wider Teleological Argument

In order to meet some of Hume's criticisms, a different form of the teleological argument was developed. The same suggestion appeared in Kant's *The Critique of Judgment* and in *The Analogy of Religion* by the prominent Anglican theologian, Joseph Butler (1692–1752).[39] It was that the laws and operation of nature further the demands of the moral law and that the best explanation of this fact is the God of Western theism. This idea provided the impetus for a new beginning that was called the *argument from the conservation of values*. When the *theory of evolution* became widely accepted, F. R. Tennant (1866–1957) and Peter Bertocci saw the possibility of incorporating that theory into this new approach. In summary, the argument maintains that the natural order not only makes possible human survival but also supports and fosters the moral and spiritual values of intelligent beings, and that this is the kind of universe one would expect a wise, benevolent, and powerful deity to have designed. Since the focus of the argument is not on the small-scale phenomena cited by Paley but on the large-scale phenomenon of the evolutionary process itself, it has become known as the Wider Teleological Argument.

The starting point of the argument is the fact of the emergence of human beings from lower forms of life and, more remotely, from inorganic material. Bertocci finds it striking that at the end of the evolutionary process, as far as we know it, intelligent, self-conscious, moral, free, and creative beings have emerged.[40] These beings have the capacity not only to appreciate beauty and goodness, but also to add creatively to the sum total of moral and aesthetic values in the world.[41] This stark fact seems to cry out for explanation. As a report of the World Council of Churches put it:

> What accounts for the fact that the design of its atoms and the laws governing their behavior made it possible finally to produce the human being within it? The cosmos did not have to be at all, and it certainly did not have to be designed in such a way as to make humanity a possibility. Such questions have no answers within science, and their contemplation leads to some sort of theological inquiry.[42]

In addition to the extraordinary fact of the development of creatures capable of increasing the sum total of good by their intelligence and power, inventing and creating new and hitherto unknown kinds of things, there is also the fact that this is the kind of creature one would expect the God of the Bible to have made. To be sure, if one accepts the theory of evolution, it cannot be supposed that when God created the universe he at that time created the human species in his image. Although God's purpose in creating the world was to create beings to share his perfection as much as possible, he has done this not at the beginning but in due time, as Irenaeus long ago suggested.

> He has made possible the kind of human being and the kind of values which come to their fulfillment when man becomes a disciplined co-creator in the realization of values. The kingdom of heaven is the communion of co-creators, finite and Infinite, who live in trust and loving mutuality.[43]

Certainly there is a great deal of dysteleology in the world. Hume was right. From the human standpoint the universe is not designed with the efficiency of a machine, but in broad outline the universe is the kind of world that the God of Christian faith might have been expected to create, especially if it is assumed that the power to create is one of the excellences that God is seeking to share with his creatures. In a perfect and smoothly running universe there would be nothing for God's creatures to improve and, hence, no new goods for them to bring into being. Imperfection is a necessary condition for perfectability.

One of the strengths of this argument is that it takes the theory of evolution as a given. It thereby avoids some of the problems of the older versions. However, it still has to face additional issues raised by Hume, the most important of which is similar to a criticism of the cosmological argument. Does nature, in this case evolution, need a further explanation? Having explained the origin of the apparent design in nature, do we really need to provide a further explanation of the theory by which the apparent design is accounted for?

The philosopher of science, Carl G. Hempel, has provided a helpful clarification of this issue in his discussion of theory construction in the natural sciences. When a systematic relationship is noted between laws describing two separate kinds of events, this correlation between *Law 1* and *Law 2* is often explained by introducing a theoretical construct or model *M*. The gas molecule theory, from which two laws concerning the behavior of gases (Boyle's law and Dalton's law of partial pressures) can be deduced, is often cited as an example. However, Hempel also notes that it is always possible to simply record the correlation between *Law 1* and *Law 2* (perhaps in terms of *Law 3*) and refrain from employing any explanatory model at all.[44]

An application of Hempel's analysis to teleological issues is found in the writings of the eminent biologist, Julian Huxley. Huxley notes the same correlation between nature and values as do Tennant and Bertocci. At times he is even more rhapsodic.

> During the thousand million years of organic evolution, the degree of organization attained by the highest forms of life increased enormously. And with this there increased also the possibilities of control, of independence, of inner harmony and self-regulation, of experience. Compared with what a protozoan or a polyp can show, the complexity of later forms of life, like bee or swallow or antelope, is stupendous, their capacity for self-regulation almost miraculous, their experience so much richer and more varied as to be different in kind.[45]

But Huxley sees no reason to invoke the God-hypothesis or model, or even to think of teleology or evolutionary purpose.[46] Let us, implies Huxley, rejoice in the vast evolutionary progress, but there is no reason to posit more.

However, a difference between the wider teleological argument and scientific theories is sometimes noted. It is argued that scientific models are adopted only when they have explanatory power in that they provide the basis for predictions which can be verified. The God-hypothesis, Hume argued, has no real explanatory power since no additional features of the natural world can be deduced from it or predicted on its basis. While it must be admitted that features of the natural world cannot be predicted or deduced from the God-hypothesis, and that this criticism of Hume's is factually sound, still the criticism is blunted when we note that historical explanations and many economic theories yield neither additional deductive consequences about the present state of affairs nor predictions about the future. Therefore, implications would seem to be *desiderata* of explanatory theories but not absolute essentials.

A Final Criticism

Up to this point, we find the controversy at a draw. Champions of teleological arguments have not been able to present a conclusive case for the existence of God, but the skeptics have likewise been unable to show that the theistic interpretation of evolution is clearly mistaken. The discussion of one last criticism will illustrate the stalemate even more clearly.

Every teleological argument rests on the conviction that an explanation of a series of events in terms of intelligent design is a more complete explanation than one that merely records these events in terms of a nonpurposive natural law. In the Fifth Way, St. Thomas clearly implies this conviction.

> The fifth way is based on the guidedness of nature. An orderedness of actions to an end is observed in all bodies obeying natural laws, even when they lack awareness. For their behavior hardly ever varies, . . . which shows that they truly tend toward a goal, and do not hit upon it by accident.[47]

St. Thomas then goes on to argue that a complete account of these invariable tendencies will demand explanation in terms of intelligence or design.

It is at just this point in the discussion that Hume focused a criticism which has impressed many commentators. Hume argued that if the order of the physical world is explainable in terms of intelligent design, why does not the order within the mind of the putative designer likewise need intelligence to explain it, and so on, ad infinitum?[48] Hume's claim is that the explanation of temporal sequence in terms of intelligent design is merely an apparent explanation. It is merely the substitution of one kind of order for another and we make no advance in the process of clarification.

In spite of the many commentators, for example, J. L. Mackie,[49] who have been impressed with this criticism, there have been many equally, or more illustrious, who have not. Like St. Thomas, Moses Maimonides was convinced that the explanation of regularity demanded an explanation in terms of the wisdom of an omniscient being that contains the reasons for all things.[50] But a rational procedure to settle the dispute between Hume and Maimonides is not easy to discover. It is hard to imagine what reasoned methods would be adequate. Yet this is not an issue on which we can remain neutral. Each of us must decide whether to accept as complete, explanations solely expressed in terms of nonpurposive laws; or whether to see such explanations as less than ideal in spite of the fact that we do not have definitive reasons for our choice.

The contemporary situation with respect to the argument from design is much the same as that of the ontological and cosmological arguments.

1. It has not been shown that belief in the existence of God is the only rational alternative. However, echoing the words of a contemporary thinker in another context, our discussion "certainly does not prove scepticism to be true. For this, a disproof of God's existence would be needed, and we do not have this either."[51]

2. The stalemate is largely due to the fact that in each argument there are premises that we can neither prove nor disprove. We do not know how to ground or to dislodge them rationally.

3. It is, therefore, as rationally acceptable to believe in God as to disbelieve in him. In addition, there is considerable evidence for the existence of God. In spite of the waste and dysteleology of the animal world, the universe still seems to be protective and supportive of values. There are moments when nature seems to be blind and indifferent to higher values, and yet there are also moments when the heavens do seem to "declare the glory of God and the firmament shows his handiwork."

4. The positive conclusion to be drawn from these considerations is that within the metaphysically possible, there is a place for God. Often atheists wrongly conclude that failure to prove the existence of God has done something to prove his nonexistence. Clearly no disproof has been established as yet.

Thus far we have been considering arguments for the existence of God. We have not as yet considered arguments against his existence. If it could be shown that the notion of God is incoherent, God would be an impossibility. Two types of arguments have been proposed to try to establish the impossibility of God. It has been held that genuine human freedom and responsibility are inconsistent with the idea of God's omniscience; if God knows ahead of time each of our thoughts and actions, then they must happen. If they must happen, then they happen by necessity and not by free choice. It has also been held that God cannot be both all good and all powerful and yet have created a world containing evil. Natural theologians have classically devoted a great deal of attention to resolving these dilemmas, and no consideration of their accomplishments is complete without an account of these endeavors.

Omniscience and Human Freedom

When St. Augustine was first converted to Christianity, he believed that human beings had free will and thus were responsible for their deeds. He also believed in God's foreknowledge of every future event, including all human actions; but he saw no conflict between human freedom and God's precognition. Late in life, while writing *The Predestination of Saints,* he came to abandon free will as a factor in salvation. He did so not because he had changed his mind about the relationship between free will and God's foreknowledge, but because he now believed that the human will was incapable of choosing and holding fast to the good. Only God's grace could heal the will wounded in Adam's fall, and so make it possible for the will to choose the good and thereby attain salvation.

Augustine's original analysis of the relationship of divine foreknowledge to human freedom, which he never abandoned, was very influential. It was not, however, all original since it had roots in Greek thought. In *On Interpretation* Aristotle sought to understand whether truth imposes necessity on the future. Take, he suggests, the statement: "There will be a sea battle tomorrow."[52] If this statement is true when uttered, then there will be a sea battle the next day; for true statements are always true. Hence, the fact that the statement is true the day before the event seems to make the event inevitable. If the statement is true today, then the event could not help but take place tomorrow. The situation is not materially altered when the truth is placed in somebody's mind as foreknowledge. Whether a true statement is known to be true by God or anybody else or remains unknown, it still seems to impose necessity on the world.

Aristotle's own solution to this problem of truth fatalism was to introduce a three-valued logic. In addition to the *true* and the *false*, Aristotle supposed that there was also the *possible*. *True* and *false* were limited to statements about the present and the past. Statements about the future were to be taken as neither true nor false, but only as possibly true or false. Since the *possible* imposes no necessity, the future could be understood as genuinely open. Aristotle's suggestion has been taken up by modern theologians, as we shall see, but was not adopted by Augustine. Augustine tackles the issue head-on in *The Free Choice of the Will*, where he rejects the doctrine that foreknowledge vitiates human freedom. "You wonder how it can be that these two propositions are not contradictory and incompatible, namely that God has foreknowledge of all future events and that we sin voluntarily and not by necessity."[53] Augustine's solution to this problem is to deny that knowledge is a kind of cause.[54] Whatever God foreknows will take place, but God's knowledge does not cause our wills to do what they do. God's foreknowledge "of tomorrow's happiness, does not take from you the will to be happy when you begin to be happy."[55]

What Augustine had in mind can be explained by an illustration. Suppose someone knows that a tree will fall in the forest tomorrow; then, as Aristotle pointed out, since it is true that the tree will fall, it will inevitably do so. However, the knowledge possessed by that person does not cause the tree to fall. Likewise, the knowledge possessed by an omniscient being does not cause an event to come to pass. If God is truly omniscient, he will know everything that will happen in the future, even events that are the results of chance or of human free choice. But the fact that the event will turn out in accord with God's knowledge of it does not destroy its chance causation or voluntary human causation any more than the knowledge that a meteorologist has of an impending storm or a seismologist has of an imminent earthquake causes these events.

Augustine and Predestination

Given this analysis, why did Augustine come to believe in predestination? He gradually did so, not because he changed his mind about the effect of God's foreknowledge on human freedom, but because he was convinced that human beings really have no freedom psychologically, that they are always torn between bad impulses (*yetzer hara*) and good impulses (*yetzer tov*), and that only the grace of God could tip the scales in favor of the good impulses. The story of his conversion exemplifies this point. Augustine's spiritual transformation was not intellectual but moral.[56] Like Paul, his problem was whether he could do what he ought to do. In his heart he echoed the words of the Epistle to the Romans: "For I do not do the good I want, but the evil I do not want is what I do . . . Wretched man that I am! Who will deliver me from this body of death?" (Rom. 7:19, 24). Augustine found his answer in another passage of Paul's. "Not in reveling and drunkenness, not in debauchery and licentiousness, not in quarreling and jealousy. But put on the Lord Jesus Christ, and make no provision for the flesh, to gratify its desires" (Rom. 13:13–14). And Augustine added: "I had no need to read further . . . for all the darkness of doubt vanished away"—doubt he could persevere and that his love for the good could be made strong by God's grace.[57]

For many years after his conversion, Augustine tried to find a place for both grace and free will. However, he gradually put more emphasis on grace. By the time he wrote *The Predestination of Saints,* he had come to believe that every movement of the will toward righteousness is the result of God's grace. In earlier works, he spoke of grace perfecting the will—"Grace cures the will whereby righteousness is freely loved";[58] but in *The Predestination of Saints,* God's grace initiates the will to love the good as well as perfecting that love. Free will is left no role to play in the pursuit of goodness. The grace of God is necessary for "the beginning," "the carrying out," and "the completion of any good work whatever."[59]

To summarize, Augustine's belief that some human beings are predestined to salvation and the rest to perdition is based on the incapacity of the human will to desire righteousness without the grace of God and is not based on a supposed necessity stemming from God's foreknowledge. Most Christians have not followed St. Augustine in this matter. Like the medieval humanist Erasmus (1455–1522), they have believed that both the grace of God and human free choice are necessary for salvation. It is also significant that Luther, Calvin, and Jonathan Edwards, believers in predestination, invoked a predestination of God's foreknowledge. Their departure from Augustine on this point was because of another issue not considered by Augustine.

How God Knows What He Knows

If God has all the perfections, then it seems that he must know every event of the future as well as of the past and present. But how could he know the future? By what process of intellection could he know what has not yet taken place? Medieval theologians began to puzzle over these questions. One possibility that occurred to them is that God knows what will take place because he knows the present state of the world and its causal laws. God can then know future events in knowing the process of their becoming.

This suggestion has awkward consequences. If every event were caused by prior events, then God could know how everything will turn out in the future, if he knows the causes. But then of course there would be no free will. However, if human freedom were a given, God could never know with precision the future state of affairs from a knowledge of present causes. By definition, a free human decision is one that is self-caused and thus not wholly determined by the state of the world or by prior internal states of mind. Hence St. Thomas concludes that God could not have certain knowledge of future events if he "knew them as future," i.e., as "known on the basis of present causes."[60] "From this it is clear that a contingent can be known as future by no cognition that excludes all falsity and possibility of falsity; and since there is no falsity or possibility of falsity in the divine knowledge, it would be impossible for God to have knowledge of future contingents if he knew them as future."[61] St. Thomas' own solution to this difficulty is to insist that God knows future contingents not as future, but timelessly. An analogy will clarify what is meant. Suppose we think of God's knowledge of past, present, and future events in terms of a movie film. Each event has its separate frame and God sees them all laid out before him in such a way that he can see them all at once. "The divine intellect, therefore, sees in the whole of its eternity, as being present to it, whatever takes place through the whole course of time."[62]

To many modern commentators, this solution has not seemed to be totally satisfactory. For one thing, it seems impossible to use this analogy to explain how God knows what time it is on earth. He sees all events at once; how then can he know that one of the frames is the frame that is now actual? He could do so if he were able to observe what is going on on earth. But this he cannot do, for then his consciousness would be changing and he would lose his immutability.[63] There is no way by which to make a correlation from God's side between God's timeless (successionless) vision and what is happening here in our world.[64]

John Duns Scotus made an interesting attempt to bridge this gap between God's timeless vision and the temporal world. In Duns Scotus' account, God's knowledge of the world begins in his knowledge of Himself. "God first knows his essence, and in the second instant he understands creatures by means of his essence."[65] What Duns Scotus had in mind was that by knowing himself God generates in his intellect the ideas of all possible beings. In terms of our analogy, God generates in his intellect every logically possible movie frame. But how does he know which frame is actual or will be actual? Duns Scotus seems to have believed that God does know because he knows which ones he has willed from all eternity to be actual.[66] Hence, by knowing only himself, God knows all events past, present, and future.

William of Ockham (1290–1349), who wrote several times on this issue, found Scotus' view no improvement. In Duns Scotus' account, God could have certain knowledge of the future if his eternal will were the sole determining cause of every event. But given free will, said Ockham, "the determination of the uncreated will does not suffice, because a created will can oppose the determination [of the uncreated will]. Therefore, since the determination of the [created] will was not from eternity, God [could] not have certain cognition of the things that remained [for a created will to determine]."[67]

A final possibility remains by which God could know the future through knowing only himself. God might know a future event by logical deduction from what he knows of his own nature. This suggestion was presented in its classic form by the distinguished philosopher Baruch Spinoza (1632–1677). However, were God to know in this way what is to happen, a complete and absolute determinism would follow. Given God's existence and the supposition that the nature and existence of everything follows logically from his nature, then the universe could not be otherwise than as God's nature determined. Again, this suggestion is inconsistent with freedom of the will. This outcome did not disturb Spinoza, but it had disturbed William of Ockham[68] and continued to disturb the majority of Christian thinkers.

How then does God know what will happen, when some events are presumed to happen by chance or by the free choice of the will? Ockham expressed the growing consensus. He confidently affirmed that God cannot know every future event by a knowledge of the present causes, or by a knowledge of what he has willed, or because the events follow deductively from his nature. But since God is described by faith as that being than which no greater can be conceived,[69] Ockham was convinced that he must have the perfection of omniscience; but "it is impossible to express clearly the way in which God knows future [events]."[70]

A Contemporary Discussion

The medieval theologians believed that God could justly reward or punish human beings for their deeds even though he knew ahead of time what they would do. They came to the conclusion that God's foreknowledge does not remove human responsibility because that knowledge does not cause us to act anymore than does our own foreknowledge of the sun's rising cause and make us responsible for the sun's movement. God's knowledge does not take away our freedom. Still, no clear account of how God knows future events was formed and so God's knowledge of the future remained a mystery.

However, another issue has emerged for the natural theologian that threatens to make God responsible along with human beings for their sins. Human beings are responsible because they are free; but perhaps God is also responsible because he created particular human beings even though he knew they would freely sin.

This issue has received a good deal of attention in contemporary philosophy because an interesting way of expressing this problem has recently been developed. It has been suggested that we think in terms of many whole worlds or universes, not just in terms of individual human beings. Most of these worlds will be "possible worlds" since only one of them is the actual world. To make matters as simple as possible, let us think of a possible world in which Jones freely sins by accepting a bribe. Let us also think of a possible world in which Jones turns down the bribe. Now let us suppose, following Alvin Plantinga, that there is a *book* for each possible world.[71] At least one such book will include an account of Jones taking the bribe and one will include an account of Jones not taking the bribe. Now, can God decide which book to open, that is, decide which possible world to actualize? If he knows that in one world Jones will freely sin and in the other world Jones will freely refrain from sinning, God has a choice of which world to create. Then he will be responsible for Jones' sinning, even though Jones will also be responsible since he freely sinned. Thus, God is responsible for every event after all.[72]

Even on its own terms, the solution reached at the end of the Middle Ages was paradoxical. If God foreknew the event, the event inevitably took place even though it was freely willed by one of us. But when the possibility of God's knowledge of possible worlds is added to this paradox, the rational pressure to accept Aristotle's solution to the problem of knowledge of the future is exceedingly strong. The future does not yet exist and hence cannot be known.[73] "Omniscience" is then defined as "the ability to be free from ignorance and error" and "to know everything that can be known." "God does not already or eternally know what we do tomorrow, for, until we decide, there are no such entities as our tomorrow's decisions."[74] More and more Christians are coming to accept this new definition of "omniscience."

Omniscience and Love

Another issue pertaining to omniscience has recently concerned theologians—the possibility that immutable foreknowledge might conflict with another of God's perfections, his love for his creatures. To recapitulate St. Thomas' thinking, God's perfection demands his absolute immutability. "The divine intellect must, therefore, be an absolutely unmoved mover."[75] Hence, God cannot know by means of discursive knowledge or ratiocination, for there can be "no succession in the divine consideration."[76] As we have seen, St. Thomas proposed that God must know everything that he knows all at once in a simultaneous present as if "in a mirror."[77] What St. Thomas means is that God sees his creatures in himself and not by observing the changing world. If he learned what he knows by observation of the temporal flux, then his consciousness would change.

This is a very striking statement for St. Thomas to make. For if God knows in this way, then he cannot know his children in the way we know each other. What St. Thomas' view amounts to is that God knows all about us, but he does not know us directly. To know us directly means that he observes our changes and thus himself changes. The intimate, personal, loving relationship between God and his children that is depicted in Scripture would, in St. Thomas' view, seem to be at best an analogy to the indirect and changeless love by the immutable being.

Christianity has always affirmed that God loves his creatures, and that in the Incarnation God entered human life to share our suffering. What could it mean for an immutable being to take mutability upon himself? More generally, if God is immutable, "he could not be affected or prompted by another nor could He respond to the needs and desires of finite beings."[78] The perfection of love would seem to negate the posssibility of God's immutability. As Charles Hartshorne has said: "Loving participation in grief, like receptivity to influence in general, is no privation but a positive power, extremely limited in us, unlimited in God."[79]

To be sure, the notion of God's immutability has important religious value. It seems to guarantee God's steadfastness and faithfulness. If God is immutable, then he can be counted on to keep his promises. If he is immutable, then his purpose and power cannot fail. If he is immutable, then he cannot fail to direct and hold up the world.

Yet in stressing God's immutability, it is not at all clear that most Christians have meant to say that God could not change in any respect whatever. Speaking for a great many, Nelson Pike suggests: "I want to propose that when the Christian says that God is immutable, what he means is that God cannot change as regards His power, benevolence, etc., . . . but God might, e.g., change His mind. More importantly, God might be moved or prompted by the prayers of the faithful. To take another example, God is immutable with respect to His omniscience, but the specific content of God's knowledge might change. It might change as the objects and circumstances that are the objects of His knowledge change."[80] Christian theologians have increasingly abandoned the traditional concept of God's immutable foreknowledge, and by adopting these modifications have continued to maintain God's essential immutability.

The Problem of Evil

The significance of the problem of evil is hard to overestimate. Because it is generated by three central, but apparently contradictory, affirmations of Christian theism, it strikes at Christianity's very heart. In his short book on the problem of evil, J. S. Whale presents the issue with force and clarity:

> The *first* axiom is the absolute sovereignty of God, maker of Heaven and Earth. Christian Theism asserts that the universe is grounded in one and only one Will which creates, sustains and orders all things. The *second* Christian axiom asserts something about the character of God; He is love, in all its goodness and holiness; One who is of purer eyes than to behold iniquity. If He were anything less that this He would not be what we mean by God. The *third* Christian axiom asserts the indubitable reality of evil in God's world. Evil, physical and moral, is a terrible fact—the fact which makes our problem.[81]

The problem of evil is not a recent concern. In ancient times, the Greek, Epicurus, and the Hebrew author of the Book of Job struggled with this same issue. Among Christian theologians, St. Augustine explored many of the issues in his *The Free Choice of the Will*. However, the problem received its most complete discussion in the eighteenth century in David Hume's *Dialogues Concerning Natural Religion*.

Hume's *Dialogues*

Hume's discussion of the problem of evil can usefully be divided into two parts. In Part X of the *Dialogues* he argues that the three propositions, "God is omnipotent," "God is benevolent," and "There is evil in the world," make a logically inconsistent triad. "Epicurus's old questions are yet unanswered. Is he willing to prevent evil, but not able? then is he impotent. Is able, but not willing? then is he malevolent."[82] In Part XI, Hume alters his stance. Even if the argument of Part X fails, he argues, the amount of evil in the world is so immense that God's existence is thereby falsified. Let us examine these two stages of Hume's argument in turn.

In spite of the brilliance of Hume's first argument, Nelson Pike has recently maintained that it is inconclusive.[83] The affirmations of God's omnipotence and perfect goodness and also of the presence of evil in the world are not mutually inconsistent if a further premise is true. If, for example, it is true that "God has a morally sufficient reason for permitting evil," then neither God's power nor his goodness are compromised. The morally justifiable reason most often advanced is the creation of free, intelligent beings, who can add to the sum total of good in the universe. Really free beings would be responsible for any evil they caused, and so the creator is released of any accountability for that evil. Thus, there is a way of blunting the first stage of Hume's argument. As a result, many modern skeptics have concentrated their attention on the second stage of Hume's critique. Is the amount of evil so vast that God's existence is proved false?

It has become customary to present this second stage of Hume's case under two headings: (1) considerations of omnipotence, and (2) considerations of benevolence. Under the first heading it is asked: To be omnipotent, must a being be able to eliminate all the many evils that afflict the world? Under the second heading it is asked: Could there ever be any morally sufficient reason for permitting the incalculable suffering endured by humanity, for example, the pain and slaughter of six million Jews? Could even the achievement of the greatest good imaginable, say world peace, excuse this most horrible crime? Add to this the countless ills of other sentient creatures and the incredible wastes of nature. How could this infinity of evils ever be justified? One can understand the loathing atheists often have for believers. To a J. S. Mill or a Bertrand Russell, anyone who continues to believe in God in the face of these evils must be either incredibly foolish or morally depraved.

Considerations of Omnipotence

It is important to realize that the concept of *omnipotence* is historically one of the last of the classical attributes of God to be analyzed. *Omniscience,* insofar as it has been distinguished from *omnipotence,* received extensive discussion in the medieval and modern periods. Discussions of omnipotence were developed more slowly.

During the medieval period, it came to be understood that an omnipotent being could not do just anything. For example, St. Thomas held that even an omnipotent being could not bring about a contradictory state of affairs.[84] God could not create something uncreated or cause a past event not to have been. Similarly, God could not lie, cheat, or steal, since such actions would be inconsistent with God's moral perfection.[85] It is surprising that, in spite of these advances in the understanding of "omnipotence," only recently another issue concerning omnipotence and the problem of evil has been explored: Could an omnipotent being create beings over which he had no control?[86] It would seem that he could not, because then he would not be omnipotent. But if such is the case, then he could not create beings with free will, or create a state of affairs in which subatomic particles or mutations of genes are subject to chance. It seems that if there is an omnipotent and omniscient being, that being would nullify any power other beings have, and all those powers would in effect be absorbed into God's power.

The issue, as J. L. Mackie has clearly seen, concerns the meaning of "omnipotence." Is there anything in the concept that gives God the ability to create free and uncontrollable beings? Mackie thinks that there is not.[87] This would be the case if "omnipotence" means "the ability to control absolutely everything." But suppose "omnipotence" means "the ability to create many different kinds of things." Surely the power to create more than one kind of thing is a greater power than the ability to create only one kind. Suppose we return to the discussion of possible worlds. For God to be able to create *both* worlds in which God can control every outcome *and* also worlds in which God cannot control every outcome, is surely to have greater power than the more limited ability to create *only* those worlds over which God has complete control. Hence, there is something in the concept of omnipotence that gives God the ability to create truly free beings.[88]

Such puzzlement over the limits of omnipotence makes Job's response to a somewhat different set of problems more intelligible. To suggest that Job, having failed to find a rational justification for evil, is simply overwhelmed by a sense of God's awful power and majesty, so that he worships only the infinity of God's might, is to miss a deeper meaning. The speeches that the poet puts into the mouth of Job need not be understood as affirming the arbitrary will of the creator, but rather as proclaiming the limitations of human wisdom to understand the fullness of God's plan. At the end of the vision Job reaffirms God's unsurpassably great power but adds: "I have uttered what I did not understand, things too wonderful for me, which I did not know. . . . Therefore I despise myself, and repent in dust and ashes" (Job 42:3–6). "Omnipotence," Charles Hartshorne has recently remarked, is not clearly enough understood "to constitute a well-defined premise from which conclusions are deducible."[89]

Considerations of Benevolence

Scripture and Christian tradition have understood God's benevolence as the gracious favor that God holds toward creation. God's universal purpose in creating the world is sometimes described as the desire to share his being and goodness as widely as possible. More specifically, it is to create beings who can be as much like him as possible, perfect insofar as created beings can be perfect. The dazzling variety of beings in the world are said to reflect his power and the plenitude of his goodness. Yet it is in intelligent beings that more of God's perfection seems to be realized. It is possible for them to be morally upright and free, as well as rational, and to share in God's creativity and increase the amount of goodness in the world. This the Scripture describes as being made "in the image of God" (Gen. 1:27).

God's sheer power, however, could not compel free creatures voluntarily to choose to exercise moral virtue or to share in God's creative enterprise. God can only accomplish this purpose by persuasion and by creating the conditions that would make it possible for human beings to fulfill their potential for personal and communal development. The voluntary nature of the believer's loving commitment was long ago recognized by St. Augustine: "It is impossible for him to believe, unless he is willing."[90] The world can be seen, then, as "a vale of soul-making," as a place where growth into the full stature of children of the most high is possible. "God does not manipulate our minds or override our wills, but seeks our unforced recognition of his presence and our free allegiance to his purposes."[91] Have we here an answer to the problem of evil?

The answer is only a partial one. It is practically impossible to relate this grand design to all the manifold individual evils, the sufferings, and the waste. The task staggers the mind and heart. But aside from this complexity, it has seemed to many that even this great good, the production of God-like human beings, is seldom accomplished. And if it could be, would even this great good justify the deaths of six million Jews in the gas chamber, not to mention the millions of others who over the centuries have suffered unjust and cruel deaths? Could it also justify the wracking pain and the destruction of natural and cultural values that both human beings and nature have wrought? To these questions, the believer and the atheist have diametrically opposed answers.

The Believer's Answer

The problem of evil is based in the triad: "God is omnipotent," "God is perfectly good," and "There is evil in the world." It has been pointed out that this triad would not be inconsistent were another premise true: "God has a morally justifiable reason for the evil found in the world." Now suppose the believer is utterly convinced of God's existence, his unsurpassable power and goodness, and also that there is evil in the world. The only possible conclusion is that God does in fact have a morally justifiable reason for the evil. Under these circumstances, no amount of evil could destroy a belief in God. And this could be true even without a full account of the morally justifiable reason that God might have for permitting evil. The believer knows the general purpose of God and that the purpose is good, but cannot see the way in which that goodness is realized in fact. Like Job, believers must simply accept their ignorance with the faith and hope that they may one day come to understand what at present they only believe.

The Atheist's Answer

Atheists must answer differently. Unbelievers look for a solution to the problem of evil so that they can decide whether or not to believe in God. These individuals cannot logically conclude that there must be a morally justifiable reason for the evil of the world even if human reason cannot find one. In the atheist's world, there is no God in whose wisdom such reasons might be present. Unable to find the answer in human reason, atheists can only conclude that theism has failed to provide itself a secure foundation.

Natural Theology: An Appraisal

The age of natural theology drew to a close at the end of the eighteenth century. Although it had not reached all of its objectives, it left a solid legacy of achievement. It succeeded in presenting a consistent and coherent version of Christian theism, and so demonstrated that the existence of God is at least a logical possibility. But it did more than that. It showed that the evidence for the existence of God that is based in nature and reason is at least as strong as that against it. Hence, it also showed that the existence of God is not only a logical possibility, but a metaphysical possibility as well. But it was unable to demonstrate that evidence drawn only from nature and reason is much more strongly in favor of the existence of God than against it.

As for attempts to show that Christianity is incoherent, natural theologians helped to outline what a consistent Christian position would be concerning the relationship between free will and God's omnipotence and omniscience. It is coherent to maintain that an omnipotent being could create beings over which he had no control and that, therefore, God could create beings with freedom of the will. However, God could not know ahead of time the results of human free choices without compromising that freedom. Natural theologians have also blunted the problem of evil by showing that there is nothing inconsistent in the triad, God is omnipotent, God is omnibenevolent, and there is evil in the world, provided that God has a morally justifiable reason for permitting evil. Although part of that reason is said to be the creation of beings who can freely choose to share in God's creative purpose to bring all things to as much perfection as possible, no complete account of God's reasons for permitting evil can be given. As we indicated in Chapter V, Christian faith in the goodness of God rests more upon belief in God's gracious action in Jesus of Nazareth to bring human life to its perfection than upon an ability to calculate a surplus of goodness in nature.

Put another way, natural theology succeeded in beating back the attacks of those aggressive critics who hoped to show that belief in God is based either on premises clearly false, or premises derived by false reasoning. This the critics have not been able to demonstrate. Nonetheless, natural theologians have been unable to fulfill their most optimistic hopes, to show that there are not only good but conclusive reasons to reject atheism. Their achievement was to show that Hume's belief that "the Christian religion cannot be believed without a miracle by any reasonable person"[92] is itself an unreasonable belief.

Both the natural theologians and their critics confined themselves strictly to considerations of nature and reason. Major thinkers of the nineteenth and twentieth centuries began to question the adequacy of these foundations, not only in the pursuit of religious truth, but also in the pursuit of truth generally. They turned more directly to epistemological issues and looked for other avenues to truth in addition to reason and the five senses. It is for this reason that the nineteenth century is described as a new beginning in Christian thought.

CHAPTER VII

Authority and Revelation

The major world religions all appeal to reason as one source and criterion of truth, but they also characteristically invoke two other sources. They appeal to experiential knowledge or inspiration— sometimes called enlightenment and sometimes, revelation. And finally, all the great world religions refer to particular writings as authoritative. These Scriptures are sometimes viewed as the repositories of an original revelation, such as was given to Moses and Mohammed. For Buddhists, the Sutta Pitaka is taken as authoritative because it is believed to contain the teachings of the Buddha himself. Sometimes the Scriptures are regarded as sources of truth because they are the products of direct divine inspiration. In some ancient texts, the Hindu Vedas are said to have been dictated by the gods, either Prajapati or Brahman. The Christian Scriptures are likewise considered to be authoritative because they are believed to be the Word of God. Some mean by this that the Bible is dictated by the Spirit.

However, in spite of these general similiarities of appeal to enlightenment or inspiration and to Scripture, each tradition differs in the way it views these elements. The Koran is especially important in Islam, which is often called "The People of the Book." At the other extreme are the Quakers, where the Inner Light or Spirit of God speaking in the Meeting is the ultimate authority. However, in classical Christianity, it is neither the Bible nor the promptings of the Spirit that are the final authority, but Jesus the Christ, who has been granted the most complete knowledge of God. "In many and various ways God spoke of old to our fathers by the prophets; but in these last days he has spoken to us by a Son" begins the Epistle to the Hebrews. And according to the Gospel of John, it is Jesus the Son of God, and not the Bible, who is God's Word, God's self-communication to human beings. The Scriptures of the Old and New Testaments are regarded primarily as the holy records of revelation and not as the original revelation. Even Christians who take the Scripture to be inerrant regard its authority to be dependent on Christ and the Spirit, and so to be derivative.

For seventeen centuries there was little reason to question the reliability of the Scriptures. Few thoughtful people in the Christian world had cause to doubt the accuracy of the accounts of creation or the stories about the Apostles and prophets, nor did doubts accrue to the Gospel accounts of the life of Christ. The Scriptures were regarded as wholly reliable. Where they spoke of matters that went beyond anything that could be known by human beings, these matters were accepted as guaranteed by Christ and the Spirit. However, during the eighteenth century, increasing doubts concerning the authority and truth of Scripture began to arise. Under the influence of John Locke (1632–1704) and David Hume (1711–1776), the philosophical doctrine known as Empiricism became popular. Empiricism's appeal to observation as the test of truth was a ready ally for the new experimental sciences that developed so remarkably in the eighteenth century. The ground was thus prepared for Hume's own influential "Essay on Miracles," which marked a first step in the modern study of the Bible.

It has been suggested that Hume launched his critique of miracles in response to the exaggerated weight placed on them by some of his contemporaries. But while Hume may have had certain contemporary works in mind as he wrote, nonetheless the appeal to miracles to support Christian claims is found as early as the Gospels, where it is frequent. St. Augustine also cites the miracles reported in the Bible as a proof of the divine inspiration of the Apostles, and St. Thomas Aquinas makes use of a similar argument with regard to Christ's authority.[1] Miracles were typically taken as God's witness to the veracity of the speakers. Hume's contemporary, Bishop Joseph Butler, who was admired as a philosopher as well as a theologian, simply carried on a long tradition when he said, "[In religion] we see distinct particular reasons for miracles: to afford mankind instruction additional to that of nature, and to attest the truth of it."[2]

As Hume's famous essay points out, the appeal to miracles as a guarantee of truth is not confined to Christianity. Most other religions use miracles in this way. However, in the Christian Gospel, one miracle carries an even more important role than this. When Paul says: "If Christ has not been raised, your faith is futile and . . . we are of all men most to be pitied" (1 Cor. 15:17, 19), he proclaims for the Resurrection a more crucial role than that of guaranteeing the reliability of Jesus as teacher. Paul saw in the Resurrection the actuality of Christ's victory over death and the means of his continued presence with his Church. It has seemed to many that possibly Christianity might dispense with other miracle stories, but it could not dispense with this one.[3] Hence, the status of miracle stories is a central concern of Christian thought.

Hume's Essay on Miracles

The issue that comes out most clearly in Hume's original essay, and the responses to it, is epistemological; that is, it addresses the question of what we can know. The issue is not primarily whether or not miracles are possible. Hume's own concept of natural law is statistical and thus natural laws do not impose the kind of necessity on the world that divine power could not alter. For Hume natural laws report only past observations and do not tell us about what is possible or impossible in the nature of things. Hence, the focus of the discussion is not on the possibility of the Resurrection, but rather on a related issue: Could there ever be sufficient reason to believe that a Resurrection had taken place? In order for an event to be taken as evidence of divine favor, it must be out of the ordinary; but paradoxically, such an event cannot be good evidence. A dead man coming to life would be a miracle because it has never been observed, but the latter fact means that there could be no reason to believe a report of it. As Hume himself put it: "There must, therefore, be a uniform experience against every miraculous event, otherwise the event would not merit that appellation. And as a uniform experience amounts to a proof, there is here a direct and full *proof* from the nature of the fact against the existence of any miracle."[4]

An obvious retort at this stage of the argument is that since miracles are not claimed to be impossible, but only not in accord with the experience of the majority, they might be established by the accounts of reliable eyewitnesses. What evidence do we have of the regularities of nature and its laws? The experience of many witnesses. But should other witnesses be forthcoming, we would abandon or severely modify these laws. Direct experience always has high evidential value. But Hume's point is that he questions the reliability of the eyewitnesses. "When anyone tells me, that he saw a dead man restored to life, I immediately consider with myself, whether it be more probable that this person should either deceive or be deceived, or that the fact which he relates should really have happened."[5] Only the most reliable of witnesses could tip the probability in favor of miracles. But are the biblical witnesses reliable?

To one who is not already a believer, they will not appear trustworthy. In order to accept their testimony, one would have to have confidence in their general reliability, their "good sense," as Hume put it.[6] One might like to know whether or not they were careful in examining the grounds for their claims and whether they were reasonably impartial. Fifty to eighty years after Hume, his doubts about both of these points had spread to students of Scripture. New Testament studies established, for example, that the Gospels were not really biographies of the life of Jesus but rather were proclamations of the Christian message. The organization of the material seemed dictated by concerns other than pure chronology. Furthermore, the writers of the Gospels did not themselves claim to have witnessed all the events mentioned but relied on the testimony of others. Belief in miracles was widespread in ancient times, and it seemed that ancient authors were more likely than modern historians to believe the unsupported testimony of others concerning such events. There was no reason to believe that they would have especially scrutinized their sources. Hence, many concluded that Scripture could not be taken as reliable.

However, the fact that Scripture could not satisfy the most rigorous canons of objective reporting is not in itself a decisive refutation of the notion that it contains accounts of genuine events. Legendary material, while it cannot pass as serious history, often has its basis in genuine happenings. Granting that the biblical witness to the Resurrection is not impartial, that people in New Testament times were disposed to believe reports of miracles and would not have subjected their sources to rigorous questioning, still we might credit their accounts if we had other reasons to believe in their general reliability. For example, we might trust their reports because of their care in discussing the spiritual life or their thoughtful evaluation of Old Testament material.

To summarize the state of the discussion, unbelievers look for evidence to convince themselves of the truth of Christian claims. Miraculous events would go a long way in providing such evidence. To believe the miracles, unbelievers must accept the testimony of the Apostles. But they have no reason to believe the Apostles unless they have reason to believe that the Apostles generally speak the truth. This is precisely what unbelievers do not have. However, believers, because they are convinced that the Apostles speak the truth when they enunciate the central doctrines of the Christian faith, have reason to trust their reports of events. Hence, many believers will give credence to reports of miracles whereas skeptics will not. Even more important, believers who already believe in supernatural agencies will expect God to reveal himself in non-natural ways. Writing some seventy years after Hume, Friedrich Schleiermacher made this point: "Once Christ is recognized as Redeemer . . . it is natural to expect miracles from Him who is the supreme divine revelation."[7]

More generally, we accept as factual only what seems probable to us. We argue from our present beliefs to our understanding of the past.[8] Those who already believe in the supernatural, and who can see a divine purpose for particular miracles in the way Butler suggested, would have reasons to credit the reports of the events, whereas the skeptic would not.

The Scientific Challenge

Hume's important critique of miracles was followed by the impact of the growing body of scientific knowledge. Hume had focused on the use of miracles as evidence, but eighteenth and nineteenth century science attacked miracles on a broader front. The physics of Sir Isaac Newton (1642–1727), which is appropriately termed "mechanistic," seemed to strengthen the case for Deism—the view that God created the world and left it to run by itself. If the world is a smoothly running machine, there would be little reason for God to interfere with its orderly operations. Yet the support for Deism given by the analogy of the machine seems not to have been as obvious to persons of the eighteenth century as it is to us now. The pioneer chemist, Robert Boyle (1627–1691), who liked to compare the universe to the clock in the Strasbourg cathedral tower,[9] accepted the miracles of the New Testament, notably the raising of Christ and Lazarus, which he thought had "proofs cogent enough to satisfy any unprejudiced person,"[10] and which demonstrated to him that God has the power to effect a general resurrection of humanity at the last day.

Likewise, the mechanistic determinism of the Baron d'Holbach, so popular in the nineteenth century, seems to have attracted little support in the eighteenth century. "All is in order in a nature, no part of which can ever deviate from the certain and necessary rules which issue from the essence it has received."[11] Perhaps in retrospect d'Holbach's views seem the dawning of a new era, but at the time they seemed merely eccentric.

However, by the middle of the nineteenth century, the situation was very different. Although nature was only rarely compared to a machine, increasingly it came to be seen as a structure of complex operations that interacted in regular and uniform patterns. Less and less did scientists look beyond nature for principles of explanation. M. LaPlace (1749–1827), who made significant contributions to the mathematical analysis of planetary motion, is often quoted in this context. His retort to Napoleon's question about God, "I have no need of that hypothesis," stands as a symbol of this growing sense of the self-sufficiency of nature.

These considerations increasingly made miracles seem out of place. Even more telling, however, was the growing divergence of nineteenth century science from the biblical accounts of the creation. In 1784 Archbishop Ussher calculated what became the most widely accepted date for the beginning of creation. Using the biblical chronology, he determined that the creation had taken place in 4004 B.C.E. It became more and more difficult, however, to maintain this young earth theory in the face of the fossil remains that were being discovered in increasing numbers. Furthermore, the great variety of extinct species represented by these remains brought into question the biblical account of the creation, in which relatively few species are mentioned. The suggestion that the biblical Flood might account for the many fossils seemed increasingly less attractive as the functioning of nature became better understood. In addition, the nebular hypothesis and its account of the formation of the earth from a planetary explosion was a respected alternative to creation by divine fiat. Finally, Charles Darwin's (1808–1882) theory of evolution made obsolete the belief that the human race had been descended from just two ancestors, and also obviated the biblical picture of separate creation of each animal species. Science presented one account of the origin of the universe and the Bible another.

This growing divergence of science and Scripture, and the recognition that natural theology had produced more limited results than its champions had hoped, led to two quite different reactions in the nineteenth century. One affirmed the traditional beliefs by an appeal to revelation. The other hoped to assimilate the scientific picture of the universe and to redirect the focus of religious concern to a realm of experience untouched by science. Both of these approaches had strengths and weaknesses, and both have contributed to twentieth century understandings of the foundations of Christian faith.

The Conservative Response

The conservative response to the growing divergence of the scientific from the biblical picture was analogous to Schleiermacher's response to Hume concerning miracles. Where most eighteenth century discussions had seen miracles as proofs of the deity of Christ, Schleiermacher saw belief in miracles as a consequence of belief in God. Miracles were taken to be the kind of actions one would expect a Son of God to perform. Hence the probability of their occurrence seemed great when set against a theistic background. In a similar way, the conservatives sought to justify the reliability of biblical revelation by appealing to prior beliefs about God. They placed emphasis on God's transcendence, his distance and difference from humanity. This view is epitomized by Søren Kierkegaard's famous phrase, "the infinite qualitative distinction between God and man."

The gap between the human and the divine seemed so great that it could never be bridged by the creature's reason. The conservative's faith was that God would choose to reveal himself in the Bible and tradition. Believing that God was also merciful and good, they concluded that God would not mislead. His revelation would be infallible. By "infallible" they meant "wholly true."

Infallibility

Doctrines of infallibility achieved prominence in the nineteenth century. Such doctrines variously located the infallible authority in Scripture, in the pronouncements of the Pope speaking *ex cathedra,* and in the Word of God, Jesus of Nazareth. In all three versions, the revelation is given in propositions, that is, the statements of Scripture, the declarations of the Pope, and the teachings of Jesus. Alternatives to infallibilist propositional theories focus on religious experience as a more direct awareness of God than is mediated through words.

All three infallibilist theories propose an authority by which proposals for belief are adjudicated and sometimes overruled. Thus, John Henry Newman (1801–1890), an Anglican clergyman who later became a distinguished champion of Roman Catholicism, describes the role of "the Church's infallibility, as a provision, adapted by the mercy of the Creator, to preserve religion in the world, and to restrain that freedom of thought, which of course in itself is one of the greatest of our natural gifts, and to rescue it from its own suicidal excesses."[12] It is not claimed that the infallible authority has spoken on all issues and enunciated all truth, but that when it speaks its pronouncements take precedence absolutely.

This doctrine was not new in the nineteenth century. St. Thomas Aquinas said: "Nothing may be asserted as true that is opposed to the truth of faith, to revealed dogma."[13] The Calvinist tradition makes the point even more explicitly. "The supreme Judge . . . in whose sentence we are to rest, can be no other but the Holy Spirit speaking in the Scripture."[14] "The Bible, therefore, does not need to be supplemented and interpreted by tradition, or revised and corrected by reason."[15]

Creation in Seven Days?

This reliance on an infallible authority does not entail a double truth theory, in which the truth of religion and the truths of science or reason are taken to be valid in their own spheres, even though they may contradict each other. It does, to be sure, assume two sources of truth, but one is superior to the other and corrects it. Hence, it is a single truth theory. Still, it is a theory with more flexibility than is sometimes recognized. Take for example the interpretation of the Genesis material on creation. Must one who accepts the infallibility of the Scripture believe that God created the world in seven days, that the human race had but two ancestors, and that it was all but destroyed in a deluge of water which fell upon the earth in the time of Noah? Many infallibilists have thought so, but not all. No one has ever believed that the Scripture is totally bereft of allegory or symbolism. No one ever took it that when Jesus said, "I am the vine, you are the branches" (John 15:5), that he literally meant that he was a vine and that his followers were twigs with bark and leaves. The question has always been: Which parts of the Scripture are symbolic and which are not? Some modern thinkers who take the Scripture to be the inerrant Word of God regard the first eleven chapters of Genesis as myth rather than science or history.[16] Moreover not all take literally stories such as that of Jonah and the great fish. When Jonah took ship to flee from God's command to preach to Ninevah, God by means of the fish returned Jonah to his point of embarkation; this is sometimes understood by infallibilists as an allegory showing that God's call is inescapable. Biblical infallibilists are more flexible than has usually been recognized.

Let us review infallibilist theories. In such theories, there are two sources of truth, revelation and reason. As useful as is science or reason, revelation is more reliable since God himself is its author. Hence, revelation always takes precedence over science and reason. By extension it can be concluded that the infallible authority, because it overrides what is learned from scientific investigation, tells us when to use reason and when not to use it. A parallel point is that reason is to be commended for use because it is a gift from God rather than because it occupies a privileged epistemological position. Many secular philosophers mistake the logic of the authoritarians' position and criticize them for inconsistency because they use reason just so far and then abandon it. But authoritarian religious thinkers are not inconsistent, because for them revelation always takes precedence over the results of reason's efforts.

John Henry Newman made this same point. When the results of scientific investigation seem to contradict authoritative doctrines, the believer has three possibilities: "He is sure, and nothing shall make him doubt, that, if anything seems to be proved by astronomer, by geologist, or chronologist, or antiquarian, or ethologist, in contradiction to the dogmas of faith, that point will eventually turn out, first, *not* be proved, or, secondly, not *contradictory,* or thirdly, not contradictory to any thing *really revealed,* but to something which has been confused with revelation."[17] The eminent Presbyterian theologian, Charles Hodge (1797–1876), made a similar point by distinguishing between what the biblical authors *intended to teach*—in which they were taken by Hodge to be infallible spokesmen for God—and what they *happened to believe*—in which they were often mistaken.[18] Hodge also echoed Newman in his rejection of Darwinism. Descent from apes seemed to Hodge not only inconsistent with biblical anthropology but also unscientific. In this Hodge has his disciples in contemporary creation scientists.[19]

These remarks can be generalized in the following way: conservative Christians believe that the criterion for deciding whether or not a proposed doctrine is really revealed is whether it plays an essential role in the structure of Christian faith. They argue that the Resurrection can reasonably be taken to play such a role. Although most Protestant biblical infallibilists accept Genesis as a book of science and history, a few of them regard the first eleven chapters of Genesis as myth. Since Vatican II, Roman Catholics have increasingly taken a similar position. Likewise, to the conservative Anglican authoritarian, J. I. Packer, an evolutionary account of cosmic and human origins does not distort the basic message of the Bible.[20]

The Limits of Reason and the Need for Revelation

By the beginning of the nineteenth century, serious doubts were expressed concerning the ability of reason to prove the existence of

God. We have seen some of the reasons for these doubts in the last chapter. The upshot of these discussions was that, on the one hand, no demonstrative proof for the existence of God was successful; and on the other hand, the strong negative case that Christian theism is incoherent also had not been made convincingly. While the existence of God had not been proved, it had not been disproved either. In these circumstances it was quite natural to turn to revelation as a source of the knowledge of God.

It was characteristic of many nineteenth century thinkers to argue that reason was more limited in its ability to attain religious truth than the eighteenth century had generally supposed. However, they did not just fall back on revelation claims in the face of reason's failure; they argued that reason failed because it was impotent to do the task which the natural theologians hoped that it would. The limits of reason were said to be intrinsic and not just accidental. Several accounts of these limits, some more far-reaching than others, were offered.

Limitations from Human Sin

In the concluding chapter of his *Apologia Pro Vita Sua*, John Henry Newman argued that the destructive effects of sin were so great that human reason was bound to go astray without the gracious and merciful gift of an infallible authority. "And first, the initial doctrine of the infallible teacher must be an emphatic protest against the existing state of mankind. Man had rebelled against his Maker. It was this that caused the divine interposition. . . . It is because of the intensity of the evil which has possession of mankind, that a suitable antagonist has been provided against it."[21] Thus Newman sees the need for an infallible authority that is an extension of God's will, in order to save human beings from their sins. Newman here echos Augustine: "Because the minds of men are obscured by familiarity with darkness, which covers them in a night of sins and evil habits, and cannot perceive in a way proper to the clarity and purity of reason, there is a most wholesome provision for bringing the faltering eye into the light of truth under the kindly shade of authority."[22] Neither Newman, nor Augustine, nor the Catholic intellectual tradition generally, denies that reason can under the right circumstances reach God. "I am not speaking here of right reason, but of reason as it acts in fact and concretely in fallen man. I know that even the unaided reason, when correctly exercised, leads to a belief in God, in the immortality of the soul, and in a future retribution; but I am considering the faculty of reason actually and historically; and in this point of view, I do not think I am far wrong in saying that its tendency is towards a simple unbelief in matters of religion."[23]

Limitations of Speculative Reason

Several nineteenth century thinkers were impressed by the fact that speculative reason when it sought to deal with the Absolute seemed to generate paradoxes and antinomies. In a well-known section of the *Critique of Pure Reason*, Immanuel Kant hoped to show that speculative reason could not be applied to matters beyond experience because even when employed rigorously it led to contradictory conclusions. Reason supported the ideas that the world both was and was not created. Kant concluded that pure reason could be employed legitimately only in the world of ordinary experience and produced nonsense when employed beyond experience. Hence reason could never lead to a knowledge of God.

In a somewhat similar way, Henry L. Mansel (1820–1871), Dean of St. Paul's Cathedral, argued that reason could not comprehend God because religious claims always involved paradox and contradiction. He thought the notions of the "Absolute," the "Infinite," and "First Cause" all involved contradictions, as did pantheistic and atheistic ideas. Hence truths about God must be attained through revelation, if they are to be attained at all.

Finally, no account of nineteenth century thinking could be complete without mention of Søren Kierkegaard. Like Kant and Mansel, Kierkegaard regarded Christianity as paradoxical and even absurd. The most striking statement of this position appears in *The Concluding Unscientific Postscript*. There is debate whether in this work Kierkegaard is expressing his own opinion or is merely exploring a view that he did not make his own. However, the view presented there has been widely influential and has had a life of its own regardless of Kierkegaard's intention.

Kierkegaard and the Absurd

Kierkegaard argued that Christianity is a matter of passionate inwardness (faith) and not a matter of dispassionate objectivity (reason). He then went on to argue that only the absurd can be embraced with passionate inwardness, and thus "the absurd is the object of faith, and the only object that can be believed." In Christianity the absurd is clearly manifest. "What now is the absurd? The absurd is—that the eternal truth has come into being in time, that God has come into being, has been born, has grown up, and so forth, precisely like any other individual human being."[24]

It might seem that what Kierkegaard is saying is that the Incarnation seems absurd to us because we are incapable of grasping the ideas or the concepts involved. But Kierkegaard specifically denies that this is the case. He argues that the absurdity or the paradox is grounded not in the limitations of human reason (as Mansel held) but in the "qualitative difference between God and man." "But the absolute paradox, just because it is absolute, can be relevant only to the absolute difference that distinguishes man from God." It is the ontological difference between the eternal (timelessness) and time that produces the contradiction and the paradox. "But the absolute difference between God and man consists precisely in this, that man is a particular existing being . . . while God is infinite and eternal."[25]

Kierkegaard produces a strong statement denying the possibility of natural theology, by insisting on the "absolute difference" between time and eternity, God and the world. Natural theology cannot succeed unless there is some continuity between the world and God. Unless there is something they share at least analogously, it will not be possible to argue from the natural order to a divine one.

But an "absolute qualitative distinction between God and the world" is not biblical. There are, to be sure, passages in the Psalms in which God is asserted to be "above all gods" (Ps. 95:3) and "his glory above the heavens" (Ps. 113:4). But nowhere is this difference described as absolute. Furthermore, a similarity between God and his creatures is affirmed in the creation story, where Adam and Eve are said to be made in God's "image and likeness." Finally, the possibility of a natural theology is expressly affirmed in a verse from the

Psalms: "The heavens are telling the glory of God" (Ps. 19:1); and in Paul's Epistle to the Romans: "Ever since the creation of the world his invisible nature, namely, his eternal power and deity, has been clearly perceived in the things that have been made" (Rom. 1:20). Hence any doctrine of an absolute distinction between God and the world and of the consequent impossibility of a natural theology is clearly unscriptural. This point is particularly telling against Kierkegaard since he had no intention of departing from Scripture.

A second part of Kierkegaard's argument against the possibility of a natural theology is that in his view God can bring about a contradictory state of affairs, for example, that the eternal (the timeless reality of God) has come into existence in time in the Incarnation of Jesus of Nazareth. The denial that God could bring about a contradictory state of affairs is, as we have seen in the previous chapter, a necessary element in any natural theology. If God can produce contradictory states of affairs, then no conclusions can be drawn about him from what he has done. Anything will be possible and nothing will necessarily be true of him. Hence, for Kierkegaard, it follows that God can be known only by revelation.

But the difficulty with this position is that it undermines itself. If God can bring about contradictory states of affairs, then he can bring it about that Peter is both damned and saved at the same time, that God's promises are both fulfilled and not fulfilled at the same time, and that a particular proposition both is and is not a revelation. The position is too sweeping and destroys itself.

Mansel did not take as extreme a position as did Kierkegaard. Instead of affirming that reality itself is paradoxical and self-contradictory, he proposed the more limited thesis that reality appears paradoxical to human beings who have only imperfect ideas and can only grasp reality approximately. Mansel argued that the concept of the Christian God is just such a paradoxical approximation.[26] But even this more restricted thesis has its difficulties. If what was argued in the previous chapter is correct, then it is possible to present a logically consistent account of theism. While there may still be some matters unexplained and unresolved, the account is substantially coherent. Whatever paradoxes remain are incidental rather than fundamental to theism. Mansel cannot really sustain his case that Christian theism is necessarily paradoxical and therefore its truth can be known only by revelation.

Revelation and Reason

By rebutting arguments like those of Kierkegaard and Mansel, we do not, however, reestablish natural theology; reason and nature are not shown to be more than a partial source of the Christian knowledge of God. The arguments for the existence of God are still not conclusive. Belief in miracles cannot be based on the ordinary study of history, and the conclusions of natural science do not authenticate the Christian witness. If Christian doctrine is to have an ultimate grounding, it must be elsewhere, in revelation or a religious way of knowing. This seems to be the conclusion of nineteenth century investigations.

Two issues remain to be discussed: (1) Is revelation propositional, as those discussed so far have thought; or is revelation an awareness of God, rather than truths about God? (2) What role does reason play in choosing among those who claim to speak in the name of God or who claim to see clearly into ultimate reality? For the most part nineteenth century thinkers were clear that, although reason could not supply the truth, it nevertheless had a role in deciding what was to be accorded the status of revelation and what was not. For example, in 1863 A. A. Hodge affirmed: "Reason establishes the fact that God speaks, but when we know what he says, we believe it because he says it."[27] And Dean Mansel suggested that there are certain facts that can provide evidences in favor of revelation.[28]

Reason in Support of Authority

An example of the use of reason "to establish the fact that God speaks" is found in discussions concerning the identification of the infallible authority. As we have already noted, the three most frequently urged candidates are: Jesus the Christ, the Scriptures of the Old and the New Testaments, and the Pope speaking *ex cathedra.*

The pronouncements of Jesus of Nazareth are often taken to constitute the infallible authority. Søren Kierkegaard expressed this conviction in his *On Authority and Revelation.* In this book, prompted by the eccentric visionary claims of a Danish Lutheran Pastor, A. P. Adler, Kierkegaard argued: "It is true that Christianity is built upon a revelation, but also it is limited by the definite revelation it has received." That revelation has its focus in Jesus, for "Christ as the God-Man is in possession of the specific quality of authority." "A Christian priest, if he would speak correctly, must say quite simply, 'We have Christ's word for it . . . therewith the matter is decided. Here there is no question either about racking one's brains or about speculation, but about the fact that it is Christ who said it, not in the capacity of a profound thinker, but with his divine authority.' "[29]

To many the simple attribution of final authority to Christ's word is sufficient. In our century the widely read Anglican layman, C. S. Lewis (1898–1963), made this stand popular in *The Case for Christianity* (Part II). But others have moved from the infallibility of Christ to the infallibility of Scripture. J. I. Packer has argued: "Christ's claim to be divine is either true or false. If it is true, His Person guarantees the truth of all the rest of His teaching (for a divine Person cannot lie or err); therefore, His view of the Old Testament is true"[30] Since the Scripture in New Testament times was the Old Testament, and since Jesus in the Gospel of John asserts "scripture cannot be broken" (John 10:35), Packer has no doubts but that Jesus accepted the Old Testament as completely authoritative[31] and that, together with the teachings of Jesus himself, the New Testament can be regarded as an extension of that infallible revelation.

Packer's presentation is a restatement of nineteenth century views. Speaking of Christ, Charles Hodge affirmed: "His authority is the ultimate and highest ground of faith and moral obligation." Like Packer, Hodge grounds belief in Scripture on faith in Christ: "We believe the Scriptures, therefore, because Christ declares them to be the Word of God. Heaven and earth may pass away, but his word cannot pass away." And finally Hodge cites the same key verse: "'The Scripture cannot be broken.' . . . This is the whole doctrine of plenary inspiration, taught by the lips of Christ himself."[32]

J. H. Newman's argument in support of the doctrine of papal infallibility can be seen as an extension of the preceding argument for biblical infallibility. Man has rebelled against his Maker and has been induced to use reason against God. Even an infallible Scripture can be misinterpreted. "The judgment, which experience passes whether on establishments or on education, . . . must be extended even to Scripture, though Scripture be divine. Experience proves surely that the Bible does not answer a purpose for which it was never intended." A merciful Deity will provide in every generation "a power, possessed of infallibility in religious teaching . . . happily adapted to be a working instrument, in the course of human affairs, for smiting hard and throwing back the immense energy of the aggressive, capricious, untrustworthy intellect."[33] Such an instrument is provided by the Pope in Ecumenical Council.[34]

The Quest for the Historical Jesus

We have discussed the authoritarian reaction to the scientific rejection of miracles—that miracles are still to be believed because they are attested to by an infallible authority. However, during the nineteenth century other Christians began to make a different response. They began to explore what Christianity would be like without the miracles. Of course they realized that if the miracles reported in the Old and New Testaments were not credible, then the reliability of Scripture as history was also called into question. Could historical investigation make it possible to sort the scriptural material into accounts of real events, folk legends, and doctrinal elaboration? This was the task that biblical scholars increasingly set for themselves. Although they attempted to apply critical methods to both the Old and New Testaments, a special focus of their work was the quest for the Jesus of history. As the contemporary New Testament scholar, Reginald Fuller, remarked: "The chief motivation . . . was to get back behind the orthodoxy of the church to the original teaching of Jesus and thus acquire a corrective to the Church's version of Christianity."[35]

These scholars saw as their task the contrasting of the traditional picture of Jesus, often called the *Christ of Faith*, with the *Historical Jesus*. They assumed that the historical Jesus whom they pursued could be discovered by ordinary historical methods, in contrast to the Christ of Faith, who could be accepted only on other grounds. These other grounds were usually some form of revelation, although not necessarily the authoritarian views just discussed.

In spite of much devoted labor, the quest for the historical Jesus turned out to be a failure. Scholars failed to provide an acceptable historical methodology by which to sort out the events from their interpretation. Because of the nature of the biblical material, a highly sophisticated methodology is needed, and this has yet to be sufficiently developed. Instead of scientific history, what the many questors provided were interpretations of the biblical material based on their own prior commitments. In every case, some prior conviction, some faith, some religious insight or revelation provided the key to the various reconstructions of the historical events. This pattern of thought is exemplified even in the most eminent recent biblical studies.

The methodology of the quest for the historical Jesus did not differ appreciably from that used by the authoritarians. The stance toward history turns out to be the same as the stance taken by Newman and Hodge with respect to the data from the sciences. By appealing to historical data, the questors seemed to be more objective than the authoritarians. In fact, they were no less apologists for their own opinions. They looked for only enough historical data to support their faith stances. This is a kind of confirmation of their beliefs, not real historical investigation. It merely shows that historical investigation does not compel one to surrender one's beliefs. It is only in this sense that the many pictures of the Jesus of history are confirmed by historical investigation.

Friedrich Schleiermacher

This method of historical investigation was exemplified in the writing of Friedrich Schleiermacher in the nineteenth century. Although he accepted the scriptural accounts of the miracles as historically true, he did not conceive of them as providing any evidence for religious belief. Rather, as we have already indicated, he believed them because he already believed in God. Schleiermacher's own account of his reasons for belief in God and in the deity of Christ provided a framework for the quest for the historical Jesus. Schleiermacher began by clarifying ideas on the nature of true religion. Then he argued that Jesus is the perfect exemplification of the true religion. As such, Christ can lead us to God and can be rightly described as Savior. And finally, this picture of the Christ is commended as the historical Jesus. This same pattern has been followed by all those who have embarked on the quest, even though they sometimes have believed that they were establishing their pictures of the historical Jesus independently of any preconceived goals.

Schleiermacher was a mystic in the sense that he thought that human beings are capable of an immediate consciousness of God, which is intertwined with self-consciousness. He turned inward, rather than outward to God. "As often as I turn my gaze inward upon my inmost self, I am at once within the domain of eternity."[36] Schleiermacher further describes this self-consciousness as "a feeling of absolute dependence,"[37] which when deepened is recognized to be a dependence on God. "To feel oneself absolutely dependent and to be conscious of being in relation with God are one and the same thing." "The God–consciousness [is] in the self-consciousness in such a way that . . . the two cannot be separated from each other."[38]

In these passages, Schleiermacher is not using "feeling" to denote sensations like pain or dizziness, but rather more broadly to denote "experience" or "awareness." He often speaks of feeling in connection with intuition. "Intuition without feeling is nothing . . . Feeling without intuition is also nothing . . . because they are originally one and inseparable."[39] The phrase "feeling of absolute dependence" would seem to indicate an "awareness of contingency" or an "experience of finitude," much as twentieth century existentialists understand it. One contemporary restatement of Schleiermacher's account of religious experience is Paul Tillich's description of the immediate awareness, in the depth of one's own being, of the power of being resisting nonbeing. For both Tillich and Schleiermacher, we come to an awareness of God precisely in the moment in which we are aware of our own powerlessness and insignificance.

For Schleiermacher, although the God-consciousness must be conceived as an "essential element in human nature," it finds its perfect exemplification in Jesus of Nazareth. Christ is distinguished from others "by the constant potency of His God-consciousness, which was a veritable existence of God in Him." So potent is "the God-consciousness in His self-consciousness" that it determines Jesus' "every moment, and consequently also this perfect indwelling of the supreme Being [is] His peculiar being and His inmost self."[40]

It is because of the purity and power of Jesus' God-consciousness that he is called Mediator and Redeemer. "The God-consciousness in the race to begin with was inadequate and impotent, and only later broke forth in perfection in Christ, from whom it continually extends its authority, and proves its power to bring peace and blessedness to men."[41] Schleiermacher believes that this ideal Jesus is amply verified as the Jesus of history. "As an historical individual He must have been at the same time ideal . . . and each historical moment of His experience must at the same time have borne within it the ideal."[42] Schleiermacher believed that he need not look beyond the Gospels for confirmation of this vision. He wrote at a time before many problems with the historicity of Scripture began to be seen. But he does anticipate the procedure of the quest for the historical Jesus. Having established the meaning of "true religion," he showed to his own satisfaction that the historical Jesus exemplified this ideal religion. By so doing, he hoped to establish once and for all the correct form of Christianity and to expose the weaknesses and mistakes of traditional supernaturalism that set God against humanity and the divine against the world. Christianity, rightly understood, could do without the miracles, for God became man in Jesus' God-consciousness.

Ritschl and Harnack

Two prominent and influential attempts to discover the historical Jesus were made by Albrecht Ritschl (1822–1889) and his disciple, Adolf Harnack (1851–1930). They sought to improve on Schleiermacher by giving more attention to historical research than had Schleiermacher. Like Schleiermacher, Ritschl and Harnack hoped to meet the challenge of contemporary science by concentrating on the religion of Jesus (the kind of religion that Jesus himself had), rather than the religion about Jesus (the Christ of Faith and its attendant supernaturalism). However, Ritschl and his disciples differed with Schleiermacher over the kind of piety they attributed to Jesus. Ritschl and Harnack rejected Schleiermacher's "mysticism" in favor of an ethical and moral faith.[43] While they agreed with Schleiermacher in stressing Jesus' God-consciousness, they understood that consciousness in a different way. To them, it consisted of Jesus' filial devotion to his Father and his resulting concern to fulfil God's plan for the world by founding an ethical kingdom or commonwealth.[44]

Both Ritschl and Harnack were self-conscious about their historical methodology and its relationship to their piety. Ritschl described his understanding of his task as follows: "The principle of theological knowledge must be a synthesis of personal religious knowledge

with the full understanding of . . . history."[45] Thus Ritschl know-
ingly interprets the past in terms of his own present experience.

All religion, says Ritschl, "is occupied with judgments of value,"
and the "acceptance of the idea of God is, as Kant remarks, a practical belief, and not an act of speculative cognition."[46] Religion, then,
is firmly based in moral and ethical concerns. God's plan for human
life is the establishment of an ethical commonwealth, and of this
plan Jesus was supremely aware. Furthermore, according to Harnack, "it is 'knowledge of God' that makes the sphere of the Divine
Sonship"; and Jesus' teaching and practice of "the higher righteousness" of God's rule secured his title as Messiah. Harnack argued that
Jesus never claimed to be divine but saw himself only as an agent
of the kingdom.[47]

The picture of Jesus that emerges for Harnack as he employs "the
methods of historical science" is of the sage. "His whole life, all his
thoughts and feelings were absorbed in the relation to God, and yet
he did not talk like an enthusiast and a fanatic. . . . He is possessed of a quiet, uniform, collected demeanour, with everything directed to one goal. He never uses any ecstatic language, and the
tone of stirring prophecy is rare. Entrusted with the greatest of all
missions, his eye and ear are open to every impression of the life
around him—a proof of intense calm and absolute certainty."[48]

The Q Hypothesis

The contrast between Schleiermacher's mystical accounts and Ritschl's
ethical accounts of the religion of Jesus forced students of the New
Testament to press further. Since the Gospel of John is the most
mystical of the Gospels and Matthew the most ethical, the former
appealed to Schleiermacher's followers and the latter to the Ritschlians. The question arose whether we could get closer to the Jesus of
history by showing that one or the other Gospel was the older.

One of the scholarly techniques which contributed a partial answer to this question was the so-called "source analysis" or "source
criticism." This analysis attempts to discover which Gospels were
the sources of other Gospels. The clearly overlapping sections of
Matthew, Mark, and Luke suggested at least some sort of partial
dependence. The puzzle presented by this overlapping material came
to be known as the synoptic problem. By the end of the nineteenth

century, the lines of a solution had begun to emerge. Matthew and Luke were dependent on Mark. However, in addition to their use of Mark, Matthew and Luke had additional material in common, which was called Q from the German word for source, *Quelle*. As we discussed in Chapter I, Q was largely a collection of the teachings of Jesus. It was not presumed that Q had to be a written source any more than it was presumed that the many short teaching sections from which Mark's Gospel was constructed were previously written down. They might well have been passed on by rote in the early Christian communities.

These findings settled the relationship between the Synoptic Gospels, but it did not directly help with the relationship between the Synoptics and John. If John were older than the Synoptics, then Schleiermacher's Jesus might be the Jesus of history. If Q turned out to be the oldest material, then Ritschl and Harnack might be right, since Q contains the ethical teachings from which this school built its portrait. Paradoxically, the argument that finally convinced the majority of scholars that John was composed after the Synoptics, late in the first century, also convinced Albert Schweitzer that the Jesus pictured by the Ritschlians never existed.

Schweitzer and Weiss

Before Albert Schweitzer (1875–1965) gave up his distinguished university career and went as a medical missionary to Africa, he wrote several theological studies. In these studies, Schweitzer took his point of departure from the ideas of Johannes Weiss (Ritschl's son-in-law) (1863–1914). Weiss noted that one of the elements in the teachings of Jesus and of the early Church that had received scant attention was the coming end of the world, the Eschaton. He concluded that the reason earlier New Testament studies had neglected these passages was that they began in the wrong place. Weiss proposed to begin his own study with the preachings of the early Church. The reason for this choice is that the Epistles of Paul are recognized by all but the most conservative to be the oldest of the New Testament writings, so it seemed natural to assume that they would be the best source of knowledge of primitive Christianity. Likewise, some of the sermons found in the Acts of the Apostles seem to contain material that predates the four Gospels in their present form. To attempt to isolate the primitive proclamation or *kerygma* seemed the soundest approach to New Testament studies.

Weiss and Schweitzer noted that Paul's Epistles give considerable evidence that an expectation of an imminent end of the world was widespread in the Christian communities to which he wrote (1 and 2 Thess.) and that Paul himself shared this expectation (1 Cor. 15). Schweitzer argued that, when the world did not come to an end in that generation, the Church survived the crisis by reinterpreting the expectation. Instead of looking to an imminent return of Christ, the Gospel of John transmuted that coming into a present reality. One key to this is the use of the phrase "eternal life." In John "eternal life" means not only "life after death," but also "a kind and quality of life in the here and now." For example, in the Gospel of John Jesus says: "This is eternal life, that they know thee the only true God" (John 17:3), and "Every one who drinks of this water will thirst again, but whoever drinks of the water that I shall give him will never thirst; the water that I shall give him will become in him a spring of water welling up to eternal life" (John 4:13–14). Weiss' followers in the eschatological school proposed that John could have been written only after it became clear that the end of the world was not coming immediately.

The eschatological interpretation of the thinking behind the primitive *kerygma* is strengthened by several additional considerations. Where did the Church get these expectations, if not from the teachings of Jesus himself? To Weiss and Schweitzer, Jesus seemed the most likely source. If this is what Jesus taught, the implication is that the Gospel of Mark is among the earliest and most accurate biblical sources. Here, as well as in Q, Jesus teaches of the coming of the Son of Man in that generation, and in Mark explicitly identifies himself as that Son of Man (Mark 14:62). "The eschatological solution . . . at one stroke raises the Marcan account as it stands, with all of its disconnectedness and inconsistencies, into genuine history."[49] Further evidence of the historical authenticity of the eschatological teachings is the last chapter of John, in which it is implied that Jesus did not explicitly claim that the world would come to an end in that generation (John 21:20–23). Since this chapter seems to be the work of an editor, it looks as if the editor is trying to reinterpret the Markan tradition by obfuscation.

Schweitzer believed that these conclusions had disastrous consequences for the quest for the historical Jesus. In his view, the Gospels were not eyewitness biographies or even newspaper accounts of events, but vehicles for teaching a point of view. Furthermore, the Gospels were composed at a time when the early Christian community was compelled to reevaluate and reinterpret its initial understanding of Jesus' mission and message. It is to be expected that the authors would be inclined to bolster their new interpretation by manipulating the group memory of Jesus' life and teaching. For these reasons, the Gospels seemed to Schweitzer to be unreliable sources for reconstructing the life of Jesus. The one thing that Schweitzer believed could be known with certainty was that Jesus was an eschatological prophet who preached the imminent end of the world and was mistaken as to its date.

Although many have concluded that Schweitzer's historical Jesus is totally irrelevant to the modern age, Schweitzer counters this conclusion with a strong affirmation of the Christ of Faith. "But the truth is, it is not Jesus as historically known, but Jesus as spiritually arisen within men, who is significant for our time and can help it. Not the historical Jesus, but the spirit which goes forth from Him and in the spirits of men strives for new influence and rule, is that which overcomes the world."[50]

For almost a generation of scholars, Schweitzer's study ended the quest for the historical Jesus. Although, as we shall see, the quest was taken up again, for most scholars the emphasis shifted to attempting to explain and account for the power that the elusive and enigmatic Christ continued to exert after so many centuries. One account of this power is given by Rudolf Otto (1869–1937) and another by Rudolf Bultmann (1884–1976).

Rudolf Otto

One of the most influential twentieth century religious thinkers is Rudolf Otto. His analysis of religious experience is profound and of lasting significance. At present we shall give only a brief summary of his ideas because they will be discussed more fully in the next chapter.

For Otto, the heart of the religious life is the sense of the Holy.

His work consisted of an analysis of this experience and its implications. Otto characterized the sense of the Holy as an experience of awe, mystery, wonder, and fascination. He considered Isaiah's vision in the Temple (Isa., chap. 6) to be a paradigm of this experience. Isaiah's sense of insignificance and unworthiness before the fearful, glorious, and exalted majesty of God is seen as the ideal awareness of God. Indeed, Schleiermacher's characterization of the God-consciousness as a "feeling of absolute dependence" is criticized by Otto as being distressingly incomplete.[51]

Otto's claim that the sense of the Holy is the backbone of biblical religion is supported by many passages in both Testaments in which feelings of awe are present. The Gospels describe the coming Son of Man in vocabulary and images chosen to evoke a sense of awe. He is pictured as coming on the clouds of heaven attended by thunder and lightning, and in the story of Jesus on the Mount of the Transfiguration, his clothes were white and glistening and his face shone. For Otto, Jesus nowhere manifests the Holy more than on the cross. "Here rational are enfolded with non-rational elements, the revealed commingled with the unrevealed, the most exalted love with the most awe-inspiring 'wrath' of the numen, and therefore, in applying to the Cross of Christ the category 'holy,' Christian religious feeling has given birth to a religious intuition profounder and more vital than any to be found in the whole history of religion."[52] Jesus is mediator between God and his children because he continues to be to us a manifestation of divine holiness. Detailed knowledge of the historical life of Jesus is unimportant. It is enough that he actually lived and was the occasion for an advance in human awareness of God.

Rudolf Bultmann

The best place to begin a discussion of Rudolf Bultmann and his influential interpretation of the New Testament is with a comparison to the authoritarian religious thinkers. He learned much from his early mentor, Karl Barth (1886–1968), whom we shall discuss more fully in the next chapter. Bultmann places the ultimate source and vindication of religious truth in revelation. Like Barth, Bultmann characterizes the religious way of knowing as a confrontation with the Word of God.[53] Like Barth but unlike the authoritarians, Bultmann identifies the Word of God with Jesus of Nazareth and not with the written text of the Bible. For both Barth and Bultmann, this identification is the starting point for Christian theology. But after this agreement, master and pupil part company. Barth believes that faith in Jesus as the Word of God—that is, as God's self-revelation—necessarily implies acceptance of the Virgin Birth and the Resurrection.[54] Barth reasons that the self-manifestation of a supernatural being must itself exhibit supernatural powers. Bultmann, however, rejects Barth's supernaturalism and, along with it, the miracles. Paradoxically, Bultmann bases his conclusions only partially on scientific and historical investigation and explains his distrust of science and history as follows: Faith demands wholehearted acceptance, whereas scientific and historical research can give us only probabilities. Moreover, even if historical research should show that Jesus in fact rose from the dead, this fact would not be sufficient to establish that Jesus was the Word of God. Historical research can establish the fact of a strange event, but not that it is religiously significant—an event that has to do with salvation. Since faith cannot come by means of science or history, it can come only by a special way of knowing, through the Word of God or his Spirit. Hence, "faith in the Word of God" cannot be tied "to the results of historical research."[55] The Gospel is an offense to reason in that reason cannot establish directly the truth of the Word. "It is not for us to question its credentials."[56] But reason and faith agree that faith is and ought to be rationally baseless. It is as much a part of Bultmann's faith stance that science and history aid faith by removing the false historical basis for Christianity, as it is a faith stance of fundamentalists that the Scripture overrides the results of science and history, or of J. H. Newman that it is at least theoretically possible to demonstrate the existence of God.

Bultmann's stance comes out clearly in his position on the quest for the historical Jesus. Since the recognition of Christ as the Word of God does not depend upon historical knowledge, Bultmann concludes that the less we know about Jesus the better. Scientific history can be pressed into service to show how little we know of him, and it can tell us about the proclamation (kerygma) of the early church.

The *Kerygma*

Like Albert Schweitzer and Johannes Weiss, Bultmann considers the eschatological expectations, the dawning of a New Age, to be central to the faith of the early church. He also accepts the view that Jesus prophesied the eschatological New Age. Bultmann thinks this is a fact of history that seems certain. But contrary to Schweitzer, he makes the astounding claim that Jesus was right—the New Age did in fact dawn. Jesus' predictions were in fact true, although the church has consistently misunderstood and all but obscured the true nature of the New Age. It is here that Bultmann believes science and history can help us in clarifying the nature of the New Age.

According to Bultmann, the early church expected the coming of the Son of Man on the clouds of heaven. History falsified this expectation and helped the early church to focus on the true nature of the coming of the Son of Man. Science has made belief in the Resurrection impossible, thereby helping us in our time to focus on the true nature of Resurrection. The New Age is not attended by the coming of a heavenly being on the clouds of heaven, nor by the performance of miracles, but by the birth of a new order of human life. The New Age is an age of spiritual transformation, not an age of either cosmic or metaphysical transformation. The early church took what was essentially a spiritual truth and expressed it in a mythological and cosmological idiom.

Bultmann's argument for this conclusion is very simple. John speaks of eternal life as both a future state and one already accomplished, of the Son of Man as coming in the future but as here already in Jesus. Likewise, Paul speaks of the death and Resurrection of Christ as an outward manifestation of the death and spiritual rebirth of the Christian. "We were buried therefore with him . . . so that as Christ was raised from the dead by the glory of the Father, we too might walk in newness of life" (Rom. 6:4). Science and history show the falsity of beliefs in a bodily resurrection. But we can see in the New Testament records the reports of spiritual transformations and feel in our own hearts the call for a decision with respect to the kingdom and the new life coming to birth in us. Thus, science and history free us for "an existentialist interpretation . . . of the New Testament."[57]

But Bultmann believes that for the early church Jesus was more than the prophet of the New Age who was crucified under Pontius Pilate. For the early Church "the Proclaimer became the Proclaimed," to use Bultmann's own words.[58] Faith in the coming of the New Age became identified with faith in Jesus as heavenly agent of that age. How did this come about? Bultmann believes that it was a result of Christian experience. Christians found that it is in the hearing of the Word that the power of the new life is discovered. The power of God for the human soul is mediated to us in the word of preaching. "The word of preaching confronts us as the Word of God."[59] Integral to that preaching is Christ the Proclaimer. Here we meet Christ not only dead but alive again. "Christ meets us in the preaching as one crucified and risen. He meets us in the word of preaching and nowhere else. The faith of Easter is just this—faith in the word of preaching."[60]

To summarize, Bultmann approaches the quest for the historical Jesus from the perspective of faith. The facts of history have no bearing on the truth of faith.[61] In the word of preaching, Christ meets us as the Word of God. What need have we then of a historically based Jesus? None at all, except the fact that he existed. Although we could know more than this of Christ historically, from the point of view of the *kerygma* we need only the fact that the Word was made flesh—that is, that Jesus actually lived, preached, and died under Pontius Pilate.[62]

Howard Kee and Norman Perrin

Studies of Jesus written since Bultmann's major work continue these themes. To several scholars, Bultmann's position did not seem entirely satisfactory. Bultmann asserted that the words of Jesus as the prophet of the New Age had in fact been realized and continue to be realized in the new life. The New Age has come. However, in Bultmann's account it is not necessary for Jesus to have realized that the New Age is a spiritual renewal rather than a physical transformation. By avoiding historical questions about Jesus' consciousness, Bultmann leaves open the possibility that Jesus did not understand the real import of his own message. Thus, the identification of the Proclaimer and the Proclaimed is merely a historical accident.

Did Jesus proclaim the same understanding, the same demythologized gospel that Bultmann found in the Gospels? Unless he did, he would seem to be an odd kind of prophet for twentieth century believers to exalt to the right hand of God. He would have been wrong about the heart of the *kerygma* that came to bear his name. It was issues like these that motivated the new quest for the historical Jesus.[63]

The work of two scholars, Howard Kee and Norman Perrin, can be taken as important examples of contemporary study of the New Testament. Both believe that, on the basis of careful historical study, it can be affirmed confidently that the actual Jesus of Nazareth understood the New Age to be a present spiritual reality. However, to arrive at this conclusion, they take radically different points of departure. Kee follows the tradition of source analysis. He argues that since Q is the earliest of our sources, one should rely on it for our knowledge of Jesus. In Q Jesus identifies himself with the work of the Son of Man as judge in heaven, but he seems not to identify himself as the one coming on the clouds of heaven.[64] In Q Jesus does speak of the future coming of the Son of Man, but since the words promising that coming in Jesus' generation are found in Mark and not in Q, there is little reason to believe that Jesus said them. Therefore, according to Kee, the Christian is spared the embarrassment of believing in a prophet who was catastrophically wrong about the date of the end of the world. More relevant to Jesus' thought, Kee believes, is the Q saying: "If it is by the finger of God that I cast out demons, then the kingdom of God has come upon you" (Luke 11:20). This passage certainly supports the conclusion that the kingdom is coming through the agency of Jesus and is now a present reality.

Perrin comes to very similar conclusions, since he also stresses the passages that suggest it was Jesus himself who preached that the kingdom was already here. He stresses the Q passage just quoted and also another from Luke: "Behold, the kingdom of God is in the midst of you" (Luke 17:21). "To say 'the Kingdom of God is among you' is to say that it is 'a matter of human experiencing,'"[65] and the context shows that Perrin means "is *now* a matter of human experience." With Kee and Perrin in such substantial agreement, it might seem that the quest for the historical Jesus has succeeded. As we shall see, however, this apparent agreement is deceptive, especially since Perrin is doubtful about Q as a reliable historical source.

The Failure of the Quest for the Historical Jesus

The purpose of both the *old* and the *new* quests was to find the real Jesus behind the Gospels. Scholars have attempted to do this because the New Testament accounts of Jesus and his teachings contain some incoherences. However, the attempt to resolve these discrepancies by using historical methods to isolate the real Jesus has proved to be a task too difficult to be accomplished.

So little is known of Jesus outside the New Testament that conclusions about him have to be based almost completely on an examination of that document. To be sure, the patterns of Jewish religion at the time of Jesus have bearing on what may reasonably be attributed to him, but this connection is always at best problematic. Since not every possible influence is a real influence, a great deal of care needs to be exercised in evaluating what we learn from contemporaneous thinking. Source analysis is also a legitimate tool and provides valuable results. Its primary usefulness is in detecting the literary relationship between large blocks of material, as for example in showing the relationships between Matthew and Luke in their uses of Mark and Q. However, the attempt to employ this type of approach to the derivation of short passages has proved inconclusive.

If we seek to find the real Jesus behind the Gospels, the usual procedure is to take one strand of New Testament thinking and try to show that it is the central strand and that the other strands can be explained by reference to it. Thus Schleiermacher selected passages that stress Jesus' God-consciousness; Ritschl and Harnack, his ethical teachings; Schweitzer and Weiss, the claim to be the heavenly Son of Man; and Bultmann, his prophesy of the New Age. Each of these scholars hoped to show by sound methods that his picture of Jesus revealed the Jesus of history. They failed because they projected their own understanding of faith back into the first century. The new questers have hoped to avoid this pitfall, but their attempt to solve the problem by source analysis is also problematic.

Howard Kee and Norman Perrin disagree on whether or not Jesus spoke of the future coming of the Son of Man. As we have noted, Kee begins his study with Q, on the grounds that Q is the oldest of the Gospel sources. However, he goes further and argues that if some saying attributed to Jesus is not in Q, then there would have to be very strong reasons to think it is an authentic saying of Jesus. For example, because Q as we have it does not contain a Passion Story (an account of the Crucifixion), and does not imply that it once had a Passion Story, the student of the New Testament can safely conclude that the Gospel material in which Jesus prophesies his own suffering and death must stem from the later reflections of the early church.[66] Correspondingly, statements in which Jesus speaks of the coming of the Son of Man are taken by Kee to be the authentic words of Jesus because they are in Q.[67]

However, Kee's argument based on Q's silence is far from convincing. By all accounts Matthew and Luke employed Q to supplement material derived from the Gospel of Mark. Since Mark already had the passion material not found in Q, there would be no reason to use Q as a source for it. Furthermore, there is no reason to hold that what we have of Q is a complete document, as Kee must do if he is to regard the passion material as a secondary development in the tradition. The argument that, because it is not in Q it is probably not in the original tradition, is not as strong as it first appears.

Contrary to Kee, Norman Perrin maintains that the use of the Son of Man imagery is not original with Jesus; rather, it is Q's putting into Jesus' mouth ideas that were in fact the conclusions of Q itself. Perrin's reconstruction of the development of Q's theology can be briefly stated:

1. Jesus preached the coming of the kingdom and himself as its God-appointed agent.
2. The Church interpreted these authentic teachings of Jesus in the light of its own experience of the Resurrection.[68]
3. The first stage in this interpretation is to see Jesus as exalted to the right hand of God, on the basis of Psalm 110:1, "The Lord says to my lord: 'Sit at my right hand, till I make your enemies your footstool.' "[69]
4. It was Q's subsequent reflection that identified the Lord Jesus with the heavenly Son of Man; this was done on the basis of

Daniel 7:13. "There came one like a son of man, and he came to the Ancient of Days and was presented before him."[70]

Perrin's evidence for this possible reconstruction is found in some of the early speeches in the Acts of the Apostles (e.g., Acts 2:32–36), where the Resurrection of Jesus is explained by reference to the above Psalm verse. However, there are at least two major difficulties in Perrin's claim that this Acts passage represents an earlier stage of theological reflection than does Q. First, in their present form these speeches in Acts are not earlier than Q; on the contrary, both Q and these speeches are found together in the same work, since by all accounts Acts is but the continuation of the Gospel of Luke. This gives no reason to argue that these speeches in Acts can reliably be considered as expressing theology that is older than Q. Moreover, at least one of the passages in Acts proclaims the theology that by Perrin's account is Q's addition and not found in the first stratum of theological reflection. At his death, St. Stephen (the first martyr) is reported to have proclaimed: "Behold, I see the heavens opened, and the Son of man standing at the right hand of God" (Acts 7:56). This and other speeches as recorded in Acts do not support Perrin's reconstruction of the stages of theological development.

Jesus Known and Unknown

Both Kee and Perrin have attempted to disentangle earlier and later strata of biblical thinking. An examination of their procedures has illuminated the inherent difficulties of the task. Literary dependence can be demonstrated where large blocks of material are concerned. But, given the fact that Luke-Acts, for example, presents a substantially unified theology, it is exceedingly difficult to isolate the single elements from which the theology was compounded. Does this mean that we know nothing of the historical Jesus? Far from it. We know a great deal from the traditions of the early Church that are contained in the New Testament. We know that Jesus was remembered as an eschatological prophet, as an ethical teacher, as a person of deep spirituality and of prayer, as a healer, as a worker of miracles, as one who taught that the Kingdom of God was not just a future hope but was also a present reality, and as one who appeared to his disciples after his Crucifixion. But what we cannot do is to penetrate behind the memories of the earliest Christians who came to worship Jesus as Lord. We know a lot about him, but what we know comes to us through the witness of the Apostles' faith that is the New Testament. Individual Christians and individual theologians may and should focus on those aspects of the tradition through which they glimpse the divine, but they ought humbly to admit that they have been unable to contain the historical Jesus in a single image.

We have moved on a bit since the work of E P Sanders?

CHAPTER VIII

Discovering the Foundations

During the twentieth century much attention has been given to exploring the epistemological and ontological foundations of Christian faith. Medieval and early modern thinkers believed that they could successfully base faith in God on reason and nature. But as we have seen in Chapter VI, although evidence for God can be obtained from these sources, it is impossible to achieve demonstrative proof.

Christian thinkers reacted to this state of affairs in various ways. Some followed Søren Kierkegaard and argued that Christian faith is antithetical to the whole enterprise of natural theology. Others argued that reason and nature are merely inadequate as foundations of faith and the real source lies in special experiences—in a religious way of knowing, sometimes called revelation. Karl Barth, Rudolph Otto, Friedrich Heiler (1882–1967), and William James (1842–1910) come to mind in this connection. Appeals to revelation or a religious way of knowing have prompted further epistemological investigations to discover what reasons can be given for believing there is this way of knowing and how we can choose when there are competing statements that claim this kind of truth. Finally, there are those like Paul Tillich and Karl Rahner who, under the influence of Martin Heidegger, have reexamined the foundations of faith in fundamental ontology.

The Priority of Faith

By the unwary, "faith" is often taken to mean merely "intellectual assent to a proposition not undisputably known to be true." In this usage to say, "I have faith in God" is to say, "I believe that God exists" in the way one would say, "I believe that it will rain tomorrow" meaning, "I think that it will rain tomorrow." But in the Bible and in Christian theology faith has never meant merely intellectual assent, but also trust, commitment, and confidence. Faith includes commitment of the heart and the will, as well as the mind.

As we shall see, several interpreters have made much of the voluntary aspect of faith in their discussions of Christian commitment. Among the most notable was Søren Kierkegaard, who based his view of faith on the conviction that between God and his creatures there is "an infinite qualitative distinction." We have already criticized this view in Chapter VII, but in the present context it is useful to add the following points. What Kierkegaard seems to have had in mind is that God's mysterious holy being makes God so different from his creatures as to make it impossible to base assent to God on knowledge; such assent can be based only on a decision. "When faith resolves to do this doubt has been overcome; in that very instant the indifference of doubt has been dispelled and its equilibrium overthrown, not by knowledge but by will."[1]

However, Kierkegaard's exaggerated emphasis on "a leap of faith," as it came to be called, is inadequately based. It is simply psychologically impossible to decide to believe without any prior preparation. One cannot wake up one morning and out of the blue just decide to believe in God. One needs, at the very least, to find belief in God attractive. This implies being able to formulate some concept of God and know something about what it would be like to live in the presence of God's mysterious holy being. Some sort of prior knowledge is, therefore, essentially involved in the decision of faith.

Another way to understand the relationship between the voluntary character of faith and knowledge about God is found in St. Thomas Aquinas' discussion of faith. St. Thomas does contrast some forms of knowledge with faith, but this is what he calls "scientific knowledge" in which "the cogency of demonstration compels" assent.[2] Such knowledge is antithetical to faith because it is involuntary. However, the person of faith has some reason for believing, such as "the authority of divine teaching" or "the inward prompting of divine invitation. Hence he does not believe lightly. But he does not have a reason such as would suffice for scientific knowledge."[3]

Thus, there is for St. Thomas both an element of freedom and an element of reason in faith's assent.

It is this combination of cognitive and voluntary elements in faith's assent that struck several twentieth century thinkers as particularly significant. Alasdair MacIntyre once remarked that "since the Christian faith sees true religion only in a free decision made in faith and love . . . any objective justification of belief . . . would eliminate all possibility of a decision of faith."[4] John Hick has come to a similar conclusion; but he adds that, given the kind of God Christians believe in, one would expect him to leave them free and uncoerced.

> We must ask: why should God want to present himself to his human creatures in such an indirect and uncertain way instead of revealing himself in some quite unambiguous fashion that would permit no possible room for doubt as to his reality? Perhaps the answer is that God is leaving men free in relation to himself. Perhaps he has deliberately created an ambiguous world for us just in order that we shall *not* be compelled to be conscious of him. . . . If the man who comes to be conscious of God in this way is to remain a free and responsible personality, the knowledge of God must not be forced upon him, but on the contrary, it must depend upon his own willingness to live in the presence of a higher being whose very existence, when we are conscious of it, sets us under an absolute claim.[5]

While this emphasis on the voluntary element of Christian commitment in faith and love was a welcome alternative to the exaggerated hunger for objective certainty that motivated many natural theologians, this account of faith is still not the whole story. The fact that faith must be voluntary does not require that every aspect of religious belief be objectively uncertain. St. Thomas Aquinas is a counter-example. He believed that he had conclusively demonstrated the existence of God. For him personally, belief in the existence of God was not a matter of voluntary assent. Yet there was room for faith in other matters—belief in the Trinity and the Incarnation, for example. Hence, every religious belief need not be a matter of faith in order to safeguard the voluntary character of Christian life. Furthermore, since we cannot just arbitrarily decide to have faith, voluntaristic accounts of belief need supplementing. But natural theology seems to be able to provide only part of this supplement. It can show that belief in God is as rational as atheism, but not that belief in God is the only rational alternative. What other reasons lead people to continue to be converted, have faith, and live the religious life with deep and abiding commitment?

In searching for other sources of faith, many discovered that the Bible and the autobiographies of saintly men and women spoke of a more direct awareness of God and of religious truth than was mediated through reason. These awarenesses were sometimes reported as visions or voices, but more often were without these manifestations, and were simply "the sense of the presence of God" or of "ultimate reality." A very significant intellectual movement began to investigate the ramifications of the view that the source of faith is found in these special awarenesses or ways of knowing, sometimes called "religious experience" and sometimes "revelation." Voices and visions were left to one side, since they cannot easily be distinguished from hallucinations.

The Reality of the Unseen World

Four types of experience have been proposed as the distinctive awarenesses from which the conviction of the reality of the unseen world is born. Although there are important differences between these experiences, the common element is more significant than the differences, as can be seen in what follows.

The Experience of the Holy

One of the most striking and influential accounts of religious experience is found in Rudolf Otto's *The Idea of the Holy*. Otto was impressed by the fact that some of the most deeply stirring happenings of Old Testament religion are characterized by a sense of awe, mystery, wonder, fascination, and human insignificance, which Otto called "creature feeling." In spite of the negative elements of dread in creature feeling, positive elements of glorious and overwhelming majesty are inseparably intertwined with it. The complex interrelationship of these positive and negative elements is present in what must have been to Otto a particularly significant example—the account of Isaiah's vision in the Temple. "In the year that King Uzziah died," begins the speaker, "I saw the Lord sitting upon a throne, high and lifted up; and his train filled the temple. Above him stood the seraphim; each had six wings: with two he covered his face, and with two he covered his feet, and with two he flew. And one called to another and said: Holy, holy, holy, is the Lord of hosts; the whole earth is full of his glory" (Isa. 6:1–3). Isaiah then continues by voicing his feelings of insignificance and unworthiness: "Woe is me! For I am lost; for I am a man of unclean lips, and I dwell in the midst of a people of unclean lips; for my eyes have seen the King, the Lord of hosts!" (Isa. 6:5). This sense of unworthiness is only temporary and soon mitigated. One of the angels takes a burning coal from the altar and touches Isaiah's mouth and says: "Behold, this has touched your lips; your guilt is taken away, and your sin forgiven" (Isa. 6:7). Finally, Isaiah is commissioned to carry a message to the children of Israel.

Isaiah's vision in the temple is not an isolated example of what Otto has in mind. Most of *The Idea of the Holy* is given over to a wealth of examples of similar experiences, not only in both Testaments, but also in the whole panoply of human religious expression—in Indian, Muslim, and primitive, as well as Christian and Jewish sources, in art, music, and literature. One need not doubt that these feelings were widespread in the past, and many psychological and sociological studies have demonstrated that they are widespread today.

Otto liked to express this sense of the Holy, this complex of feelings of overwhelming majesty and human insignificance, in the Latin phrase *mysterium tremendum et fascinans* (a mystery, tremendous and fascinating). He also called it the "numinous experience." Otto was convinced that this experience is the focus of human awareness of ultimate reality. Otto speaks of a "'feeling of reality,' the feeling of a 'numinous' *object* objectively given" which is to be taken as "a primary immediate datum of consciousness."[6] Otto provides further amplification with a quotation from William James' *The Varieties of Religious Experience*: "But the whole array of our instances leads to a conclusion something like this: It is as if there were in the human consciousness *a sense of reality, a feeling of objective presence, a perception* of what we may call *'something there,'* more deep and more general than any of the special and particular 'senses' by which the current psychology supposes existent realities to be originally revealed."[7] Otto sees in numinous experience the source and foundation for belief in the reality of the unseen world; and like Isaiah, he identifies the numinous presence with the God of the Scriptures.

Mystical Union

It has become customary to reserve the term "mystical" for a range of experiences in which feelings of unity with the divine reality are paramount. Mysticism thus defined is very widespread and is to be found in every religious tradition. There are Hindu, Buddhist, and Muslim, as well as Christian and Jewish mystics. Although the mystical tradition is very ancient and has been continuously represented in each tradition, it has attracted special attention in our time because of the new interest in religious experience. Among the most influential twentieth century interpreters are the Christians, Evelyn Underhill (1875–1941) and W. R. Inge (1860–1954) (Dean of St. Paul's Cathedral in London), the Jewish authority, Gershom Sholem (1889–1982), the philosopher, William James, and the philosopher, W. T. Stace (1886–1967), whose sympathies lie with Hindu and Buddhist rather than with Jewish or Christian thinking.

The phrase "I and God are one" comes easily to those who report these mystical experiences, although closer examination reveals that several different ideas can be meant by this phrase. Hindu mystics often use it to affirm that there is but one reality of which each soul is a part, and that they have discovered that unity in experience. Others have said that in the experience they are not aware of a difference between God and the self, but that the two are different in reality. Julian of Norwich (b. 1343) is sometimes cited as exemplifying this view. In her fourteenth Revelation she says: "And I saw no difference betwixt God and our Substance: but as it were all God; and yet mine understanding took that our Substance is in God: that is to say, that God is God, and our Substance is a creature in God."[8] Still others seem to imply that they are aware of a difference between God and the soul in the experience, but that God seems to have become so much a part of one's consciousness that he is said to abide or dwell in the soul. Meister Eckhart (1260–1327) is sometimes given as an example of this type of mysticism. "Some simple people think that they will see God as if he were standing there and they here. It is not so. God and I, we are one. I accept God into me in knowing; I go into God in loving."[9]

In two of the mystical types just mentioned, no distinction between the self and God is said to be experienced, although the third type does make such a claim. On the basis of this evidence, W. T. Stace, among others, has asserted that the experiences of the Hindus and Julian of Norwich are in fact identical. He cites the following passage from the *Mandukya Upanishad* as a typical description of this kind of experience.

> Beyond the senses, beyond the understanding, beyond all expression. . . . It is the pure unitary consciousness, wherein awareness of the world and of multiplicity is completely obliterated. It is ineffable peace. It is the Supreme Good. It is One without a second. It is the Self.[10]

What is described here is a state of consciousness in which the multiplicity of ordinary experience has been transcended. Gone are the many distinctions of color, shape, sound, and smell. It is like being aware of light, just light, of one thing only. Hence the phrase "pure unitary consciousness" is particularly appropriate.

In addition to its unitary character, the experience is described as one of "ineffable peace." In words that mark it off from Otto's experience of the holy, the Buddhist text *Milindapañha* declares that "It is to be recognized through freedom from distress, danger and fear, through peace, calm, bliss, joy, abundance, purity, coolness."[11] To have the experience is, it is said, to possess if only for a moment the *summum bonum*, or greatest good.

Often this experience is taken directly as an experience of ultimate reality or God. However, other mystics claim that it is a matter of inference or interpretation that here one glimpses God or ultimate reality. Because they already believe in God or in an undifferentiated reality that is the source of all things, they come to the conclusion that this mental state must be an awareness of God or the Absolute. We shall discuss these interpretations below. In the present context we are interested in those who hold that this experience is

in itself an awareness of reality in much the same way physical seeing is an awareness of something real. William James cites a particularly interesting account of such an experience.

> The impression had been so profound that in climbing slowly the
> slope I asked myself if it were possible that Moses on Sinai could
> have had a more intimate communication with God. I think it well
> to add that in this ecstasy of mine God had neither form, color,
> odor, nor taste; moreover, that the feeling of his presence was ac-
> companied with no determinate localization. It was rather as if my
> personality had been transformed by the presence of a *spiritual
> spirit*. But the more I seek words to express this intimate intercourse,
> the more I feel the impossibility of describing the thing by any
> of our usual images. At bottom the expression most apt to render
> what I felt is this: God was present, though invisible; he fell under
> no one of my senses, yet my consciousness perceived him.[12]

This passage is reminiscent of many classical mystical sources. The
Hindu Shankara (700–750) speaks of the unitary consciousness as
"awareness of Brahman." Plotinus (205–270) calls it "an apprehen-
sion of the infinite," and in the context of a similar experience the
Muslim, Baba Krihi of Shiraz (eleventh century), speaks of "seeing
God." Many mystics believe that in the experience of the unitary
state God or the Absolute is experienced not as an inference but in a
direct awareness analogous to seeing with the eyes.

It is important to stress again that the third group of unitive mystics mentioned above believe that, although they come to know God
directly in the experience, they do not lose awareness of self. They
do not have a unitary consciousness, because they are still aware of
a distinction between the self and God. Sometimes when Jan van
Ruysbroeck (1293–1381) speaks of "union" with God, he says that
"the creature in its inward contemplation feels a distinction and an
otherness between itself and God."[13] Eckhart is often cited as expressing a similar view when he says that the soul is "not satisfied"
with what it has found of God, but seeks for what is in the Godhead
and in the essence of His proper nature,[14] thereby implying that the
soul never loses its sense of separation from God. This type of unitive mysticism is not significantly different from the personalistic
type of religious experience that has been discussed in the writings
of Martin Buber.

Personalistic Mysticism

The most influential twentieth century representative of personalistic mysticism is Martin Buber (1878–1965). Although a devout Jew, Buber was impressed by some aspects of the New Testament, particularly the figure of Jesus of Nazareth, whose teachings reflected what Buber thought was the finest flowering of Hebrew religion. Buber's version of Judaism is found in the New Testament passages that emphasize the presence of the divine in close relationships between human beings. "Where two or three are gathered in my name, there am I in the midst of them," said Jesus (Matt. 18:20). And the First Epistle of John states explicitly: "If any one says, 'I love God,' and hates his brother, he is a liar; . . . for God is love" (1 John 4:20, 8). Buber found these same emphases in ancient Judaism.

In putting these ideas into his own words, Buber drew a distinction between two stances or attitudes toward the world: I-Thou and I-it. The I-it attitude is one in which we approach another human being or inanimate thing as an object of use, as something from which we gain some advantage, as something to be controlled. But the I-Thou stance is one of mutuality and respect, like the respect and mutuality that ideally ought to exist between human beings. Buber sometimes calls this relationship "dialogic."

For Buber, "it is also only in the relation I-Thou in which we can meet God at all." It is here that God is "glimpsed." It is not that the glimpse gives us information about God. "Man receives, and he receives not a specific 'content' but a Presence, a Presence as power." "The Word of revelation is *I am that I am*. . . . That which is *is*, and nothing more. The eternal source of strength streams, the eternal contact persists, the eternal voice sounds forth, and nothing more."[15] Buber regards information and factual knowledge as belonging to the sphere of I-it, since thinking of the length of another's nose or the color of the skin interferes with and distances us from the deepest encounter between persons and so would prevent or break off the mutuality that is central to the I-Thou relationship.

Although Buber thinks that we can have I-Thou relationships with natural phenomena, inanimate objects, plants, and animals, and through them catch a glimpse of God, it is clear that he thinks of the I-Thou relationship between human beings as the most frequent context for a glimpse of God. He speaks of the "mysterious intercourse between two human worlds," and "Only when two say to one another with all that they are, 'It is *Thou*,' is the indwelling of the Present Being between them."[16]

Like the unitive mystics and Otto, Buber describes the glimpse of God as the source of light and life. "You know always in your heart that you need God more than every thing. . . . You need God, in order to be."[17] We cannot sustain this relationship for long, but brief though it may be, that presence is the inexhaustible source of strength. So important is the relationship with the Eternal Thou that our ethical relationship with other human beings and our love for them are reinforced and made full by it.[18]

The Theology of Revelation

The most influential Protestant theologian between the two world wars was Karl Barth (1886–1968). There are surely many differences between Barth and the other thinkers treated in this section. Indeed, Barth would have objected strenuously to being grouped with them, since from his perspective they emphasize our search for God at the expense of God's search for us. What he shares with them is the conviction that the divine reality is to be known directly in acts of awareness. But where Buber thought that the Eternal Thou was to be glimpsed in I-Thou relationships, and Otto in numinous encounters of awe, mystery, wonder, and fascination, and the mystics in the practice of meditation, Barth spoke of God's revelation of himself in his Word. For Barth, the Word of God manifests itself in three forms: the Words of the preacher, the Word written in Scripture, and Jesus of Nazareth, called the Word in the Gospel of John.[19] However, the Word of God is not precisely identical with any of these manifestations, but rather is God's self-communication, using these three forms in somewhat the same way that a speaker uses "languages."[20] The Word of God is God's speaking to us—God's making himself known. "Knowledge of God takes place where there is actual experience that God speaks, that He so represents Himself to man that he cannot fail to see and hear Him . . .

man sees himself faced with the fact that he lives with God and God with him, because so it has pleased God."[21]

Barth was an implacable enemy of natural theology and of any suggestion that ultimate truth could be realized from comparative religion. For Barth, God speaks definitively only in Christianity, and he does so uniquely. Knowledge of God "differs completely from anything else which man calls knowledge, not only in content, but in mode of origin and form as well." Indeed, it is so different that "the real believer will be fain to acknowledge that even his consciousness of faith is human darkness." For Barth, the knowledge of God is not reached by argument, but comes from a sense of God's presence so powerful that believers feel grasped, possessed, and overwhelmed. "Its trueness has come home to them personally, has become their property." And he adds that "knowledge of God is a knowledge completely effected and determined from the side of its object, from the side of God. But for that very reason it is genuine knowledge."[22]

For Barth, Scripture is not simply and without qualification the Word of God; nonetheless, God does speak his Word through its pages. Barth is, however, not like the authoritarians discussed in the last chapter, since not every message in Scripture need be taken as a source of divine revelation. Nevertheless, Barth is conservative in his interpretation of the Bible. He believes in the miracles of the Virgin Birth and the Resurrection. Because the Word of God as written and the Word of God speaking in our hearts are the same God speaking, God is known as he is portrayed in Scripture—as the almighty, all good and gracious, loving, sovereign power. Barth goes so far as to say that since God is the paradigm of these virtues, we will not know what true love and true goodness are if we do not know God. God is not only the source of our knowledge of him, but also the source of our knowledge of what is most important for human life.

A Religious Way of Knowing

These four types of twentieth century perspectives are united by a common conviction of the presence of an unseen reality. This conviction springs not from inference or interpretation, but from experiences of such power and force that they are called awareness. This unseen reality is experienced as immensely valuable; it is described variously as "holy," "glorious in majesty," "highest good," "love," and the "source of human goodness and strength." There are, however, important differences between the various descriptions of these experiences. Otto's awe, mystery, wonder, and fascination do not feel like the peace, calm, and unspeakable bliss of the mystics. The context and content of Buber's glimpse of the Eternal Thou in I-Thou relationships are certainly different from Barth's knowledge of the Word of God in the pages of Holy Writ. Furthermore, insofar as these authors acknowledge the existence and validity of the other types of experience we have discussed, they devalue them differently in comparison with the one that appears to them to be the most important. For example, Martin Buber, who once believed the unitary consciousness to be an awareness of God, came to regard it as a snare leading one to excessive concern with the self and thus away from God and the life of communion with others.[23] And W. T. Stace, who regards highly the mysticism of the unitary consciousness, regularly explains away the testimony of people like Julian of Norwich and Jan van Ruysbroeck as attempts to avoid the appearance of pantheism in order to satisfy the guardians of Christian orthodoxy.[24]

Yet, these differences may not be as significant as they first appear. Perhaps they reflect only partial glimpses or different perspectives on the same reality. The awareness of a mysterious and holy being might be colored by the context in which the divine reality is perceived, much in the same way that stained glass filters the light of the sun. And the identification of that mysterious presence with the personal God of the Bible or with an Undifferentiated Absolute might be due to theological and philosophical considerations derived from sources other than those given in the momentary experiences. However, all these issues, important as they are, are less significant than the common claim that in these experiences, so forcefully and overwhelmingly described, there is a glimpse of ultimate reality. The crucial question is whether it is a real possibility that the claim is true. Singling out mysticism as a particular example, William James replied affirmatively:

1. Mystical states, when well developed, usually are, and have the right to be, absolutely authoritative over the individuals to whom they come.

2. No authority emanates from them which should make it a duty for those who stand outside of them to accept their revelations uncritically.

3. They break down the authority of the non-mystical or rationalistic consciousness, based upon the understanding and the senses alone. They show it to be only one kind of consciousness. They open out the possibility of other orders of truth, in which, so far as anything in us vitally responds to them, we may freely continue to have faith.[25]

By what kind of argument could James' conclusion be supported?

The Foundation Theory

In the passage just quoted, William James suggested that Empiricism, the view that the only avenue to truth is through the senses and reason, is unduly restrictive and that there are kinds of truth other than empirical truth. James' proposal raises important epistemological issues that have concerned twentieth century philosophers. For example, what considerations would show whether or not Empiricism is too restrictive? This question is discussed in terms of three general theories of truth: the *Foundation*, the *Coherence*, and the *Pragmatic Theories*. There is, however, a further question: Which of these three general theories of truth is most satisfactory? In some form, these epistemological questions are as old as philosophy itself. They have been discussed by Plato, Aristotle, and all the great thinkers, but have never been settled in a generally acceptable way. Hence, they have been addressed in every age. In our present discussion, we shall first explain Empiricism briefly and then proceed to the foundation theory of truth.

The classic formulation of Empiricist doctrine is found in the writings of the English eighteenth century philosophers, John Locke and David Hume. Empiricism fell out of favor in the nineteenth century, but during the first decade of the twentieth century it was revived with great success by G. E. Moore (1873–1958) and Bertrand Russell (1872–1970). Indeed, so successful were they and their followers that Empiricism became the dominant philosophical view in the English-speaking world. In addition to its implications for the foundation theory of truth, Empiricism has been commended as the philosophy of common sense. We have all become suspicious of those who claim to be in touch with the dead, or read the minds of others, or foretell the future, and the like. We also know of many who claim to have special insight or to have been given supernatural revelation. It has been shown that many of these individuals have preached falsely and have been dangerous to human welfare, as the horrible events of Jonestown have demonstrated. We are suspicious when someone cannot cite as evidence for their beliefs observations based on the senses and subjected to the scrutiny of reason. Moreover, this empirical method of inquiry has produced impressive results in modern science. Is it any wonder, then, that the advice: "Stick close to the observations of the senses and to reason" should be so appealing?

Concern about the terrible and destructive consequences of error has fostered an alliance between Empiricists and proponents of the foundation theory of truth because, more than all other theories of truth, it promises a way to be free of error. Briefly, the foundation theory proposes to divide our beliefs into two types: basic or foundation beliefs, which can be known indubitably and infallibly, and all other beliefs. The latter beliefs must be justified by our basic or foundation beliefs.[26] Ideally we will have no beliefs that are not securely grounded, for they are either indubitable or have been justified by indubitable beliefs. Thus Bertrand Russell, who is both an Empiricist and a champion of the foundation theory of truth, confidently asserted in 1912: "Philosophy may claim justly that it diminishes the risk of error, and that in some cases it renders the risk so small as to be practically negligible."[27]

The link with Empiricism can now be made clear. The two most plausible candidates for foundation beliefs are beliefs based on the truths of logic and those based on the observation of the five senses. I certainly can know without fear of contradiction that "All bachelors are unmarried males," provided only that I know the meanings of the terms. "Unmarried male" is what "bachelor" means. There seems no possibility of error here. However, we do not learn very much from such beliefs because they tell us only what words mean. What infallible beliefs can we have about the world around us? The most likely ones are beliefs based upon the evidence of the five senses. For example, it seems that I can be certain that the paper on which I am writing is white, provided only that we know the meanings of the words "paper" and "white." With this knowledge, how could we be mistaken about the color of the paper? There it is right in front of us and what could take away from us our belief that it is white? The evidence of the senses seems so clear, so forceful, so definite, so insistent.

Unfortunately, the foundation theory fails in the end because no evidence about the external world is in fact infallible or incorrigible, even the testimony of the senses. Some have thought that the foundation theory also fails because truths of logic cannot be infallibly known either. But leaving that issue aside, it is quite easy to show that there are no infallible beliefs about the external world. Let us return to the example of the white paper. There is something infallible about the whiteness of the paper, namely that it seems white to you and to me. But the belief that it is actually a piece of white paper is always corrigible, for I might be having a hallucination or an illusion and so might you. Of course we can get evidence that this is not the case, but it will not be incorrigible or infallible evidence. To be infallible, this next evidence must be based on the senses, but it also might be only illusory or hallucinatory, and so on without end. Our investigation will never lead to assured statements about the external world. We can infallibly report our feelings and sensations, but whether these feelings and sensations form a bridge to the external world is always open to doubt.[28]

The Coherence Theory of Truth

The last discussion leads us directly to a consideration of the coherence theory of truth, the only promising alternative to the foundation theory. Recognizing that no judgment is incorrigible, the theory asks, "How is it that we support or undermine our beliefs about what is the case?" And then it replies, "By seeing how they are supported by or in conflict with our other beliefs." When I came to the conclusion that this is in fact a white piece of paper before me, I brought to bear on the situation a great many other beliefs that I held, including beliefs about how to tell hallucinations and illusions from reality, and beliefs about the reliability of sight when in a normal state of mind. Since any of these other beliefs is capable of being mistaken and our investigation might go on interminably, we must rest at the point when we are reasonably convinced that there is no advantage in investigating the possibility of error further. We are content that nothing has arisen in our other beliefs to call this particular belief into serious question. We cannot be certain that there are no false beliefs lurking somewhere among our beliefs. We can only trust that they will be eliminated by the rest of what we believe. As Nicholas Rescher has recently put it: "The criterion thus assumes an entirely *inward* orientation: it does not seek to compare the truth-candidate directly with other facts *outside* the given epistemic context; rather, having gathered as much information (and this, alas, will include misinformation) about the facts as is possible, it seeks to sift the true from the false *within* this body. The situation arising here resembles the solving of a jigsaw puzzle with superfluous pieces that cannot possibly be fitted into the orderly picture in whose construction the 'correct solution' lies."[29] In summary, every belief is corrigible. We correct our beliefs with the evidence of other beliefs. It is only thus that we come to a unified, consistent, coherent view of the world and of reality.

The Pragmatic Theory

The coherence theory is more satisfactory than the other rival alternative, the pragmatic theory, which has been particularly attractive to American philosophers. William James and John Dewey (1859–1952) were prominent defenders of the pragmatic theory, which holds that the test of truth is its usefulness. "The true is the name of whatever proves itself to be good in the way of belief, and good, too, for definite, assignable reason."[30]

Whatever virtues the pragmatic theory may have, it will always be a more complex view than the coherence theory. In order to decide whether or not something is good for definite, assignable reasons, some knowledge of the world will be required. The usefulness of believing a particular proposition will depend on what we think the consequences of that belief might be. For example, Pragmatists might urge belief in God's providence on the grounds that that belief has the useful consequence of mitigating anxiety. Should, however, Pragmatists be challenged to support the claim that faith actually reduces anxiety, they appeal to psychological and empirical observations of human behavior and not to further considerations of utility. Pragmatists do not urge us to accept their own arguments because it is useful to do so, but because these arguments are valid and true. Hence the pragmatic theory is not a complete theory and needs to be supplemented by evidence of a more traditional kind.

Coherence and Integration

The discussion of the weaknesses of the foundation theory helps us to understand why religious experience can be seen as a way to truth. The foundation theory cannot satisfy our desire for certainty, as it first promised. It cannot protect us from error by trying to base truth on the senses and reason alone. Hence if Empiricism cannot provide certainty, there is no reason to refuse to recognize nonempirical experience as an avenue to truth. Moreover, we have seen that the sense of the presence of an unseen reality seems as insistent, extrinsic, overwhelming, and not to be thought away by an act of will, as does the experience of reality provided by the senses. The reports of religious experience are clear on this point. "I could not any more have doubted that *He* was there than that I was. Indeed, I felt myself to be, if possible, the less real of the two."[31] This is so typical an example that one need not quote others. Here lies part of the "authority" of mystical states mentioned by William James.[32]

But the coherence theory gives added reason to value religious experience, when it breaks down empiricist and rationalistic consciousness, and to see such experience as a path to truth. This is the construction aspect of the coherence doctrine mentioned by Rescher above. Under the coherence theory, truth is built up out of the bits and pieces of our beliefs and experiences. Truth is like a rope in which one strand overlaps and strengthens another, or a geodesic dome in which the parts fit together to support the whole. Coherence is thus a guide to theory building as well as a negative test of what to exclude from our beliefs. If we had independent reason to think that there is a transcendent and nonempirical reality, we would have added reason to believe that religious experience that comes to us with such force is in fact an awareness of unseen reality. These two strands would fit together to integrate our vision of reality. To have provided this independent evidence is one of the achievements of the theologies of the Protestant, Paul Tillich, and the Roman Catholic, Karl Rahner.

The Fascination with Being-itself

Both Paul Tillich and Karl Rahner were impressed by the thinking of the German philosopher, Martin Heidegger (1889–1976), who early in his career called for a new direction in the philosophical investigation of the nature of what *is*. This division of philosophy has traditionally been called *metaphysics* or *ontology*. Heidegger was fascinated with Being. He saw that the specialized disciplines—astronomy, biology, physics, anthropology, economics—were given over to the study of particular kinds of entities, or aspects of them. What fascinated Heidegger, as it had fascinated the Greek philosophers in ancient times, was not these beings, but "the Being of beings." What is being-itself—that which the special objects that we encounter so easily in daily life have in common and manifest? Heidegger considered it his philosophical task to uncover being in such a way that it would no longer be hidden from our view, but would be manifest to us in the objects of daily life, which are scrutinized by the specialized sciences.[33]

Paul Tillich and Karl Rahner both came to know of Heidegger's thinking while they were at the University of Marburg, where he taught. Though both admired him, neither followed him slavishly. Heidegger had briefly studied for the Roman Catholic priesthood, but he devoted little attention to the philosophy of religion. Among the few passages in his works in which he discusses theological issues is one in which he explicitly refuses to identify God with being-itself. Instead, Heidegger thinks of God as one of the special beings. Neither Tillich nor Rahner follows him here. They learned much from Heidegger about being, but they see their investigation of being as central to the theological enterprise because both of them identify being-itself (alternatively expressed as the power of being, or the ground of being) with God. Rahner and Tillich differ on many issues. But on the nature of being and its centrality for the establishment of theological foundations, they are in wholehearted agreement.

The Reality of Being-itself

A convenient place to begin this discussion is a question often used as a starting point by Heidegger, Tillich, and Rahner: "Why is there something rather than just nothing at all?" We encounter many entities in our experience, and we can explain why there is this or that particular entity in terms of other entities. "Why the French Revolution?" is explained in a discussion of the conditions in France during the eighteenth century. "Why elephants?" is explained in a discussion of earlier forms of life and the evolutionary process. We always explain the existence of particular beings in terms of other beings. But why is there anything at all rather than just an empty void? The answer given is that there exists a power of being in whatever is, a power to resist non-being, which keeps beings in existence as long as they exist. As Tillich puts it: "Everything finite participates in being-itself and in its infinity. Otherwise it would not have the power of being. It would be swallowed by non-being, or it never would have emerged out of nonbeing."[34]

Thus far nothing controversial has been said. Whatever the ultimate constituents of the universe (atoms, subatomic particles, or whatever), because they exist they have a power to resist non-being, at least as long as they continue to exist. But what is the nature of this "being as such" that they all have in common? How can this "act of being"[35] be described?

The Mystery of Being

Being as such, or being-itself, is common to all things. It therefore cannot be described by the properties of any particular entity; it escapes description in terms of beings. As Tillich puts it: "Being-itself infinitely transcends every finite being. There is no proportion or gradation between the finite and the infinite. There is an absolute break, an infinite 'jump.'"[36] What Tillich has in mind here needs careful explanation. Tillich does not say that we can have no idea at all about being or God, but that these ideas are indirectly achieved. First, we can speak of the relationship of being to the rest of reality. God or being-itself can be described as the source of all things. It is "the power of being," or "ground of being," the "power to resist non-being in everything which has being." Second, we can discover something about the ultimate mystery by distinguishing it from what it is not. Things are finite and hence have a beginning and an end. "This is true of everything except being-itself—which is not a 'thing.' As the power of being, being-itself cannot have a beginning and an end. Otherwise it would have arisen out of non-being. . . . Being . . . is its own beginning and end, the initial power of everything that is."[37] Hence Tillich sometimes describes God as "the Unconditioned" or "the Absolute."[38]

Being cannot be described directly in terms of the distinguishing properties of things, but only negatively. If we try to get at what everything has in common, we must empty our minds of what is peculiar to particular objects or even kinds of things. If we go up in a scale from particular ideas to more general ideas, we find that the more general ideas are sparer than the particular. The idea of animal has less content than the ideas of horse or dog, and the idea of physical object even less than that of animal. Hence our idea of what is common to all things, being, will be emptied of all these particular contents. It will be without any of the contents proper to entities or things. Rahner makes the same point in a more discursive style: "Every object of our conscious mind which we encounter in our social world and environment, as it announces itself as it were of itself, is merely a stage, a constantly new starting-point in this movement which continues into the everlasting and unnamed 'before us.'"[39] God is beyond exact human conceptualization, and he is ultimate mystery. However, Tillich and Rahner disagree about what further can be said about him. Since Tillich is the more radical, we shall examine his view first. Rahner's view will be treated later as a modification of Tillich's proposal.

Being and the Holy

Both Tillich and Rahner give us reason to believe that religious experience is really an awareness of ultimate reality and not a feeling or an illusion, for both have shown that there is an ultimate reality of which religious experience might be a perception. However, since Tillich and Rahner are each deeply affected by different types of experience (Tillich by Otto's description of the Holy and Rahner by the mystical tradition), each correlates being-itself with religious experience in a different way.

It is clearly evident that Tillich finds Otto's account of numinous experience congenial. Central to every one of Tillich's works is a discussion of the Holy. References to the Holy are to be found in discussions of ethics and religious symbols as well as in discussions about our knowledge of God. As for the latter, Tillich asserts that "the sense of the numinous presence" is in fact an awareness of the ground of all being, although Otto himself did not describe the divine in this way.

> When Otto calls the experience of the holy "numinous," he interprets the holy as the presence of the divine. . . . When he describes the mystery of the holy as *tremendum* and *fascinosum*, he expresses the experience of "the ultimate" in the double sense of that which is the abyss and that which is the ground of man's being. This is not directly asserted in Otto's merely phenomenological analysis. . . . However, it is implicit in his analysis, and it should be made explicit beyond Otto's own intention.[40]

The ground of being is a tremendous mystery, of which there is no doubt. That it also fascinates us is clear; for we are tantalized by the question: Why is there something rather than nothing? And we are driven by that question to search for meaning. But Tillich believes that the idea of the Holy is much fuller and richer in significance than is being-itself. It is infinitely more fascinating and its mystery more strongly tinged with awe than is the mystery of the incomprehensible source of all. Part of the reason for this is that throughout the history of religions the numinous presence is always reported as personal. Tillich is much concerned with this fact. In *Biblical Religion and the Search for Ultimate Reality,* his most complete discussion of the relationship between the Holy and being, Tillich is troubled by the apparent contrast between what he has said of the Holy and of being: "Whenever the holy is experienced, the person-to-person character of this experience is obvious."[41] Person-to-person relationships are dynamic, interactive, and involve mutual give and take. In short, they are reciprocal. In contrast, since being-itself cannot be described by properties which differentiate one thing from another, it cannot be described as active or passive, as personal or impersonal. "Nothing," adds Tillich "seems to contradict the ontological concept of 'being' more than this reciprocity between God and man."[42] How to resolve this contrast?

In discussing this matter, Tillich makes two points that echo the general thesis of this chapter. First, for the seeker after wisdom, religious experience is much more momentous than is philosophical discussion, even philosophical discussion about the power of being in everything that has being. The truly wise are those whose reason has been enlightened. "They have experienced a saving transformation and an illuminating revelation. Only because this has happened to them can they seriously and successfully ask the question of ultimate reality. Ontology presupposes a conversion, an opening of the eyes, a revelatory experience."[43]

Tillich means to say here that the priority goes to religious experience and not to philosophy; this is borne out by a second point. The experience of the Holy is richer than the contributions of ontology and so takes precedence over them. The intimations of the Holy concerning ultimate reality can absorb the findings of philosophical speculation. "Religiously speaking, this means that our encounter with the God who is a person includes the encounter with the God who is the ground of everything personal and as such not *a* person."[44]

It is at this point that we need to provide the modification in Tillich's views promised earlier. Tillich has to leave the question of God as person in a paradoxical state, as spelled out in the last quotation, because of what he believes about being-itself. Being-itself is not a thing like other things; and hence, Tillich concludes, it cannot be described by any of the properties of things.[45] But here he seems to be in error. The principle by which he came to this conclusion was that, if being is what stones and people have in common, the commonality cannot be characterized by what distinguishes them, which is personhood or consciousness. But if it should be the case that consciousness, at least in some minute degree, is a property not only of God and of human beings but also of everything that exists, there is a way out of Tillich's dilemma. If at least some small measure of consciousness is to be found in everything, personhood could be attributed to God and God would still be "being" or the "power of being" in everything. Another philosopher of being, Karl Rahner, has taken just this alternative. In a bold act of speculative synthesis, he asserts that being and knowing are simply identical and, hence, that ultimate reality is mind.[46]

Being and Mystical Awareness

Like Tillich, Rahner is more interested in religious experience than in the philosophical quest for being. This concern is shown in the fact that in his writings he expends more energy on leading his readers to a sense of the incomprehensible mystery of reality than on ontological analysis. However, unlike Tillich, he is more impressed with the Catholic devotional tradition than with the *mysterium, tremendum, et fascinans* of Rudolf Otto. He praises the mysticism of St. Ignatius of Loyola (1491–1556), the founder of the Society of Jesus (Rahner's own religious order), as a life lived always in the presence of God, in "the simple illuminated darkness of God."[47]

Rahner makes it clear that he is not referring here to the unitary consciousness. He devotes a whole essay to the thesis that the awareness of self does not disappear in Christian mystical consciousness, but that self and God are experienced as correlates of each other.[48] After a long meditative passage in which he hopes to lead the reader to a realization of the divine mystery, Rahner describes this awareness as "the mysticism of everyday life, the discovery of God in all things; there is the sober intoxication of the Spirit, of which the Fathers and the liturgy speak, which we cannot reject or despise, because it is real."[49]

The way by which Rahner hopes to lead his readers to an awareness of God demonstrates his own spirituality and how he uses philosophical discussion about being to convince his readers that God is found in all things. Rahner's usual method of meditation is to ask the reader to consider some one of the sciences, and then he leads the reader to realize that we very quickly come to the end of our knowledge in that area of science. The specialized sciences—anthropology, psychology, biology, sociology—all have something to contribute to our knowledge of human beings. But because of the complexity of the undertaking we can never produce the unified view of humanity for which we strive. Humanity is a mystery to itself. In whatever we undertake we deal merely with the surface, the incidental, the trivial; the whole escapes in an unending series of further questions.[50] In these enterprises, "man is forever occupied with the grains of sand along the shore where he dwells at the edge of the infinite ocean of mystery."[51]

For Rahner the key to finding God is to recognize that this sense of mystery, of incomprehensibility, is itself truly the awareness of God and is our beatitude. "We must let ourselves go into this inconceivability as into our true fulfilment and happiness, let ourselves be taken out of ourselves by this unanswered question. This incomprehensible venture, which sweeps all questions aside, is customarily referred to as the (devout) love of God."[52]

But how do we know that this venture "apparently into the void"[53] really puts us in touch with reality? The experience certainly seems to be the awareness of being as such, that escapes attempts to describe it in terms of the distinguishing properties of ordinary finite objects. According to Rahner, the conclusion that this sense of infinite mystery is in fact the awareness of ultimate reality is based on the prior conviction that there is an ultimate reality and that that reality is incomprehensible mind.

The Liturgical and Spiritual Revival

One of the most striking aspects of the life of Christian faith in the twentieth century is the special attention devoted to public services of worship or liturgy, in addition to the practice of private prayer and meditation. To be sure, Christians from earliest times have gathered for worship and praise of God and engaged in private devotions. But during the twentieth century worship became an object of study in a new way and attention to its principles and practice became a subject for seminary education. Why was so much interest lavished upon it? The answer is that the stress on religious experience as a foundation of the spiritual life brought about a changed concept of the relationship between belief and prayer. For centuries it had seemed obvious that prayer implied belief. One prayed to God because one believed that he was almighty and good, and because he was the creator and ruler of the universe. But now when the question was more insistently asked, Why believe in God? the answer was given: Because one *experiences* him, and it is in worship that one does so. "Here man responds to the impact of Eternity, and in so doing learns the existence of Eternity; accepting his tiny place in that secret life of Creation, which consists in the praise, adoration, and manifestation of God."[54]

It should not be surprising that these are words from a book entitled *Worship* and were written by Evelyn Underhill, one of the most widely read authorities on mysticism in the first half of this century. Likewise, it is not surprising that Friedrich Heiler should have titled his classic study of both mysticism and numinous religion *Prayer*, and that he called prayer "the experience of the Divine presence." Heiler quotes two other authors whose spirituality he admires: Prayer is "no mere earthly power but a power which reaches to the heavens"; and, "in the depths of our inner life we have not a mere echo of our own voice, of our own being, resounding from the dark depths of personality, but a reality higher and greater than our own, which we can adore and in which we can trust."[55]

Prayer, worship, and meditation were commended as a source of faith, "for worship is an acknowledgment of Transcendence; that is to say, of a Reality independent of the worshipper, which is always more or less deeply colored by mystery, which is there first."[56] The emphasis on public worship is easy to understand. Although there are always those, like A. N. Whitehead (1861–1947) and William James, who find congenial Plotinus' remark that true religion is "the flight of the alone to the alone," the majority feel the presence of God most readily in the company of others. It is in services of public worship, in the gathering of the people of God, that the presence of the divine seems most readily manifest. "Where two or three are gathered in my name, there am I in the midst of them," says Jesus in the Gospel of Matthew (18:20). These words express a universal truth about the presence of the divine. The swelling chorus of angels and archangels in the Book of Revelation pictures the place where the divine seems most evident. These same thoughts are reflected in a bishop's advice to his clergy:

The man who leads his congregation in worship must himself be so lost in the contemplation of the majesty and beauty of God,

must so obviously himself be worshipping, that, through him, even
the careless person will catch the inspiration which radiates from
him, and the whole church will be filled with the consciousness of
the Presence of the Eternal.[57]

Recapitulation and Prospectus

In this chapter, we have discussed twentieth century explorations
into the foundations of Christian faith. We have followed recent
examinations of the nature of faith, of religious experience and its
sense of the presence of an unseen world of incalculable worth. We
have investigated the possibility that the philosophy of being-itself
provides support for the intimations of an unseen world found in
religious experience. We then examined the related revival of interest in prayer and worship. In discussing the nature of truth we
discovered that the coherence theory not only commends itself as a
general theory, but also has particular relevance for the enterprise
of faith. One of the most important aspects of the theory is the
proposal that integration is a test of truth. The attempt to discover
truth is more like assembling a geodesic dome into a self-supporting
and coherent whole than it is like finding infallible starting points
for further thought. However, there are still many pieces not yet
integrated into the whole. Some considerable coherence has been
achieved. Some alternatives have been sorted through, some kept
and some discarded. Not every view about the Trinity, the Incarnation, and the Atonement has been retained, although there are a
good many alternatives that still claim attention.

The next two chapters will focus on subjects that have proved
even more divisive than those discussed thus far—the sacraments
and the Church and the ministry. These issues have sharply divided Christians in the West, at least since the Reformation. Indeed, the disagreements were so profound that they largely caused
the schisms among the Anglican, Lutheran, Presbyterian, Congregationalist, Baptist, Quaker, and Roman Catholic churches. However, in the last hundred years these divisions have become a source
of distress, and new efforts have been made to examine their origins
and propose a reconsideration that many hope will lead to a reunion
of the separated churches.

CHAPTER IX

The Sacraments

Sacraments are broadly described as rites or ceremonies performed to symbolize or help bring about a transformation in the lives of those who participate in them. Since New Testament times the Christian Church has had two central sacraments, Baptism and the Supper of the Lord, also called the Eucharist, Mass, and Holy Communion. Other rites and ceremonies have also been called sacraments. For example, the Western tradition identified five other sacraments—Confirmation, Matrimony, Penance, Unction, and Ordination—making seven in all.

In what follows, we shall concentrate on baptism and the Eucharist because by all accounts they are the most fundamental; they are closely associated with Jesus' own ministry, as well as with the redemptive role of the Church in the life of the individual Christian. In the Gospel records, Jesus commanded his followers to teach and baptize all nations, and also to reenact the Supper he ate with his disciples the night before his crucifixion. We shall treat the other sacramental rites less extensively. Confirmation and penance will be dealt with in connection with baptism. Ordination, matrimony, and unction will be deferred until the chapter on the Church and the ministry, where they will be discussed briefly or mentioned only in passing. It is also convenient to postpone until then the rationale for the choice of seven as the number of these rites.

The meaning of the word "sacrament" developed through several stages. In its original meaning as "sacred sign," it was used in the Roman army as the name for the oath to the Emperor. "Sacrament" does not appear in Christian writing until the early third century.

Apparently Tertullian was the first to use the term and did so to denote not only particular signs, like the water of baptism, but also the whole rite of which the sign was a part. This extension of the meaning of *sacramentum* was encouraged by the fact that it was used as a translation for the Greek term *musterion* (mystery). Christians had already borrowed the latter term from ancient Hellenic religion, where it was a name for sacred ceremonies. Quite naturally, Latin Christians used "sacrament" in a similar way. The phrase "Holy Mysteries" when applied to the Eucharist reflects this etymology. Finally, "sacrament" came to mean more than simply "sign" or even "ritual," and carries with it the idea that sacred action changes the lives of the participants. A sacrament brings about that of which it is a sign. It was with these ideas in mind that sacraments have often been described as outward and visible signs of inward and spiritual graces and as means through which these graces are received.

Before we begin our discussion of baptism and the Supper of the Lord, it will be helpful to set these two sacraments more fully in the context of Jesus' life and teaching and thus give a partial account of their centrality to Christian faith. Jesus began his ministry with the proclamation of the good news that God's kingdom was about to be realized. "Repent, for the kingdom of heaven is at hand" (Matt. 3:2). However, Jesus not only called his followers to a new way of life, but also assured them of his continuing presence. In the Gospel of Matthew, the last words of Jesus to his disciples are recorded as, "Lo, I am with you always" (Matt. 28:20). These two themes of transformation and presence find expression in the two major sacraments, the former especially in baptism and the latter especially in the Eucharist. It is the common conviction of Christians that these sacraments carry on Jesus' ministry, but in what way?

Since New Testament times, Christians have sought to deepen and make more precise the ways in which the Eucharist and baptism are effective signs and means of Christ's presence and of a transformed life. We have already encountered a similar process of faith seeking understanding in our discussions of the Trinity, the Incarnation, and the Atonement. We proposed that these doctrines are best understood as the Church's way of making more precise the words of Paul, "God was in Christ, reconciling the world to himself." Now we turn our attention to the way in which the sacraments carry on Christ's mission and purpose. However, the wide measure of assent that has been accorded the doctrines about God in Christ has not been forthcoming in regard to theories about the sacraments. As we shall see, and especially since the Reformation, important and fundamental disagreements have been the rule. Indeed differences over the understanding of the sacraments and of the nature of the Church have been the precipitating causes of the formation of a number of Christian denominations. In our own time, the Ecumenical Movement has sought to reassess these disagreements. Although many of them have been resolved, several still pose questions for the future.

The Universality of Sacramental Rites

Every culture engages in sacramental activities. Every culture has symbolic ceremonies used not only to mark important occasions, but also to rekindle the loyalty and commitment of its members. Fourth of July ceremonies in the United States and the May Day parade as observed in the former Soviet Union are but two examples of ritual actions that perform this dual role. In each case, they commemorate the founding of the nation and summon forth renewed dedication to the ideals of the society. In ancient times, New Year's Day celebrations were a time of new beginnings, as they are today; but they often represented a re-creation of the whole cosmos, thus symbolizing the most radical and thoroughgoing new beginning possible. [1] As the participants symbolically relived the original creation, they felt their own lives reborn. As we examine the Christian sacraments, we need to keep in mind the natural tendency of human beings to express themselves in ritual action. We also need to be aware of the rich symbolic language that is part of our cross-cultural heritage. Many of the Christian symbols have analogues in other cultures.

Each religious tradition draws from the ritual language of its general cultural setting, although it may also develop symbols of its own. For example, the ancient Hebrews took much from the Canaanites, altering and reinterpreting their borrowings in the light of the Covenant at Sinai. Several Psalms seem to have been adaptations of Canaanite hymns of praise. [2] Whole Canaanite festivals seem to have been taken over. Tabernacles and Succoth are often cited as examples. Circumcision, widely practiced in ancient times, also seems to have been derived from non-Jewish sources. In addition, the Hebrew sacrificial system bears striking similarities to Canaanite practice, and there seems little doubt that much was derived from Canaanite ceremonies.[3] These are but examples of a much broader pattern of borrowing by one culture from another.

In every culture rites or ceremonies often use particular basic elements, which are usually objects of everyday use like the water of baptism. Over the centuries people in various cultures have found water especially rich with meaning. In many ancient rituals the emphasis is on the cleansing and life-sustaining properties of water. Water is also associated with the waters of chaos out of which many peoples believed the world was formed. Finally, water is associated with death—that is, death by drowning. Each of these meanings has found expression in baptismal liturgies.

The basic elements of the Eucharist also derive much of their significance from universal symbolic language. The natural symbolic meaning of food as a source of strength is used in the Eucharist to express the central Christian conviction that the risen Christ continues to be present with his people, strengthening and empowering them to join with him in his plan to redeem humanity and the world. It is said that just as bread and wine sustain and give life to our bodies, so Christ's body and blood give life to the soul. Of course "body" and "blood" do not fully describe the gift, for they in turn signify the whole Christ of which they are but parts. Sometimes Christ's self-giving in the Supper has been coupled with his sacrificial self-giving on the cross, because the eucharistic terms "body" and "blood" suggest a connection of the sacrament with Jesus' death. However, such coupling of communion and sacrifice has not always been greeted with approval. This complex issue will be treated in later contexts; for the moment it has been enough to note some of the ways in which universal symbolic language has been used in the service of the Gospel.

Ritual in the Hebrew Scriptures

The early Christian community's immediate sources for symbolic and ritual action were, of course, the traditions of Hebrew religion.

As we noted earlier,[4] the Torah achieved its present form about the year 250 B.C.E. It was with the completed Torah that we began our study of Hebrew religion, and we will do the same in our discussion of Hebrew ritual, rather than speculate about what Hebrew worship was like in pre-Biblical times or the extent of its dependence on Canaanite sources.

The Hebrew Bible is rich in material on a variety of ceremonies—the rite of initiation (circumcision), rites of purification, sacred meals, and sacrifices—but by far the most frequent and elaborate discussions of ritual worship are devoted to sacrifice. As described in the Torah, the sacrificial system was a complex set of ritual offerings. Sacrifices were made at solemn moments in the life of Israel, when the nation or an individual recognized the need to draw nearer to God. Various kinds of animals and cereal grains were specified as suitable objects to be offered. Occasions requiring sacrifice were specified, as were the individuals who must offer them. One type of immolation, however, was specifically forbidden. Although neighboring tribes practiced human sacrifice, such offerings were vigorously condemned in later parts of the Hebrew Scriptures (2 Kings 16:3, 21:6; Jer. 7:31; Ezek. 16:20, 23:37–39). In what follows, we will discuss the forms of sacrifice in terms of the purposes for which they were performed, rather than develop a classification of sacrifices in terms of their material components or persons required to offer them, as is frequently done.

Propitiatory Sacrifices

It is often assumed that the main purpose of sacrifice in the ancient world was to propitiate the gods. We find this idea clearly stated in Homer, where Odysseus gave the purpose of a sacrifice offered to Apollo by explaining, "by this means we may appease the [god]."[5] However, the Hebrew Scriptures nowhere explicitly state appeasement as a purpose of sacrifice. In the prophetic literature the wrath of God is often vividly described (Amos 1, 2; Isa. 7), but when God denounces Israel for its sins, as he frequently does, he characteristically calls for a return to the keeping of the Covenant (Jer. 3:12–14; Hos. 6:1–6). Sacrifices alone will not allay his wrath. To be sure, sacrifices for specific sins are required (Lev. 4; Num. 15:22–31). The rituals for the Day of Atonement (Lev. 16:1–34) are particularly striking examples, but even these are for the purpose of showing proper repentance and are not commanded as acts of appeasement. In this spirit, Psalm 51:17 asserts: "The sacrifice acceptable to God is a broken spirit; a broken and contrite heart, O God, thou wilt not despise." Still, it is difficult to keep the idea of appeasing God's wrath totally divorced from the notion of sacrifice. As we shall see below, Thomas à Kempis, among others, used the language of appeasement in describing the sacrifice of the Mass.

Thanksgiving Sacrifices

In the Hebrew Scriptures far more attention is given to sacrifices as acts of public and private thanksgiving than as sin offerings. Public sacrifices were offered as acts of thanksgiving at the end of battle (Josh. 8:31; 1 Sam. 13:9), and by David to celebrate the safe arrival of the Ark in Jerusalem (2 Sam. 6:17–18). The sacrifices marking the sealing of the Covenant between God and Israel (Exod. 24:5) and at the dedication of the Temple (1 Kings 8:64) were acts of public thanksgiving as well as acts of consecration. In addition, the daily sacrifices, the sacrifices required on the Sabbath and the new moon, and the sacrifices on the days of the great festivals— Unleavened Bread, First Fruits, Trumpets, and Booths (Tabernacles)—had thanksgiving as an essential ingredient. Private sacrifices often had this character (Lev. 7:12–15, 22:29; Ps. 56:12–13, 107:22, 116:17), as did the offering of the first fruits at the time of harvest (Exod. 23:19, 34:26; Lev. 2:14, 23:20) or at the birth of a first child (Exod. 13:1–16). Thanksgiving sacrifices must have been very frequent.

Burnt Offerings and Peace Offerings

The Peace Offering or Communion Offering (*zevach*) was also a frequent form of sacrifice. In contrast to a Burnt Offering (*'olah*), where the sacrificial animal or cereal was totally consumed by fire, at a peace offering part was burned and part removed from the fire and eaten by the worshipers in a communion meal. Both peace offerings and burnt offerings were as widely practiced in the rest of the ancient world as they were in Israel. The procedures to be followed for both types of sacrifice were laid out in elaborate detail (Lev. 1–3).

The peace offering provides an obvious analogue to the Eucharist, in which the bread and wine are offered to God and later consumed by the congregation. However, some have also drawn a parallel between the Eucharist and the burnt offering. While the peace offerings symbolized the unity of God and human beings in the living community founded on the Covenant, burnt offerings signified the complete surrender of the worshiper to God. Although an animal or cereal was placed on the fire, it was ultimately the worshiper himself who was being offered. This identification was expressed by the suppliant laying his hand on the sacrificial animal before it was slaughtered (Lev. 1:4). One might draw the conclusion that it was the self that was reduced to ashes. While Jews generally did not draw this inference, Hindus often did, which is how the mystical Vedanta tradition developed from the Brahmin religion of sacrifice. The whole imperative of Vedanta is to lose the self in God or, more accurately, to discover that Atman (the self) is not different from Brahman (God). Sometimes Christian writers have voiced a similar idea. "In the presence of God . . . everything [including the self] must be reduced to ashes. . . . It is the sign of our religion that we offer everything in sacrifice to God."[6] This idea found classic expression in late medieval ideas of the Eucharist.

Another important connection between peace offerings, burnt offerings, and the Eucharist ought to be noted. Occasionally, a particularly important ceremony included both peace offerings and burnt offerings. One such observance took place at Sinai at the giving of the Covenant. That story also includes an account of Moses catching the blood of the sacrificial animals and, in an act of purification, pouring out some of it on the steps of the altar and the remainder on the people (Exod. 24:4–8). The pouring out of the blood in connection with the giving of the Covenant will be echoed in New Testament accounts of the Last Supper (Matt. 26:28; Mark 14:24; Luke 22:20).

Sacred Meals

Sacred meals are very much a part of the Jewish tradition. The mere fact that every meal began with a thanksgiving for God's bounty and goodness showed that at a basic level it was a sacred event. Other sacred meals included *chaburah* or brotherhood meals, when, for example, a rabbi and his disciples gathered for food and fellowship. In addition, part of the peace offering was a sacrifice to God and part was a sacred meal shared by the people. But by far the best known Jewish sacred meal is the seder or Passover meal, which has been celebrated continuously since ancient times as a commemoration of the Exodus from Egypt.

As the seder is described in the Torah, each household supplied a lamb, which was killed in a sacrifice at the Temple in Jerusalem; it was then eaten in family groups after having been roasted whole (Exod. 12:1–28, 43–49; Deut. 16:1–8). In New Testament times the crowds celebrating the Passover in Jerusalem must have been very great. The Jewish historian Josephus, for example, estimated that for the celebration of 65 C.E. "not less than three million" were present.[7] However, after the destruction of the Temple by the Romans in 70 C.E., the offering of the paschal lamb came to an end, and the connection of the seder meal with the sacrificial system became only a memory. In its modified form, however, the seder has continued as a central rite of Judaism.

Initiation and Purification

At the time of the composition of the Torah, initiation and purification were clearly distinguished. Circumcision was the rite of initiation of males into the Jewish community of faith. Other rites were designed to remove impurities that severely impaired the relationship between God and human beings. By the beginning of the Common Era, certain initiatory rites came to include a purificatory component. This came about because converts to Judaism were thought to be contaminated by their gentile background and needed to be purified before they could take their places among the people of the Covenant.

Circumcision is a very ancient practice, well established among many peoples of the world. However, it played and still plays a special role in Judaism as its initiatory rite. According to the Biblical account, Abraham at age ninety-nine circumcised himself and the males of his household at God's command. "Every male among you shall be circumcised . . . and it shall be a sign of the covenant between me and you" (Gen. 10:11). Although rabbinic tradition was aware that circumcision was known before Abraham, the Abraham story gave the practice divine sanction,[8] so much so that only cir-cumcised males could share in the Passover sacrifice (Exod. 12:44, 48).

Directions for the many purification rites are found primarily in the Holiness Code in Leviticus, although they can also be found in other places in the Scripture. Ritual uncleanness stemmed from many sources. Contamination came from contact with a corpse or a tomb, diseases such as leprosy, or running sores, as well as from sexual impurities like incest (Lev. 11–15; Num. 19:11–22). We have already seen how bodily discharges were regarded as polluting be-cause they were breaches in the stable order of things.[9] Even such natural occurrences as the emission of semen or menstrual blood regularly required purification (Lev. 15:16–30). These ideas were to have momentous consequences for the role of women and the exal-tation of the celibate life. For all these impurities, rites of purifica-tion were prescribed. Rites involving water were the most numerous—objects regarded as unclean were plunged in water (Lev. 11:32) or just sprinkled (Lev. 14:7). Sometimes a man's entire body was washed (Lev. 15:5–13, 18; Deut. 23:10–11). Even when no impurities were present, similar rites were sometimes required as a preparation for coming into the divine presence (Exod. 19:10, 14; 29:4; Lev. 16:4). Against this background, it is easy to see why baptismal purification was regarded as an essential step in the pro-cess of gentile conversions to Judaism.

Gentile Conversion

There is ample evidence that at the beginning of the Common Era gentile converts to Judaism were not uncommon. Not only are there several references in the New Testament to Jews making proselytes of Gentiles, but rabbinic tradition also mentions the practice. The rabbinic references are particularly interesting for their bearing on Christian initiation. The Babylonian Talmud records a rabbinic controversy that goes back to New Testament times. Rabbi Eliezer required both circumcision and ritual immersion for the admission of a proselyte, whereas Rabbi Joshua held that a proselyte needed only ritual immersion.[10] While it is noted that the majority of authorities sided with Rabbi Eliezer, the minority opinion must

264 / A SHORT HISTORY OF CHRISTIAN THOUGHT

have been significant enough to have been recorded. In any event, when the early Church became convinced that the circumcision of gentile converts was not necessary before inclusion in the community of faith, there was precedent for centering its rite of initiation in purification by water.

The Jewish purification rites took on special significance in the Essene communities and in the activities of John the Baptist. The Essene communities, of which many scholars believe the Dead Sea Scrolls community was an example, were noted for their practice of frequent immersion in water as an act of ritual purification. According to Josephus, their concern for ritual purity was such that they refused to take part in the Temple sacrifices,[11] presumably because they feared contamination from an impure priesthood.[12] Rather, they preferred to offer sacrifice in their own communities. In addition to noting that entrants into the community were required to undergo an initiatory immersion, Josephus also wrote that participation in the noonday meal required a daily ritual bath.[13] So religiously significant was this meal that initiates were not immediately admitted to it, but had to serve a probationary period of three years.[14] These arrangements are cerainly suggestive of later Christian practices.

It is against the Essene background, and the background of Jewish purification rites in general, that the activities of John the Baptist ought to be placed. John the Baptist is a pivotal figure, not only because he baptized Jesus, but also because in all four Gospels he introduced Jesus' ministry. John preached the coming of a New Age—an age for which sinful, impenitent persons were not ready. He called for repentance, to be followed by a purifying immersion in water (Mark 1:4). The kind of baptism that John proclaimed was a true rite of passage, marking as it did the transition from one form of existence to another. Unlike the Holiness Code in Leviticus, but like both the Prophets and Jesus, John's concern was primarily for moral purity rather than ritual purity (Luke 3:10–14). From the Christian point of view John remains a figure of the Old Covenant and not the New, since before his death at the hands of Herod he had not become one of Jesus' disciples. However, his call for a renunciation of one's past way of life and the adoption of a new way—that is, one marked by an ethical seriousness—was an essential element in the Christian gospel.

Baptism in the New Covenant

Deeply embedded in the New Testament is the conviction that not only the celebration of the Eucharist (1 Cor. 11:23–26), but also the practice of baptism (Matt. 28:18–19) can be traced to Jesus' own ministry. As previously noted, Jewish sacred meals, particularly the Passover, and Jewish rites of initiation and purification formed the background of primitive Christian practice, but new meanings were added to these ritual actions. While preserving the Jewish significances, Christian understanding, especially in the Pauline writings, deepened and enlarged the meaning of baptism beyond what we know of the Jewish heritage. We can see this amplification in the account of Jesus' own baptism (Mark 1:9–11). There three elements stand out: the descent into the water, the coming of the spirit, and the adoption by God of Jesus as his son. The threefold pattern of action and meaning described in Jesus' baptism are repeated in almost all New Testament accounts of this rite. [15]

Like John the Baptist, early Christian sources emphasized the need for repentance and forgiveness, in the words "Repent and be baptized." However, they added "receive the gift of the Holy Spirit" (Acts 2:38). In Christian baptism, as in the Jewish baptism of converts, the candidate was adopted into a covenant of faith. The early Church soon came to agree with Rabbi Joshua in his debate with Rabbi Eliezer and decided to follow the practice of Paul, requiring only water baptism, and not the practice of the church at Jerusalem, which required circumcision as well (Acts 21:17–26). As if to emphasize the sufficiency of baptism alone, Colossians asserted that in baptism Christians "were circumcised with a circumcision made without hands" (Col. 2:11).

Paul added considerably to Jewish ideas about baptism. Using a favorite metaphor that likened the Church to the body of Christ, Paul said, "For by one Spirit we were all baptized into one body" (1 Cor. 12:13). To emphasize the radical change of existence associated with baptism, Paul connected it with death and new life. He regarded total immersion as a symbol of death by drowning, and compared the descent into and ascent from the water with the death and resurrection of Jesus. "Do you not know that all of us who have been baptized into Christ Jesus were baptized into his death? We were buried therefore with him by baptism into death, so that as Christ was raised from the dead by the glory of the Father, we too might walk in newness of life" (Rom. 6: 3–4). Rebirth, this time without a parallel emphasis on death, was also a favorite theme in the Gospel of John: "Unless one is born of water and the Spirit, he cannot enter the kingdom of God" (John 3:5). In both Paul and John, Christian initiation is seen as a radical passage from an ordinary to a sacred existence.

The Eucharist in the New Testament

The New Testament accounts of the Eucharist continue the Jewish tradition of sacred meals. On the night before his crucifixion, Jesus ate such a meal with his disciples, although the Evangelists do not agree about its type. The Synoptic Gospels state that it was the Passover meal, whereas the Gospel of John implies that it was a *chaburah*, a fellowship meal between a rabbi and his disciples. In John the crucifixion took place on Passover at the time the sacrificial lambs were slain, and the Last Supper took place the night before. Thus it could not have been the seder. In any event, however, the meal would have begun with a benediction and concluded with a blessing of the wine.[16]

All four Evangelists associate the Last Supper at least indirectly with Passover and its themes of liberation and deliverance. But the New Testament finds in the Last Supper a set of meanings not found in Jewish sources. Although the reenactment of the Passover gives devout Jews a vivid sense of the Exodus, the New Testament makes the stronger claim that Christ himself will be present whenever the Christian community reenacts the Last Supper. He will be present retrospectively as his actions are memorialized, as implied by the words of Jesus: "Do this . . . in remembrance of me" (1 Cor. 11:25); and he will be present prospectively as the Messianic banquet in heaven is anticipated, as implied by Jesus' words at the Supper: "I tell you I shall not drink again of this fruit of the vine until that day when I drink it new with you in my Father's kingdom" (Matt. 26:29; Mark 14:25; Luke 22:18; see also Luke 22:28–30 and Matt. 19:28). In addition, Jesus is said to be at the Supper in the present, as a participant in the meal. For example, in a story that takes place after Jesus' death and burial, an unknown man who has been walking with two disciples on the Emmaus road is revealed to them to be Jesus as they eat supper together at an inn (Luke 24:28–32). Finally, and most strikingly, Jesus is said to be present in the eucharistic elements themselves. The early Church understood the words "This is my body . . . this is my blood" (Matt. 26:26–29; Mark 14:22–25; Luke 22:19–20; 1 Cor. 11:23–26) to be Christ's promise to be present in the bread and the wine every time the Eucharist was celebrated. Paul made this explicit. "The cup of blessing which we bless, is it not a participation in the blood of Christ? The bread which we break, is it not a participation in the body of Christ?" (1 Cor. 10:16; see also 1 Cor. 11:27, 29). John shared the same conviction and added to it when he represented Jesus as saying, "I am the bread of life. . . . Unless you eat the flesh of the Son of man and drink his blood, you have no life in you" (John 6:48, 54).

The New Testament language concerning the Eucharist has an even wider resonance. In addition to the symbolism of presence in the account of the Last Supper, the fact of Jesus' impending death links the Eucharist with the symbolism of sacrifice. As already noted, John connects the death of Jesus with the slaying of the *Pesach,* the paschal lamb. Paul makes the same identification: "Christ our paschal lamb has been sacrificed. Let us therefore celebrate the festival" (1 Cor. 5:7–8). The author of Revelation does likewise when he uses the symbolism of the lamb to refer to the risen Christ (Rev. 5:6–14). Through this imagery of the paschal lamb, a close connection between the sacrificial death on Calvary and the Eucharist is forged. Just as the lamb was sacrificed and then eaten at the Passover meal, so too is Jesus both the lamb that was slain and the body and blood taken and eaten in the Eucharist.

The Gospels also present another sacrificial theme in the Last Supper. The words Jesus spoke after the blessing of the cup, "This is my blood of the covenant, which is poured out for many for the forgiveness of sins" (Matt. 26:28; see also Mark 14:24), recall the blood of the sacrifices Moses poured out on the altar steps and on the people at the solemn ceremony that sealed the Covenant of

Sinai (Exod. 24:6–8). The Epistle to the Hebrews stresses this identification (Heb. 9:20). Such sacrificial images were to have far-reaching influence the Christian experience.

Finally, two additional and closely connected meanings of the Eucharist are expressed by Paul and John. Both describe the Eucharist as a bond of union, John as a communion or interpenetration of Christ and the believer, "He who eats my flesh and drinks my blood abides in me, and I in him" (John 6:56), and Paul as a source of union with the Church, "Because there is one bread, we who are many are one body, for we all partake of the one bread" (1 Cor. 10:17). At various times and places, all of these New Testament themes find expression in the life of the Church.

Baptism and the Eucharist before the Accession of Constantine (312)

During the first centuries of the Christian Era, the Church was primarily a missionary community. From time to time it also underwent persecution. However, after Galerius issued the Edict of Toleration in 311, Constantine and succeeding Emperors increasingly supported the Church. The situation changed so dramatically that by 600, far from being a persecuted minority, the Church was the dominant religious force in the empire. From that time forward it lost the character of a missionary community and became the established religious institution. Church life was therefore far different before Constantine than it was afterward.

We can catch a glimpse of what the ceremonies of the pre-Constantine Church were like by singling out for discussion the church of Rome at the time of Hippolytus (c. 170–235). At that time, the initiatory rites, Baptism and First Communion, were administered together on Easter Evening. In the Acts of the Apostles, baptism was often administered as soon as one professed one's belief in Jesus as the Christ, but by the third century the pattern had changed to a more deliberate process. In Rome a three-year period of instruction preceded baptism.[17] On Easter Eve the candidates were brought to the water, where they waded into a pool and had some of it poured over them. In most parts of the early Church, the water baptism was followed by an anointing. (In Rome, a later second anointing by the Bishop was the rule.) Following the anointing, the candidates made their first communion at the first Eucharist celebrated on Easter.[18] In Rome, at least, this pattern continued until about the year 800.

The early Fathers gave the range of New Testament meanings to baptism, although with different emphases by different thinkers. For example, the Shepherd of Hermas emphasized death and resurrection. We descend into the water "dead" and come out "alive."[19] In the Epistle of Barnabas, washing away of sin was stressed,[20] and Clement of Rome spoke of the "one spirit of grace poured out upon us."[21] Justin Martyr described baptism as effecting regeneration, illumination, and remission of sins.[22] Finally we might mention Irenaeus, who wrote, "We have received baptism for the remission of sins in the name of God the Father, and in the name of Jesus Christ the Son of God, Who was incarnate and died and rose again, and in the Holy Spirit of God." In baptism we are washed, have the spirit of God conferred on us, and receive "the image of the heavenly."[23] All of this was of course in the context of being made a member of the Church.

Tertullian's *On Baptism*, written in the early years of the third century, represents something of a landmark, as the first treatise about either of the Gospel sacraments. However, it is in *Against Marcion* that Tertullian gave a convenient summary of the Church's teaching on baptism. There he explained that baptism consists of four gifts: remission of sin, deliverance from death, regeneration, and bestowing of the Holy Spirit.[24] Yet, all was not serene. Tensions in the doctrine of baptism began to develop, particularly with regard to the role of the Spirit. Since the extent of these difficulties was not fully apparent until the next century, we shall take them up in that context.

As in discussions of baptism, the frequent use of New Testament images by the early Fathers can be seen in descriptions of the Eucharist. Although the service became increasingly formal, with fixed prayers and elaborate ceremonial, it maintained its rootage in the Last Supper. To be sure, the practice of celebrating the Eucharist as part of a larger meal (1 Cor. 11:17-34) had all but been abandoned in the middle of the second century,[25] but the Eucharist retained its character as a meal in that bread was eaten and wine consumed. Yet it was not "ordinary" bread and wine but, as the

Didache stated, "holy" food.[26] More specifically, Ignatius of Antioch declared that "the eucharist is the flesh of our Savior Jesus Christ, which suffered for our sins and which the Father in his goodness raised."[27] Sacrificial terminology was also quite common. Writers as diverse as Justin Martyr, Clement of Alexandria, Tertullian, and Cyprian (200–258) all referred to the Eucharist as a "sacrifice."[28] Justin Martyr described the Eucharist as the pure offering prophesied by Malachi (1:11),[29] and Cyprian made an explicit identification between the Eucharist as a sacrifice and Christ's death on Calvary. "As to our mention of his passion in all of our sacrifices—for it is in the Lord's passion that our sacrifice consists—we ought to do nothing other than he himself did."[30]

Controversies over Baptism

To recapitulate, the early practice was to baptize with water on Easter Eve, followed by anointing and first communion. For adults, before these solemn rituals there was a lengthy period of preparation, often as long as three years. This *catechesis*, as it was called, included learning, training, probation, and real but limited participation in the community's worship. In short, it was an extended period of spiritual formation, intended to bring about a radical reorientation of the candidate's life. However, by the end of the second century, problems had arisen that threatened this early practice.

The Epistle to the Hebrews states that sins after baptism cannot be forgiven. "For it is impossible to restore again to repentance those who have once been enlightened, who have tasted the heavenly gift, and have become partakers of the Holy Spirit" (Heb. 6:4; see also 10:26–31.). The Shepherd of Hermas spoke with approval of "certain teachers" who insisted that the only forgiveness available to Christians is found in baptism.[31] To be sure, during this same period there is also evidence of a different attitude toward sin after baptism. Ignatius and Polycarp believed that the fallen may become reconciled after a proper repentance.[32] The Second Letter of Clement emphasized God's mercy and urged the baptized not to put off seeking forgiveness until death "when we can no longer confess and repent."[33]

These disagreements continued into the fourth century. In the East, *The Apostolic Constitutions* laid down a procedure for the reconciliation of sinners after baptism.[34] At the same time the view that such sin could not be forgiven was widespread. In the West, many accepted the rigorist views of Novatian (c. 250), who argued that after baptism there could be no forgiveness because the Church could not remit mortal sins.[35] Ideas like these led many to postpone baptism until their deathbeds in fear of sinning after this forgiveness. The Emperor Constantine is perhaps the most famous example of this practice, and Novatian himself seems to have sought baptism only when he believed he was near death.[36] However, the rigorist position gradually lost ground until it completely fell from favor by the turn of the millennium.

What brought about this changed view was the growing prevalence of infant baptism. This practice in turn received dramatic support from developments in the doctrine of original sin. In the early days of the Church, the vast majority of candidates for baptism were adult converts, although there is some evidence that infants were baptized along with their parents. The New Testament suggests as much in Paul's words, "I did baptize also the household of Stephanas" (1 Cor. 1:16; see also Acts 16:15), if it is presumed that "the household" included the small children as well as the servants. Such was probably the practice in much of the early Church, as witnessed by Hippolytus in the *Apostolic Tradition*.[37] However, infant baptism became the rule only when the conviction had taken hold that baptism washed away original sin as well as actual sin. Given the debilitating effects of original sin, it seemed only prudent to begin the process of regeneration as early as possible.

Although Tertullian laid much of the groundwork for the doctrine of original sin, he was not particularly taken with the practice of infant baptism. He recorded the practice, although he personally preferred that baptism be postponed until the age of discretion.[38] It is in the writings of Augustine that we find an argument for infant baptism based on the need to remove original sin. Time and time again he criticized Pelagius not only for his failure to affirm the universality of human infection brought about by Adam's fall,[39] but also for his failure to understand that infants should be baptized for the express purpose of nullifying "the ancient and original sin."[40] It was largely through Augustine that the doctrine of original sin became an indispensable part of the theology of baptism in the West.

Later Repercussions on Penance, Confirmation, and First Communion

The growing prevalence of infant baptism was bound to have an effect on other aspects of church life. One such effect was the further undermining of the rigorist's position on sins after baptism. It became increasingly impossible to maintain the view that the grace of baptism was such that one could be expected to live without subsequent sin. It was unrealistic to hope that children, baptized as infants, could remain sinless thereafter. In response to this situation, penitential systems began to evolve. However, the view that confession ought to be a regular part of spiritual discipline was slow in developing. At first it was assumed that confession would be a public act and that it could take place only once. Ambrose (338–397) reflected this point of view. "Just as there is one baptism," he observed, "so there is but one public penance."[41] Other developments in the fourth and fifth centuries were pastorally more sensitive. Not only was reconciliation permitted more than once, but public confession was not always required. Augustine allowed bishops discretion in assessing which sins demanded public penance and which sins might be dealt with in private. It is, however, not until the Third Council of Toledo (589) that we find mention of private confession, though here it is labeled "a detestable presumption."[42]

Nevertheless, it is not in these fragments that we find the origins of regular private confession. This practice, together with public or private penance and spiritual direction by a confessor, began sometime in the early Middle Ages and is traceable to the monks of Ireland, Wales, and England.[43] This purely local monastic practice was first extended to the laity and then spread by Celtic missionaries to the continent. Behind these developments lay practical pastoral concerns that were modifying the understanding of the sacraments. Perfection of life was still the Christian's goal but, instead of assuming that it could be had all at once, it was recognized that it must be achieved by stages. The practice of frequent confession seemed an obvious means to that end.

Such thinking not only lay behind the development of Penance as a separate sacramental observance, but also supported the similar development of Confirmation. The evidence from the New Testament and the early Church is clear that the Holy Spirit is given in baptism. Still, gifts of the Spirit were occasionally said to be mediated through anointing and the laying on of hands. A passage in Acts seems to suggest that baptism by itself is incomplete and must be supplemented by the gift of the Spirit through the laying on of hands (Acts 8:14–17). Tertullian apparently echoed this view when he said, "Not that we obtain the Holy Spirit in the waters, but having been cleansed in the water under the ministry of the angel, we are prepared for the Holy Spirit."[44] Of course we are not here speaking of a separate rite. The descent into water and the laying on of hands and anointing (by a bishop if present) were all parts of the same initiatory ceremony. Evidence for confirmation as a separate rite is not found until the end of the fifth century in southern Gaul.[45] A Gallican homily of the fifth or sixth century provides what became the almost universal justification for its separate status: "The Holy Spirit, who comes down upon the waters of Baptism with health-giving descent, in the font gives His fullness to produce innocence, in Confirmation affords an increase to produce grace. In Baptism we are regenerated so as to attain to life; after Baptism we are strengthened for battle. In Baptism we are washed; after Baptism we are made strong."[46] In the Middle Ages, Peter Lombard (1100–1164?) made a similar distinction: "The virtue in Confirmation is the gift for strength of the Holy Spirit who was given in Baptism for remission."[47]

What lay behind the development of confirmation as a separate rite was the recognition of the need for Christian nurture after baptism. Many baptized as infants seemed to make lackluster adults. They seemed to need additional empowerment to lead a Christian life. Furthermore, in the interest of inculcating a proper reverence for the Holy Mysteries, there was mounting pressure to postpone first communion to the age of discretion or reason. In this atmosphere, a rite of passage to this new status began to seem necessary. As we have noted, in the early Church the initiatory rites of baptism, anointing with chrism, laying on of hands, and first communion all took place late on Easter eve and early Easter day. The practice of admitting to communion all the baptized continued even after infant baptism became frequent. Augustine argued strongly in favor of this practice. Speaking of baptized children, he said, "They are infants, but they are his members. They are infants, but they receive his sacraments. They are infants, but they are partakers of his table, that they may have life in themselves."[48] This practice seemed inappropriate to St. Thomas Aquinas, who argued that the sacrament ought to be withheld from the baptized until they "begin to have some use of reason so as to be able to conceive some devotion for the sacrament."[49] Although St. Thomas did not mention it, he seems to have had in mind Paul's warning about those who partake of the Lord's Supper unworthily: "For anyone who eats and drinks without discerning the body eats and drinks judgment upon himself" (1 Cor. 11:29).

By the Middle Ages, the Christian imagination was captured by the idea that progress in the Christian life must be delimited in a series of stages marked ritually and sacramentally. At the Reformation and again in our time, these issues and the medieval solutions have come under review.

Eucharist Thinking in the Fourth and Fifth Centuries

Christian thinkers of the fourth and fifth centuries continued to describe the Eucharist as a sacrifice as well as a communion. They also continued to refer to the bread and wine as the body and blood of Christ, which they sometimes gave a realist and sometimes a symbolic interpretation. For example, Ambrose affirmed both a realist and a symbolic interpretation of the words "This is my body." On the one hand he said, "Before the blessing of the heavenly words another nature is named; after the consecration the body is denoted."[50] On the other hand, he elsewhere described the offering of the bread and wine as "the figure of the body and blood of our Lord Jesus Christ."[51] Ambrose's interpretation was a continuation of the practice of the pre-Nicene Church, where "figure," "symbol," and "representation"[52] were used concurrently with statements affirming an identity between the bread and wine and the body and blood of Christ.[53]

These contrasting descriptions proved uneasy bedfellows. Sometimes they came to be taken as alternative and not as complementary characterizations. Either the bread and the wine were symbolic representations of the body and blood or they had in some mysterious way been transmuted into the body and blood of Christ. This dichotomy later broadened into the contrast between objective and subjective interpretations of Christ's presence in the Eucharist. In objectivist views, Christ was believed to be present as an extramental reality. In subjectivist views, he was said to be present in the way in which something is said to be present when it is brought to mind, perhaps through a symbol or through memory. However, this dichotomy developed in stages and was not immediately recognized. A decisive step toward this recognition was taken in the writings of Augustine.

Although, like Ambrose, Augustine continued to use both realist and symbolic language in describing the presence of Christ in the Eucharist, he began to clarify the discussion by introducing a distinction between *the sacrament or sign* and *the thing of which the sacrament was a sign*. Sometimes he put it in terms of the *sacrament* and its *power*. "The sacrament itself is one thing, and the power of the sacrament another."[54] At other times he put it in terms of what is *seen* and what is *understood*. "They are called sacraments because one thing is seen in them, another understood."[55] The distinction between *sacramentum* and *res sacramenti* became important in subsequent efforts to refine and explain the nature of the eucharistic presence because it enabled the discussion to focus on the question of what the relationship is between the *sacramentum* (the bread and the wine) and the *res sacramenti* (the body and blood of Christ). Three possible positions suggested themselves. First, the bread and the wine are identical with the body and blood of Christ because at the prayer of consecration they become the body and blood of Christ substantially. Second, the bread and the wine on the altar are not substantially the body and blood of Christ, but symbolize them; the true body and blood are in heaven, belonging to the ascended Christ. Third, the bread and the wine symbolize the body and blood of Christ, but the body and blood of Christ are present not only in heaven but also here on the altar along with the bread and the wine, their presence being a spiritual, nonphysical one. During the early Middle Ages attention was focused on the first two of these possibilities. It was only later that the third option clearly emerged as a distinct position, although some scholars detect it in the writings of St. Augustine.

In spite of Ambrose's occasional use of figurative language, most scholars have concluded that his settled view represented the first position—the bread and the wine are converted into the body and blood and thus become substantially the body and blood of Christ. "The sacraments," he wrote, "by means of the mystery of the holy prayer are transformed into flesh and blood."[56] This idea had already taken root in the East. For example, Gregory of Nyssa said that the "bread which is consecrated by the word of God is transmade into the body of God the Word."[57] A noteworthy quotation from Justin Martyr is sometimes cited as an early example of this position. "Just as our savior Jesus Christ was made flesh through the Word of God . . . so also we have been taught that the food which has been eucharistized by the word of prayer . . . is the flesh and blood of the incarnate Jesus."[58]

Many students of Augustine believe that he, like Ambrose, asserted the first position—the conversion of the substance of the bread and wine into the body and blood.[59] Among passages cited in support of this interpretation are the following: "Not all bread, but that bread which receives the blessing of Christ, becomes the body of Christ,"[60] and "the bread is the body of Christ and the chalice is the blood of Christ."[61] However, other students of Augustine find support for the second position—a symbolic interpretation of the words "This is my body."[62] "What you see on the altar is bread and wine, as your eyes tell you, but an informed faith asserts that the bread is the body of Christ, and the wine his blood."[63] A symbolic interpretation is also suggested in a passage from the *Epistles:*

> If the Sacraments had not any likeness to those things of which they are Sacraments, they would not be Sacraments at all. And from this likeness for the most part also they receive the names of the things themselves. As then after a certain fashion the Sacrament of the body of Christ is the body of Christ, and the Sacrament of the blood of Christ is the blood of Christ.[64]

In these passages, at least, Augustine suggested that the bread and wine on the altar are not the body and blood of Christ substantially, but because of a certain likeness symbolize the body and blood and for that reason are called the body and blood. To make matters even more complicated, other scholars believe that Augustine's teachings on the Eucharist as sacrifice suggest the third alternative, that Christ is really present on the altar, but in a spiritual and heavenly manner.[65]

Augustine and Ambrose on the Eucharistic Sacrifice

Ambrose's realistic interpretation of the words "This is my body" shaped his thinking on the Eucharist as sacrifice. Since he believed that the bread and the wine were converted into the body and blood of Christ, he also believed that Christ offered his own physical body on each altar. "For even though Christ no longer seems to be offering sacrifice, nevertheless He Himself is offered in the world wherever Christ's body is offered. Indeed He is shown to be offering in us, since it is His word which sanctifies the sacrifice which we offer."[66] Augustine also taught that in some sense the Eucharist is a sacrifice and that what is offered is the body of Christ, but his views are complicated by his frequent use of the phrase "body of Christ" in three contexts—the body of Christ in the Eucharist, the body that Christ offered on Calvary, and the body of Christ that is the Church. If we ask what it is that is offered as sacrifice at the Eucharist, Augustine implies that we offer all three bodies in the same action because they are mystically identical. "The selfsame Christ Who was slain there [at Calvary] is in a real sense slaughtered daily by the faithful, so that the sacrifice which was offered once for all in bloody form is sacramentally renewed upon our altars with the oblation of His body and blood."[67] But in this same action, the body that is the Church is offered. "This is the sacrifice of Christians: we who are many are one body in Christ. The Church celebrates [this sacrifice] in the sacrament of the altar . . . [where] in what she offers she herself is offered."[68] But these offerings are one because the body of Christ that is the Church is identical with the body of Christ on the altar. "There you are upon the table, there you are in the chalice," Augustine once said to the newly baptized at their first communion at Easter.[69]

Augustine did not explain the way in which these three bodies of Christ are identical. He left behind an ambiguous body of material that could be interpreted in a variety of ways. Later thinkers with diverse views regularly cited him as an authority. He did, however, provide the Church with the rudiments of a coherent view, the shape of which has become clearer in recent ecumenical discussions.

After Augustine and Ambrose

Lines hardened between those who followed Ambrose's realism and those who developed the symbolic aspects of Augustine's thinking. However, it was not until the ninth century that a full-blown controversy over the Eucharist developed. The dispute seems to have developed inadvertently. On his election as Abbot of the monastery at Corbei in 844 and in an effort to obtain royal patronage, Paschasius Radbertus revised an earlier treatise of his, *The Lord's Body and Blood,* and sent it with a new dedication to the Emperor, Charles the Bald. Charles must have been sufficiently puzzled by its doctrine that he in turn asked the opinion of a certain Ratramnus, also a monk of Corbei, about Radbertus' work. Ratramnus replied in a work of similar title, *Christ's Body and Blood.*

Radbertus had given a careful exposition of the essentials of Ambrose's position, affirming that the flesh of Christ in the Eucharist is "obviously none other than the one that was born of Mary, suffered on the cross, and rose from the grave."[70] He also adopted Ambrose's "transformationalism." The color and taste of bread and wine do not change, but these are "the mere figure of bread and wine." After the consecration what remains is "nothing other than the flesh and blood of Christ."[71]

Ratramnus was disturbed by what he took to be Radbertus' crude realism. He repudiated both aspects of the position taken by Radbertus. "For as regards the substance of the creatures [the bread and the wine], they are after consecration what they were before. Bread and wine they were before, and after they have been consecrated, they are seen to remain in the same nature."[72] Nor is there an identity between the body of Christ's earthly ministry and the eucharistic body. "The difference is great which distinguishes the body in which Christ suffered . . . from this body which is daily celebrated by the faithful in the mystery of the passion."[73] Ratramnus' positive doctrine seems to have been a kind of virtualism. "So far as they are corporally handled, their nature is that of corporal creatures; but according to their power, and as they have been spiritually made, they are the mysteries of the body and blood of Christ."[74] Though they are still bread and wine, they are in effect—that is, have the power of—the body and blood of Christ.

The ninth-century controversy ended inconclusively, only to be revived in the eleventh century in the persons of Berengar of Tours (d. 1088) and Lanfranc (d. 1089), later Archbishop of Canterbury. Berengar took Ratramnus' position and Lanfranc, Radbertus'. This time the controversy was much more bitter, finally coming to an end only after about thirty years. Although Berengar defended his position with great erudition and had many powerful supporters, including at one time Pope Gregory VII, he was finally asked to recant at the Council of Rome (1079). Whether he later recanted the recantation is still a matter of dispute, but it was clear to him that his position had been repudiated.[75] He lived the remainder of his life in quiet obscurity at Tours, although his ideas and those of Ratramnus would receive new life at the Reformation.

Peter Lombard and St. Thomas Aquinas

In the High Middle Ages, the realistic view achieved greater and greater sanction. In his *Sentences*, the influential compendium of medieval theology, Peter Lombard asserted that the bread and the wine are converted into the body and blood of Christ, although he reported that he was unable to decide whether it was a substantial or a formal change, or change of some other kind.[76] Essentially, Peter Lombard's position was taken at the Fourth Lateran Council, held in 1215. There the change was described as "transubstantiation," but no explicit definition of the meaning of the term was given. No one really questioned this formulation until Reformation times, although the precise meaning given "transubstantiation" was then still a matter of discussion. For example, St. Thomas Aquinas held that the substance of the bread and wine was converted into the body and blood of Christ, the accidents such as color and taste being allowed to remain.[77] This theory depended on an ancient philosophical view that any physical object possesses an underlying substratum, its substance, in which its empirical properties, its accidents, inhere. Although substances and their accidents are inseparable in nature, God could by an exercise of his power separate substances from their accidents, making substances to be present without their accidents and accidents to remain without their substances. William of Ockham gave a somewhat different account. While holding this same philosophical view of the relationship between substances and accidents, he modified St. Thomas' explanation of transubstantiation as a conversion of the substance of the bread and wine into the substance of the body and blood, by proposing that God simply destroyed the substance of the bread and wine, while making the substance of the body and blood to be present along with the accidents of the bread and wine.[78] Although these attempts to make more precise the nature of the supposed change may seem to be but minor variations on an ancient philosophical view, they provided the concepts and vocabulary in which the Reformation discussion was couched.

The views of St. Thomas Aquinas provide a convenient summary of eucharistic thinking in the Middle Ages. As explained above, St. Thomas not only embraced the language of transubstantiation but interpreted it to mean that at the moment of consecration the substance of the bread and the wine is "converted into" the substance of the body and blood of Christ.[79] For the sake of future discussion, it is important to realize that the relationship between the substance of the body and blood of Christ and the accidents of the bread and the wine was seen as an extrinsic one. "It is obvious," St. Thomas wrote, "that those accidents do not inhere in the substance of Christ's body and blood," adding that it is not possible "that Christ's body, now glorious and immune from suffering change, should be so altered as to receive these qualities."[80] It is also significant that St. Thomas believed Christ's presence in the Eucharist to be a noncorporeal one (in the ordinary sense of "corporeal"), a presence "above the nature of a localized body. In no sense is the body of Christ pinned down to a spot in this sacrament."[81]

In addition to providing an account of transubstantiation, St. Thomas also reaffirmed the belief that each Eucharist participates in the sacrifice of Christ enacted once and for all on Calvary. "Just as what is offered everywhere is the same identical body, not many, so the sacrifice is one and the same with his."[82] And finally, because each eucharistic offering participates in Christ's offering on Calvary, it too is a propitiatory offering, and propitiatory benefit could be increased by increasing the number of Masses. "The offering of sacrifice . . . is multiplied in many masses, and so the sacramental and sacrificial effect is increased."[83] Given the fact that propitiation plays a negligible role in Old Testament accounts of sacrifice, the almost exclusive medieval emphasis on this kind of offering is striking. Undoubtedly the popularity of Anselm's theory of the Atonement, where Christ's death is seen as a payment to satisfy God's justice,[84] made propitiation the dominant sacrificial motif. The stress on the need to satisfy God's justice made it almost inevitable that good deeds would be seen to tip favorably the scales of God's justice and that attendance at Mass would be viewed as a particularly meritorious good dead, since each Mass was a participation in Christ's own sacrifice. These eucharistic ideas, which seemed the logical outcome of centuries of Christian thought and practice, surprisingly would become ready tinder for the conflagration we know as the Reformation.[85]

Eucharistic Piety in the Late Middle Ages

In late medieval piety, the Mass continued to be regarded as a propitiatory sacrifice. It also continued to be regarded as an opportunity for the worshiper to identify with Christ in his sacrificial offering. In popular piety this identification was not taken as the ontological unity that St. Thomas implied when he said, "What is offered everywhere is the same identical body,"[86] but rather was a psychological identification. Sometimes the idea of the Mass as recalling Christ's suffering was stressed, a notion taken up by many of the Reformers. For example, Gabriel Biel spoke of it as "the most perfect memorial of the Lord's passion."[87] At other times participation in the Mass was regarded as a way to copy Christ's offering, as implied by the title of Thomas à Kempis' book *The Imitation of*

Christ. In the Mass we too must do what Thomas à Kempis believed Christ did, sacrifice our entire selves to God. For à Kempis, Christ's sacrifice was not only the dedication of himself to God's service, but a self-annihilation.

> As I willingly offered Myself to God the Father for thy sins, with My hands stretched out upon the Cross, and My Body naked, so that nothing remained in Me which was not completely turned into a sacrifice to appease the divine wrath; even so oughtest thou willingly to offer thyself to Me daily in the Mass, as intimately as thou canst, with thy whole energies and affections, for a pure and holy oblation. . . . Offer thyself to Me, and give thy whole self for God, and thy offering shall be accepted. . . . But if thou wilt stand upon self, and not offer thyself freely to my will, thy offering is not complete, nor will there be an entire union between us.[88]

Several of the ideas expressed here are reminiscent of Old Testament ideas of sacrifice. As we noted earlier, it is possible to see in the sin offerings a propitiation of God's wrath, and in the burnt offerings the notion that the worshiper must yield up the entire self, "nothing remaining in me not turned into sacrifice." It is natural that when the Mass was so closely associated with the sin and burnt offerings, the ideas associated with the peace offering tended to be forgotten. It is not surprising that in this context the notion of the sacred meal almost disappeared and the noncommunicating Mass became the rule.

While the ideal of total self-abnegation has had its supporters in every age, it was one of the elements of late medieval piety that several of the Reformers found objectionable. Of course, not every medieval thinker taught this kind of self-abasement. Bernard of Clairvaux is a case in point; in describing his third and highest stage of love for God, he urged us not to disparage the self too much, but to learn to love and value the self for God's sake.[89] However, Bernard's guidance is severely undercut by à Kempis' advice to those who would follow Christ. In his early days as a monk, Luther followed a path like à Kempis', but he gradually came to the conclusion that self-abnegation was not the road to peace with God, but rather the opposite, the road to despair and loss of faith.

The Reformation

In 1517 when Martin Luther nailed his 95 Theses to the door of the church at Erfurt, no one, not even he, imagined the far-reaching consequences of this act. The catalyst for Luther's anger was the sale of indulgences by the Dominican monk Tetzel. The belief behind this practice was that the apostle Peter and his successors the Popes were given the keys to heaven and hell. This view had come to mean that the Pope could grant indulgences, that is, remit the penalties for sin and thus excuse an individual from serving a specified number of days in purgatory. Indulgences could be purchased not only for oneself but also for others, so that a penalty for sin could be remitted without any change of heart on the part of the perpetrator. To Luther this practice seemed odious in itself, but it was rendered even more so by the jingle with which Tetzel hawked his wares.

> When the money in the coffer rings,
> The soul from purgatory springs.

Luther soon realized, however, that his objections to the sale of indulgences applied with equal force to Masses offered on behalf of the dead.[90] Like indulgences, Masses were bought and sold in the belief that remission of penalty would be granted to individuals in purgatory without regard to the state of their souls.[91] Furthermore, the idea that the frequency of celebration increased the efficacy of one's offering provided added motivation for the buying and selling of Masses. It is not surprising, then, that the notion of the Mass as a propitiatory sacrifice, as expressed by St. Thomas Aquinas and the main-line medieval teaching, soon came under review.

Luther's Problems with Self-Sacrifice

In addition to questioning the idea that the Mass could be offered as a propitiation on behalf of others, Luther's own experience led him to question another link between the Mass and sacrifice. Thomas à Kempis saw sacrifice of the self as the paradigm of the Christian life. Thus he urged the devout to sacrifice the self daily in the

Mass. As already noted in our discussion of the doctrine of justification by faith,[92] Luther had come to reject such notions. In his life as a monk Luther had attempted to appease God's wrath by a life of self-denial. Yet whatever he did in the way of fasting, the offering of Masses, and other devotional exercises seemed inadequate to win God's grace and favor. Suddenly, while in a state of despair and depression, Luther had a moment of enlightenment. He came to realize that faith, and not sacrificial deeds, is the essence of the Christian life. Good works do not win God's love, but good works spring naturally from a faith-filled heart. "Lo, thus from faith flow forth love and joy in the Lord, and from love a joyful, willing and free mind that serves one's neighbor willingly."[93]

As we shall see, several of the Reformers transferred these ideas directly to their sacramental theories, but with differing emphases. Luther's attack on the selling of indulgences convinced them all that they must preserve two principles. First, salvation is not a human achievement, but depends on God's grace, favor, and action. Second, God's grace will not be efficacious irrespective of a person's state of mind. Faith and repentance are required of those receiving God's favor. With regard to these matters, the Reformers were agreed that late medieval thinking and practice were defective. However, they did not agree among themselves about the way in which piety was to be reformed. Some put more weight on God's grace and favor, others on faith and repentance.

Reformation Views on the Eucharist

As doubts about the reliability of the medieval tradition deepened, the Reformers turned to the Scripture as the only standard of belief and practice. This move led them almost immediately to reject the idea that there were seven sacraments. They found only two, baptism and the Eucharist, with sure Scriptural warrant. They also began to question the idea that the Mass was a sacrifice. In the Epistle to the Hebrews they found what seemed an authoritative statement countermanding the medieval teaching that each Eucharist was propitiatory. Three times Hebrews affirms that Christ made only one sacrifice, and that sacrifice was sufficient for the sins of the whole world: "We have been sanctified through the offering of the body of Jesus Christ once for all" (10:10); "Christ . . . offered for all time a single sacrifice for sins" (10:12); and finally, "By a single offering he has perfected for all time those who are sanctified" (10:14). Having accepted these passages from Hebrews as a definitive rejection that each Mass was a sacrifice or that it participated in Christ's sacrifice, the Reformers preserved in varying degrees other elements of medieval teaching on the Mass. For example, they all affirmed the presence of Christ in the Eucharist, but they gave quite different accounts of the way in which he was present. Some thought that Christ was substantially or objectively present. Others affirmed that, although Christ was not objectively present, he was subjectively present, present insofar as we have him in mind. As we shall see, several variations on these positions were proposed.

Luther and Consubstantiation

On the eve of the Reformation, transubstantiation was the official explanation of the presence of Christ in the Eucharist, having been promulgated at the Fourth Lateran Council. The Reformers rejected transubstantiation, along with their rejection of the Mass as sacrifice. Luther's discussion of the issues is indicative of the thinking of others. Luther took the position that the body of Christ was present as substance, but not because the substances of the bread and wine were converted into the body and blood of Christ. Rather, he argued, the substance of the body and blood of Christ was present without any accidents (color, shape, weight, etc.), and also the substances of the bread and wine were present together with their accidents. In a famous passage from *The Babylonian Captivity of the Church,* he wrote:

> Some time ago, when I was drinking in scholastic theology, the learned Cardinal of Cambrai gave me food for thought in his comments on the fourth book of the *Sentences.* He argues with great acumen that to hold that real bread and real wine, and not merely their accidents, are present on the altar, would be much more probable and require fewer superfluous miracles—if only the Church had not decreed otherwise.[94]

Did Luther really teach consubstantiation — No! He did teach the ubiquity of Christ's body.

Luther's view was that in the sacrament the bread and wine remained whole and entire, possessing both substance and accidents; Christ chose to be present, but in substance only and without the accidents of his body and blood. Although this was not William of Ockham's own view, he had discussed it as a logical possibility, calling it consubstantiation, to distinguish it from transubstantiation.[95] Luther also used other ways to describe the presence of Christ in the sacrament. In addition to speaking of Christ as present along "with" the bread, he also spoke of him as present "in" the bread and perhaps even "under" the bread.[96] Noting the similarity with Christ's original incarnation, Luther sometimes called the presence an "impanation," literally "imbreadedness."[97] Luther's several ways of speaking of Christ's presence all stress the notion of a conjunction between Christ's substantial presence and the substances of the bread and wine. Luther's view found many adherents in England as well as in Germany, where consubstantiation was adopted by many of the reform minded. However, as we shall see, several of the Reformers were dissatisfied with Luther's doctrine and proposed more radical solutions.

Virtualism

This is a traditional name for the view that Christ is truly present in the sacrament but his presence can best be described as a presence in "power" and "effect," which was the original meaning of "virtue."[98] In our contemporary vocabulary, we would call this a "dynamic" presence. John Calvin's position is often cited as an example of this view. According to Calvin, Christ's body is in heaven, and therefore cannot be present as a substance is present.[99] In the first place, it is not a large enough body to extend over such a vast distance. Second, since a body is necessarily circumscribed in time and place, it cannot be in more than one place at the same time. Calvin was looking for a way to explain how Christ in heaven could be present and active over vast distances of space and time. The explanation had to be that the presence and activity are noncorporeal and nonlocalized, but could Calvin give a more positive statement about the nature of that presence? He began to speak of Christ as present dynamically, that is in power and in effect. He also spoke of Christ as spiritually present. To be sure, he occasionally spoke of the presence as "substantial," but here he seems to have meant only that the presence is objectively real, since he also denied that the substance of Christ's body is eaten by mouth. Calvin made several of these points in the following passage.

> The explanation to be adopted then will be that substantially we become partakers of the flesh of Christ—not that any carnal mixture takes place, or that the flesh of Christ brought down from heaven penetrates into us or is swallowed by the mouth, but because the flesh of Christ, in virtue of its power and efficacy, vivifies our souls just as the substance of the bread and the wine nourishes our bodies.[100]

In order to make this point clearer, Calvin added,

> The body of Christ is given to us in the Supper spiritually, because the secret virtue of the Spirit makes things separated in space and time to be united with each other, and accordingly enables life from the flesh of Christ to reach us from heaven. This power and faculty of vivifying might not improperly be said to be something abstracted from the substance, provided it be truly and distinctly understood that the body of Christ remains in heaven, and yet from its substance life flows and comes to us who are pilgrims on earth.[101]

Distinguishing his position from Luther's, Calvin remarked, "The body of Christ is [not] given us under the bread or with the bread, because it is not a substantial union of corruptible food with the flesh of Christ that is denoted, but sacramental conjunction."[102] Calvin's general position can be summarized by an analogy: Just as the sun through its heat is present here on earth even though it is high in the sky, so Christ in heaven is present in our world as a vivifying power.

A similar position was given eloquent expression by Thomas Cranmer (1489–1556) in England. Like Calvin, Cranmer affirmed that although Christ is corporeally present in heaven, the believer eats spiritually yet truly of his body and blood.

> God grant, that all contention set aside, [all] parties may come to this holy communion with such a lively faith in Christ, and such an unfeigned love to all Christ's members, that as they carnally eat with their mouth this sacramental bread and drink the wine, so spiritu-

ally they may eat and drink the very flesh and blood of Christ, which is in heaven, and sitteth on the right hand of his Father; and that finally by his means they may enjoy with him the glory and kingdom of heaven.[103]

Objectivist and Subjectivist Views

The Idea of an Objective Presence

As we have said, some views assert that Christ is present in the Eucharist as an objective or external reality, while other views maintain that he is present as a subjective or internal reality, a mental reality. Both objectivists and subjectivists claim that Christ is present in the sacrament, but give very different accounts of the manner of his presence. In order to make the differences between objectivists and subjectivists more perspicuous, it is helpful to keep four points in mind. First, both objectivists and subjectivists assume that Christ is now present in heaven at the right hand of God. Second, both groups take cognizance of the material components of the sacrament, the bread and the wine, and more largely the celebration of the Supper. Third, both groups recognize that in connection with their participation in the Supper believers have certain subjective states of mind—thoughts about Christ and feelings of love and perhaps awe. However, in addition to these three elements, objectivists propose a fourth, the presence of another reality, variously described as the substance of Christ's body, or his vivifying power, or his spiritual but real presence. Sometimes objectivists describe the sense of Christ's presence as an encounter with Christ or as Christ actively penetrating our hearts. It is Christ himself who is the cause of the subjective states of the believer and who awakens in the believer a conviction of his holy presence. Subjectivists describe the situation differently. They speak of the Supper, of Christ's presence in heaven and of the believer's thoughts about Christ. They do not speak of the fourth element described above. They see no need to affirm an additional reality present in the sacrament. For the subjectivist, Christ is present to the believer internally, mentally, as an idea is said to be present in someone's mind.

Historically, objectivist views have emphasized the symbolism of

Get the christology first, then look at the view of the sacraments.

eating. For example, Calvin wrote in 1536, "Just as bread nourishes, sustains and strengthens the life of our body, even so is the body of Christ the nourishment and protection of our spiritual life."[104] Objectivists have also stressed another aspect of eating, the idea of incorporation, in which Christ becomes a part of us and we of him. Thomas Cranmer emphasized this notion in the 1549 Book of Common Prayer where the celebrant prays

> that we, and all others who shall be partakers of this Holy Communion, may worthily receive the most precious Body and Blood of thy Son Jesus Christ, be filled with thy grace and heavenly benediction, and made one body with him, that he may dwell in us, and we in him.[105]

By the act of communion, the lives of Christ and the worshiper are no longer separated from each other, but so interpenetrate that they can be described as becoming one body.

Subjectivist Perspectives

Great stress on Koinonia.

Some Reformation positions are clearly subjectivist. For example, Ulrich Zwingli held that Christ's presence in the Eucharist is identical with our collective consciousness of him. In explaining his view, he insisted that the Eucharist is fundamentally a memorial service. "The mass is not a sacrifice," he said, "but is a remembrance of the sacrifice and assurance of the salvation which God has given us."[106]

Zwingli's position here is more powerful than it first appears. In the dramatic recollection of the Last Supper, the events of the passion become present to us. We become Jesus' contemporaries. As Charles Harold Dodd put it:

> Past, present, and future are indissolubly united in the sacrament. . . . At each Eucharist we are *there*—we are in the night in which He was betrayed, at Golgotha, before the empty tomb on Easter day, and in the upper room where He appeared. . . . History has been taken up into the suprahistorical, without ceasing to be history.[107]

Temporal rather than spatial.

In reenacting the Lord's Supper, the temporal distinctions between then and now are erased, and we are with him and he with us. In

This is a modern view of anamnesis.

this way, the memorial reenactment of the Last Supper is a means of grace. It awakens in us a vivid consciousness of Christ.

Zwingli's subjectivism is made even clearer by his identification of Christ's presence with a particular state of consciousness. Drawing a distinction between two ways of eating the body and blood of Christ, the one sacramentally and the other spiritually, he proposed that to eat sacramentally was only to eat the bread which is a symbol of Christ's body. "To eat the body of Christ spiritually," Zwingli continued, "is equivalent to trusting with heart and soul upon the mercy and goodness of God."[108] Alternatively Zwingli put it, "To feed on him is simply to believe on him."[109] These words might be taken to suggest that physically eating the bread and wine is unnecessary for one who has achieved spiritual communion. However, Zwingli seems not to have drawn this inference, continuing to believe that the physical eating might still be a means of grace because it helps to stir us to a vivid consciousness of Christ. Hence, the physical eating can be said to awaken a sense of Christ's presence.

Anabaptists departed from Zwingli at just this point. They thought that he had not sufficiently freed himself from objectivist thinking because he still regarded the Eucharist as a means of grace. Although he no longer thought of the substance of the body and blood as an intermediary, Zwingli still thought of the enactment of the Supper as faith building. Luther's doctrine of grace and good works helps to illuminate the Anabaptist point of view. Just as the good works of Christians are not a means of salvation but a result of faith, so Anabaptists regarded the celebration of the Lord's Supper not as a means of grace but as the sign of a grace already given. Believers eat the bread and wine because they already have faith in Christ and therefore want to obey his commands. They also, of course, testify to their faith before the Christian community. As Conrad Grebel (1498–1526) wrote, "Although it is simply bread, yet if faith and brotherly love precede it, it is to be received with joy, since, when it is used in the church, it is to show us that we are truly one bread and one body, and that we are and wish to be true brethren with one another."[110] Later in this passage Grebel stressed the strengthening of community and fellowship that takes place among those who eat the Lord's Supper. However, such ideas were common among all schools of thought. In England, Thomas Cranmer also emphasized this aspect of eucharistic celebration.

> Christ ordained the sacrament to move and stir all men to friendship, love, and concord, and to put away all hatred, variance, and discord, and to testify a brotherly and unfeigned love between all them that be the members of Christ.[111]

Although we have described the best known subjectivist expositions of the Lord's Supper, we have not yet exhausted their possibilities. A logical, if not chronological, next step is found in the thinking of the American Baptists, who further restricted the import of the Eucharist in their Confession of 1688. All references to the Supper as a means of grace are omitted, and its celebration is commended solely on the grounds that Christ commanded it.[112] There is no clearer way of affirming the Anabaptist principle that the sacraments are but the signs of a grace already given.

A final view carries the emphasis on faith and spiritual communion with Christ to an even more extreme conclusion. Deeply Christ-centered, George Fox, the founder of the Quakers or the Society of Friends, focused his preaching on the "Inner Light" or, as he also called it, "The Light of Christ."[113] From this emphasis on the inner light followed the Quaker abandonment of any ritual observance, including the celebration of the sacraments. George Fox was adamant on this point. The Gospel has to do with the inner life and not outward ceremony. He made this clear throughout his Journal.[114] Water baptism does not cleanse, said Fox to a group of Baptists. "I told them that they must find these things in their own hearts."[115] For faithful Quakers ceremonial is a barrier and not an opening to a devout and holy life.

Reformation Views on Baptism

Beginning with New Testament times, Christians associated baptism with the gifts of the Holy Spirit, with the washing away of sin, with death and resurrection, and with initiation into the Christian fellowship, the Church. Later, when Christians began to emphasize original sin, they came to believe that baptism removed it as well as actual sins. The Reformers reversed this development and described baptism as the early Church did, omitting all references to "the washing away of original sin." Indeed, as we shall see, the major Reformers, Luther, Calvin, and Zwingli, were in remarkable agreement. Only the Anabaptists struck out on their own, but there the focus of controversy was the Anabaptist rejection of infant baptism.

The Continental Reformers all repudiated the idea that in baptism original sin was removed; our natural egoism seemed just as powerful after baptism as before. Thus Calvin denied

> that by baptism we are loosed and liberated from original sin and the corruption that is inherited from Adam by all his posterity, and that we are restored to an original righteousness and purity of nature, the same that Adam would have had if he had remained always in the integrity in which he had first been created.[116]

Luther, Zwingli, and the Anabaptists all agreed. The exception was England, where the Thirty-Nine Articles by their silence permitted one to follow medieval tradition at this point. With the repudiation of the belief in the cleansing of original sin, the main theological reason for infant baptism was removed. Should the practice itself be abandoned? Anabaptists said it should. However, some Reformers developed other rationales for infant baptism.

In the Reformers' discussions of baptism, we observe a tension between objective and subjective poles similar to the one encountered in regard to the Eucharist. On the objective pole, discussion centered on what is offered to us in baptism. On the subjective pole, the focus was on the attitude the candidate brought to baptism. In his 1520 treatise, *The Babylonian Captivity of the Church*, Luther began to work out the implications of his insight that we are saved by grace through faith. In a text from Mark, he found an emphasis on both of these poles. "He who believes and is baptized will be saved" (Mark 16:16). The subjective pole, the emphasis on faith, is found *in the text*, while *the text as a whole* expressed the objective pole, God's promise of salvation.[117] Likewise, the rite of baptism itself contains the two poles, proclaiming the promise and calling for faith. These themes are treated in a similar way in both Zwingli's and Calvin's treatises on baptism.[118] In addition, Zwingli and Calvin stressed baptism's role as "an initiatory sign or pledge with which we bind ourselves to God, testifying the same to our neighbor."[119]

With so much emphasis on the faith of the recipient, how is it possible to justify infant baptism? The Anabaptists, appealing to Mark 16:16 as decisive, insisted that only believers could be baptized and called for the rebaptism of all who had been baptized as infants.[120] In the face of this logic, what kind of arguments did the major Reformers give for the practice of infant baptism? To this question all three gave very much the same answer. Not to allow infant baptism was to put too much emphasis on the subjective pole and not enough on the objective. In short, to deny infant baptism is a return to a religion of works and not of grace.[121] Faith is important, but faith may be awakened in the infant after baptism. As Luther put it, "Infants are aided by the faith of others, namely, those who bring them for baptism. For the Word of God is powerful enough, when uttered, to change even a godless heart, which is no less unresponsive and helpless than any infant."[122] Of course "the faith of others" included the faith of the Christian fellowship that mediates God's Word and Promise to the growing child. Zwingli and Calvin followed suit with similar stress on the influence of the Christian fellowship.[123] Calvin sought to round out the argument for infant baptism by securing a Biblical basis for it. He found precedent for it in the rite of circumcision, the reception of children into the people of God in the Old Testament, and in Jesus' welcoming of the little children.[124] For Calvin, baptism, like circumcision, was a sign of the covenant.

Reformation views on confirmation were quite mixed. On one extreme were those who rejected confirmation entirely. The Anabaptist insistence on believers' baptism obviated the need for it. In this they were followed by the Mennonites, Amish, Hutterites, and American Baptists. Zwingli also rejected confirmation because it was not instituted by Christ.[125] However, Calvin took quite a different view. Purged of medieval superstition, he believed that it could play a useful role in the spiritual development of those baptized as infants. He saw the need for "a catechetical exercise, in which children or youths [would] deliver an account of their faith in the presence of the Church."[126] In this matter Calvin may well have been influenced by the late medieval reformers, John Wycliffe

(1320–1384) and Jan Hus (1373–1415), and their followers among the Bohemian Brethren.[127] However, it is largely through Calvin that adolescent confirmation as a supplement or completion of infant baptism took root in so many post-Reformation churches. Although some in the twentieth century have concluded that the theology of confirmation is confused, it continues to be regarded by many as a necessary adjunct to the practice of infant baptism.

The Council of Trent

The Reformation began with Luther's attack on the selling of indulgences. It soon focused on two principles: salvation is solely dependent on God, and grace is available only to those who are right minded. In the light of these two principles, much of medieval thinking seemed flawed. In addition, since the Reformers thought that a good deal of medieval tradition was false to Scripture, a radical rethinking of the essentials of the Gospel had to be attempted. This rethinking led, as we have seen, to a rejection of much of the medieval sacramental theory.

In order to meet these criticisms, the Pope called a council. The council first met in Bologna, but was later transferred to Trent and came to be known as the Council of Trent. In its three sessions, which met from 1547 to 1562, it took up all the major areas of controversy. While the debate was wide ranging, and some present hoped to embrace several of the Reformers' positions, the mood was defensive and conservative. Most of the resulting decrees reflected medieval thinking.

This conservatism was especially prominent in discussions of the sacraments. Trent not only reaffirmed the number of the sacraments as seven, but also asserted that they were all instituted by Christ. Marriage might seem to be the most difficult one to meet this test. To support the contention that it was every bit as much a sacrament as were baptism and the Eucharist, the council appealed to the authority of Jesus and Paul, first to Christ's presence at the wedding in Cana, and then to the fact that Paul spoke of marriage as a "mystery," translating this latter word in the manner of the early Church as "sacrament" while assuming that the early Church

Fathers gave the word all of its medieval significance. Against several of the Reformers, Trent asserted that baptism was a means of regeneration from original sin as well as a gift of the Holy Spirit and an incorporation into the body of Christ.

As for the Eucharist, the council insisted that it be regarded as a propitiatory sacrifice on behalf of the living and the dead, a very important disagreement with the Reformers, all of whom had rejected this notion. Is the Eucharist a continuation of the Incarnation, as several of the Reformers taught, or is it primarily a continuation of Christ's sacrifice, the view favored at Trent? To put it another way, does this rite focus on presence and communion, or on immolation and oblation? Trent made it clear that it regarded the Eucharist as a real sacrifice, and not just a Holy Communion. "If any one saith, that in the mass a true and proper sacrifice is not offered to God; or, that to be offered is nothing else but that Christ is given us to eat: let him be anathema."[128]

Consistent with its conservatism, Trent also insisted on transubstantiation as the true account of Christ's presence in the Eucharist. Certainly the notion of a sacrifice coheres comfortably with the idea of a substantial presence. If the bread and wine have become the body and blood of Christ, then it can be said more easily that Christ is truly offered in the Mass for the sins of the world. The Reformers had no need of the transubstantiation theory since Christ's presence as holy food needed only a spiritual or nonphysical presence. In Calvin's thinking, it was sufficient to have a "sacramental conjunction" between the bread and wine and Christ in a "dynamic presence."

Trent and the Passion

The Reformers understood the medieval position to be that each Mass was a new sacrifice in addition to the sacrifice on Calvary. As already noted, their study of the Epistle to the Hebrews led them to several passages that seemed to contradict the medieval notion. In Hebrews Christ's sacrificial death is called "the offering of the body of Jesus Christ once for all" (Heb. 10:10). Furthermore, that death is a full and sufficient sacrifice. "For by a single offering" continues

Hebrews, "he has perfected for all time those who are sanctified" (Heb. 10:14). In meeting this Scriptural challenge, the Council of Trent said that the Reformers misunderstood the nature of the eucharistic sacrifice. Like St. Thomas Aquinas, the council denied that each Mass constituted a new sacrifice and said it was simply the reactualization at another time of the original sacrifice on the cross. The Mass "surely cannot be either an independent addition to that of Golgotha or its intrinsic complement; it can only be the one self-same sacrifice of the Cross."[129] Trent explains the grounds for this identity through the identity of the victim. "For the victim is one and the same, . . . the manner alone of offering being different."[130] It further argued that since each Mass participated in the sacrifice on Calvary, it also participated in Calvary's propitiation and expiation.

But how was what Christ did at the Last Supper related to his sacrifice? Was the Supper a sacrifice in its own right, or was it merely a symbolic calling to mind of the death on the cross? The delegates wished to affirm that in the Last Supper Jesus offered himself. However, they believed that the offering in the Last Supper was not merely, as the Protestants held, Christ's offering of himself to his disciples in a holy communion, but rather had a propitiatory character. But how could this notion be explained? Two possibilities presented themselves. It might be said that the Last Supper was itself a sacrifice to God and that the propitiatory character of the offering of the Mass was somehow grounded in what Christ did in the Supper. Alternatively, it might be said that the Last Supper was one part of a sacrificial action that found its culmination and completion at Calvary. While the Decrees of the council do not explicitly favor one or the other of these possibilities, several delegates favored the second alternative during the debate preceding the final formulations. For example, Caspar de Casala, the Bishop of Leiria, following the lead of St. Thomas Aquinas,[131] argued that Christ perfected his passion in several stages, of which the Supper was an intermediate and the Cross a final stage.[132] Thus he argued that the Supper and Cross were parts of a larger sacrificial action. The other alternative, that the Supper itself was a sacrificial action, gained increasing favor in the years between Trent and Vatican II.

Roman Catholic Eucharistic Theology between Trent and Vatican II

Between Trent and the mid-twentieth-century Second Vatican Council there was little change in Roman Catholic or Protestant thinking on baptism. However, there was considerable discussion in Roman Catholic circles with respect to the Eucharist, in which attempts were made to expand and make more explicit the implications of Trent's theology. Roman Catholics continued to affirm that the Mass was a propitiatory sacrifice. They stressed the idea that Roman Catholic priests were different from Protestant ministers in that they were specifically ordained to a sacrificial priesthood.[133] Furthermore, some theologians coupled the sacrificial priesthood with the requirement for a celibate clergy. Noting that Old Testament law required of its priests a period of sexual abstinence before they were permitted to sacrifice (Lev. 22:3, 15:2), these theologians argued that this requirement was most fully observed in a celibate priesthood. Finally, they saw the Last Supper as itself a sacrifice. "The Mass," said one theologian, "is nothing else than a continual repetition, commanded by Christ Himself, of the Sacrifice accomplished at the Last Supper."[134]

The case for regarding the Last Supper itself as a propitiatory sacrifice was grounded in the designation in the Epistle to the Hebrews of Christ as a "priest forever after the order of Melchisedech" (Heb. 5:10).[135] Noting that Melchisedech, the priest-king of Salem, greeted Abraham with an offering of bread and wine, it was affirmed at Trent that Melchisedech here acted in his priestly role and that this offering foreshadowed Christ's offering of bread and wine.[136] However, to many Roman Catholics, Trent failed to explain how the Last Supper was a propitiatory sacrifice because it did not take a stand on whether or not Christ could be said to have died at the Supper. This issue had been raised at Trent in the form of one of the questions set forth for debate (question 12 of the 1562 Sessions) but was not commented upon in the Canons and Decrees. After Trent various theories were advanced to defend the idea that in the Last Supper Christ died a sacrificial death. Some identified the death with the act of communion, the eating of the body of Christ by the priest; others identified it with the act of consecration, the moment that the bread and wine became the body and blood of Christ.[137] To the theologian Joseph Pohle, writing in 1911, neither of these views seemed wholly satisfactory. The communion theory seemed odd because it located the sacrificial death inside the body of the celebrant and not on the altar. The consecration theory seemed to confuse creation with destruction, for in the moment of transubstantiation Christ's body is not destroyed, but created. Pohle favored the view that identified the death of Christ in the Supper with the separation of Christ's blood from his body, a separation that ensures the death of the victim. He grounded the separation on the fact that at the Supper Christ consecrated the bread as his body, and the wine as his blood in two separate blessings. Indeed, he argued "the double consecration is an essential element of the Mass as . . . sacrifice."[138]

Protestant Developments

Reformation thinking about the Eucharist shaped Protestant discussions for two hundred and fifty years. However, toward the end of the eighteenth century a new element influenced Protestant thinking—Immanuel Kant's critique of metaphysics. This important development in the history of thought reinforced the Protestant rejection of transubstantiation and the idea of the Mass as sacrifice. As to the first, the medieval explanation of the conversion of the bread and the wine in terms of the categories of substance and accident was rendered ineffective because Protestants now rejected the metaphysics in which these categories are rooted. Second, Kant's critique reinforced their rejection of Roman Catholic views of the Mass. Protestants regarded as an "evasive suggestion"[139] Trent's claim that each Mass was but an extension of the original sacrifice on Calvary on the grounds that at Calvary and on each altar "the body was the same." Without the substance/accident metaphysic, there was no way to ground the claim that they were identical.

Rather than grounding Christian doctrine in metaphysics, men like Friedrich Schleiermacher sought to base a coherent theory of the Lord's Supper on the Protestant conviction that it is a communion with Christ in feeling or experience. "Our paragraphs," begins his discussion of the Lord's Supper, "ought in every case to contain simply the expression of our Christian consciousness."[140] In other words, the discussion ought to grow out of the experience of "the fellowship of each soul with Christ" and "the fellowship of believers with each other."[141] It is in this connection that we are to understand the words of institution, "This is my body; this is my blood." These words signify a self-giving which is one with "the whole redeeming love of Christ."[142] Hence, in partaking of the supper, we experience "a repeated nourishing of personal spiritual life out of the fullness of Christ's life."[143]

To be sure, Christ's nourishing life can sustain us apart from the bread and wine. But this fact does not render them less effective as instruments of Christ's presence. Bread and wine, "linked together by the Word,"[144] provide "a new influx of living spiritual power out of Christ's fullness."[145] In this way, they convey special graces to the recipients.

The Ecumenical and Liturgical Movements

Recent thinking about the sacraments has been profoundly influenced by two twentieth-century events—the flowering of the Ecumenical Movement and its counterpart the Liturgical Movement. We shall discuss the Ecumenical Movement in some detail in the next chapter on the Church and the ministry, but a brief mention of it here will help to explain the direction of sacramental thinking.

The nineteenth century was a century of worldwide missionary expansion. It was among these mission churches that the Protestant impetus for church unification saw its first real stirring. One result of the feeling that denominational competition was becoming futile, at least in the mission field, was the development of the Faith and Order Movement, which was later reconstituted as a Commission of the World Council of Churches at its First Assembly in Amsterdam in 1948. This Commission met from time to time to work on issues of ecumenical interest—in particular, issues concerning the Church, the ministry, and the sacraments. Its work culminated in a document entitled *Baptism, Eucharist, and Ministry,* which was given its final form at a meeting in Lima, Peru in 1982.

written
by
S. Wainwright.

This document provides a convenient summary of much of the sacramental thinking of the twentieth century.

In the meanwhile, concerns with sacramental theology emerged among Roman Catholics in what came to be called the Liturgical Movement. Its beginnings have been traced to France, in the refounding of the monastery at Solesmes by Guéranger in 1832. A second phase of the movement began in Belgium, when Dom Lambert Beauduin called for a revitalization of the liturgical practices of the church at a Congress in Malines in 1909. In Germany a similar agenda to invigorate church life and liturgy was adopted at Maria Laach, under the leadership of Abbot Herwegen. [146]

The impetus behind the Liturgical Movement was deeply devout. We have already noted[147] how the nineteenth-century revival of interest in worship complemented and reinforced the stress on religious experience as the foundation of the spiritual life. It was in worship that God's presence seemed most palpable. Ideally the individual at prayer would be swept away from the petty concerns of ordinary life and would, for a moment at least, be transformed in mind and spirit. There true joy was to be found.

It is no wonder that the Liturgical Movement soon reached out to the wider Christian community, since Christians of other denominations shared the desire to strengthen Christian worship, especially eucharistic worship. Scholars of many denominations began to work on various aspects of liturgy. Many of them knew each other and closely followed each other's works. These included Biblical studies and studies of doctrine as well as music and conduct of the service. It was in this atmosphere that Pope John XXIII (1958–1963) called the Second Vatican Council, which met from 1962 to 1965. At the council, the Roman Catholic church turned from an attitude of isolation to one of engagement with other Christian groups and the world. The willingness expressed at the council to reopen old issues that had divided Christians for centuries and to develop a fresh approach bore immediate fruit in the establishment of several Bilateral Consultations with other denominations— Anglican, Lutheran, Methodist, and Reformed. All of these consultations discussed baptism and the Eucharist as well as other matters of concern. Often a substantial measure of agreement was reached, at least among the participants. However, as we shall see, many issues and problems have lingered to dash the hopes of those who want to see organic union, or at least universal intercommunion, achieved in the near future.

Baptism and Confirmation in Contemporary Discussion

Protestant ecumenical discussions have revealed a large measure of agreement concerning baptism. The section on baptism approved in the report of the Faith and Order Commission of the World Council of Churches at Lima in 1982 is fairly typical. That the authors reaffirmed the Biblical understanding of baptism is revealed in its section headings: Participation in Christ's Death and Resurrection; Conversion, Pardon, and Cleansing; The Gift of the Spirit; Incorporation into the Body of Christ; and The Sign of the Kingdom (which anticipates the time when all peoples will be united in their recognition of Jesus as Lord). However, there still remain areas of profound disagreement. One such area concerns whether infants ought to be baptized, or whether baptism ought to be restricted to those who have made a profession of faith. A second area of disagreement concerns baptism and original sin. Is baptism a rite of forgiveness, removing only the taint or stain of actual sins, or does it remove original sin by a process of regeneration? Both of these issues have divided Christians for centuries.

To these two, we might add a third issue—the relationship of baptism to confirmation. The Lima report noted that at the present time there are three types of practice. First, there is the Baptist model. Baptism is administered only after a personal profession of faith; a rite of confirmation is deemed superfluous. Second, there is the Eastern Orthodox model. In the belief that the Holy Spirit is fully given in baptism and the accompanying anointing with chrism, infant baptism is the rule. Children receive communion at an early age, and there is no additional rite of confirmation. Finally, there is the process model. Here baptism is administered at an early age followed later by personal confession and commitment. The commitment is normally solemnized at confirmation.[148] Sometimes the person is admitted to communion before confirmation and sometimes after.[149]

These are still "burning issues."[150] Can we say anything that may help to resolve them? As we have seen, Luther, Calvin, and Zwingli all feared that the denial of infant baptism and the insistence on believers' baptism could easily lead to a new kind of works righteousness. What was needed, they thought, was a recognition of the priority and prevenience of God's grace (the objective side of the sacrament) as distinguished from the subjective side of the sacrament (the human response to that offer of grace). In contrast, the Baptist and Anabaptist traditions have always feared that too much stress on the objective side of the sacrament could lead to a quasimagical concept of grace. Both of these dangers are avoided in the process model described above. There, both the priority and prevenience of God's grace and the personal confession and commitment of the individual are given liturgical and ritualistic expression—the former in infant baptism and the latter at confirmation. It is perhaps for this reason that the process model grew in favor among Protestants during the nineteenth century.[151]

However, this practice has been questioned in recent times because it has usually been linked to the view that the gift of the Spirit is given in confirmation while the grace of baptism is confined to the regeneration from sin. The Scriptural justification for this interpretation is the story in Acts, in which the believers in Samaria had "only been baptized in the name of the Lord Jesus," but when Peter and John came and laid their hands upon them "they received the Holy Spirit" (8:14–17). Earlier in the chapter we noted that this passage from Acts is atypical and that the understanding of the majority of New Testament and early Church writings is that the Spirit is given at baptism, thereby seeming to remove the rationale for confirmation.[152] But this seems an unnecessary conclusion. There is no need to deny the gifts of the Spirit in baptism in order to find a place for them in confirmation, nor to deny them in confirmation in order to ensure their place in baptism. After all, the New Testament often speaks of gifts of the Spirit apart from baptism, as does the theological tradition when it recognizes ordination and penance as sacraments or sacramental rites. Moreover, while the Spirit is given at baptism, strengthening gifts of the Spirit are often mediated to us through a variety of occasions, including solemn ritual occasions.

The last area of disagreement concerning baptism involves the washing away of original sin, the traditional justification for infant baptism. At the Reformation, most Protestant groups concluded that baptism did not remove original sin. It did not restore human beings to the perfection Adam and Eve had before the fall. Experience taught that the effects of the fall, the tendency to selfishness and egoism, remain after baptism. However, the Reformers also believed that baptism could begin a process whereby the self-centering dispositions could be gradually dissipated. They believed that the candidate, by being made a member of the Christian community, was brought into a special environment. Ideally, those baptized as children, growing up in the community of faith, will have the grace of God mediated to them by their parents and the Church, and will be immersed in the life of the Gospel, thereby undercutting the negative inheritances that encourage self-centeredness. Recent thinking about both baptism and original sin has narrowed the gap betweeen the heirs of the Reformation and those who stress the radical effects of baptism on the candidate. Modern formulations of the doctrine of original sin still speak of inherited dispositions to sin. However, these are taken to be not the results of a fall from a state of perfection, but the products of our evolutionary or cultural inheritance, or perhaps even of our finitude.[153] If the need is not the restoration of a lost excellence but the overcoming of a natural condition, then it seems plausible that the perfecting of human life is accomplished only gradually. In these circumstances, it makes good sense to regard baptism as initiating a process of overcoming the egoism and selfishness that are the effects of original sin, rather than completely removing them. The gap then between those who think of the grace of baptism as regeneration from the effects of original sin and those who stress the importance of becoming a member of the Church at baptism is dramatically reduced.

Rethinking the Eucharistic Presence

The Eucharist has become a central focus of contemporary Protestant discussion in large measure because its celebration has become increasingly frequent. In the eighteenth century, almost all Protestant churches celebrated the Eucharist only three or four times a year. While even today this practice still continues in some congregations, monthly, if not weekly, celebrations are becoming the rule. With the revolution in piety, encouraged in large part by the Liturgical Movement, the theology of the Lord's Supper has again become a central concern. The historic controversies over presence and sacrifice have continued to be at the heart of contemporary discussions. Since almost all traditions have affirmed that Christ is present in some manner in the Eucharist, we will begin our discussion with the nature of the presence. What is striking about the bilateral reports is the manner in which the traditional vocabulary has been avoided. Words like "transubstantiation" and "consubstantiation," so prominent in sixteenth-century polemic, and "receptionism" and "virtualism," later adopted as descriptive of sixteenth-century positions, hardly appear. The Final Report of the Anglican Roman Catholic International Commission, commonly called The Windsor Statement, is typical. "Communion with Christ in the eucharist presupposes his true presence, effectually signified by the bread and wine which, in this mystery, become his body and blood." At this point appears a note on "transubstantiation," which "should be seen as affirming the *fact* of Christ's presence and of the mysterious and radical change which takes place. In contemporary Roman Catholic theology it is not understood as explaining *how* the change takes place."[154] A similar point was made earlier in the joint Lutheran–Roman Catholic statement.[155]

What lay behind these statements was a growing dissatisfaction on the part of many Roman Catholic theologians with the substance/accident metaphysics inherited from the Middle Ages.[156] If this metaphysics was unsatisfactory, an alternative account of Christ's presence in the Eucharist was needed. Roman Catholic theologians began to search for new ways to express their conviction of an objective reality, and a variety of proposals were made. Edward Schillebeeckx spoke of the Eucharist as "an encounter" with Christ.[157] For Odo Casel, the operative idea was "mystery," expressing as it does the hidden yet manifest character of God. Just as God communicates himself to us in Christ, so in the Eucharist Christ gives himself as "a presence of power, a dynamic presence."[158] Echoing the opening verses of John's Gospel, Louis Bouyer described Christ as "the Word of God," God's dynamic Son active in the world as creator and revealer. It is as this active Word that Christ is present in the Eucharist. "The whole reality of the eucharist proceeds from the one divine Word, uttered in the Son, who gives us his flesh to eat and his blood to drink."[159]

While each of these views intends to affirm an objective presence without exclusive dependence on the doctrine of transubstantiation, they leave unclear the relationship of Christ's presence to the bread and the wine. All three of the views are consistent with Calvin's sacramental conjunction and Luther's consubstantiation, and even Trent's transubstantiation is not specifically ruled out. It was to address this issue, the relationship of Christ to the bread and wine, and to affirm a more Catholic position that spoke of an ontological change of the bread and wine, that J. de Baciocchi spoke of a "transfunctionalisation, transfinalisation, and transsignification" of the eucharistic elements.[160] By this he meant that the bread and wine undergo a change of being since they are given new functions, purpose, and meaning. A whole group of theologians began to explore the implications of these new ideas.

It should surprise no one, however, that some people fear that such statements ignore important issues and concerns. Transubstantiation still mattered to Pope Paul VI (1963–1978), who in his encyclical *Mysterium Fidei* (1965) found words like "transignification" and "transfinalization" to be unsatisfactory. Rather then preserving an objectivist perspective, they seemed to focus only on what the bread and wine mean to us at the moment. To Paul VI, "transignification" and "transfinalization" seemed to signal only a subjective change in human consciousness and not a real change in the bread and wine. He reemphasized Trent and its dogma as a way of explaining as well as affirming the real presence.[161] In this the Pope was but one of a number of influential thinkers in all communions who found the older terminology to their satisfaction even when they disagreed among themselves about the correct understanding of the Eucharist.

Those who agree with the thrust of the more contemporary formulations have not yet provided a persuasive theological justification for them. As a start in that direction, let us begin by reexamining the views classified as objective. As noted above, there are three basic positions. First, there is the view called transubstantiation in which it is affirmed that the substance of the bread and wine are converted into the substance of the body and blood of Christ. Second, there is the view that no change of substance takes place in the bread and wine, but that Christ is substantially present under or along with the bread and wine (consubstantiation). Third, there is the view that Christ is virtually present or "dynamically present," that is, present in power and effect in a spiritual or noncorporeal way. Here the bread and wine are seen as divinely chosen instruments for mediating Christ's presence. Still, the following question presses on us: Is the *presence* affirmed in each theory really different, or do the theories under scrutiny amount to the same thing? When their meanings are closely examined, "the dividing-lines between the old doctrines are becoming more and more difficult to trace."[162]

Let us first look at transubstantiation versus consubstantiation. There is an important difference between these two theories, but the difference has to do with what happens to the bread and wine and does not affect the description of Christ's presence. In both views, the kind of presence affirmed is a nonempirical and noncorporeal one. In both views, the substance of Christ's body is said to be present without its accidents, that is, without color, weight, taste, size, smell, etc. That a noncorporeal presence is being affirmed is made clear by the fact that the whole undivided Christ is said to be present under each of the species of bread and wine and to be present on many altars at the same time. This idea St. Thomas brought home with the words, "In no sense is the body of Christ to be pinned down to a place in this sacrament." Thus there seems to be no important difference between the manner of Christ's presence in transubstantiation or consubstantiation. Still, there may be a real difference between these accounts of Christ's presence and the spiritual or dynamic account favored by Calvin and by much of Cranmer's writing. We shall argue that there is not.

The problem that Calvin and Cranmer faced was to understand how Christ's body could be in heaven and at the same time on the many eucharistic tables on earth. The only way they could explain this paradox was to say that the presence was a spiritual one. In spite of some Roman Catholic misunderstandings,[163] "spiritual" here does not mean figurative or metaphorical but rather "real," "nonempirical," and "noncorporeal." For example, Calvin wrote:

> Even though it seems unbelievable that Christ's flesh, separated from us by such great distance, penetrates to us, so that it becomes

our food, let us remember how far the secret power of the Holy Spirit towers above all our senses. [164]

He later explained that the flesh can reach us because it does so in a noncorporeal way. Describing the heavenly kingdom where Christ sits at the right hand of God, Calvin continues:

> This Kingdom is neither bounded by location in space nor circumscribed by any limits. Thus Christ is not prevented from exerting his power wherever he pleases, in heaven and on earth. He shows his presence in power and strength, is always among his own people, and breathes his life upon them, and lives in them, sustaining them, strengthening, quickening, keeping them unharmed, as if he were present in the body. In short, he feeds his people with his own body, the communion of which he bestows upon them by the power of his Spirit. In this manner, the body and blood of Christ are shown to us in the Sacrament. [165]

By the action of the Holy Spirit, Christ is present in a noncorporeal way, a way that transcends space and time, in short, a spiritual presence, just as in transubstantiation and consubstantiation. In modern times, the idea of a spiritual presence has strong appeal to those who no longer regard heaven as a place nor view Christ's resurrected body as being made up of physical parts. For Calvin, heaven was still a location and Christ's resurrected body an empirical object. But for those for whom heaven is not a locality, nor Christ's resurrected state a corporeal entity, the idea of a spiritual presence in the Eucharist seems an obvious conclusion and in no way lessens the reality of Christ's presence.

Finally, we should say something about the relationship between Christ's presence and the bread and wine. All objectivists speak of the bread and wine as the body and blood of Christ. In what sense are they that body? In each of the three objectivist accounts, the connection between the bread and wine and the body and blood is an extrinsic and not an intrinsic one. That is, the bread and the wine are not related to the body and blood as a heart is to an animal or even as a hand is to a body; rather, they are related in the way in which tools are related to a hand. That the relationship is external and extrinsic is immediately apparent for the theories that reject the doctrine of transubstantiation, maintaining that the bread and wine remain in their integrity; in consubstantiation and in Calvin's

dynamic view, the relationship is not an intrinsic or inherent connection but a conjunction or association. But the relationship is also
extrinsic for the doctrine of transubstantiation. St. Thomas illustrates this point nicely. As noted above, he denied that the body and
blood of Christ are new subjects in which the accidents of the bread
and wine inhere. By divine power the accidents of the bread and
wine are kept in existence standing free of any substance.[166] The
remnants of the bread and wine are thus no more closely connected
to the body and blood in St. Thomas' view than in Luther's consubstantiation or Calvin's dynamic view. In all these views the visible
bread and wine are only functionally Christ's body and blood, that
is, they are instruments chosen by Christ to carry on his work in
the world.[167] We have, therefore, good reason to conclude that the
three objectivist theories of Christ's presence converge and are
essentially the same.

Subjectivist Views Reconsidered

Whereas objectivist views propose that our realization of Christ's
presence at the Eucharist is mediated to us by some aspect of his
being—the substance of his body and blood (Luther) or his life-
giving power (Calvin)—subjectivists deny that his presence is con-
veyed in this way. Rather, they affirm that Christ is present because we have him in mind. Christ's presence is thus identical to
some state of consciousness—to remembering him or believing in
him. These memories need not be pale shadows, but can be vivid,
powerful, and transforming states of mind, as many eucharistic
mystics have attested. Subjectivist views are devoid of metaphysical
postulates and exhibit such common sense that they appeal to many
Christians today. This fact suggests that a reconsideration of subjectivist views might prove fruitful.

We begin such a reconsideration by asking whether there is a
real distinction between the main subjectivist views proposed since
the Reformation—Zwingli's view and the Baptist view. Both views
rely on collective memory, but ostensibly on different memories.
We can distinguish three possible memories: the Supper itself, the
cross and passion, and finally the command issued at the Supper,
"Do this in remembrance of me." Although these memories can be

distinguished, they all are indissolubly interconected and merge
into one another; on reflection there appears to be no real difference
between Zwingli's view and the apparently more extreme American
Baptist view. Baptists assert that we ought to celebrate the Eucharist solely because Christ commanded it. However, in order to carry
out the command, we must be mindful of it. Yet we do not just call
it to mind, but call it to mind in the context in which it was uttered,
at the Last Supper itself; and in calling to mind the Supper, we
cannot ignore the context in which the Supper took place, the
passion and Christ's death on the cross. In keeping the commandment, then, we are drawn into the whole series of events of which
the Lord's Supper is but a part. We are there, and Christ is here in
our lives, with us and in us. The interconnection of the various
memories makes it impossible for one to operate without the other.
Thus the Baptist view cannot be understood apart from the wider
context provided in Zwingli's view and in the end fosters the same
state of mind. In keeping Christ's commands, Baptists too rejoice in
a lively sense of his presence in their lives.

While it may be possible to resolve the apparent conflicts within
both the objectivist and subjectivist views, it seems evident that
these two types of views cannot be reduced to a common core. To be
sure, in both types Christ's presence is a spiritual and not a corporeal one. His continuing presence on earth transcends both space
and time. But still an important difference remains. In subjectivist
views, the sense of Christ's presence is thought to be a mental
creation. We create a kind of mental picture of him as we call him
to mind. In objectivist views, a real and living Christ confronts us
from outside. Experientially this difference can be made clear with
an example. After the death of a loved one, some people report that
they have a sense of a real presence. The loved one seems near at
hand, just as she did in life. Others, however, have a sense of a real
absence. The loved one is called to mind, but she is no longer felt to
be nearby. *Is that really an analogy?*

Memory functions in different ways, which fact further exemplifies the difference between subjectivist and objectivist views. A
memory is often a kind of re-creation. An object destroyed long ago
is brought to mind and in this way given a new lease on life. For
skeptics who believe that Christ's death on the cross was the end of
his existence, or for those like Zwingli who believe that Christ is

Time as important as Space.

now ascended into heaven and is unable to appear here on earth, our collective memories of him must also be re-creations of someone who is no longer present. But for those who are open to the possibility that Christ may appear to them as a living reality, a memory need not be a reconstruction, but can be an avenue of awareness. This difference can be made clear by two examples. I find a picture of a grade school teacher whom I have not seen since childhood. I call something of her to mind, but it is a struggle and I suspect that my "memories" are as much a present creation as they are veridical recollections. Now contrast this with another event. I am musing about my old teacher when a person comes into the room and stands near me. At first I do not recognize her, but I gradually become aware that she is the teacher about whom I have just been thinking. I move over to her and shake her hand and realize that I could not have recognized her had I not very recently called her to mind. Memory here is not the exclusive content of the awareness, but an avenue of awareness. Without the memories, I would not have known who she is; with the memories, she is no longer a stranger.

Of these two accounts of memory, the second better reflects many believers' grasp of Christ's presence in the Eucharist. In the New Testament, the story of the disciples on the road to Emmaus (Luke 24:13–35) exhibits this same structure. Two disciples walked along a road when they were joined by a stranger. In the process of the conversation, they rehearsed the recent events in Jerusalem at the time when Jesus was crucified. They also talked about the meaning of the Scripture from Moses to the Prophets. At supper, against this background, they came to recognize that this stranger was Jesus himself. Christ was there all the time, but they recognized him only after their memories had been refreshed. Here again memory was not the content of the awareness, but the doorway to awareness. Christ's risen self transcends space and time and yet is ever near to us waiting to be recognized—a recognition that can be triggered by our collective memories of him.

The Eucharist as Sacrifice

In addition to the continuing controversy over the manner of Christ's presence in the Eucharist, the other main area of current disagreement concerns the sacrificial aspect of the Eucharist. Medieval thinkers described each Mass as a propitiatory sacrifice, while the Reformers rejected this doctrine as contrary to the teaching of the Epistle to the Hebrews, which spoke of Christ's death on Calvary, as the one, perfect, and sufficient sacrifice for the sins of the world. Following St. Thomas Aquinas, the Council of Trent sought to resolve the apparent contradiction between Hebrews and the medieval tradition by teaching that each Mass, although separate in space and time, was really identical with the sacrifice on Calvary. There matters have stood until quite recently. Roman Catholics took their stand on Trent; and, like Schleiermacher, most Protestants regarded Trent's teaching as an evasion. Still, some notion of sacrifice was an important part of Protestant thinking, as Melancthon remarked in the *Apology of the Augsburg Confession.*

> We are perfectly willing for the Mass to be understood as a daily sacrifice, provided this means the whole Mass, the ceremony and also the proclamation of the Gospel, faith, prayer, and thanksgiving. Taken together, these are the daily sacrifice of the New Testament.[168]

Most Protestants were content to see the Eucharist as a sacrificial offering of themselves in praise and thanksgiving. Of course Roman Catholics did not deny this idea, but added to it the further claim that Christ himself was offered on each altar.

What is striking about the present ecumenical conversations is the attempt to break out of this deadlock by finding a different way to explain how our offering is to be identified with Christ's offering of himself on Calvary. To this end The Windsor Statement affirmed, "The Church's offering of herself is caught up into his [Christ's] one offering."[169] Our sacrifice of praise and thanksgiving is taken by Christ and offered to God as part of his offering. Bishop Alan Clark, who headed the Roman Catholic delegation that produced The Windsor Statement, explained, "The Commission wishes to underline that we do not offer ourselves apart from Christ, but 'enter into the movement of his self offering'—for he alone is the ever acceptable Victim to the Father."[170]

In understanding The Windsor Statement it is helpful to relate the idea of the eucharistic sacrifice to the work of salvation. One possibility is to look at the relationship as part and whole. As St. Thomas urged that we see the Last Supper as a stage in Christ's passion that reached its culmination and completion on Calvary, so we should see the passion as a stage or part of the divine plan for the world. Thus the Incarnation, the teaching and healing ministry, the Last Supper, death on Calvary, the resurrection, and the intercessory prayer of the ascended Jesus are parts of one total, complete, and unreserved dedication to the Father. This unqualified and comprehensive commitment to God's will for the salvation of the world constituted Christ's sacrifice at its deepest level. This is what Thomas à Kempis meant when he said, "All Christ's life was a sacrifice and a martyrdom." If Christ's sacrifice embraces the whole of his saving activity, then St. Thomas' definition of sacrifice as involving the death or substantive alteration of the victim is too narrow. A broader understanding of sacrifice as dedication and costly offering, sometimes including but not limited to the death of the victim, is the more satisfactory account.

These considerations provide a background for the idea expressed in The Windsor Statement that in heaven Christ unites in one great sacrifice the several offerings he made and continues to make on earth. That great offering includes the offering of his body once made on the cross. It includes his continuing oblation of his body the Church, and so it also includes the sacrifices all Christians make when they dedicate themselves to God's service. Finally, the one great sacrifice includes Christ's offering of his body and blood in communion whereby he draws us ever closer to himself in order that we may continue his life of self-dedication. In this notion we find many elements of the tradition drawn together into a unified and coherent whole. And because they are drawn together, each has a significance it does not have separately. Here we find a unity of conception that includes Scripture and the thinking of the Fathers and the Reformers. In the Epistle to the Hebrews, Christ, the High Priest, is described as offering himself on Calvary "once to bear the sins of many" (9:28). He continues his role as High Priest by entering the Holiest of Holies, not "a sanctuary made with hands, a copy of the true one, but into heaven itself, now to appear in the presence of God on our behalf" (Heb. 9:24). Ambrose seems to have had a part of this unified concept in mind when he spoke of Christ as eternally making his sacrifice in heaven. Augustine had

another element of it in mind when he wrote that we see ourselves
there on the altar in the offering of bread and wine, and Cranmer
another part when he described, in the Book of Common Prayer,
the Eucharist as an offering of "ourselves, our souls and bodies, to
be a reasonable, holy, and living sacrifice." The Windsor Statement
synthetizes all these traditional elements.

In spite of its virtues, The Windsor Statement seems unduly
complex and overly subtle. Doubts about it were expressed in the
report of the *Anglican–Lutheran International Conversations*. There
it was noted:

> Many Anglicans and some Lutherans believe that in the Eucharist
> the Church's offering of herself is caught up in his [Christ's] one
> offering. Other Anglicans and many Lutherans do not employ the
> concept of sacrifice in this way.[171]

Similarly, the agreed statement of the Roman Catholic/Lutheran
World Federation records that Evangelical Lutherans still prefer
"to avoid even today any mention of 'sacrifice of the Mass'"[172]
because it seems to support the idea that the priest has special
sacrificial powers and to undermine the role of all the faithful in the
eucharistic celebration. Other Protestant groups have also expressed their own reservations. Methodists fear that our inclusion
in Christ's self-offering

> would imply that Christ is still being sacrificed. . . . Methodists
> prefer to say that Christ has offered one sacrifice for sins and now
> lives to make intercession for us, so that we in union with him can
> offer ourselves to the Father making his sacrificial death our only
> plea.[173]

There have been reservations, though of a different sort, in the
Roman Catholic church at the highest level. Although Pope John
Paul II has consistently written of the eucharistic sacrifice as the
Church's sharing in Christ's self-offering, in the letter *Dominicae
Cenae* he also insisted on a fundamental distinction between the
offering of the priest and the offering of the congregation. The
priest's is the true sacrificial offering and the people's a subjective
one, in mind and heart only,[174] thus confirming the fears of the
Evangelical Lutherans mentioned above. Furthermore, in this

same letter the Pope put special stress on sacrifice as propitiatory,[175] a notion bound to alarm the churches nurtured by the
Reformation.

Conclusion

In spite of the tremendous progress that has been made toward
union, deep cleavages remain and many issues are unsettled. While
perhaps no longer mistrustful of each other's motives, many on all
sides are still apprehensive. Although areas of misunderstanding
have been cleared away and new possibilities of agreement have
been opened, several of the central concerns about baptism and the
Eucharist are unresolved. However, even if they were worked out
to the satisfaction of all, differences concerning the Church and the
ministry would need to be tackled. To some, these have seemed
even more difficult to resolve and demand even greater patience and
wisdom.

CHAPTER X

The Church and the Ministry

At the close of his earthly ministry, Jesus left behind a community of disciples and a band of apostles, chosen leaders for the community. He also left behind a body of teaching; the teachings were oral rather than written, entrusted for safekeeping to the community's memory. Hence, when the New Testament appeared as a written document, it was a product of the community as much as the community was a product of Christ's words. In the very early days the Church shaped the Scriptures; in later times the Church was shaped by the Scriptures.

From the first, the community was called *ecclesia,* and is so named in the Epistles of Paul and the Acts of the Apostles. In English we translate this term by the word "church." In the Septuagint, the Greek translation of the Hebrew Scriptures, the Jewish scribes used the word *ecclesia* to designate a congregation or assembly called together for religious purposes. Thus we read in Psalm 26:12, "In the great congregation I will bless the Lord." Although *ecclesia* soon dropped out of Jewish usage, the Christians continued to use it as the Septuagint had. In other respects as well the earliest Christian communities naturally followed Jewish precedents, since they saw themselves as Jews. For example, the early chapters of Acts record that the Jerusalem community worshiped regularly in the Temple. However, the Temple disappeared as a center of worship among Jews and Christians when it was destroyed by the Romans in reprisal for the 68–70 C.E. uprising and, along with the destruction of the Temple, the Jewish priesthood disappeared as a dominant force in religious life. No early Christian leader is recorded as having been a Temple functionary, and the religious training of the early Christian leadership seems to have occurred in the synagogues. In this situation, it was natural that Christians drew heavily from synagogue models and so organized their own communities with governing bodies of elders. The elders, also called presbyters (from the Greek word for elders, *presbuteroi*), constituted a local leadership that apparently functioned alongside the apostles, who Acts tells us were primarily traveling missionaries. Like Peter and Paul, the apostles established churches in various cities. Whether they usually appointed the elders or whether the elders were usually chosen by the local congregations is a matter of conjecture. Given the variety of practices revealed in the writings of the early second century, it is prudent to conclude that no single method of choice obtained in the local churches.

The Spirit-Filled Community

Continuity with Jewish institutions does not fully explain the emerging conception of the Church. Grounded in Jesus' promise of a New Convenant (Matt. 26:28; Mark 14:24; Luke 22:20), the Church soon saw itself as quite different from the synagogue. The synagogue was first and foremost a vehicle for instruction, a school. The faithful also gathered there for religious services on the Sabbath, but the teaching of the Law was its primary mission. However, from the beginning, the emerging Christian Church saw itself as a community energized by the Holy Spirit. This idea dominates the Acts of the Apostles, especially the early chapters. At a meeting on the feast of Pentecost, the Apostles were so "filled with the Holy Spirit" that they began to speak in tongues (Acts 2:4). The Holy Spirit is given to those who obey God (Acts 5:32). When Peter and John preached, "all [were] filled with the Holy Spirit and spoke the word of God with boldness" (Acts 4:31). Likewise, Stephen is said to speak with "wisdom and the Spirit" (Acts 6:10). Finally, the Apostles looked for men "full of the Spirit and of wisdom" (Acts 6:3) when they appointed assistants to aid them in their eucharistic ministry.

Paul also stressed the presence of the Spirit in Christian fellowship. The professions of faith made by Christians were said to be prompted by the Spirit. "No one can say 'Jesus is Lord' except by the Holy Spirit" (1 Cor. 12:3). Paul saw the Spirit as the source of the many gifts by which the Church was strengthened and advanced. The powers of healing, prophecy, wisdom, knowledge, the working of miracles, speaking in tongues, and the interpretation of tongues were all works of the Spirit (1 Cor. 12:8–11). Since apostolic times, there have been those who protested against conventional Christian life by appealing to New Testament accounts of charismatic gifts. Such protests often arise in times of crisis or despair. At such times these gifts of the Spirit have seemed to be signs of the New Age and portents of Christ's impending return. Their absence has been taken as a sign of apostasy.

The Church as the Body of Christ

In addition to speaking of the Church as the Spirit-filled community, Paul also described the Church as God's plantation (1 Cor. 3:6–9), as God's building, whose foundation is Christ (1 Cor. 3:9–15), as God's sanctuary (1 Cor. 3:16), as a new creation (2 Cor. 5:17), as the kingdom of God's beloved son (Col. 1:13), and as the bride of Christ (2 Cor. 11:2–3). Other descriptions are found scattered throughout the New Testament. The Church is called the pillar of truth (1 Tim. 3:15), God's flock (1 Pet. 5:2–3), God's people (1 Pet. 2:10), and God's household (Eph. 2:19), to name only a few.[1] Especially striking is Paul's metaphorical depiction of the Church as the body of Christ (Rom. 12:4–5; 1 Cor. 10:16–17, 12:12).

Paul's descriptions of the Church as Christ's mystical body and as the Spirit-filled community have been his most influential characterizations. Of course the two ideas can be united, since in another metaphor the Church can be described as the body of which the Spirit mediated through Christ is the animating principle. Whether this was in Paul's mind is difficult to say, since he nowhere makes this point explicitly. In the extended Pauline corpus, only Ephesians suggests this concept in its statement that "there is one body and one Spirit" (Eph. 4:4).[2] However, by combining the metaphor of the Church as the body of Christ with the idea of the Spirit mediated through Christ as its animating principle, it was natural that later thinkers developed the idea that the

Church is a continuation of Christ's Incarnation. Accordingly, the Church has been taken to be, like the Eucharist, a quasiphysical embodiment of Christ's continued presence in the world.

However, this view of the Church as the continuation of the Incarnation has tended to absolutize the institution and has sometimes been in conflict with the notion of the Church as the Spirit-filled community. Writing about 200, Irenaeus sought to integrate the two ideas by remarking, "Where the Church is, there is the Spirit of God; and where the Spirit of God is, there is the Church and all grace."[3] Many, however, have emphasized only one of Paul's descriptions of the true Church: Some, like Tertullian and the Montanists, emphasized the need for the manifest presence of the Spirit; others, following Cyprian, used the idea of all Christians as part of the same body to express institutional continuity with the apostolic community.[4]

The Ministry in the New Testament

As we have said, Jesus left behind not only a community, a church, but also a band of leaders. The Gospels call them *apostoloi* or "ambassadors" in the Greek usage of the time. In the New Testament the word "apostle" is not confined to the Twelve (Matt. 10:2–4); it is also used with a wider group of pioneer leaders, especially Paul, but also such people as Barnabas, Andronicus, and Junius, who were all commissioned to preach the gospel (Acts 14:14; Rom. 16:7; Gal. 1:1). In addition to the apostles, the New Testament also speaks of other forms and offices of ministry, for example, bishops, elders or presbyters, and deacons.

Several New Testament scholars detect a change of emphasis between the undoubted Epistles of Paul and the Epistle to the Ephesians, which is often credited to one of Paul's disciples.[5] In Galatians, Paul speaks of his call to be an Apostle as deriving from an inner revelation of Jesus directly to him (1:16–17). As we should expect, Christ is declared by Paul to be the foundation of the Christian community (1 Cor. 3:11). Later, Ephesians records a subtle shift from Christ to the Apostles as the Church's foundation; the Church is described as "built upon the foundation of the apostles and prophets, Christ Jesus himself being the cornerstone" (Eph.

2:20). As further evidence of a change, some scholars point to what appears to be an expanding institutionalization, which is manifested in a growing concern to clarify the relationship between the various ministerial offices.[6] For example, Paul speaks of "bishops and deacons" (Phil. 1:1) but not of "elders," and Acts uses "elders" (11:30), but not "bishops" and "deacons." The relationships between Acts' elders and Paul's bishops and deacons are unclear and the different responsibilities are not spelled out. Perhaps these were two separate ways of organizing ministerial responsibility—rule by a group of presbyters following the synagogue model, and the bishops and deacons expressing a different development in Hellenistic congregations.[7] However, by the early second century we find in the Pastoral Epistles, and especially in First Timothy, that the responsibilities of these ministers are described in much greater detail (3:1–13, 5:17–22). Here the first steps in combining the two models can be seen, though it is unclear just how this was accomplished. Some scholars believe that "bishop" and "elder" were different terms for the same office, while other scholars believe that the threefold ministry of bishops, presbyters, and deacons had already begun to take institutional shape.

The Ministry at the Turn of the First Century

Many students of the New Testament believe that the First Epistle to Timothy was not written until after the year 100.[8] This time frame would make it contemporaneous with a group of Christian writings that were widely respected in the early Christian community but did not find their way into the New Testament. These include: The Epistles of Ignatius of Antioch, The Didache (or Teaching of the Twelve Apostles), The Shepherd of Hermas, and the slightly earlier First Epistle of Clement. These writings are noteworthy because they give us much information about early Christianity and, in particular, about the evolving conception of the ministry. The threefold ministry of bishops, presbyters, and deacons receives further specification, even though considerable variety is still apparent.

The Didache speaks of bishops and deacons as local elected officials,[9] but there is no mention of presbyters. Apostles are mentioned and are distinguished from the local leaders; they are members of that wider group of traveling missionaries identified in the New Testament as apostles.[10] A different pattern emerges in The Shepherd of Hermas. As in The Didache, the traveling apostles appear,[11] and the leaders of the local community are called presbyters (elders).[12] Bishops and deacons are also mentioned, but are described as teachers and protectors of the poor, respectively.[13] Clement of Rome, however, described a close connection between the bishops and the Apostles. Addressing the unruly church at Corinth, whose peace and concord were threatened by schism, Clement wrote that everyone ought to submit to the authority of bishops because they were appointed by the Apostles.[14] As the successors of the Apostles, once commissioned they ought not to be deposed.[15] However, this did not mean that bishops were being raised above presbyters, indeed Clement on occasion seems to use these titles interchangeably.[16] For Ignatius of Antioch, the bishop was clearly central. He spoke of the bishop as surrounded by the presbyters,[17] but the bishop was paramount. "We ought to regard the bishop as the Lord himself,"[18] and Christians "should do nothing apart from the bishop."[19] While deacons clearly appear to have been different from the bishops and presbyters, it seems that the relationship between presbyters and bishops may have varied from one local church to another. Nevertheless, there is evidence that these offices were gradually being differentiated. For example, separate rites of ordination to these offices are reported in The Apostolic Tradition of Hippolytus, written in 215.[20] These rites follow the New Testament pattern (Acts 6:6), the laying on of hands together with prayer for the gifts of the Holy Spirit.

Apostolic Succession

By the middle of the third century the two primitive patterns of local church government, governance by bishops or by presbytery, had completely coalesced.[21] The ministry of bishops as chief pastors assisted by presbyters and deacons had emerged as the universal pattern. The term "priest" was not yet assigned to the presbyterate. When "priest" was used, it was used of the bishop as the normal celebrant at the Eucharist.[22] However, presbyters were beginning to celebrate the Sacred Mysteries in the absence of a bishop. The bishops were almost universally designated as "successors to the Apostles." This phrase meant "succeeding to the apostolic office," and had a less specific meaning than a similar phrase used today. In modern times to say that a bishop is "in the apostolic succession" means that the bishop was consecrated by bishops who stood in a line of bishops whose consecrations could be traced directly back to the Apostles.

But how had the bishops emerged as the "successors to the Apostles"? Students of this period have held widely different views as to how the bishops were given this title. A partial answer lies in the need to establish authorities to settle matters threatening the unity of the Church. Clement himself is an example of this dynamic. He wrote to the church in Corinth as the leader of one church to another, urging them to maintain their unity by respecting the leaders appointed by the Apostles. The appeal to a succession by appointment was an attractive anchor on which to ground the authority of bishops. But why appointment, since in some parts of the church, bishops and other ministers were elected by the local church and not appointed?[23] And why was the authority vested only or primarily in bishops, since Clement indicates that presbyters also were appointed by the Apostles? A different and more important notion of "successor to the Apostles" must have been operative. Recall that in the second century the New Testament had not yet taken its present form and the Ecumenical Creeds had not yet been adopted, so that the safeguarding of tradition was in the hands of the church leadership. But who among these leaders were most likely to be able to do so? Those who had been taught by the Apostles. Irenaeus argued that this lineage was most clearly exemplified in the case of bishops. As noted earlier,[24] he used himself as an example. Irenaeus was a disciple of Polycarp, who was a disciple of John.[25] The Bishop of Carthage, Cyprian, put forth a similar argument. Cyprian held that the bishops stand in the place of the Apostles as teachers and pastors, and thus that the Church is founded on the bishops[26] and is "united and held together by the glue of the mutual cohesion of the bishops."[27] The authority of men such as Irenaeus and Cyprian must have been impressive. By the time of the Council of Nicea in 325 it was assumed that bishops were the appropriate persons to attend the council and pass judgment on the issues. The fact that the bishops were a smaller group than the presbyters may also have been important. Over three hundred bishops attended; the larger group, including the presbyters and deacons, would have been completely unwieldy. Thus when the peace and unity of the Church were threatened, it was the group of bishops that came to be relied on to preserve the apostolic tradition.

The Church as Catholic

The Nicene Creed as amended at Constantinople spoke of the Church as One, Holy, Catholic, and Apostolic. These marks of the Church have functioned both as descriptions and criteria of churchly authenticity. The true Church was the one that possessed these characteristics. In the first few centuries of the Church's life, the most pressing concerns centered on apostolic continuity. During this period the Church was expanding rapidly and, because of the persecutions, contact between parts of the Christian community was sometimes extremely difficult. The appeal to the standard of apostolicity was a way to define doctrine and safeguard the Church's corporate unity. However, this appeal turned out to be insufficient. Galerius' Edict of Toleration (311) opened lines of communication that had been closed, and no sooner had they been opened than it became clear that disagreements over the contents of the apostolic tradition had been developing for some time. We have already noted earlier[28] how deeply the Church's unity was threatened by the Arians and the followers of Athanasius. To meet this threat, Constantine called the Council of Nicea. Bishops from all parts of the Church came together to discuss and resolve their differences. Here in this universal council, the appeal to catholicity was implicit.

The word "catholic" or "universal" was used as a description of the Church from very early times. As he faced death, Polycarp prayed for "the entire Catholic Church throughout the world."[29] The idea was that each congregation was part of the living unity of the Christian fellowship. However, it was not long before catholicity, like apostolicity, was used as a criterion for the testing of doctrine. In 434, during a hiatus between the Councils of Ephesus and Chalcedon, Vincent of Lérins wrote:

We shall conform to the principle of universality if we confess as alone true the faith professed by the entire church throughout the world; to that of antiquity if we deviate in no particular from the tenets manifestly shared by our godly predecessors and the fathers; and equally to that of consent if, relying on former ages, we make our own the definitions and opinions of all, or at any rate the majority of, bishops and teachers. [30]

In another formulation he proposed as a criterion for the Catholic faith "what has been believed everywhere, always and by all."[31] The appeal to universality as a test of doctrine was widely taught. Somewhat earlier Augustine wrote in *The Utility of Belief*, "I have believed no one except the affirmed opinion and widespread report of peoples and nations. . . . In this matter . . . I believed a report which had strength of numbers, agreement and antiquity."[32] A century later the treatise *On the Catholic Faith*, attributed to Boethius, carried the same theme. "This catholic church, then, spread throughout the world, is known by three particular marks: whatever is believed and taught in it has the authority of the Scriptures, or of universal tradition, or at least of its own and proper usage."[33]

Occasionally the appeal to universality seemed in danger of supplanting the appeal to apostolicity. Jerome appealed to the confession of "all the churches . . . one great horde of people from Palestine to Chalcedon."[34] Athanasius vindicated his position by claiming the support of "so many bishops in unanimity,"[35] and Augustine in contention with the Donatists wrote, "The judgment of the whole world is reliable."[36] Summarizing the view that catholicity is not only a necessary but also a sufficient criterion of faith, John Cassian concluded, "The consensus of all ought then of itself to be enough to refute heresy."[37] But this extreme view never took root. The majority favored a position that combined catholicity and apostolicity.

The Church as Holy

If an understanding of what it meant for the Church to be apostolic was examined in the Patristic age, and what it meant for the Church to be catholic was largely worked out in the period of the

Four Great Councils, the meaning of the Church as holy received significant definition in the Middle Ages. There is much to be said for placing St. Augustine at the beginning of this development. Almost from the moment he became Bishop of Hippo, he was embroiled in a controversy with the Donatists, a controversy that focused on the holiness of the Church. The Donatists, who were Augustine's neighbors in Africa, were appalled by the readiness of the mainstream church to welcome back into the fold those bishops and clergy who had abjured their Christianity during the persecutions. The Donatists considered the ministry of these lapsed clergy to be invalid, and required them and all whom they had baptized to be rebaptized. The controversy involved both a narrow and a wider issue. The narrow issue was the validity of the ministry of immoral clergy. Augustine argued that since such presbyters or priests, as they were usually called by then, were but instruments of the Holy Spirit, their immoral characters did not affect the efficacy of the sacraments. This became known as the *ex opere operato* doctrine and has been an important element of Catholic ministerial theory ever since. However, the wider issue in the Donatist controversy was the nature of the Church's sanctity, an issue that surfaced again during the Reformation. The issue is made acute by the inevitable tension between the Church as catholic and the Church as holy.

A classic discussion of this issue is found in Ernst Troeltsch's famous work *The Social Teachings of the Christian Church*. There he draws a distinction between the *church type* and the *sect type* of ecclesiastical organization. The guiding principle of the church type is inclusiveness or catholicity. It recognizes that the gospel is addressed to everyone, and it tries to reach as many as possible. Conversely, the guiding principle of the sect type is holiness. It regards the Church as a community of saints and seeks to maintain a high standard of rectitude and to cut itself off from everyone who fails to meet this high standard. In the Reformation period the Anabaptists offered a striking example of the sect type.

During the Middle Ages, a historically important solution to the tension between the catholicity and the holiness of the Church was worked out. This was the development of a hierarchical notion of the Church. The Church was broad enough to include everyone, even those who were not yet saints, and yet ideally it had holy men and women at its core. The moral standard of the clergy was to be

What
Monachism = P. 327v

high, as evidenced and symbolized by the growing regard for celibacy as a holier estate than matrimony, and by the growing belief that the fullness of sacramental ministry was concentrated at the top in the papacy and from that source diffused throughout the Church. These ideas were grounded in a Neo-Platonic vision of the nature of the divine presence in the world, a vision given a Christian form in the writings of the Pseudo-Dionysius (c. 500).

We know nothing of this man who exerted such a powerful influence on the church in the West. Although he was reputed to be Dionysius, the disciple of Paul recorded in Acts (17:34), scholarly opinion has been that his works, *The Celestial Hierarchy, The Ecclesiastical Hierarchy,* and *The Divine Names,* must have come from a much later period. The organizing principle of the Neo-Platonic vision is what early in this century Professor Arthur Lovejoy of Harvard called the Great Chain of Being. Being and Goodness are found in their fullness in the Divine Reality, and from it are dispersed in a descending order to the world. Macrobius, an early fifth-century Neo-Platonic thinker, described this hierarchical descent as follows:

> Since, from the Supreme God Mind arises, and from Mind, Soul, and since this in turn creates all subsequent things and fills them all with life, and since this single radiance illumines all and is reflected in each, as a single face might be reflected in many mirrors placed in a series; and since all things follow in continuous succession, degenerating in sequence to the very bottom of the series, the attentive observer will discover a connection of parts, from the Supreme God down to the last dregs of things, mutually linked together and without a break. And this is Homer's golden chain, which God, he says, bade hang down from heaven to earth.[38]

Dionysius gave this vision so impressive a Christian form that it influenced generations of theologians, not the least of them Thomas Aquinas, who wrote a commentary on *The Divine Names* and often cited *The Celestial Hierarchy.* St. Thomas defined "hierarchy" as a "sacred rule" or regimen,[39] and Bonaventure, as "an ordered power of sacred and rational realities."[40] It was the hierarchical organization of the universe and, in particular, the organization of the celestial hierarchy that St. Thomas adopted from Dionysius as the proper model for the organization of the Church. "The hierarchy in the Church is modelled on that in heaven."[41] Dionysius had argued that the celestial pattern of three (three orders of angels within each of three hierarchies of angels) was the model for the three orders of ministry: bishops, priests, and deacons.[42] In Dionysius' time it had not yet been universally accepted, as it was in the Middle Ages, that the ministerial hierarchy included not only the three major orders but the minor orders of subdeacon, acolyte, exorcist, and doorkeeper.

Once can detect the importance of the hierarchical concept in the movement to exalt the papacy. This development is already apparent in the twelfth century in the writings of men such as Bernard of Clairvaux, but reached its height in the writings of Giles of Rome (Aegidius Romanus) (1247–1316). Bernard drew the parallel between the orders of "angels and archangels arranged under their one head, who is God," and the clergy and prelates who are arranged "under one supreme pontiff."[43] Writing in 1301, Giles argued that the supreme pontiff has plenitude of power. Just as God himself has plenitude of all power and is the source of all powers of created things, so in matters of authority in the Church the supreme pontiff can "act without other agents, because the power of all agents is contained in him, so that in him is all the power of all the agents in the church; and therefore it is said that in him there is a plenitude of power."[44] He even extended the Pope's plenitude of power from the Church to the state. "All temporal things," he wrote, "are placed under the dominion and power of the church and especially of the supreme pontiff."[45]

We have just cited from authors writing in the High Middle Ages, but the ideas they expressed had their roots in an earlier time. As we shall see, these late medieval authors stood at the end of a long period of development, a development that received powerful impetus from the writings of St. Augustine. Augustine's emphases on the Church as Christ's kingdom, as his mystical body and his bride, and as the mother of Christians were important for succeeding generations,[46] but his thinking about other aspects of the Church's life was also influential. His ideas on celibacy, on the hierarchical ordering of the ministry, and papal primacy were cited again and again to support what became the distinctive Roman Catholic position in the controversies spawned by the Reformation.

Clerical Celibacy

In *Of the Good of Marriage,* St. Augustine cited with approval Paul's preference for virginity over marriage (1 Cor. 7:1–8) and praised "the greater sanctity of the unmarried woman . . . because she thinks only of this, how she might please the Lord."[47] Like Paul, Augustine believed that marriage was ordained by God for the procreation and nurture of children. However, Augustine also believed that sexual desire was a product of the fall and the procreative act was therefore impure,[48] something Paul himself never explicitly stated although Augustine certainly believed that he faithfully represented Paul's view. It was upon considerations like these that Augustine based his strong conviction that the clergy, called to exemplify a holy life, should not be married.

Despite Paul's undoubted authority, the early Church certainly was not unanimous in acting on Paul's plea, "I wish that all were as I myself am" (1 Cor. 7:7). The New Testament itself bears witness to the existence of married clergy. In First Timothy it is prescribed for a bishop that he be "the husband of one wife" (3:2). In Titus the same requirement is laid on presbyters (1:5–6). To be sure, in early times these verses were not taken as unqualified endorsements of clerical marriage, but rather were nearly always interpreted as prohibitions against remarriage.[49] Still, there were other important voices supporting clerical marriage. Clement of Alexandria argued that marriage, if properly used, could be a way of salvation for all, clergy and lay people alike.[50] And Gregory of Nazianzus at the funeral of his own father, who was a bishop, gave a moving picture of the sanctity of the latter's married life.[51] At the Council of Nicea, Paphnutius, although celibate himself, gave an impassioned plea against imposing it on presbyters.[52]

Despite voices to the contrary, however, the ideal of the celibate life for the clergy continued to gain ground. Local synods, Elvira in Spain (306) and Carthage in North Africa (419), made it mandatory. The reputation of the monastic life continued to gain in respect. For much of the Middle Ages, especially in those places where diocesan structures were weak, the monastic houses were the centers of learning, worship, discipline, and missionary activity. The celibate monks seemed to exemplify Christian life at its most committed. Added to this were the persuasive voices of celibacy's out-spoken champions, monks like Ambrose, Jerome, and Augustine. Together these forces not only ensured the place of celibacy within the Church as a manifestation of holiness but led almost inevitably to its universal imposition on the clergy of the Church in the West at the First Lateran Council in 1123. A different practice had long obtained in the East. Since the time of the Emperor Justinian I (527–565), the Church had permitted marriage among presbyters and deacons but had required that bishops be celibate.[53] This difference between the Eastern and Western churches may in part be explained by the greater prevalence in the West of Augustine's belief that sexual intercourse was impure. This characterization of the sexual act was supported by the passage drawn from the Torah that regarded sexual acts, even when not sinful, as defiling and needing ritual purification (Lev. 15:16–18). It was on such principles that Pope Damasus I (366–394) concluded that marital acts are repugnant to sacred ministry.[54] Only the celibate are fit to offer the eucharistic sacrifice. *So much for Peter!!*

Seven Sacraments and Seven Orders of the Ministry

The tradition of the seven orders of the ministry began to form fairly early. In a letter to Fabius, Pope Cornelius I (251–253) noted that in Rome there were one bishop, forty-six presbyters, seven deacons, seven subdeacons, forty-two acolytes, and fifty-two exorcists and doorkeepers.[55] This is the listing that became standard. Although Augustine nowhere provided a full roster, he did mention each of these orders somewhere in his writings. Bishops, priests, deacons, and subdeacons appear in several listings; the three remaining orders are discussed but not placed in a formal roster.[56] Still, universal acceptance of Pope Cornelius' list came only during the High Middles Ages. Until then the number of orders vacillated widely. The *Statuta Ecclesiae Antiqua*, late fifth-century Gaul, had nine orders; in the eighth century, the codifier of Eastern Orthodox thought, John of Damascus, listed five; and Pope Innocent III in the thirteenth century listed six.

If there is an early beginning to the notion of the sevenfold orders of ministry, the beginning of the sevenfold division of the sacraments was longer in coming. Various listings vied for acceptance. Otto of Bamburg, writing in 1139, was apparently the first to adopt the number seven, and Peter Lombard was the first to provide the list that became standard: Baptism, Eucharist, Confirmation, Confession, Ordination, Matrimony, and Unction. It is striking that the number seven became so important in medieval lists of various kinds. In addition to seven orders of the ministry and seven sacraments, there were seven gifts of the Holy Spirit, seven virtues, seven deadly sins, seven penitential psalms, and seven sorrows of the Virgin, as well as various other septads. Why was the number seven so popular? The answer lies in two directions. Classical as well as Biblical sources provided the theory that the universe was structured according to numerical patterns. Biblical and other Jewish sources provided the idea that the number seven is a symbol of completion or perfection. Let us briefly review the foundations of these two beliefs.

The doctrine that the key to understanding the cosmos was the numerical relationship of part to part has been called Pythagoreanism, after the name of one of its earliest exponents, Pythagoras of Samos (c. 540–c. 510 B.C.E.). This idea was remarkably influential, in part because it found expression in Plato's *Timaeus*. It was re-echoed by Philo as well as by Platonists generally, and was deeply embedded in the thought-worlds of Augustine and Dionysius.[57] Augustine loved to quote a passage from the Wisdom of Solomon, "He has arranged all things according to measure, number, and weight" (11:20), and he understood this text to assert the Pythagorean doctrine of the Platonists. St. Augustine believed that the numerical pattern of the universe was ultimately grounded in God himself. "Where all these come from, I don't understand, unless from the highest measure and number and order, which dwell in the immutable and eternal sublimity of God himself."[58]

However, Augustine regarded six rather than seven as the perfect number,[59] and Dionysius, three.[60] The choice of seven as the number for perfection seems to have had its origin in Sumer, perhaps in connection with the seven planets. Seven is especially prominent in the Hebrew Scriptures as well as in the New Testament. God created the world in seven days; Jacob served seven years for Leah and seven years for Rachel; in the dream Joseph interpreted for Pharaoh, he saw seven years of plenty after seven years of famine; indentured servants were to be released in the seventh year, and so on. The New Testament carried on this tradition, especially the Book of the Revelation. Jewish sources also continued to think in terms of seven. *The Fathers According to Rabbi Nathan* (fifth century) contains a lengthy discussion of the numerical properties of things but gives a special emphasis to the number seven.[61] For example, Rabbi Nathan listed seven heavens and seven types of created things, as well as seven rules of interpretation. The Venerable Bede (672–735) also referred to seven heavens,[62] although there seems to have been no connection between him and Rabbi Nathan. Joachim of Fiore (1145–1202) gave great prominence to patterns of seven, speaking of seven world ages and using seven in a visual representation of God, in which he combined the four letters of the Hebrew word for God, YHWH, with three circles representing the Persons of the Trinity.[63] John of Salisbury's (1125–1180) treatise *Seven Subdivided by Seven*[64] listed seven kinds of knowledge, seven powers of the soul, seven stages of life, seven aspirations of the soul, seven virtues, seven kinds of contemplation, and finally seven principles of things. These examples demonstrate the fascination the number seven had for minds that sought to interpret reality in terms of Pythagorean doctrine.

By the High Middles Ages there was almost universal acceptance of Dionysius' principle that human life and the natural world reflect and ought to reflect the celestial patterns. That the patterns were largely numerical was also taken for granted. Many details of the design of the medieval cathedrals, with their concern for numerical ratios, reflect this principle.[65] We have seen the number seven's increasing popularity as exemplified in the many lists employing it. In justifying the number of the sacraments as seven, many thinkers appealed to the similarity of pattern with other lists. Bonaventure simply correlated the seven sacraments with the seven virtues, and Albert the Great correlated them with the seven deadly sins. Similar correlations were made for the seven sacred orders. However, Thomas Aquinas believed that a stronger justification for these two important sevenfold lists had to be given. He justified the seven orders of the ministry, not by a Dionysian appeal to heavenly patterns, but by a need for a division of labor in the proper administration of the Holy Mysteries, some sacramental duties falling to bishops, others to priests, and so on.[66] He justified the seven sacraments with the notion that each sacrament has a special role in the battle against sin.[67] However, although St. Thomas down played Dionysian principles in explaining the number of sacraments and orders of the ministry, he continued to affirm in other contexts that "the hierarchy in the Church is modeled on that in heaven."[68]

The Rise of the Papacy

We have already alluded to another area of church life in which Augustine's influence was substantial—the role of the papacy. He was a champion of the Popes as the successors of Peter, and as the ever-present symbol of the unity of Christ's body and its appointed leaders. The Roman church was, for Augustine, the seat of Peter "to whom the Lord after His resurrection entrusted the feeding of His sheep,"[69] and the church "in which the primacy of the apostolic chair has always flourished."[70] In support of papal primacy, Augustine joined his contemporaries, Jerome, Ambrose, and Optatus,[71] in appealing to the text from Matthew, "You are Peter, and on this rock I will build my church" (Matt. 16:18). Throughout history this text has been given a variety of interpretations. Augustine himself did not always see these words as a commissioning of the man Peter; sometimes he took it as a commendation of Peter's faith.[72] However, even if the text from Matthew is taken as the appointment of Peter to be the leader of the Apostles, it does not follow directly that a similar primacy ought to be accorded to the church that tradition says Peter founded in Rome. How was the case for this latter idea made?

The most reasonable explanation is that many came to see the need for a symbol of unity and an arbiter of perplexing problems. There were several reasons why the choice for this role should have been the bishop of Rome, some of which we have already mentioned. First, there was the tradition linking Rome to Peter and his role in launching the Church. The early chapters of Acts show Peter as a leader matched only by Paul. Second, Rome was the capital of the Empire during most of the formative years of the Christian movement. It was natural that the city at the center of the civilized world should be accorded a special role. Finally, and perhaps most important of all, there was a series of early bishops of

Rome, beginning with Clement I and climaxing with Leo I (440–461), who earned the respect of the rest of the Church because in theological disputes they so often lent their weight to the side that was eventually recognized to be in the right. Thus Augustine's claim, quoted above, that in Rome "the primacy of the apostolic chair has always flourished" seemed to be verified by actual history. Leo I summarized the developing consensus that the primacy of Peter among the Apostles had implications for the government of the Church in succeeding centuries:

> While the election of all of them [the Apostles] was equal, yet it was given to one [i.e., Peter] to take the lead of the rest. From this model has arisen a distinction of bishops also, and by an important ordinance it has been provided that everyone should not arrogate everything to himself, . . . [but] through them the care of the universal church should converge toward Peter's one chair, and nothing anywhere should be separate from its head.[73]

However, the acknowledgment of papal primacy in the West was matched by Eastern reserve. The Council of Chalcedon (451) provides an interesting example of the ambivalence and developing opposition to the notion of papal supremacy in the East. While the bishops at Chalcedon received with appreciation Leo's *Letter* about the Incarnation (which they were debating) declaring "Peter speaks through the mouth of Leo,"[74] they refrained from granting the papacy the primacy that Leo claimed for it. In one of its twenty-eight canons the council placed "Constantinople on a practical equality with Rome."[75]

The Papacy in the Middle Ages

As the Middle Ages progressed, increasing power was vested in and claimed by the papacy. This double thrust was in large measure the result of the need to justify the papacy's role in the Church's missionary activity and in reform. These forward-looking initiatives were increasingly attractive to the progressive elements of the ecclesia. The Popes had taken the lead in the evangelization of the Germanic peoples. Gregory the Great (590–604) sent Augustine of Canterbury to convert the Angles and Saxons in England. Gregory

II (715–731) sent Willibrod to Frisia and later to Germany, and Gregory III (731–741) dispatched Boniface to Germany.

The Popes were also primary agents of the far-reaching reforms of the eleventh and twelfth centuries. Hildebrand, later Gregory VII (1073–1085), was in the forefront of the reform movement under his predecessors. He saw as dangers to the Church the lack of order and discipline among the clergy and the control exercised by the lay nobility. During his pontificate, canon law was extensively codified. In addition, he attempted to bring the higher clergy everywhere under his control and enforced clerical celibacy to a degree unknown up to then. He also fought a series of battles with the secular authorities over church control, most notably with Henry IV of the Holy Roman Empire. About one hundred years later, Innocent III (1198–1216) undertook a similar program of reform, again supporting it by reaffirming the claims of his predecessors that the Pope, and not the local bishops and princes, was responsible for the primary direction of the Church. Innocent's pontificate is regarded as a high-water mark in the exercise of papal power, and after his death there began a decline in actual effective papal control. This did not, however, prevent the Popes from reaffirming their claims. Boniface VIII in the Bull *Unam Sanctam* (1302), which is perhaps the summit of papal claims to supremacy, declared "it is altogether necessary for salvation that every human being be subject to the Roman pontiff."[76]

The Plenitude of Papal Power

Apologists for the papacy supported its claims by an appeal to the idea of the plenitude of papal power. As noted above, this idea found support in the hierarchical thinking of Bernard of Clairvaux and flowered in the writing of Giles of Rome and Augustinus Triumphus (1243–1328). It was argued that in granting Peter the keys of heaven and hell (Matt. 16:19), Christ gave Peter and his successors full jurisdiction over both church and state. Thus it was not possible in this life "to appeal from the pope to God or man."[77] Proponents of this theory went so far as to assert that although the Pope might be mistaken, "his error creates right."[78]

In his treatise *The Catholic Concordance*, Nicholas of Cusa (1401–

1464) summarized this view. Just as the universe is a multitude of singular objects that derives its order and stability from God, so the Church must have a similar source of stability and order. The papacy fulfills the same function in the Church that God fulfills in the universe. As an example to illustrate what he had in mind, Nicholas compared the relationship of the papacy to the Church with the action of a magnet on iron filings. The magnet not only attracts iron filings to itself but confers the power of attraction to some of the filings, which in turn attract other filings, until an end is reached at which the filings at the outer edge of the mass are able to adhere to the mass but cannot attract more filings to themselves. He then likened the Pope to the magnet and the clergy to the intermediate filings and implied that the laity were to be relegated to the last group, who lack power over others.[79] To summarize, the doctrine of the plenitude of papal power asserted that all sacerdotal power and all jurisdictional power, whether ecclesiastical or secular, must be funneled through the papacy. This doctrine was so extreme that it could not help but undergo scrutiny at the Reformation.

The City of God

When Augustine titled his great treatise "The City of God," he had no way of knowing the full results of this choice of words. "City" was used to take the place of "kingdom" in the Gospels and, like it, had a rich store of symbolic resonance. It called to mind the Heavenly City or the New Jerusalem of the Book of the Revelation, which Augustine contrasted with the Earthly City, exemplified by Rome and Babylon. Human beings can be inhabitants of either city, and they establish their citizenship by committing themselves to the aims of either city—the service of God or the service of mammon and the self. Hence, in Augustine's view, the City of God contained all those who were dedicated to God and God's will for the world. Because the Church on earth was created for God's service and contained so many devoted disciples, it was a part, but only a part, of that grander and loftier commonwealth, the Heavenly City.

In spite of its origins in the Book of the Revelation, "city" as a metaphor for the divine society contained within it the seeds of a different fruit. That fruit was gradual absorption of state-like characteristics by the Church. History testifies to the process. When the Roman Empire in the West collapsed, the Church increasingly stepped in to fill the governmental void. In many parts of the West, the bishops were sometimes the only effective administrators of the political subdivisions or dioceses. The appropriation of the term "diocese" for a bishop's jurisdiction (originally a Roman civil subdivision) seemed another sign that the Church was the heir of the Roman Imperium. The so-called Donation of Constantine, a spurious document that surfaced sometime during the eighth century, added to this growing idea. This document, which purported to be the Emperor's gift to the Popes of "the city of Rome and all the provinces, districts, and cities of Italy or of the Western regions,"[80] was universally accepted as genuine until the fifteenth century, no doubt in large part because it merely confirmed what was in fact the case. The Pope had become the Emperor's successor as the focus of unity and allegiance in the West. The spurious Donation thus gave a kind of legal justification to the Pope's claims for temporal power.

By the time of James of Viterbo (d. 1308), the idea that the Church was a visible kingdom had become firmly established. The title of his work *The Christian Government*, sometimes credited as the first separate treatise on the Church, indicated as much. The recovery during the twelfth century of a significant portion of Roman Law, contained in the *Corpus Juris Civilis* of Justinian, furthered this process. This body of law provided concepts and precedents to organize and rationalize the structure of offices within the Church. Increasingly the Church looked more and more like a state.[81] Although not without important opposition from within and without the Church, increasingly the Popes hoped to make good the claim that they succeeded to the mantle of Constantine and the old Roman Imperium. However, the idea that the Church was like the empire, a "visible kingdom," was to be strongly challenged at the Reformation.

The Church Falls on Evil Days

Jesus said, "By their fruits you shall know them." If the Church is to be known by its fruits, then at the end of the Middle Ages its fruits were arguably not unity, holiness, catholicity, and apostolicity. Its claims to catholicity and apostolicity were jeopardized by the doctrinal pluralism that was becoming more and more evident. Nicholas of Cusa's words about the multiplicity of views concerning the Last Judgment were symptomatic of the increasing proliferation of opinion. "Everyone has an abundance of his own interpretations, and no one agrees with anyone else."[82] Jean de Gerson (1363–1429) also lamented that the learned had produced "a confusion of idioms and languages that are mutually unintelligible, as at the tower of Babel."[83] It had become increasingly difficult to see any application of the rule of faith—universality, antiquity, and consent—that was favored by Augustine and Vincent of Lérins.

Even more visible to everyone was the shattering of the unity of the Church caused by the Avignon Schism. For nearly seventy years (1309–1377) there were two Popes, one at the French city of Avignon and one in Rome. The Western church was divided in its loyalties between these claimants. The ideal of unity, as well as the prestige of the papacy which had come to symbolize that unity, was badly tarnished. It became necessary to struggle to reestablish it. With longing, Jean de Gerson spoke of "the quest for the unity of the church with one undoubted vicar of Christ."[84] To heal the schism was one of the goals of the Conciliar Movement of the fifteenth century. The Council of Constance (1417–1418) succeeded in doing so, although it failed to reach agreement on a thoroughgoing program of reform, as it had hoped.

During the remaining years of the fifteenth century, the papacy was brought into further disrepute with a series of very worldly Popes. The Popes had by then come to rule a territory in Italy known as the Papal States. They became embroiled in a series of wars with their neighbors and thus became increasingly indistinguishable from temporal princes. The papacy fell to its lowest point during the pontificate of Alexander VI (1492–1503). A man of unbridled immorality, he had obtained the papacy through bribery and openly made great efforts to advance his bastard children Lucrezia and Cesare Borgia.[85] It is no wonder that such Popes were called Antichrists.

Laxity of morals was not confined to the higher clergy. Simony and clerical concubinage were often singled out for criticism. Things had not changed since Marsilius of Padua (1270–1342) wrote, "Because the governance of the church is so infected, the entire mystical body of Christ is sick."[86] Likewise Ubertino of Casale's lament that among the clergy "discipline is very defective today and intolerable evils are being tolerated" still rang true.[87] When Desiderius Erasmus (1466–1536) ridiculed the ignorance and superstition of many of the clergy in *The Praise of Folly,* he merely acknowledged what everyone believed.[88] Furthermore, scandals like the sale of indulgences by unscrupulous hawkers like Tetzel increased the unrest within the Church. In the face of these scandals, how could the Church claim to be "one, holy, catholic, and apostolic"?

The Reformation

The movement for ecclesiastical reform had been gathering momentum for a long time. While the need for change was widely recognized, there was disagreement as to the extent. Some believed that the problem lay with people and not with the system; others in varying degrees thought that the problems were systemic and that a drastic overhaul of the institution was needed. The more conservative remained in the Roman Catholic church. The more radical found even Lutheranism and Calvinism too timid and halting in their movement toward reform. In spite of the wide diversity of opinion, the spectrum of views on the Church and the ministry from Luther to the Quakers can be presented systematically.

Martin Luther

Perhaps the most significant element in Luther's view of the Church was his strong conviction of the priesthood of all believers. Echoing 1 Peter 2:9, "You are a chosen generation, a royal priesthood, and a priestly kingdom," Luther concluded, "Therefore, we are all priests, as many of us as are Christian."[89] By this he meant that all Christian people are called to teach as well as to bear witness to the gospel.[90] However, he did not mean that an ordained ministry was superfluous, for he added, "But the priests, as we call them, are ministers chosen from among us, who do all in our name."[91] By emphasizing the phrase "chosen from among us,"

Luther meant to imply that the traditional hierarchical view of the Church was to be discarded. He made this clear elsewhere. "All Christian men are priests, all women priestesses, be they young or old, master or servant, mistress or maid, learned or unlearned. Here there is no difference."[92]

Luther never doubted that the Church was a means of salvation. However, because it was always in danger of being corrupted, it was important to be able to recognize the true Church here on earth.[93] In 1530, Philip Melancthon summarized Luther's teaching on this point in the Augsburg Confession. "The church is the congregation of saints (the assembly of believers) in which the Gospel is rightly and purely taught and the sacraments are rightly admininstered." Adding what became one of the most notable features of most Reformation churches, Melancthon went on to say, "For the true unity of the church it is enough to agree concerning the teaching of the Gospel and the administration of the sacraments." Whereas the Fathers at Trent believed that the Gospel would be truly preached in the right Church, Lutherans were convinced that the true Church could be found only where the Gospel was rightly preached. And finally, Melancthon revealed the moderation of the Lutheran Reformation. "It is not necessary," he added, "that human traditions or rites or ceremonies, instituted by men, should everywhere be alike," thus implying that departures from the practices of the primitive Church were not to be condemned automatically.[94]

Calvin and the Reformed Tradition

To distinguish them from the followers of Luther, the Swiss and neighboring German Protestant congregations have come to be known as the Reformed churches. Their leaders, Ulrich Zwingli, Heinrich Bullinger (1504–1575), and, even more forcefully, John Calvin committed themselves to the first two points of Melancthon's summary, the priesthood of all believers[95] and the marks of a true Church, right preaching and right administration of the sacraments,[96] but they departed from the Lutherans on the third point. Luther was willing to tolerate extra-Biblical tradition provided that it was not expressly forbidden in Scripture. The Reformed Tradition, however, insisted that the New Testament provided the only guide and model for the ministry. "I approve of no human constitutions," wrote Calvin, "except such as are founded on the authority of God, and deduced from the Scripture, so that they may be considered as altogether Divine."[97] In the *Ecclesiastical Ordinances* of 1541, Calvin lists four offices that he derived from the New Testament: pastors, teachers (doctors), elders, and deacons. Here he provided the foundation of the Presbyterian form of church government, which has been adopted by a great many Protestant bodies.

There were several distinctive elements in Calvin's understanding of these roles. He regarded the office of Apostle as a temporary one, restricted to the first generation of believers. Hence, bishops had no right to claim that they were the Apostles' successors in that office. In Reformed churches where the title "bishop" was used, it was almost always used for a superintending pastor. Sometimes the same individual was permitted to occupy two offices, such as pastor and teacher. The pastors were ordained for life; the elders, who administered discipline, and the deacons, who served tables and visited the poor, held temporary appointments. In a dramatic departure from the traditional reading of early Church history, Calvin regarded elders and deacons as lay officials.[98]

This polity became known as Presbyterian, from the word "presbyter," which surprisingly was used as a synonym for "pastor" rather than "elder." Groups of local congregations and their pastors were combined into larger units called Presbyteries and Synods, which legislated for the member churches. Congregationalism sprang up among Calvinists who rejected Synods and Presbyteries, believing that the local congregation was the only legitimate seat of religious authority; ideally each congregation was to be a fully independent entity. Leaving aside for the moment the question of the accuracy of Presbyterian and Congregationalist accounts of ministry in the early Church, their forms of church government have proved remarkably successful in practice.

The Radical Reformers

Conrad Grebel and other Anabaptist leaders saw as their goal the restoration of New Testament Christianity. They accepted the three points of the Reformed Tradition: the priesthood of all believers; right preaching of the word together with right administration of the two sacraments as marks of the true Church; and the New Testament as the guide and model for the ministry. However, they added a fourth emphasis: the Church was to be a congregation of saints. Separation of the Christian community from the world was to be the rule. One can detect this tendency as early as 1527 in the Schleitheim Confession of Faith.[99] Michael Sattler (1490–1527), the chief author of the Confession, was burned at the stake for heresy by the Catholic Austrian authorities soon after its composition. Three of its articles are particularly noteworthy. First, it insisted on believers' baptism. Baptism was to be given only to "those who have learned repentance and amendment of life." Second, the Confession established the Ban, or the excommunication of sinners. Third, it advocated separation from ordinary society. "A separation shall be made from the evil and from the wickedness which the devil planted in the world. . . . we shall not have fellowship with them [the wicked]." Withdrawing from the world in order to preserve the purity of the community as a people of God is the most striking mark of the Anabaptist movement. The Amish, who are followers of Jacob Amann (seventeenth-century Mennonite bishop), are perhaps the purest form of what Ernst Troeltsch called "the sect type," as opposed to what he called "the church type" of organization. Here was a complete repudiation of the medieval attempt to unite holiness and catholicity in a single institution. Holiness of life was the goal, and if it meant complete separation from the world, then complete separation must be achieved.

The Quakers

Finally, among radical reformers we ought to mention the Society of Friends, the followers of George Fox (1624–1691). Early in his career, Fox came in contact with Anabaptist ideas. These strongly influenced him and his movement, and for at least two centuries the Quakers saw themselves as living a separate existence. Although living in the world, they were not of it. As we have already noted, Fox took a stand against outward observances like baptism and the Eucharist, but he also stressed the absolute equality of everyone before God. The stand against outward forms and the stand for human equality militate against a separate ministry.[100] Perhaps this explains in part why Fox was so critical of those whom he called "priests," those who accepted money for preaching, and why Quakers ever since have been suspicious of a paid ministry. To be sure, in most parts of this country Meetings are now served by paid ministers, but many Quakers regard this as a departure from the ideal.

The Council of Trent

The reforms undertaken by the Roman Catholic church at the Council of Trent (1545–1563) were much more conservative than those advocated by Luther and the other Protestants. Protestants were of the opinion that the evils within the Church were organic, and so they advocated measures to change its structure. The Roman Catholic reformers diagnosed the problem differently. They believed the failures of the late medieval Church lay in the weaknesses and corrupt practices of individuals and not in the ecclesiastical structure. It is not surprising, then, that Trent reaffirmed much that the Protestants criticized. It reaffirmed the seven sacraments,[101] the seven orders of the ministry,[102] the centrality of the papacy,[103] in short, the hierarchical concept of the Church that had flowered during the Middle Ages. Describing the Church as understood at Trent, Robert Cardinal Bellarmine (1542–1621), the distinguished apologist, wrote, "The one and true church is the community of men brought together by the profession of the same Christian faith and conjoined in the communion of the same sacraments, under the government of the legitimate pastors and especially the one vicar of Christ on earth, the Roman Pontiff."[104] Roman Catholics also continued to assert a structural similarity between the Church and a secular kingdom. The Church, Bellarmine wrote, is a society "as visible and palpable as the community of the Roman people, or the Kingdom of France, or the Republic of Venice."[105] Protestants disliked this characterization. Melancthon spoke for them all when he wrote that the Church was not "the supreme outward monarchy of the whole world."[106] The Anabaptist emphasis on believers' baptism further differentiated church and state. Membership in a church was voluntary, whereas membership in a state was an accident of birth.

As a final contrast with the Reformers, Trent reaffirmed the sacrificial character of the priesthood.[107] The emphasis on the priest as sacrificial agent, coupled with passages from the Hebrew Scriptures calling for the purification of the priest before the sacrifices, naturally supported the ideal of celibacy. On the Protestant side, Richard Hooker's (1554–1600) voice was typical: "Seeing then that Sacrifice is now no part of the Church Ministry,"[108] the word "priest" must be divested of all sacrificial connotations. Since in his opinion this was difficult to do, it is not surprising that he preferred the term "presbyter" to that of "priest."

Anglican Thinking on the Ministry

Anglicans have maintained the threefold ministry of bishops, priests, and deacons, but have disagreed among themselves as to whether bishops are essential or not. Undoubtedly the most influential Anglican writer of the late Reformation period was Richard Hooker. Believing that the Church was Christ's creation and "his body mystical,"[109] that the ministry was of divine appointment, and that bishops were the successors of the Apostles,[110] he nonetheless held that episcopacy was not of the essence of the Church, but had commended itself over time as being a very satisfactory instrument of church leadership. Against both Calvinists and Roman Catholics, he argued that the New Testament models of ministry need not be closely followed. Since there is no passage in Scripture indicating that any model of ministry was legislated by Christ as universal for all time, Hooker concluded that "laws touching matters of order are changeable by the power of the Church; articles concerning doctrine not so."[111] Indeed, he further argued that the Church has the power to legislate for occasions not anticipated by the early Church.

> All things cannot be of ancient continuance which are expedient and needful for the ordering of spiritual affairs; but the church being a body which dieth not hath always power, as occasion requireth, no less to ordain that which never was, than to ratify what hath been before.[112]

In retrospect, many find in Hooker's views a sane interpretation of the confusing and conflicting evidence from the first three centuries of the Church's life. However, Hooker's was not the only Anglican voice. There were others who believed that the New Testament model of ministry was binding on future generations, and that the threefold ministry of bishops, priests, and deacons was the New Testament model. This was the view of the English Archbishop William Laud (1573–1645), who argued that episcopacy is no "human device," but "the institution of Christ himself."[113] It was on the basis of this conviction that Laud attempted to introduce bishops into Presbyterian Scotland, an action that certainly stoked the unrest that erupted in the English Civil War and the reorganization of the Church of England by Parliament along Presbyterian lines. In the process Laud was tried and beheaded, as was King Charles I. When the monarchy was restored, soon after the death of Oliver Cromwell (1599–1658), episcopacy was also restored to the Church of England and attempts to introduce it in Scotland were abandoned. However, Anglicans continued to differ on the rationale for the episcopate, the Broad and Low Churchmen following Hooker, the High Churchmen, Laud.

Five Models of the Church for the Modern World

From the Reformation Era until the beginning of the nineteenth century, confessional lines were strengthened and maintained. Episcopal, presbyterian, and congregational polities all vied with each other. Although there were occasional proposals for church unity—one notable scheme was proposed by the philosopher G. W. Leibniz (1646–1716)—most believed that church unity was possible only if all could accept one of the polities already laid down. Since the issues continued to be discussed pretty much in the same terms as they had been in the sixteenth century, it is not surprising that the thinking on church and ministry remained static. The ideal of reestablishing the New Testament pattern still dominated ecclesiastic thinking, but a definitive solution to the conflicting New Testament evidence remained elusive. A case in point was the rationale behind John Wesley's decision to ordain clergy for the evolving Methodist church. He did so with great reluctance in order to supply a desperate need for clergy in the colonies. After much soul-searching, and although still a priest of the Church of England, he concluded that, because the New Testament makes no clear distinction between bishops and presbyters, he as a presbyter had the same powers as did any bishop. This conclusion was of course rejected by most Anglicans and Roman Catholics.

At the beginning of the nineteenth century, however, some ferment can be detected. With hindsight we can identify five emerging models of the Church. The use of models to analyze church life was suggested by the work of Avery Dulles.[114] Although we will not follow Dulles in detail, like him we take "models of the Church" to mean conceptual structures that are expressed in terms of missions or tasks to be undertaken. Each of the five models identifies a different function as the primary mission of the Church. These are, respectively, Worship, Preaching of the Word, Community Building, Social Action, and Institutional Renewal. Corresponding to these missions are differing analyses of the problems facing the Church in the modern world. Those who see worship as the primary activity of the Church believe that the pressing need is to be transformed by a sense of the presence of God, to be open to dimensions of spiritual awareness that are so often dulled by everyday existence, in brief, "to praise God and enjoy him forever." Those who see proclamation as the primary mission of the Church seek to challenge the flaccid, conventional Christianity that they believe is prevalent among the majority of church people. They hope to arouse the vital, living faith that they see as characteristic of New Testament Christianity. Those who see community building as the Church's first obligation believe that society is dominated by a sense of fragmentation and alienation, and they hope to reestablish the inclusive community—the community of faith and love—that they believe was founded by Jesus. Those who believe that the attempt to establish social justice is the primary task of the Church see the lack of such justice as the primary ill of modern society. Finally, those who seek institutional maintenance and renewal see a strong and vibrant institution as the only bulwark against an increasingly secular culture, which they believe is driven by self-centered and indulgent concerns. Only an institution that is concerned about every aspect of life, from education to health care, from pastoral counseling to caring for the poor, can possibly save human beings from being overwhelmed by a materialistic culture.

Of course each of these models draws on themes already deeply embedded in Christian consciousness and they are not mutually exclusive, although they sometimes are thought to be so. As each model focuses on what it sees as the central mission of the Church, it unifies the Church's concept of itself. Around it other themes are organized and arranged so as to bring them into a coherent whole.

Worship

The lengthy discussion of worship in the preceding two chapters should in itself be an indication of its importance in the life of the individual and the life of the Church. To recapitulate, worship makes real a sense of God's presence, and by means of this awareness the life of the worshiper is transformed. In these moments of adoration, we are taken out of our humdrum existence and focus on a reality vastly more glorious than we ourselves are. Thus the *Shorter* Westminster Catechism declares, "The chief end of man is to glorify God and enjoy him forever."[115] Likewise, Evelyn Underhill described worship as a devout "proclamation of the splendor, the wonder, and the beauty of God";[116] or as St. John of the Cross explained, it consists "in considering the Beauty of God, and in rejoicing that He has such beauty."[117] For those for whom a sense of the presence of God is the supreme fulfillment of human aspirations, the Church ought to be first and foremost a worshiping community.

Of course, worship plays a role in each of the four other models of the Church, but in them it is secondary. In the Proclamation model, it is derivative, a natural concomitant of the hearing of the Word. Where the primary emphasis is on community building or on social justice, worship is often seen as supportive or a necessary starting point for these other activities.

Preaching of the Word

Preaching and teaching have always been important aspects of Christian ministry and there have always been famous preachers.

From an earlier time, Ambrose of Milan and Bernard of Clairvaux spring readily to mind. However, as a result of the Protestant Reformation, the Sunday sermon became the central focus of every parson's ministry. Preaching reached a high art, substantial in scholarship as well as skilled in oratory, in the sermons of men like John Donne in the seventeenth century, Jonathan Edwards, John Wesley, and George Whitefield in the eighteenth, and Frederick William Robertson and Phillips Brooks in the nineteenth century, to mention only a few. Alongside these men were the popular revivalists of the nineteenth and twentieth century. In both the scholarly sermon and the popular revival, the words of the preacher mediated the Word of God, and in hearing the Word the listener was moved to repentance and amendment of life. Those who heard God's call were united by their response to that call into a single fellowship of service. A striking statement of the centrality of proclamation is found in the Düsseldorf Theses of 1933. "The holy Christian church, whose only head is Christ," the first thesis declared, "is born from the word of God; in this it abides, and it does not harken to any alien voice."[118]

The circumstance of this declaration was the growing threat of the "alien voice" of the Nazi movement in Germany. The Nazis wanted to incorporate the Christian Church into their campaign for world hegemony under the leadership of Adolf Hitler and the pure Aryan German nation. As Führer, Hitler was to be more important even than Christ. But the Evangelical response is noteworthy. It was an appeal, not to the Church as an institution, but to a renewed preaching of the word. Indeed, in this view the Church as an institution is created by the hearing of the word. Nowhere in the twentieth century has this view been given more compelling form than in the writings of Karl Barth, whose thought has been described as a theology of the Word of God.[119]

The Evangelical response to Naziism took shape in the Düsseldorf Theses and also the Barmen Declaration which followed the next year. Both documents identified the apathy of the merely conventional Christians, those who had accepted Christianity as only a part of the culture into which they were born, as the real danger to Christianity. Many saw at the time and continue to see in similar situations an imperative to reconstitute the Christian community. However, among those who take proclamation and hearing the

Word of God to be the central elements in Christian faith, there have always been people who have responded individualistically. Almost a century before the Barmen Declaration, Søren Kierkegaard called Christians to renounce their comfortable, conventional faith for the sterner creed of the New Testament. In *The Attack upon "Christendom,"* written as a series of articles between 1854 and 1855, Kierkegaard decried the religion fostered by the established church of Denmark. To him the so-called Christian nation of Denmark was anything but Christian. "When all are Christians, Christianity *eo ipso* does not exist."[120] The real Christian, the true Christian, stands alone before God and is not an intimate of any human group. The genuine Christian is made such from outside the self and outside human culture, and thus can never really be comfortable with the world.[121] To be sure, Kierkegaard's individualistic stance is extreme, but many will regard as authentic his call to the kind of faith he found exemplified in Abraham, a vital and living faith called into being by God's singular summons to each person.[122]

A Community United in Faith and Love

While Kierkegaard stressed the individual's relationship with God, his near contemporary Friedrich Schleiermacher (1768–1834) emphasized the community. For Schleiermacher there are no solitary Christians. The Church, which is equivalent to "the fellowship of believers," is the means whereby the individual is brought to a new life in Christ. "The truth is," wrote Schleiermacher, "that the new life of each individual springs from that of the community, while the life of the community springs from no other individual life than that of the Redeemer."[123] The marks of this fellowship are faith and love fed by the Holy Spirit. Such love is inclusive, a love directed not only to Christians, but "a universal love of humanity, [that] we know only as one and the same thing with the will for the Kingdom of God in its widest compass."[124] Like Thomas Cranmer at the Reformation, Schleiermacher declared that the nurturing of universal love is one of the effects of participating in the Lord's Supper. Partaking of the body and blood of Christ not only "conduces in the case of all believers to confirm their fellowship with

Christ,"[125] but "is also bound to exert [its effect] on our fellowship with each other."[126] "As each knows that the others are being united more closely with Christ, he feels himself more closely united with them."[127] Finally, because universal love is the essence of true Christianity, the latter has within it a dynamic striving toward unity. "Whensoever separations actually occur in the Christian Church, there can never be lacking an endeavor to unite the separates."[128]

In our century many have adopted Schleiermacher's fellowship or community model of the Church. For example, Jürgen Moltmann speaks of the Church as "the community and fellowship of Christ." Like Schleiermacher, he also describes this community and fellowship as the product of "the Holy Spirit."[129] However, unlike Schleiermacher he gives the love imperative an ecological focus by extending the imperative beyond the whole human race. "The church participates in the uniting of men with one another, in the uniting of society with nature and in the uniting of creation with God." "The true church," he adds, "is the fellowship of love."[130] Again like Schleiermacher, he emphasizes solidarity with Christ,[131] and like Schleiermacher he understands the Eucharist as a celebration of the presence of and comradeship with Christ.[132] However, unlike Schleiermacher, Moltmann gives the Eucharist an eschatological dimension, "a token of the future," a foretaste of the eschatological banquet. "The groups which celebrate the supper in this sense," he continues, "understand it as a love feast for the celebration of life, fellowship, hope and work for peace and righteousness in the world."[133]

The idea of the Church as community has wide appeal in the late twentieth century. Disillusioned with the individualism and self-centeredness of much of contemporary culture, an increasing number of voices have argued the need for community. From quite different perspectives, Robert Bellah in his sociological investigation of American life, *Habits of the Heart,* and Alasdair MacIntyre in his study in moral theory, *After Virtue,* both find hope for humankind in the actualization of "community," the former in the parish setting,[134] and the latter in a rebirth in modern form of the "communities" pioneered by St. Benedict at the dawn of the dark ages.[135]

Moltmann's
theology reflects
that of the
Liberation
theologian.

The Church as an Agent of Social Justice

Moltmann's view of the Eucharist as a celebration of hope and work for peace and righteousness leads directly into the model of the Church as an agent for social justice. Moltmann has been a tireless advocate of what has come to be called Liberation Theology, which has placed social justice centrally in its agenda. In his case, the ideas of the Church as community and as agent of social change shade into each other and are not easily distinguished in theory or in practice. "Creative love," he writes, "is the true reality of the Christian church. . . . The church is indeed no religious or dogmatic community of Christians who all think and feel the same, but the concrete overturning of exclusive and repressive societies at their boundaries. Only then can this community break down and destroy the fences built between men, by anxiety and contempt."[136]

This idea of the Church as an agent of social justice is, of course, not a recent development. The history of the Church in the Middle Ages is the story of the Church's involvement in affairs of state, not the least of which was the attempt to organize kingdoms and principalities in accord with Christian moral principles. Bishops often had temporal as well as religious duties. Sometimes they were Chancellors and Prime Ministers, and sometimes heads of state, like the Pope in the Papal States. In England bishops sat, and still sit, in the House of Lords. In these varied roles, it was assumed that church leaders would bring Christian influence to bear on the affairs of state and help to see that justice was done. However, when in 1891 Pope Leo XIII wrote *Rerum Novarum* with its recommendations for economic and social reform, and when forty years later Pius XI in *Quadragesimo Anno* and again seventy years later John XXIII in *Mater et Magistra* applied the principles of *Rerum Novarum* to more recent developments, no one assumed that they placed the issues of social justice at the top of the Church's agenda. But this is what Liberation Theologians have urged. Describing what he called a new ministry, José Comblin wrote, "We find that the rights of the human person are the very nucleus, the center of the Christian message."[137]

Liberation Theology's understanding of the Gospel has three aspects. First, it regards the establishment of the kingdom of God on earth as the heart of Jesus' teaching and sees that the duty of every Christian is to work for the coming of that kingdom. Second, it gives the phrase "kingdom of God" a social and political interpretation. Christian duty then translates into the obligation to strive to organize society in such a way that political and economic justice are assured. Third, it regards the Church as a primary agent for the realization of God's kingdom. The first two of these themes received powerful expression in nineteenth-century writing, but not until the Social Gospel Movement of the twentieth century was the Church seen as a primary and direct agent of social change.

Kant, Ritschl, and Harnack

The nineteenth century began with a call to social justice. In *Religion within the Limits of Reason Alone,* Immanuel Kant fastened on the phrase "kingdom of God" as encapsulating Jesus' ideal for humanity. He gave "kingdom of God" a social and moral interpretation, conceiving it as "an ethical commonwealth" or "people of God under ethical laws."[138] Kant did not identify the Church with the kingdom of God, but saw the Church as subordinate to the kingdom. The Church was but a part of the larger society and was to bend its efforts to realizing the ideal of the pure ethical commonwealth.

Later in the nineteenth century, Albrecht Ritschl echoed these Kantian themes. "The kingdom of God," wrote Ritschl, "is through and through a religious concept," but it is also "the fundamental idea of ethics" as well, and ethics is the foundation of a just society.[139] Though the establishment of a just society is the obligation of all Christians, they should do so directly through ordinary political channels. "It is necessary," said Ritschl, "to distinguish between viewing the followers of Christ, first, under the conception of the Kingdom of God, and secondly, under the conception of the *worshipping community* or the Church."[140] As worshiping community, the Church is only an indirect agent of social change.

Finally, in his immensely influential *What Is Christianity?* Adolf Harnack declared: "The Gospel is a social message, solemn and overpowering in its force; it is the proclamation of solidarity and brotherliness, in favor of the poor."[141] Furthermore, "Jesus' disciple ought to be able to renounce the pursuit of his rights, and ought to cooperate in forming a nation of brothers, in which justice is done, no longer by the aid of force, but by free obedience to the good, and which is united not by legal regulations but by the ministry of love."[142] Although the message is social, the kingdom of God is, in Harnack's view, a state internal to the individual. It is through converted individuals that a just society will be realized. Effectively, the Church as institution plays no direct role in bringing about social justice. However, the problems of the industrialized society, as it developed at the end of the nineteenth century and the early twentieth century, brought a change in the views of many nurtured by the liberal Protestant tradition.

The Social Gospel

The American Social Gospel Movement was the heir to earlier social reform impulses. The Anti-Slavery Movement, spearheaded by Evangelicals like William Wilberforce (1759–1833) and the Earl of Shaftesbury (1801–1885) in England, found noteworthy champions in America among Quakers and Congregationalists, John Woolman (1720–1772) being an example of the former and Henry Ward Beecher (1813–1887) of the latter. However, the best-known exponent of the Social Gospel Movement was Walter Rauschenbusch (1861–1918). The son of a German Baptist professor, he was able to draw on the German liberal tradition, but eleven years as pastor of a church in one of the poorest sections of New York City gave him deep insight into the evils afflicting industrial society. Echoing Ritschl and Harnack, he wrote, "To those whose minds live in the social gospel, the kingdom of God is a dear truth, . . . calling for equal rights and complete justice."[143] His experience in the slums convinced him that a radical reform of the social fabric must be undertaken. "As long as a man sees in our present society only a few inevitable abuses and recognizes no sin and evil deep-seated in the very constitution of the present order, he is still in a state of moral blindness and without conviction of sin."[144] It is the Church that must undertake this radical reform. The Church "does not exist for her own sake; she is simply a working organization to create the Christian life in individuals and the kingdom of God in human society."[145]

Martin Luther King, Jr.

Martin Luther King told us that early in his career he was impressed by the interpretation of the Gospel offered by Walter Rauschenbusch and others of a similar persuasion. He was also impressed by the nonviolent protests of Gandhi and soon saw how to implement a Christian social program by Gandhian means.

> As I delved deeper into the philosophy of Gandhi, my skepticism concerning the power of love gradually diminished, and I came to see for the first time that the Christian doctrine of love, operating through the Gandhian method of nonviolence, is one of the most potent weapons available to an oppressed people in their struggle for freedom.[146]

Implicit in the wedding between the Social Gospel and Gandhian action was the mobilization of the Christian Church in the struggle for social and racial justice. "If the church accepts the challenge with devotion and valor, the day will be speeded when men everywhere will recognize that they 'are all one in Christ Jesus.'"[147] It is significant that the umbrella organization that King and others put together was called the Southern Christian Leadership Conference, implying that the clergy would play a leading role, as indeed they did.

Liberation Theology

Liberation theologians had a somewhat different lineage. Whereas King was nurtured by the Social Gospel Movement, the liberation theologians were nurtured by the papal social encyclicals. Like Rauschenbusch, they were appalled by poverty and suffering, in their case by the ills of so many of the third world peoples, particularly in South America. Like the liberal Protestant tradition of the nineteenth century, they gave the kingdom of God a political and social focus and, like Rauschenbusch and the Social Gospel Movement, they saw the Church as a primary agent of social change. Gustavo Gutierrez, the best known of the liberation theologians, put it thus: "Since the Church is not an end itself, it finds its meaning in its capacity to signify the reality in [virtue] of which it exists . . . this reality is the Kingdom of God which has already begun in history."[148] He described poverty as "a scandalous condition," "incompatible with the coming of the Kingdom of God, a Kingdom of love and justice."[149] And he calls for "solidarity with the poor" in the form of "a real protest against the poverty of our time."[150]

It is well known that some of the foremost liberation theologians were much impressed with the Marxist analysis of the ills of western capitalism, and they joined forces with Marxists at the local level. Furthermore, many of their grass roots churches, the "base communities," contained within them individuals who regarded themselves as Christian Marxists.[151] It was this Marxist connection that was a primary focus of criticism from the Vatican in 1984. The "Instruction on Certain Aspects of 'Liberation Theology,'" signed by Cardinal Ratzinger, is a case in point. Among other things, it argued that Marxism, rather than Christianity, was the real driving force of the movement and cautioned Catholics not to be seduced by outward appearances. Liberation theologians replied that, while they have drawn on Marxist writings, it has only been for an analysis of the problems and for programs of action, and that otherwise their connection with Marxism is peripheral.[152] They contended that the concept of the kingdom of God was drawn from the Bible and papal encyclicals and not from Marx. At this level the liberation theologians fairly easily rebutted the Vatican criticisms. However, Cardinal Ratzinger and other critics may have had in mind a different concern when they criticized the liberation theologians for being too heavily influenced by Marxism. The fault as they saw it was a focusing of the mission of the Church primarily on political and social issues. This seemingly secular focus is what alarmed so many critics. They feared that what the liberation theologians really wanted was to turn the Church into a political party, or perhaps something akin to a labor union.

Institutional Renewal

Another vision sees the Church as embattled by modern culture. To many, modern culture is not a liberator, but an idol that promotes self-centeredness and indulgence and fails to provide the human spirit with the means to raise itself to its highest potentiality. The widespread changes in sexual morality, the increasing use of abortion as a means of birth control, the rise in violent and white collar crime, all seem to reflect the bankruptcy of the modern age. The remedy proposed is to alert Christians to their peril, to heighten the differences between Christians and their secular neighbors, and to concentrate their energies on renewing the vitality of traditional Christian faith and life in the face of these corrosive influences.

In the nineteenth century, Pope Pius IX (1846–1878) represented a particularly forceful example of this point of view. "Pius IX," wrote William Ward, "took up the position that Christianity had apostatized. The appropriate action for Catholics was immense loyalty to the central power, unity among themselves, and separation from the outside world."[153] In order to achieve his ends, Pius IX called the First Vatican Council in 1870. What the Pope wanted from the council was help in uniting the Church against the forces that would, he thought, destroy not only Christianity but civilized society as well. He believed that only the Catholic church, united by a strong papacy, could be effective in rolling back the forces of decay. As a way to unite the Church behind the papacy, he urged the adoption of the doctrine of papal infallibility. After much deliberation, the council finally acceded to his wishes and affirmed that when the Pope speaks *ex cathedra,* that is, when he formally defines "a doctrine regarding faith or morals to be held by the universal Church," he is "possessed of that infallibility with which the divine Redeemer willed that His Church should be endowed"; and therefore, such decrees are "irreformable."[154]

Pius IX's program for the Church and for society is summarized in *The Syllabus of Errors* (1864). It was an uncompromising attack on modern trends that the Pope found destructive. Among the errors condemned were the ideas that the state ought to be separated from the Church, that public schools should be exempted from the authority of the Church, and that freedom of religion should be guaranteed. A fitting summary to the *Syllabus* is the concluding error it cites, that "the Roman Pontiff can, and ought to, reconcile himself, and come to terms with progress, liberalism, and modern civilization."[155]

Protestant Fundamentalism

At the heart of Protestant Fundamentalism are some of these same themes.[156] For these Protestants, belief in the infallibility of Scripture functions in much the same way that infallibility of the Pope does for Roman Catholics. By "guaranteeing" the rightness of the Biblical faith, powerful support is given those who seek to model their lives on the Scripture. Again like Pius IX, these Evangelicals have urged a divorce of Christianity from contemporary culture. "Liberalism is not Christianity," wrote J. Gresham Machen in 1923. Because liberals and evangelicals are to be found in the same churches, the Christian witness is made ineffectual. Thus "a separation between the two parties in the Church is the crying need of the hour."[157] In the minds of the Fundamentalists, a consequence of this confusion is moral decay, prompting Biblical Infallibilists like William Jennings Bryan (1860–1925), presidential candidate and secretary of state, to call for "moral reform."[158] Similarly, Jerry Falwell recently urged his followers "to bring back decency to America."[159] "The world, in this view," wrote Richard Hofstadter, "is 'an arena for conflict' between absolute good and evil."[160]

Modern science, in the view of most Fundamentalists, contributes directly to our social and modern decay. Contemporary infallibilists almost universally follow in the footsteps of William Jennings Bryan in repudiating the theory of evolution. Their criticism of this theory concentrates on what seems to them to be its social and moral implication: the denial of a unique status to human beings as children of God. The view that, rather than being specially created, human beings gradually evolved from simpler forms of life seems to depreciate the significance of human life. Hence, the theory seems to reduce, if not eliminate, the duty to treat our neighbors as persons and encourages the self-centered, pleasure-seeking way of life that so many have come to deplore.

Fundamentalism's attack on evolution has had wide appeal because it provides ordinary people with a focus for a critique of modern culture.[161] It is this disillusionment with modern society that fuels many conservative protests, such as the Right to Life Movement and the movement to restore school prayer in the public schools, as well as the movement to counteract the teaching of evolution. This disillusionment has also brought an increase in the popularity of Christian academies. It is a sign of the times that Protestant Fundamentalists and conservative Roman Catholics have joined forces in several of these endeavors.

The Ecumenical Movement

Our discussion of the five different models of the Church might suggest that the Christian movement is fragmenting, but there are equally strong forces pulling it together. In the last hundred and fifty years there has been a ground swell of longing for the reunification of the Christian churches. This desire is expressed in the Rule of Taizé, a Protestant religious community located in France. "Never agree to the scandal of Christian divisions, that glibly proclaim love for their neighbor but remain divided. Have love for the unity of Christ's Body."[162] This longing was given a theological focus at the Fourth Assembly of the World Council of Churches in Upsala in 1968. "The purpose of Christ is to bring people of all times, of all races, of all places, of all conditions, into an organic and living unity in Christ by the Holy Spirit under the universal fatherhood of God."[163]

The contemporary Ecumenical Movement is not without historical precedent. Although the schism between the Eastern and the Western church and the divisions engendered by the Reformation seemed too deep to overcome, schemes of reunion were sometimes proposed; but they came to nothing. However, a promising change took place in the last quarter of the nineteenth century. For the first time, a major, worldwide denomination took a serious and concrete step toward church union. The Anglican Bishops, meeting at Lambeth Palace near London in 1888, adopted what has come to be called the Lambeth Quadrilateral. In it the bishops proposed as a basis for reunion the acceptance of the following: (1) the Old and the New Testament as "the rule and ultimate standard of faith"; (2) the Apostles and Nicene Creeds as "the sufficient statement of the Christian faith"; (3) "the two Sacraments ordained by Christ Himself," baptism and the Lord's Supper; and (4) "the Historic Episcopate."[164]

The Lambeth statement did not directly inaugurate the modern Ecumenical Movement, however much it may have encouraged it.

Rather, the modern movement has had three different sources, which were eventually combined in the World Council of Churches. The first strand was the missionary concern, which was the reason for the Edinburgh Conference of 1910. All over the world, the various denominations had competing missionary projects. This state of affairs seemed counterproductive, especially in countries where the Christian community was a small minority. It was these struggling missionary churches that called increasingly for an institutional structure to unite them in their common task.

The second strand came to be known as "Life and Work." It had as its architect and driving force the Swedish Lutheran Bishop Nathan Söderblom (1866–1931). Söderblom worked tirelessly to effect an international conference because he was convinced that it was the deep-seated and long-standing divisions in the Christian Church that prevented it from drawing individuals to Christ and dealing effectively with social ills. He achieved his goal when the Universal Christian Conference on Life and Work was convened in Stockholm in 1925.

The third strand was known as "Faith and Order." This time the initiator was an American, Charles Brent (1862–1929), the Episcopal Bishop first of the Philippines and later of Central New York. Although Bishop Brent first proposed an international meeting in 1910, it was not until 1927 that the first World Conference on Faith and Order met in Lausanne. The work of this body has continued under the auspices of the World Council of Churches, since its First Assembly in Amsterdam in 1948. Although purposely not a superchurch, the World Council has been a center for discussions on reunion and the coordinator of worldwide Christian, if mainly Protestant, concerns. The World Council has met approximately once every ten years since its founding. Some measure of the strength of the desire for unity is indicated by the number of mergers that have taken place. Between 1925 and 1966, 42 union churches were formed from 131 separate bodies.[165] Since then several more large mergers have taken place. Included among the more notable new churches worldwide are the Church of South India and the United Church of Canada. In the United States, the United Methodist Church, the United Church of Christ, the Presbyterian Church (U.S.A.), and the Evangelical Lutheran Church in America are among the largest newly merged denominations.

The Roman Catholic Church and Vatican II

Longing for the union of all Christians into one Church was equally strong among Roman Catholics. "If it could be truly said," wrote Pope Leo XIII, "that we were pushing towards the coming of the time promised by God when there will be but one flock and one shepherd, then we would arrive at the complete fulfillment of our desires."[166] However, what Leo had in mind was reunion of schismatics with the Roman Catholic church and not a union of legitimate independent churches. This traditional Roman Catholic attitude toward other Christian bodies remained the official position until the pontificate of John XXIII. In his long career as a papal diplomat, John had seen these other churches at work and had come to have great respect for their commitment to Christian faith and zeal in living out that faith. Many other Roman Catholics had come to share the Pope's conclusions. Pope John, therefore, in his person and in his actions, was much more open to the possibility of reunion on more equal terms than any of his predecessors since the Reformation. This same attitude carried over into the planning for and the meetings of the Second Vatican Council (1962–1965). In a striking departure from previous practice, observers from other Christian bodies were invited to attend, and issues concerning church unity had an important place on the agenda. The work of the Holy Spirit in other Christian bodies was acknowledged in the council's formulations, where it was recognized that "some, even very many, of the most significant elements or endowments which together go to build up and give life to the church herself can exist outside the visible boundaries of the Catholic Church."[167] It broke with the past by referring to non-Catholic Christians as "separated brethren," and their religious organizations as "Christian communities"[168] and "churches or church communities."[169] It spoke of the longing for reunion as a work of God. "Everywhere large numbers have felt the impulse of this grace, and among our separated brethren also there increases from day to day a movement, fostered by the grace of the Holy Spirit, for the restoration of unity among all Christians."[170] In the previous chapter, we noted that the longing for reunion resulted in the appointment of a series of bilateral consultations with various Protestant churches. There we discussed the proposals of the bilateral consultations and the Lima document of the Faith and Order Commission concerning baptism and the Eucharist. Let us now turn to issues concerning the Church and the ministry.

Issues Concerning the Ministry after Vatican II

The euphoria over schemes for the reunion of the Christian Church remained high for some years after the Second Vatican Council, but it has since subsided. There are several reasons for this turn of events, the main one being that not much progress was made in resolving the differences over the ministry, the nature of the Church, and the role of the papacy. Each one of these issues seemed increasingly intractable.

Little advance was made in the discussions about the ministry. From the first, participants in the bilateral discussions were urged to take seriously the emerging consensus among Biblical scholars that several models of ministry were exemplified in the New Testament and in the early Church. "The New Testament," notes the Lima document, "does not describe a single pattern of ministry which might serve as a blueprint or continuing norm for all future ministry in the Church."[171] The historical evidence seems to indicate that the threefold order of bishops, priests, and deacons emerged only after a period of experimentation. Even when the threefold order had been accepted, there was considerable divergence for several centuries in the way bishops were chosen and the responsibilities they were assigned. It would seem, then, that Richard Hooker was correct in his judgment that the details of church ministry had been largely in the discretion of local church bodies and that the threefold ministry evolved as the best solution to problems facing the Church in its first several centuries. However, Hooker-like thoughts on the origins of the Church's ministry, far from settling the issues, have left the ground open for all the traditional proposals for the organization of the Church. Episcopal, presbyteral, and congregational forms of church government each had champions, and strong voices proclaimed each system "to be essential to the good order of the Church."[172] No lasting progress has been made in resolving the disputes. To be sure, some schemes for church union have been arranged in such a way that they will preserve the episcopal form of government and require that, after a brief transition period, all future bishops will be ordained by bishops in apostolic succession. The plan for the Church of South India and the similar one for North India are outstanding examples of this approach. While these unions have been very successful, their solution to the problems of church government has provoked little enthusiasm elsewhere. The schemes to preserve apostolic succession while allowing a period of transition appear to be based on nothing stronger than a principle of accommodation. Arguments for accommodation certainly cannot persuade those who are convinced congregationalists or presbyterians, or those who are convinced that apostolic succession is an essential ingredient of the Church and so oppose the transition period on principle.

The Church United?

The five models of the Church discussed above have vocal and active champions on the contemporary scene, who are often very aggressive missionaries for their points of view. This is not an easy time for those who long for reunion. A favorite metaphor for the Church, "the body of Christ," might seem to provide some common ground between the contending parties, but even here there is disagreement as to what it means. Cardinal Bellarmine spoke of the Church as *Christus prolongatus*[173] or, in the words of J. A. Möhler, "the continuing incarnation of Christ."[174] However, this interpretation of the phrase "body of Christ," although traditional, has recently come under renewed criticism. The Roman Catholic Hans Küng and the Lutheran Jürgen Moltmann both fear that it divinizes the Church, making it too much of a sacred reality. As the continuing incarnation, the Church runs the danger of an over-identification of itself with Christ. To Moltmann and Küng, a sharper distinction between Christ and his Church seems necessary in order to avoid an ecclesial idolatry in which the Church's weaknesses and continual need of reform are underplayed.[175] For Moltmann and Küng, the Church is still Christ's body because the Spirit of Christ dwells in it,[176] but the difference between the sinlessness of Christ's original Incarnation and his presence in an often sinful community needs continual emphasis. Indeed, Paul Tillich made this distinction the very essence of the Protestant principle. "The central principle of Protestantism is . . . that no individual and no human group can claim a divine dignity for its moral achievements, for its sacramental power, for its sanctity, or for its doctrine."[177] The Church as "body of Christ" can be given another interpretation, however. Instead of being conceived as the continuing incarnation of Christ, it can be understood to mean that the Church is Christ's instrument in the world in the way that "members" of a body, that is, legs and arms, can be regarded as implements or tools. No resolution among these alternative interpretations has been reached. While the lack of agreement on this issue is not an insuperable barrier to church unity, it certainly is not an encouragement to those who seek it.

The Papacy Today

What role should the Pope play in a reunited church? No issue looms larger or is seemingly more intractable. Must the papacy be the focus of unity in the emerging great Church, or is it better to ground the unity of the Church in occasional ecumenical councils or in bodies like the World Council of Churches? Such questions have not received the attention that discussions on the sacraments or other aspects of ministry have. Vatican II just assumes that the Pope will continue to play a central role in the future, while the Lima document does not discuss the papacy at all. The Lutheran–Roman Catholic bilateral discussions gave it scant attention. Only in the Anglican–Roman Catholic bilateral documents is there an extended treatment of this issue.

These latter documents recognize that historically the Pope has been the symbol and focus of unity for the church in the West. The several reasons for this were noted earlier. The facts that Rome was the capital of the empire, that its Christian community owed its beginnings to the apostles Peter and Paul, that it was the source of missionary activity to most of Europe, and that the Pope played a leading role in the settling of disputes gave the institution of the papacy a well-earned prestige. In the two hundred years before the Reformation, the good will built up over time was largely lost. Can this good will be restored so that the Pope can again effectively lead a united Christendom? The Anglican–Roman Catholic documents suggest that it can. The suggestion made was not very different from that so often proposed by the Orthodox, that the Bishop of Rome be considered as the first among equals in the College of Bishops.

However, before such a resolution can be effected, the issue of papal infallibility must be dealt with. It seems that no scheme for church union will succeed unless the Roman Catholic church is willing to modify its stand on this issue. As the majority of Protestants see it, the problems that engendered the Reformation were largely due to the centralization of power in the papacy, and institutional safeguards against abuse of papal power are still necessary. The doctrine of papal infallibility seems to exempt the papacy from these necessary safeguards, and its assertion that the *ex cathedra* decrees of the Pope on faith and morals are protected by God from error, and are therefore irreversible, seems to betray the Protestant principle that the Church must always be open to reformation. It was with considerable anticipation that the Protestant community waited for the Roman Catholic reaction to Hans Küng's book *Infallible? An Inquiry.*

In his study, Küng concluded that the Church must give up all claims to infallibility, both that special infallibility said to protect the Pope in his teaching office and a similar and more general infallibility of the Church when performing the same office. Instead, Küng proposed that the term "indefectibility" be substituted.[178] While "infallibility" implies that the Church is free of error in faith and morals, "indefectibility" has a more restricted significance. It implies that although the Church may err from time to time in its doctrinal or moral teachings, nonetheless it cannot stray so far from the truth that it ceases to be the ark of salvation. "What is meant here then," adds Küng, "is that the church remains in the truth and this is not annulled by the sum total of individual errors."[179]

Küng came to the conclusion that many of the papal decrees that were declared to be infallibly true were clearly not so since they are now recognized to be false.[180] Rather than give a lengthy summation of them, Küng analyzed one recent decree of Paul VI, *Humanae Vitae* (1968), which according to Küng met all the formal requirements for an infallible decree set forth at Vatican I.[181] However, it seemed clear to Küng that this encyclical, which condemned the use of artificial means of birth control, was radically mistaken. In the face of this conflict between the satisfaction of the formal requirements and the falseness of the conclusion, Küng concluded that the best solution was to abandon the claim to infallibility and to adopt the more modest claim of indefectibility.

Küng's proposal was not greeted with approval at the Vatican or by many Catholic theologians. While many agreed with Küng's alarm at the teachings of *Humanae Vitae,* they merely concluded that, under these circumstances, it could not be an infallible pronouncement. Indeed, Harry McSorley and others have argued that it failed to fulfill the requirements of Vatican I for an infallible decree.[182] Although a vigorous discussion was carried on for a short time, in the end the Roman Catholic authorities censured Küng by refusing to grant credit toward ordination to students who took his courses at the university of Tübingen. Since then voices in support of the infallible status of *Humanae Vitae* have become stronger.[183]

This hardening of the Roman Catholic position on papal infallibility dampened enthusiasm among many supporters of the Ecumenical Movement. In spite of the significant mergers to form new Protestant churches, a similar rapprochement with Rome seems increasingly far off. In addition, the large-scale growth of conservative evangelicalism, with its emphasis on personal piety and largely congregational polity, has made the Ecumenical Movement seem irrelevant. New issues have also come to the fore. The ordination of women in many Protestant denominations, which the Vatican and many evangelical groups vigorously oppose, and the continuing disagreements over birth control and abortion have further widened the gaps between the churches. However, in spite of these serious divisions, both formal and informal discussions on ecumenical issues continue, so much so that one must conclude that hope for genuine unity among the churches is still a potent factor in twentieth-century church life. With the hope of clarifying one of these issues, we will take up the question of women's ordination in the Epilogue.

CHAPTER XI

Epilogue

We have not reached the end of the history of Christian thought but have turned a new page and begun another chapter. In the last third of this century, several issues have emerged to challenge accepted perspectives and conclusions. "New occasions teach new duties; Time makes ancient truth uncouth," wrote James Russell Lowell. At least what has passed for truth is made uncouth as old ideas are rethought and fresh ones born.

Important contemporary challenges to Christian thinking have come about through deeper and more extensive contacts with other religions and through the movement for women's equality. Long dormant issues have lately sprung to life and have become increasingly insistent, fed by feelings of anger, resentment, marginalization, and oppression. Adherents of other religions have resented Christianity's sense of its superiority. Following World War II, revelations about the Holocaust have intensified Jewish bitterness toward Christians, making Jews more critical of Christian attitudes toward them. Later in this century, many feminists focused their own criticisms on Christianity. Faced with so many obstacles to advancement in the world of business and the professions, they saw the same patterns of male domination in the churches. Some doors have been opened for women within the Church, but ordination was blocked for many years and still is in several Christian bodies. Many women have become convinced that their marginalization is to be traced to the exaltation of the male encouraged by the nearly exclusive use of masculine images of God. Thus important roots of their rejection and devaluation are perceived to lie in false consciousness. A conceptual reformation on several fronts, it is argued, is needed to effect a change of practice.

In what follows, we will not attempt to address the secular issues relating to these conflicts. Instead, we will focus on the reasons internal to Christianity itself that impel Christians to take these concerns seriously. Even in a brief discussion it is important to show how profoundly these issues challenge Christian thinking, not only from without, but also from within, striking chords that resonate deep within the Christian tradition.

Christianity and Other Religions

In earlier times, the relationship between Christianity and other religions was not a primary focus for discussion. However, an increasingly existential interest in other faiths began to develop early in the nineteenth century. The vast colonial expansion in that century and extensive missionary activity brought with them dramatic expansion of our knowledge of other cultures and gradually increasing respect for them. In addition, the growing economic interdependence of nations fostered a greater sense of the unity of all humanity. As we in the West developed a new regard for the civilizations of Asia and the Near East, so also has our appreciation grown for their religious traditions—Hinduism, Buddhism, and Islam. Similarly, extended contact with pre-modern cultures has revealed that they and their religions are much more sophisticated than our grandparents believed. Furthermore, as colonial peoples began to win independence after World War II, they became aware of the extent to which their own cultural and religious traditions had been diluted by their contacts with colonial powers. In the process of reasserting their own heritages, they came to view Christian missionaries as mere tools of colonialism. As a result, Christians have begun to reexamine their attitudes toward other religions and, in particular, to consider seriously the charges that Christian missionary activity resulted in cultural and religious imperialism. We shall postpone discussion of the relationship between Christianity and Judaism until later because it has unique features that do not obtain to the relationships between Christianity and other faiths.

Beliefs about Salvation

A central issue in the relationship between Christianity and other religions is whether people of other faiths will be saved. Christian theologians have given differing answers to this question. Some have held that no one who does not have an explicit and active faith in Jesus can be saved. Others have held that an active faith in Jesus is not required of all, that is, salvation is available to the righteous and deeply spiritual of other faiths.

The restrictive doctrine finds classic expression in one of Peter's sermons in the Acts of the Apostles. "And there is salvation in no one else, for there is no other name under heaven given among men by which we must be saved" (Acts 4:12). Similar passages are found in the Johannine literature. "No one comes to the Father, but by me," states Jesus in John's Gospel (14:6), and John in his First Epistle wrote, "He who has the Son has life; he who has not the Son of God has not life" (5:12), where the context makes it clear that "having the Son" means to "believe in him."

Thomas Aquinas is often cited as a classic exponent of the inclusivist position. He held that active faith in Jesus Christ is not necessary for salvation for those who are invincibly ignorant of God's revelation about Jesus.[1] In this context, "invincible ignorance" means the "incapacity or lack of opportunity" to hear the Gospel. St. Thomas' stance can also be supported by Scripture. In the Epistle to the Romans, Paul certainly assumed that invincible ignorance excuses an obligation, although he does not say so explicitly. His assumption is apparent in the following argument: No one merits salvation because all, both Jew and Gentile, have "sinned and fall short of the glory of God" (Rom. 3:23–25). All are guilty and without excuse since all knew what was morally required of them (Rom. 2:1). The Jews had the law revealed to them by Moses, and although the Gentiles did not know the law in this way, still they had the moral precepts of the law "written on their hearts" (Rom. 2:15). Since Paul concluded that both the Jews and the Gentiles were without excuse *because* they both knew the law, he tacitly assumed that ignorance is an excuse; those ignorant of the law could not be expected to meet its demands. Perhaps it was with such texts in mind that St. Thomas concluded that God gives grace to those who "do what is in them."[2]

What are we to make of these conflicting perspectives? Without going into details, let me suggest that we see here a tension between an emphasis on God's fairness and justice and a conviction of the unique importance of Jesus and his mission. The first emphasis leads to the more inclusive stance, the second to the restrictive. In the face of this tension, many Christians have given their assent to one or the other perspective, but there have always been those who have attempted to reconcile the apparent contradictions between them.

Traditional Resolutions

One way to resolve the contrasts between the two stances is to show that, in spite of appearances, the seemingly exclusivist texts do not negate the inclusivist position. A careful examination of the relevant passages reveals that they fall into two types. Some texts assert that salvation is possible *only through Christ's mediation.* Other texts assert that without *explicit faith in Christ,* no one can be saved. In the first group belong passages like, "No one comes to the Father but by me" (John 14:6), whereas in the second group belong texts like, "He who does not believe is condemned already, because he has not believed in the name of the only Son of God" (John 3:18). These two types are very different in underlying meaning.

The first type of text is perfectly consistent with the inclusivist position because these texts do not assume that to be saved a person must have a knowledge of Jesus, much less have faith in him. Rather they assert that those who are saved, are saved by Christ whoever and wherever they are. We can explain this point more clearly by reference to the doctrines of the Trinity and the Incarnation. In their classic formulations, it is the second "person" of the Trinity who becomes incarnate in Jesus of Nazareth. There are then two natures in Christ, the human and the divine, which remain distinct and unconfused, although inseparably united. To which nature does the passage in the Gospel of John refer when it says: "No one comes to the Father but by me"? If it is the human nature, then it could be argued that only those who approach God through Jesus of Nazareth can be saved. However, if it is the divine nature, the second "person" of the Trinity, to which this passage and others like it refer, then we would have a quite different result.

In the classic account of the doctrine of the Trinity, the second "person" (called Son and Logos in the Gospel of John) is not only incarnate in the historic Jesus, but is an active power whose dominion reaches to the outer limits of the cosmos. The description of the divine Logos includes everything that can be said about God in relationship to the world; that is, it is only through the Logos that we can know God. The Logos is then creator, redeemer, inspirer, and enlightener. The Logos includes the Spirit, for the Spirit is generated from the Father through the Son. Christ in his deity, as Logos, is thus at work everywhere, in everything and in everybody. To say, then, that no one comes to the Father but by the mediation of Christ in his deity is to say that whoever is saved, whether they be within Christian faith or outside it, is saved by God's grace and power. It says nothing about being saved by any knowledge of the ministry of Jesus of Nazareth.

But what of the passages that affirm that no one can be saved without faith in Jesus? They too are consistent with the inclusivist position because they apparently are directed to those who already know about Christ and his mission. Those condemned for their lack of faith are censured because they have rejected an explicit revelation. For example, those condemned by John in his First Epistle are censured because they have "not believed in the testimony that God has borne to his Son" (1 John 5:10). This passage says nothing about those who are invincibly ignorant, such as those who have never heard of the Gospel or who are incapable of appreciating the Gospel because of their cultural conditioning.

The Contemporary Debate

The traditional discussion of the relationship between Christianity and other religions focused on whether someone outside Christian faith can be saved, and it did not entertain seriously the possibility that other religious traditions might have some positive contribution to make to Christian understanding or that the great traditions might be convergent rather than divergent. These ideas are now being increasingly explored. To some they seem controversial; to others they seem but a simple inference from elements deeply rooted in the tradition. The Gospel of John describes the Son and Logos as "the true Light that enlightens every man" (John 1:9), which is to say that the divine Logos is the source of all truth. This description of the Logos is echoed in the creedal formula of Irenaeus previously discussed and also in Augustine. To put the matter another way, wherever there is truth, the eternal Word is at work teaching and leading humanity forward. It is ideas like these that underlie Karl Rahner's belief that non-Christian religions, although incomplete, may be genuinely salvific,[3] and C. S. Lewis' suggestion that "those who are at the heart" of their different traditions "are closer to one another than those who are at the fringes."[4]

In spite of the historical roots of these proposals, they are still regarded by many as radical. People still disagree about the proper attitude to take toward non-Christian religions. But even among those who, like Karl Rahner, believe that there is Scriptural warrant for investigating and appreciating non-Christian religions, there is no consensus on what Christians ought to learn from these sources. If it is agreed, for example, that God is at work in Buddhism, it is not agreed which aspect of Buddhism reflects the Wisdom of God. There is also no agreement on the implications of these ideas for missionary activity. Some interpret Rahner as implying that missionary activity should be continued vigorously, since other faiths need to be completed in Christianity. Others conclude, as does Antony Fernando,[5] that the best missionary strategy is to help Buddhists to be better Buddhists, and Hindus, better Hindus; only in that way can the human family discover its religious unity in the Creator of all.

Today we can be fairly certain of one thing—the dialogue of Christianity with other religions is being conducted on such a wide scale that there is no turning back. Surface indications of the breadth of the dialogue are exhibited in the popularity of the books of Thomas Merton, the Trappist monk who wrote extensively on Buddhist spirituality, and the impact the Dalai Lama has made during his lengthy visits to the United States.

Judaism and Christianity

The relationship between Judaism and Christianity is unique. Both Christians and Jews see themselves as the children of Abraham.

Furthermore, the impact of Judaism on the emerging Christian faith is incalculably great, and the separation between these faiths that took place in ancient times has left emotional scars on both. But why should Christian concern with Judaism far outweigh, at least in contemporary times, a similar concern with Islam, since Moslems also see themselves as children of Abraham? Without doubt, the answer to this question is that for many centuries there have been Jewish communities in every Christian country, and their proximity made Christians constantly aware of them. This awareness has been heightened by events in the twentieth century. Christian consciences were shaken by the Holocaust. The complicity of a great many Christians in this event involving the extermination of six million Jews brought home the need for a special reexamination of Christian attitudes toward Judaism. It is of course an exaggeration to blame all Christians for these heinous crimes, but it is true that certain Christian concepts and ideas fed the fires of bigotry. Thus anti-Semitism is perceived by some contemporary critics to result from Christian teaching and to be woven into the very fabric of the intellectual and emotional life of Christians.

It was in this atmosphere that the Second Vatican Council reexamined Christian attitudes toward Judaism in the fourth section of its Declaration on the Relation of the Church to Non-Christian Religions. Among other issues, the Declaration addressed two notions that have been used to support anti-Semitism among some Christians—the supposed guilt of the Jewish nation for the death of Jesus and the idea that God has rejected the Jews because they did not and do not accept Jesus as the Messiah. As to the first, the Declaration stated that whatever the complicity of Jewish leaders in Jesus' crucifixion, only they and not their descendants, much less the Jewish people as a whole, could be guilty of Christ's death. As to the second issue, the Declaration noted that, in Paul's mind at least, God did not reject the Jews or abandon his covenant with them even though they opposed the preaching of the Gospel (Rom. 11:28–29). Whatever enmity the Jews harbored toward the emerging Church, they were still loved by God. Both of these conclusions echo and are echoed by many other Christian bodies.[6] Still, in these views there is no thought that the Covenant with the Jews is of equal status with the New Testament Covenant. That possibility is being explored in what is called Two-Covenant theories.

Two Covenants or One?

Very early on, Christians began to stress the idea that the new, second Covenant inaugurated by Christ (Matt. 26:28; Mark 14:24; Luke 22:20) was better and more complete than the old Covenant. "For if the first covenant had been faultless, there would have been no occasion for a second" (Heb. 8:7). From this verse it seemed natural to conclude that the Jews who had clung to the old Covenant had put themselves outside the company of the truly faithful and would someday suffer for it. It was but a short next step to conclude that God has abrogated the old Covenant and rejected the Jews for their hardness of heart.

The view that the Covenant with Israel is abrogated by the Covenant in Christ has been called a One-Covenant theory. The view that the Jewish and Christian Covenants are coordinate and parallel, each with its own integrity, neither having primacy over the other, is a full-fledged Two-Covenant theory. A modified Two-Covenant theory asserts that, although the Covenant with Israel is still in force alongside the Christian Covenant, it will lose its significance when, at the Last Judgment, Jesus' messiahship becomes clear to all. On the Jewish side, something like a full Two-Covenant theory seems to lie back of Martin Buber's call for Jewish-Christian dialogue.

> An Israel striving after the renewal of its faith through the rebirth of the person and a Christianity striving for the renewal of its faith through the rebirth of nations would have something as yet unsaid to say to each other and a help to give one to another—hardly to be conceived at the present time.[7]

Christian proponents of a full Two-Covenant theory look for support to the eleventh chapter of Romans. There Paul insisted not only that, in spite of Israel's unbelief, God has not rejected his people (v.2), but also that Israel remains a "holy" people and a holy "root" (v.16), and "beloved for the sake of their forefathers"(v.28). For "the gifts and the call of God are irrevocable" (v.29). Furthermore, Christians are now being "grafted" into that same root (v.24). Clearly, the argument continues, the implication is that, far from superseding Israel, the Church is a parallel branch of the same tree. It may be that the reason Paul did not mount a campaign to

convert Jews, but turned his missionary efforts to the Gentiles, was
that he believed that "all Israel will be saved" (v.26) because God
still honors his Covenant with Israel.

In the light of Romans 11, Paul could not have held a One-
Covenant theory, but whether or not he held the stronger of the
Two-Covenant views is more controversial. Given Paul's deep conviction of the necessity of faith in Jesus as the Messiah, many
people think that a modified Two-Covenant theory more faithfully
reflects his view. In any event, the new salience of Paul's teaching
that God's Covenant with Israel is irrevocable has practical consequences. Certainly it fosters a new respect for the Jewish people
and further undercuts anti-Semitism. It seems to many that missionary work among Jews is rendered inappropriate. Increasingly
Christian bodies have condemned "proselytizing." Some have condemned any form of missionary activity among Jews, while others
have limited it to witnessing to Christian faith.[8] However, many
others are not convinced that Paul's words about God's abiding love
for and continuing Covenant with Israel entail the abandonment of
a mission to the Jews. It is argued that Jews still need to learn of
Jesus the Messiah even though they remain Jews. The "Jews for
Jesus" movement builds on these ideas.

The Movement for Women's Rights

Like the complaints against Christianity voiced by peoples of other
religions, feminist concerns have their roots in a consciousness of
oppression. For centuries women have been discriminated against.
They have been denied equal opportunity in political, economic,
and domestic life. It is only in this century that women have been
granted the right to vote, and only comparatively recently have
significant numbers been employed at the managerial level. Only a
few have reached the highest levels of responsibility in business and
government. The perspective of history makes the recent gains
seem impressive, but full equity has yet to be achieved. Attitudes of
inferiority or dependence on the part of women and superiority or
dominance on the part of men have been insidious and pervasive
and have failed to yield entirely to feelings of equality and mutuality, although women have argued the feminist cause for over a

hundred years. The failure to achieve closer parity with their male counterparts has recently provoked a searching analysis of the cultural and psychological roots of male dominance and female acquiescence.

Feminists generally accept the conclusion that male dominance is very deeply embedded in our culture, but they go beyond this. It is not just that masculine superiority finds expression in legal codes, nor that men and women have separate and unequal status in occupation, recreation, and public life. All of these are said to keep sexual inequality a matter of civil rights. Rather, it is said to be the case that "the problem of patriarchy is conceptual. . . . Patriarchy has erroneously conceptualized and mythed 'Man's place' in the universe and thus—by the illusion of dominion that it legitimates—it endangers the entire planet."[9] What is of special relevance to the study at hand is that many Christian concepts have played a major role in that process of legitimation. Scripture and tradition have been used to provide concepts to justify male supremacy.

Almost patly — but w^e go on w^k k argument. ok.

Equality and the Bible

The movement to accord equal rights to women has grown in strength since its small beginnings in the eighteenth century. In 1790 Condorcet, the influential French humanist, gave eloquent expression to the fundamental precept of all such movements, the principle of universal and equal respect. The principle can be briefly put as the requirement to treat equals equally. After noting that women, like men, are beings with sensibility, reason, and moral discernment, Condorcet added:

> So women, having these same qualities, have necessarily equal rights. Either no individual of the human race has genuine rights, or else all have the same; and he who votes against the rights of another, whatever the religion, color or sex of that other, has henceforth abjured his own.[10]

The mention of Condorcet suggests that the equal rights movement is secular in origin and intent. However, this is far from the case. The concern for equality has deep roots in the Bible and in Christian consciousness, so much so that the movement to abolish slavery received much of its impetus from deeply committed Anglo-Saxon Christians, like Woolman, Wilberforce, and Shaftesbury. Among African-Americans the civil rights movement was similarly nurtured by the Biblical heritage. In spite of the fact that in both Testaments there is toleration of slavery as a social arrangement and absence of an explicit condemnation of racism, the vast majority of contemporary Christians, basing their view on Biblical principles, conclude that these practices are contrary to the will of God.

A similar point can be made with regard to the relationship between men and women. Although many passages in Scripture assert or imply the superiority of men over women, other passages imply their equality. These latter passages, many argue, are theologically more fundamental. Often cited passages denigrating women include the creation of Eve from Adam's rib (Gen. 2:21–23) and the unequal provisions for men and women in the Holiness Code in Leviticus, where it is laid down that when a boy is born the mother is unclean for seven days, but after the birth of a girl she is unclean for fourteen days (Lev., chap. 12). The New Testament likewise has passages that assert male supremacy. Men and women are treated hierarchically in the Epistle to the Colossians; although husbands are commanded to love their wives, wives are commanded to obey their husbands (Col. 3:18–19). Yet in spite of these patriarchal passages, most have come to believe that the equality of men and women is a Christian principle.

When the Bible speaks of the origin and destiny of the human race, it speaks of the equality of men and women. At the creation, both men and women were made in the likeness of God. "God created man in his own image . . . male and female he created them" (Gen. 1:27; see also 5:1–2). Similarly, when humanity shall have fulfilled its destiny, all gradations based on race, class, and gender will be seen to be without foundation. "There is neither Jew nor Greek, there is neither slave nor free, there is neither male nor female; for you are all one in Christ Jesus" (Gal. 3:28). The idea that in God's eyes each human being is of equal dignity with every other human being is so prominent in the practice and teaching of Jesus that we can say that it reflects the mind of Christ. Everywhere his ethical teaching implies equality in that every person is loved by God. Furthermore, the Gospels are filled with stories of Jesus' respectful encounters with people from all parts of society.

He welcomed, for example, not only the outcasts, the publicans and sinners, the lepers and the mentally diseased, the poor and the destitute, but also those with social standing, the lawyer and the rich young man. And, strikingly in a patriarchal culture, he added women as well as men to his most intimate circle. Mary, Martha, Salome, and Mary Magdalen seem every bit as close to him as Peter and John. In the words of one commentator, "Women [as well as men] interact with Jesus in mutual respect, support, comfort, and challenge, themselves being empowered to acts of compassion, thanksgiving, and boldness."[11]

The principle of universal and equal respect—that is, the requirement to regard all people as of equal value—is also deeply embedded in Jesus' teaching about love of neighbor. This connection Kierkegaard put especially forcefully. "To honor every man, absolutely every man, is the truth, and this is what it is to fear God and love one's 'neighbor'. . . . And the 'neighbor' is the absolutely true expression for human equality. In case every one were in truth to love his neighbor as himself, complete human equality would be attained."[12] Paul Tillich echoed this same understanding. For him the principle of universal and equal respect is located in the recognition of every other as a person, which in turn is a requirement of justice,[13] and justice is an aspect of love. "Justice is taken into love if the acknowledgement of the other person as person is not detached but involved. In this way, love becomes the ultimate moral principle, including justice and transcending it at the same time."[14] However, the question remains: How does the principle of universal and equal respect affect the choice of persons to serve in the ministry? Ought women be ordained? Although there are many who say Yes, there are also many who say No.

The Ordination of Women

The case against women's ordination can be briefly stated. First, although the New Testament does not record any teachings of Jesus on the ordination of women, the Gospels describe him as calling only males to be Apostles. Second, we should expect him to have done so since the Bible generally places men above women. This subordination of women to men is directly applied to religious functions in both the Old and New Testaments. For example, the Old

Testament provided for no women functionaries at the Temple, and the New Testament prohibits women from speaking in church (1 Tim. 2:11–14; 1 Cor. 14:33b–36). Third, the clergy perform a dual representative function; they represent the people to God and God to the people. While there is no bar to a woman representing the people to God, she cannot, it is argued, do the reverse.[15] Since Jesus was a male, and God is symbolized as male, a woman cannot signify God. "Sacramental signs," St. Thomas argued, "represent what they signify by natural resemblance."[16] Women lack the natural resemblance necessary for playing the priest's iconographic role. It could be argued that Mary, the mother of Jesus, plays a very important iconographic role, but it is not the icon of priest or pastor, even though Mary has sometimes been called "Mediatrix." She does not primarily represent God to the people, but the people to God. She was not made an Apostle, and although she is said to be exalted to the right hand of God, she is there as an intercessor for us with her Son and not as a primary agent of salvation. Hence her traditional role is not a precedent for the ordination of women.

At first sight, the arguments against the ordination of women seem formidable, but they are less so on examination. The claim that Jesus, in spite of his close friendships with women, made his will about church leadership known by choosing only men to be Apostles is far from secure because the meaning of his choice of men is not clear. The opponents of women's ordination assume that he intended this action to indicate a universal mandate, but they have no real evidence for this conclusion. Furthermore, if his choice of men as Apostles indicates a universal mandate, why is it not also a mandate to call only Jewish males, since the twelve were all Jewish males? Are we to take his actions as limiting church leadership in this respect as well?

At this point opponents of women's ordination appeal to the practice and teachings of the New Testament Church. They argue that the Epistles of Paul and the Acts of the Apostles make it abundantly clear that the Church believed itself authorized to choose church leaders from Gentile as well as Jewish backgrounds, but did not believe itself authorized to select women for this leadership. Indeed, as we have already noted, Paul and the author of the First Epistle to Timothy forbade women to speak in church.

However, the situation is more ambiguous than these Biblical references make it appear. Earlier, in First Corinthians (11:4–5), Paul commented on what was clearly the practice of the Corinthian church, women praying and prophesying in the services of worship. He did not criticize women for these practices, but only for not having their heads covered when they did so.[17] Furthermore, at the end of the Epistle to the Romans, Paul commended Phoebe, a Deaconess of the church in Cenchereae, to his readers. He also asked them to extend his greeting to his "fellow workers in Christ," Prisca and Aquila (Rom. 16:1–4a). All this is fully in accord with Paul's words in Galatians that in Christ "there is neither Jew nor Greek, there is neither slave nor free, there is neither male nor female" (3:28).

What seems to be the case is that the New Testament Church at first granted leadership roles to women but later drew back from this position. Paul appears to be a pivotal figure in this transition. Gradually his egalitarian impulses seem to have given way before the power of the subordinationism of his culture,[18] and subordinationist arguments begin to dominate the Epistles. Subordinationist arguments like man is "the glory of God; but woman is the glory of man" (1 Cor. 11:7) were used to justify the veiling of women in church and the lower status of women in marriage (1 Cor. 7:1–16, 11:2–16). And it is subordinationist arguments that moved the author of First Timothy (2:13–14).[19] However, as already noted, appeals to ancient Hebrew and Christian subordinationist thinking have in large measure lost their power to shape thinking today. The conviction that the egalitarian ideal more truly reflects the mind of Christ and the inner logic of the Gospel than do subordinationist ideas has steadily gained acceptance.

The final argument about women's ordination can now be addressed. Can a woman represent God to the Church and the world? The argument that she cannot has been represented as primarily iconographic. Since in the tradition God has almost universally been described by male images, it has seemed that a woman cannot appropriately represent God. However, symbolizing God is not the only way by which to represent God. In the Hebrew Bible the prophets represent God, and, as just noted, the New Testament Church recognized women as prophets. These facts undercut much of the theological basis for denying that women can represent God and explain why so many nuns, who represent God to the people as teachers, pastors, and prophets, have become restive in the churches that still deny women ordination.

The preceding considerations seem to many to amply justify the ordination of women. Some would like to go even farther and fully address the iconographic argument. In doing so they are led directly to consider the aptness of inclusive language about God. Perhaps women can symbolize God because God is properly pictured as Mother as well as Father.

Female Symbols of God

Feminists have begun to champion the use of female images of God. They have spoken of God as Mother as well as Father and use the pronoun "she" as well as "he." These proposals have sometimes touched raw nerves and have evoked strong negative reactions. Many of the issues are not well understood, and aspects of the subject are murky and confused, but in spite of the confusions, clarification is possible.

The reasons for the proposals are fairly straightforward. Symbols divinise that from which the symbol is taken. Paul Tillich made this point with characteristic insight.

> If God is symbolized as "Father," he is brought down to the human relationship of father and child. But at the same time this human relationship is consecrated into a pattern of the divine-human relationship. If "Father" is employed as a symbol for God, fatherhood is seen in its theonomous, sacramental depth.[20]

By depicting God with male images, both Scripture and tradition seem to exalt manhood. Such divinisation seems to many feminists to be a form of idolatry. "It is idolatrous," wrote Rosemary Ruether, "to make males more 'like God' than females. It is blasphemous to use the image and the name of the Holy to justify patriarchal domination."[21]

Some feminists have concluded that traditional theism is so patriarchal that it must be abandoned. Speaking for them, Naomi Goldenberg has written, "A culture that maintains a masculine image for its highest divinity cannot allow its women to experience themselves as the equals of its men."[22] Reactions like this have prompted several proposals. Some have been attracted to Native American spirituality, where the characterizations of the Great Spirit and its manifestations in male and female spirit-beings seem more egalitarian. Others have turned for inspiration to ancient polytheisms, for similar reasons. Not only are the gods and goddesses on a more equal footing, but the virtues exemplified by the various divine figures (love, justice, wisdom, etc.) are recognized for their intrinsic worth and are not placed in a hierarchy. Some neo-polytheisms are only half-hearted, since their gods and goddesses are not real beings, but "images" which "impose psychological interpretations on reality."[23] Alternatively the gods and goddesses are taken to be expressions of something deep within, something fundamental to human experience that is "initially perhaps more easily recognized in outward projections like those of ancient cult and myth."[24] In such views, religion tells us much about humanity and only very indirectly about ultimate reality. Indeed, the nature of the truly real seems only of peripheral concern to such feminists.

Another, quite different response calls for rethinking the meaning of the Christian concept of God in light of feminist concerns. Can God be equally described as female as well as male, Mother as well as Father? Prominent among those who have argued in favor of adding feminine images to our traditional masculine ones are Anne Carr, Sallie McFague, Rosemary Radford Ruether, Elisabeth Schüssler Fiorenza, and Elizabeth A. Johnson.[25] Because their thinking is deeply grounded in Christian theology, their proposals may well take root in it.

Earlier we mentioned how difficult it is to get a clear vision of the issues. One of the murkiest areas is the formation of our concepts of gender. One theory holds that these concepts are primarily based on reproductive biology, that the different reproductive systems of men and women shape their thinking and feelings about themselves and each other. Another theory holds that definitions of gender spring primarily from the unconscious, and that the unconscious ultimately determines the ways in which our thought patterns and our cultural expressions are ordered. Another theory holds that gender is primarily a social construct. Because men and women are perceived differently in different cultures, gender seems more malleable than either of the other theories recognizes. Each of these theories undoubtedly contains a measure of truth, but assigning them their proper weights seems to be impossible at present. Therefore, in what follows, we will reflect on the possible uses of female images of God without solving the problem of gender origins. We will draw heavily on points made by Elizabeth Johnson in her recent book *She Who Is,* since her contribution is the most recent of those mentioned, and she has been able to build on the pioneering work of the others.

The first step is to ground inclusive language about God in a firm doctrinal base. Deeply embedded in the theological tradition is the statement in Genesis that both men and women are created in the image of God (1:27). If they are, the initial presumption must be that metaphors for God can properly be drawn from women's life and experience as well as from men's.[26]

On several occasions the Scripture does precisely that. In Isaiah, God likens himself to a mother suckling her infant and comforting Israel like a child (Isa. 49:15, 66:13). Indeed, the maternal imagery is sometimes quite vivid.

> For a long time I have held my peace,
> I have kept still and restrained myself;
> now I will cry out like a woman in travail,
> I will gasp and pant. (Isa. 42:14)

Several scholars find the image of God as mother in Jeremiah. When God is said to "show mercy" on Israel, they argue that a better translation is "I will truly show motherly-compassion upon him" (Jer. 31:20).[27] The single New Testament example is contained in Jesus' lament over Jerusalem. "How often would I have gathered your children together as a hen gathers her brood under her wings, and you would not!" (Matt. 23:37; Luke 13:34).

Along with these scattered Biblical texts there is also a medieval tradition that speaks of Jesus as mother. Echoing Jesus' own words, Anselm prayed, "But you too, good Jesus, are you not also a mother? Are you not a mother who like a hen gathers her chicks beneath her wings?"[28] Julian of Norwich compares the food of the Eucharist with a mother feeding her young.

> The mother can give her child to suck of her milk, but our precious Mother Jesus can feed us with himself, and does, most courteously

and most tenderly, with the blessed sacrament, which is the precious food of true life.[29]

And Bernard of Clairvaux often described Jesus as mother. "He will be your mother, and you will be his son," he wrote in one of his letters.[30] The same theme is found in two other Cistercian abbots, Guerric of Igny and Aelred of Rievaulx.[31]

It can be argued that these examples from Scripture and from medieval spirituality concern only God's actions and do not touch deeply the divine nature. Thus they only suggest something relatively uncontroversial, that God does some of the things that women do, but not that God's being deeply reflects the feminine. Such a view would not really address the feminist concern that a dominantly male characterization of God, with only occasional deviations, seems to divinise patriarchy and subjugate women. Is there a theological foundation for commending the use of both male and female images in an equivalent fashion so that patriarchy is thoroughly undercut?

The Case for Equivalence

The case for equivalence begins with a stress on the mystery of God. All of our descriptions of God are halting and inadequate, but nevertheless we cannot just be silent. Although we must say that God is beyond any descriptions of which we are capable, and so is most truly neither male nor female, we cannot avoid gendered speaking of God. It is unavoidable because one of the most deeply held convictions of Biblical religion is that God is a "person." This doctrine places us under a severe constraint because "predicating personality of God . . . immediately involves us in questions of sex and gender, for all persons we know are either male or female."[32] The theological tradition has chosen to speak of God in masculine images, but has always immediately qualified this usage. The "Fatherhood of God" is regularly regarded as an analogy.

Feminists propose that we expand our list of analogies by calling God by both female and male names and using them equivalently.[33] In practice this will mean fulfilling four desiderata. The female names used for God must be grounded in the theological tradition. These names must be used directly of God and not simply of God's actions. Male and female titles must be used equivalently, that is, be of equal force and significance. Finally, they must be genuinely female, not incidentally or accidently female. Can these desiderata be met? Feminists argue that they *are* met by the doctrines of the Trinity and the Incarnation.

In these doctrines a female image is used directly of God. In our earlier discussion, we noted how Sophia (Wisdom) was conjoined with Logos (Word) as names for the second "person" of the Trinity, the divine element in Jesus of Nazareth.[34] It is noteworthy that Sophia is feminine and Logos masculine, and that they are used correlatively and interchangeably, not only in pre-Christian sources like the Wisdom of Solomon, but in much Christian writing of the Patristic age. We also find this same pattern reflected in the New Testament. In the Gospel of John, what has come to be called the second "person" of the Trinity is described by the masculine noun "Word," and in the Epistles of Paul, by the feminine noun "Wisdom." Thus three of the desiderata are met. Feminine predicates are used directly of God, and this usage is deeply embedded in the theological tradition. Furthermore, male and female titles are used equivalently. But is Wisdom centrally or only accidentally characterized as feminine?

In the Hebrew tradition, there is no doubt that the Wisdom of God is a female principle. For example, in Ben Sirach, Wisdom says, "I am the mother of beautiful love, of fear, of knowledge, and of holy hope" (Ecclus. 24:18). This is not an isolated example; wisdom is regularly called "she" and not "he." Nor is this practice a mere accident of the Hebrew language, since wisdom is normally feminine in the languages of the ancient world. This custom seems to reflect something deep-seated about the way in which human beings characterize their world.

Jesus the Man

As we have seen, Christian feminists have not set out to substitute feminine images of God for masculine ones, but have tried to show that both masculine and feminine descriptions ought to be used equivalently. Up to this point, we have sketched arguments that tend to enhance our perception of female characterizations of God. In addition, feminists hope to de-emphasize male titles and descriptions. To do so they want to reduce the significance of Father as a name for God and the fact that Jesus was a man. Success here is thought to be especially important since the fatherhood of God and the manhood of Jesus are primary pillars of the case against the legitimacy of inclusive language for God.

Of course no one seriously questions that Jesus was a man. The evidence from the New Testament, the tradition, and the few references to Jesus from non-Christian sources all agree that Jesus was male. At the same time, it is argued, this fact ought not be taken as sacralizing masculinity. In becoming incarnate, God had to become either a man or a woman, but God did not thereby necessarily grant men a special status. Elizabeth Johnson put the point more generally.

> The historical particularities of Jesus' person, including his sex, racial characteristics, linguistic heritage, social class, and so on do not signify that God is more appropriately incarnate into these realities than into others. [35]

Other parts of the tradition seem to sacralize manhood by prominent and persistent use of "God the Son" for the second "person" of the Trinity. However, this usage is not as significant as it first appears, since it derives largely from the fact that Jesus the man is called "Son of God" to emphasize his special relationship to God and not out of a desire to divinise manhood. [36] Furthermore, as Elizabeth Johnson has pointed out, the classic formulations of the doctrine of the Incarnation encouraged this usage. "The close union between the human and divine natures—a hypostatic union—coupled with confession of Jesus the Christ's personal identity as 'God from God' has tended to allow the sex of the human being Jesus to be transferred to God's own being." [37]

God the Father

In the creeds and in the tradition generally, the first person of the Trinity is called Father. This usage has two sources—discussion about the Trinity and the fact that calling God "Father" is one of the distinctive elements of Jesus' teachings on prayer. However, these two considerations do not count decisively against the use of inclusive language. In Trinitarian doctrine the Father is said to generate the son. The metaphor here is "giving birth," and is used to express the conclusion that the second "person" is also God. "What is begotten of God is God," declared Origen.[38] Undoubtedly the reason the generator is said to be the Father and not the Mother is because of mistaken notions about the generative process. In the ancient cultures of the Near East, the role of the father was likened to the planting of the seed, and the mother was merely the bearer of the seed, providing food and a warm place for the fetus to grow. Given this inaccurate biological account of procreation, it is not surprising that early Christian theologians neglected the mother and thought only in terms of the father as the generator. Were the doctrine of the Trinity formulated in our own time, it is more than likely that the title Mother would be given a prominent place in Trinitarian thinking.

The second source of the title of God as Father derives from the prayers of Jesus. It has been argued that Jesus' use of *Abba* as the name of God is one of the most certain parts of the tradition. Do not the words of Jesus validate without question the masculinity of God? Again Elizabeth Johnson tempered this conclusion.

> However often Jesus may have used the father symbol in speaking of God, its meaning when he did use it is not in dispute. In context the Aramaic *'abbâ* connotes an intimacy of relation between Jesus and God, along with a sense of God's compassion over suffering, willing good in the midst of evil. Made concrete in Jesus' preaching, life-style, and relationships with others, this idea of God is subversive of any form of domination.[39]

Jesus called God "Father," but Jesus did not encumber God with the trappings of patriarchy.

An Open Question?

Feminist theologians recognize that their constructive proposals are tentative. Many of them are novel and must be evaluated further and perhaps refined before they can be integrated into the main-stream of Christian thought. These ideas are just too new to find their final place within Christian theology. However, the complexity of the arguments in favor of inclusive language for God prompts us to ask again, Is such language really necessary? If its use is motivated only by the need to safeguard women's equality, perhaps not. As Bernard Häring has put it:

> Surely, anyone who wants to overemphasize Christ's maleness in order to establish prerogatives of males ("priests") over females has not understood Jesus as the liberator of all people, men and women, and has not understood the way he liberated us.[40]

Nonetheless, many will not be satisfied even though Häring's emphases lead men away from patriarchal practices. Without the approbation that inclusive language confers on women, many of them will continue to feel devalued and marginalized.

Conclusion

The ferment of the last thirty years illustrates again the logic of the development of Christian thinking. The life of faith is often described as a pilgrimage. The individual journeys from the profane to the sacred, from earth to heaven. However, the corporate intellectual expression of faith's journey has had a different character. It began with the conviction that God was reconciling the world to himself in a real historical event—the life, death, and teaching of Jesus of Nazareth. From this beginning, Christian understanding deepened by exploring the intellectual grounds of its basic commitment, and broadened by developing the implications of its beliefs. As Christian thought moved through new centuries and vastly different cultural contexts, it confronted new questions and issues. Our short history reveals the vitality of Christian faith as it reached out to meet these new challenges and in the process was enlightened and renewed. It has learned much along the way from philosophy, from science, and from people's experience as they have struggled to realize their humanity, always because it found new life in him from whom it took its start. The Word Incarnate is far richer and more complete than our partial understanding can ever be. How incomparable, said St. Augustine, is the "Word, our Lord, who abides in himself for ever, yet never grows old and gives new life to all things."[41]

Notes

Introduction

1. Alfred North Whitehead, *Religion in the Making*, pp. 50f.
2. Ibid., p. 50.

Chapter I. Scriptural Sources

1. Theodorus Christiaan Vriezen, *An Outline of Old Testament Theology*, p. 151.
2. Martin Buber, *Moses: The Revelation and the Covenant*, p. 16.
3. Book of Enoch, chaps. 45–51.
4. Genesis Rabbah, chap. 2, sec. 4; cited in Harry A. Wolfson, *The Philosophy of the Church Fathers*, vol. 1, p. 158.
5. Book of Enoch, chap. 48.
6. Although some scholars have done so, there is no warrant for relying on what we have of Q to give us a tradition about Jesus more historically secure than Mark. See Chapter VII.
7. Book of Enoch, chap. 48.
8. Cf. J. Jeremias, *New Testament Theology*, vol. 1, pp. 62–68.
9. Those who believe Paul teaches that the law is to be supplanted put too much emphasis on a text from Galatians, "If you are led by the Spirit you are not under the law" (5:18), and neglect the long discussion of these issues in Romans where the keeping of the law is linked to life in the Spirit. Paul does not urge us to love God and do what feels right, as do some modern advocates of "situation ethics."
10. The Mishna, Ketuboth, chap. 5, sec. 6; 1 Cor. 7:1–7.
11. Paul's own celibacy is not typically Jewish, but is represented in

tradition by Simon ben Azzai in New Testament times (Talmud, Yebamoth, sec. 63b, and Tosefta, Yebamot, chap. 8, sec. 7).

12. For other examples see E. P. Sanders, *Paul and Palestinian Judaism*, and J. T. Townsend, "1 Corinthians 3:15 and the School of Shammai," *Harvard Theological Review*, vol. 61 (1968), pp. 500–504.

13. For a different interpretation, see Krister Stendahl, "The Apostle Paul and the Introspective Conscience of the West," in *The Writings of St. Paul*, comp. Wayne Meeks, pp. 422–434. Stendahl rejects this type of introspective interpretation of Paul largely on the grounds that in Philippians 3:6 Paul declares himself "as to righteousness under the law blameless." However, Stendahl does not seem to see the importance of Romans 7:8, "Sin, finding opportunity in the commandment, wrought in me all kinds of covetousness." These words are the heart of the introspective interpretation and contradict Philippians 3:6.

14. The Apocrypha is placed between the Old and the New Testaments in some editions of the Bible.

15. Talmud, Pesahim, sec. 54a, cited in Wolfson, *Church Fathers*, vol. 1, pp. 157ff.

16. *The Allegorical Interpretation*, bk. 2, chap. 21, sec. 86.

17. Athanasius, *The Incarnation of the Word of God*, chap. 1, sec. 1.

Chapter II. The Mystery of the Trinity

1. James A. Pike, *A Time for Christian Candor*, p. 127.

2. Athanasius, *The Incarnation*, chap. 1, sec. 1.

3. Ibid., chap. 1, sec. 5.

4. Ibid., chap. 1, sec. 11.

5. Samuel Sandmel, *Philo of Alexandria: An Introduction*, p. 157.

6. Philo, *The Allegorical Interpretation*, bk. 2, chap. 1, sec. 1.

7. Philo, *The Special Laws*, bk. 1, chap. 5, sec. 30, quoted in Harry A. Wolfson, *Philo, Foundations of Religious Philosophy in Judaism, Christianity, and Islam*, vol. 1, p. 171f.

8. Philo, *The Virtues*, chap. 39, sec. 214; *Allegorical Interpretation*, bk. 2, chap. 1, sec. 2; *Allegorical Interpretation*, bk. 2, chap. 1, sec. 2; all as cited in Wolfson, *Philo*, vol. 1, pp. 171ff.

9. Philo, *Abraham*, chap. 28, sec. 143; *The Change of Names*, chap. 2, sec. 11; chap. 3, sec. 15; *The Worse Attacks the Better*, chap. 44, sec. 160.

10. Philo, *The Posterity and Exile of Cain*, chap. 9, sec. 28.

11. Philo, *The Change of Names*, chap. 3, sec. 15.

12. L. Urban and P. Henry, " 'Before Abraham Was I Am': Does

Philo Explain John 8:56–58?" *Studia Philonica*, vol. 6 (1979–80), pp. 174ff.

13. Philo, *The Cherubim*, sec. 227f.

14. Philo, *Husbandry*, secs. 50–52.

15. Wolfson, *Church Fathers*, vol. 1, p. 177.

16. E. R. Goodenough, *An Introduction to Philo Judaeus*, p. 100.

17. Sandmel, *Philo*, pp. 94–97.

18. Philo, *Who Is the Heir?* chap. 52, sec. 206.

19. Wolfson, *Church Fathers*, vol. 1, p. 585.

20. J. N. D. Kelly, *Early Christian Doctrines*, pp. 102f.

21. Irenaeus, *Proof of the Apostolic Preaching*, chap. 6, quoted from Kelly, *Early Christian Doctrines*, p. 89.

22. Kelly, *Early Christian Doctrines*, pp. 102ff.

23. Ibid., p. 130.

24. Ibid., p. 128.

25. Justin Martyr, *First Apology*, chap. 10, sec. 2; chap. 57, sec. 7; chap. 59; cited in L. W. Barnard, *Justin Martyr: His Life and Thought*, pp. 111f.

26. Philo, *The Creation*, chap. 2.

27. Clement of Alexandria, *The Exortation to the Heathen*, chap. 4.

28. Tertullian, *Against Praxeas*, chap. 3.

29. Kelly, *Early Christian Doctrines*, p. 116.

30. G. W. H. Lampe, *God as Spirit*.

31. See Kelly, *Early Christian Doctrines*, pp. 115–119.

32. Tertullian, *Against Praxeas*, chap. 1.

33. Jürgen Moltmann, *The Trinity and the Kingdom*, pp. 59f.

34. Kelly, *Early Christian Doctrines*, p. 122.

35. Wolfson, *Church Fathers*, vol. 1, pp. 314ff.

36. Ibid., p. 318.

37. Basil, *Epistles* no. 38.

38. Wolfson, *Church Fathers*, vol. 1, p. 343.

39. Augustine, *The Trinity*, bk. 7, chap. 6, sec. 11. Later Anselm, who views genus and species (the universals) as themselves material substrata (cf. *The Incarnation of the Word of God*, chap. 1), combines the two approaches, as did Basil (Wolfson, *Church Fathers*, vol. 1, pp. 343f). The unity of God can be spoken of as a unity of genus because the unity of genus is itself the unity of a material substratum. Thus the Fathers explained the Son's unity with God the Father as the sharing of the "same material essence," where "essence" means both "substance" and "genus." They further associated this idea with the scriptural assertion that the Son is "begotten" of God, that is, that the Godhead (the material substratum) differentiates itself.

40. In the same way that Anselm conceived of the universals as continuous, spiritual realities, a "material essence," but manifest in many individuals (Anselm, *The Incarnation,* chap. 1). Similarly, the Medieval Arabs conceived of the active part of the human intellect as one and the same in all people, and Hindus view the individual self as one with the universal self of all. In both conceptions, the universal agent, intellect, or self, is viewed as one gigantic subterranean pool of molten lava which extrudes itself into individual human bodies as through fissures in the earth's crust.

41. Kelly, *Early Christian Doctrines,* p. 115.

42. Wolfson, *Church Fathers,* vol. 1, p. 333, citing Hippolytus.

43. Wolfson, *Church Fathers,* vol. 1, pp. 339, 320. The issue of the meanings of these terms is extensively discussed in G. L. Prestige, *God in Patristic Thought,* pp. 157–178.

44. R. C. Gregg and D. E. Groh, *Early Arianism: A View of Salvation,* pp. 14–23 passim; cf. Kelly, *Early Christian Doctrines,* pp. 226ff.

45. William G. Rusch, *The Trinitarian Controversy,* p. 31; Gregg and Groh, *Early Arianism,* p. 53.

46. Kelly, *Early Christian Doctrines,* p. 227; Rusch, *Trinitarian Controversy,* p. 32.

47. Cited by Athanasius, *Orations Against the Arians,* no. 3, chaps. 26f.

48. Quoted from Kelly, *Early Christian Doctrines,* p. 232.

49. Augustine, *Against Maximus,* chap. 2, sec. 6.

50. Cited by Athanasius, *Orations,* no. 1, chap. 33.

51. Cited ibid.; Athanasius, *The Defense of the Decrees of the Council of Nicea,* chap. 30.

52. Athanasius, ibid.

53. Augustine, *The Trinity,* bk. 5, chap. 3, sec. 4.

54. Ibid., bk. 5, chap. 11, sec. 12; bk. 2, chap. 5, sec. 9; bk. 5, chap. 13, sec. 14.

55. Ibid., bk. 6, chap. 7, sec. 9.

56. Cyril C. Richardson, *The Doctrine of the Trinity,* p. 77; Karl Rahner, *The Trinity,* pp. 11f.

57. Augustine, *The Trinity,* bk. 9, chap. 2; bk. 14, chap. 17, and chap. 27.

58. Richard of St. Victor, *The Trinity,* chap. 3.

59. Richardson, *Trinity,* pp. 92f.

60. Quoted from Jürgen Moltmann, *The Trinity and the Kingdom,* p. 144.

61. Richardson, *Trinity,* pp. 93f.

62. Moltmann, *Trinity*, p. 177; cf. Claude Welch, *In This Name: The Doctrine of the Trinity in Contemporary Theology*, pp. 287f.
63. Moltmann, *Trinity*, p. 177.
64. Ibid., p. 176. A Patristic source for this "unity of Light" can be found in Ambrose, *The Holy Spirit*, bk. 1, chap. 15.
65. Moltmann, *Trinity*, pp. 177f.
66. Ibid., pp. 88; 125f.
67. Ibid., p. 148.
68. Thomas Aquinas, *Summa Theologica*, pt. 1, q. 29, a. 1.
69. Thomas Aquinas, *Summa Theologica*, pt. 1, q. 29, a. 3–4 in c.; *The Power of God*, q. 9, a. 3 ad 1; *Commentary on the Sentences*, bk. 1, d. 23, q. 1, a. 4.
70. Moltmann, *Trinity*, pp. 139ff.
71. Richardson, *Trinity*, pp. 135ff.
72. Rahner, *Trinity*, p. 11n.
73. Augustine, *The Trinity*, bk. 5, chap. 3, sec. 4.
74. One element of the Augustinian–Western conception of the Trinity that differentiates it from the Nicene Trinity and from the thinking of Eastern Orthodoxy is the addition of a clause to the Nicene Creed. This clause concerns the Holy Spirit and affirms that it proceeds not from the Father alone, but "from the Father and the Son." These words added at the council of Toledo in 586 C.E. are found only in the West. In writing and discussing this subject, Eastern Orthodox theologians have often said that they would be quite happy with an alternative reading "from the Father through the Son" (cf. Moltmann, *Trinity*, pp. 185, 187). This proposal reflects the fact that in the East the earlier Trinitarian view has never gone out of style, for the phrase "from the Father through the Son" is an expression of the relationship as discussed in the progress of the Church toward Nicea (see Gregory of Nyssa, quoted in Rusch, *Trinitarian Controversy*, p. 155).

Chapter III. The Mystery of the Incarnation

1. Søren Kierkegaard, *Kierkegaard's Concluding Unscientific Postscript*, p. 188.
2. Tertullian, *The Flesh of Christ*, chap. 5, sec. 4.
3. Henry Bettenson, ed., *Documents of the Christian Church*, p. 73.
4. Kelly, *Early Christian Doctrines*, p. 141.
5. Wolfson, *Church Fathers*, vol. 1, p. 553.
6. Ibid., p. 552.

7. Kelly, *Early Christian Doctrines*, p. 140.

8. Wolfson, *Church Fathers*, vol. 1, p. 553.

9. Kelly, *Early Christian Doctrines*, p. 144.

10. Shepherd of Hermas, Similitude 5, chaps. 5–7.

11. See Kelly, *Early Christian Doctrines*, pp. 56–60.

12. Ibid., pp. 53–60.

13. Jean Paul Audet, "Affinités litteraires et doctrinales du *Manuel de Discipline.*"

14. Augustine, *Diverse Questions*, chap. 48.

15. Kelly, *Early Christian Doctrines*, p. 149; Aloys Grillmeier, S.J., *Christ in Christian Tradition*, vol. 1, pp. 115f.

16. Tertullian, *Against Praxeas*, chap. 16, quoted from Kelly, *Early Christian Doctrines*, p. 151.

17. Origin, *First Principles*, bk. 2, chap. 6, sec. 2, quoted from Kelly, *Early Christian Doctrines*, p. 154.

18. Malchion, quoted from Kelly, *Early Christian Doctrines*, p. 159.

19. Grillmeier, *Christ*, vol. 1, p. 130; Wolfson, *Church Fathers*, vol. 1, pp. 387–396.

20. Origen, *Against Celsus*, chap. 3, sec. 41, quoted from Wolfson, *Church Fathers*, vol. 1, p. 392.

21. Apollinarius, *Fragments* no. 2, quoted from Kelly, *Early Christian Doctrines*, p. 292.

22. Apollinarius, *Epistle to Dionysius*, quoted from Kelly, *Early Christian Doctrines*, p. 293.

23. Apollinarius, *Epistle to Diocaesarius*, quoted from Kelly, *Early Christian Doctrines*, p. 293.

24. Pseudo-Athanasius, *Against Apollinarius*, quoted from Kelly, *Early Christian Doctrines*, p. 296.

25. Gregory of Nyssa, *Against Eunomius*, quoted from Kelly, *Early Christian Doctrines*, p. 297.

26. Theodore of Mopsuestia, *Against Eunomius*; Leontius of Byzantium; both quoted from Grillmeier, *Christ*, vol. 1, pp. 432f.

27. R. A. Norris, Jr., *The Christological Controversy*, p. 115.

28. Cf. Kelly, *Early Christian Doctrines*, p. 314.

29. Norris, *Christological Controversy*, pp. 123–131.

30. Ibid., pp. 124f., 137.

31. Nestorius, *The Bazaar of Heracleides of Damascus*, quoted from Kelly, *Early Christian Doctrines*, p. 314.

32. Kelly, *Early Christian Doctrines*, p. 315; Grillmeier, *Christ*, vol. 1, p. 463; Wolfson, *Church Fathers*, vol. 1, p. 455.

33. Grillmeier, *Christ*, vol. 1, p. 461.

34. Grillmeier, *Christ*, vol. 1, p. 459; Wolfson, *Church Fathers*, vol. 1, pp. 461ff.

35. Aristotle, *Metaphysics*, bk. 5, chap. 6, p. 1016a.

36. Kelly, *Early Christian Doctrines*, pp. 328f.

37. Grillmeier, *Christ*, vol. 1, p. 482.

38. Pope Leo I, *Tome of Leo*, sec. 6, quoted from Norris, *Christological Controversy*, p. 154.

39. Eranistes, quoted from Wolfson, *Church Fathers*, vol. 1, pp. 445f.

40. Eranistes, quoted ibid., p. 446.

41. Pope Leo, *Tome of Leo*, sec. 4, quoted from Norris, *Christological Controversy*, p. 150.

42. Ibid.

43. Ibid., p. 148.

44. Norris, *Christological Controversy*, p. 158.

45. Bettenson, *Documents*, p. 73; cf. Norris, *Christological Controversy*, p. 159.

46. John Hick, ed., *The Myth of God Incarnate*, p. 4.

47. Michael Goulder, ed., *Incarnation and Myth: The Debate Continued*, p. 48.

48. Paul Tillich, *Systematic Theology*, vol. 2, pp. 142, 148.

49. John of Damascus, *The Orthodox Faith*, bk. 3, chap. 14, quoted Wolfson, *Church Fathers*, vol. 1, p. 468.

50. Norris, *Christological Controversy*, p. 151.

51. Thomas Aquinas, *Summa Theologica*, pt. 3, q. 9, a. 3 in c.

52. Ibid., pt. 3, q. 9, a. 2 in c.

53. Ibid., pt. 3, q. 10, a. 2 in c.

54. Ibid., pt. 3, q. 13, a. 1 in c.

55. Ibid., pt. 3, q. 12, a. 2 in c.

56. Quoted in J. I. Packer, *"Fundamentalism" and the Word of God*, p. 83.

57. P. E. More and F. L. Cross, eds., *Anglicanism*, p. xxviii.

58. Tillich, *Systematic Theology*, vol. 2, p. 138.

59. Ibid.

60. Thomas Aquinas, *Summa Theologica*, pt. 3, q. 2, a. 2 in c.

61. W. N. Pittenger, *The Word Incarnate*, pp. 90, 100–103.

62. Thomas Aquinas, *Summa Theologica*, pt. 3, q. 2, a. 2 in c.

63. E. L. Mascall, *Via Media*, p. 97.

64. Meister Eckhart, *Commentary on the Gospel of John*, quoted from E. Colledge and B. McGinn, *Meister Eckhart: The Essential Sermons, Commentaries, Treatises, and Defense*, p. 54.

65. Hans Küng, *On Being a Christian*, p. 446.

66. Goulder, *Incarnation and Myth*, p. 43.

67. Schubert Ogden, *The Point of Christology*, pp. 41, 79, 87, 146.

68. Goulder, *Incarnation and Myth*, p. 43.

69. Ibid., p. 48.

Chapter IV. The Atonement

1. Leonard Hodgson, *The Doctrine of the Atonement*, p. 68.

2. Athanasius, *The Incarnation*, chap. 1, sec. 5.

3. Paul Tillich, *The Courage to Be*, chap. 2.

4. Irenaeus, *Against Heresies*, bk. 5, preface, quoted from Kelly, *Early Christian Doctrines*, p. 172.

5. Athanasius, *The Incarnation*, chap. 2, sec. 9.

6. Ibid., chap. 4, sec. 20.

7. Epistle of Barnabas, chap. 5, sec. 1, quoted from Kelly, *Early Christian Doctrines*, p. 165.

8. Tertullian, *Answer to the Jews*, chap. 13; *Antidote for the Scorpion's Sting*, chap. 7, quoted from Kelly, *Early Christian Doctrines*, p. 177.

9. Basil, *Homily on the Psalms*, chap. 28, sec. 5.

10. Justin Martyr, *Dialogue with Trypho*, chap. 85, sec. 1.

11. Ibid., chap. 41, sec. 1, quoted from Kelly, *Early Christian Doctrines*, p. 169.

12. Origen, *Against Celsus*, chap. 7, sec. 17, quoted from Kelly, *Early Christian Doctrines*, p. 185.

13. Since all views discussed suppose that the taking of Christ's life is a terrible crime, it is important to point out that his death on Calvary provides no grounds for anti-Semitism. In the Gospels, guilt for his death is located only in part in the religious authorities of the time and in the vacillating crowd, but ultimately in Roman civil authorities, since Pilate could have prevented the execution. Moreover, in many early views these actors are but the tools of Satan. Also significant is the New Testament passage: "He himself bore our sins in his body on the tree" (1 Pet. 2: 24). The Gospel seems to imply that it is the sins of our common humanity that put him there—fear for self, anger, greed, and self-seeking impulses. Only an accident of history places us in this century and Caiaphas and Pilate in the first. A frequent theme of Good Friday sermons, "Were Christ to come among us as he did of old, he would be crucified afresh by us," is voiced in Johann Hermann's 1630 hymn.

> Who was the guilty?
> Who brought this upon thee?

Alas, my treason, Jesus,
hath undone thee.
'Twas I, Lord Jesus,
I it was denied thee:
I crucified thee.

14. Irenaeus, *Against Heresies*, bk. 5, chap. 21, sec. 3, quoted from Gustav Aulén, *Christus Victor*, p. 51.

15. Irenaeus, *Proof of the Apostolic Preaching*, chap. 37, quoted from Aulén, *Christus Victor*, p. 36.

16. Kenneth Kirk, *The Epistle to the Romans*, p. 52.

17. Athanasius, *The Incarnation*, chap. 5, sec. 27.

18. Hodgson, *Atonement*, p. 146; H. A. Hodges, *The Pattern of Atonement*, p. 37; John Macquarrie, *Principles of Christian Theology*, p. 286; Tillich, *Systematic Theology*, vol. 2, p. 171.

19. Aulén, *Christus Victor*, pp. 68–70.

20. Great Catechism, quoted from Aulén, *Christus Victor*, p. 65.

21. Origen, *Commentary on Matthew*, chap. 26, sec. 8.

22. Anselm, *Why God Became Man*, bk. 1, chap. 7; Peter Abelard, "Exposition of the Epistle to the Romans (An Excerpt from the Second Book)," *A Scholastic Miscellany: Anselm to Ockham*, pp. 280–283.

23. Augustine, *Exposition on the Psalms*, Ps. 149, sec. 10.

24. Athanasius, *The Incarnation*, chap. 4, sec. 25.

25. George Fox, *The Autobiography of George Fox*, p. 2.

26. Ibid., p. 6.

27. Ibid., p. 7.

28. Søren Kierkegaard, *Christian Discourses*, pp. 78–79.

29. Friedrich Schleiermacher, *The Christian Faith*, pp. 424–438.

30. Moltmann, *Trinity*, p. 69; Edward Schillebeeckx, *Jesus: An Experiment in Christology*, p. 256.

31. Tillich, *Systematic Theology*, vol. 2, p. 134.

32. Ibid., p. 138.

33. Ibid., p. 155.

34. M. L. King, Jr., *Strength to Love*, p. 172.

35. M. L. King, Jr., *Why We Can't Wait*, p. 88.

36. Ibid., p. 30.

37. Ibid., p. 28.

38. Quoted from Hodgson, *Atonement*, p. 80.

39. Anselm, *Why God Became Man*, bk. 1, chaps. 6–7.

40. Ibid., bk. 1, chaps. 11–12.

41. Ibid., bk. 1, chap. 19.

42. Ibid., bk. 2, chaps. 22ff.

43. Ibid., bk. 1, chap. 15.

C. F. W.
Dillistone

44. Ibid., bk. 2, chaps. 2ff.

45. Ibid., bk. 2, chap. 10.

46. Ibid., bk. 2, chap. 11.

47. Ibid., bk. 2, chap. 14.

48. Abelard, "Epistle to the Romans," p. 282.

49. Thomas Aquinas, *Summa Theologica*, pt. 3, q. 48, a. 1–2.

50. Ibid., pt. 3, q. 46, a. 6.

51. Ibid.

52. John Duns Scotus, *Commentary on the Sentences*, bk. 3, d. 29.

53. John Calvin, *Calvin: The Institutes of the Christian Religion*, bk. 2, chap. 16, sec. 10.

54. Hastings Rashdall, *The Idea of Atonement in Christian Theology*, pp. 422f.

55. Tillich, *Systematic Theology*, vol. 2, p. 172.

56. R. C. Moberly, *Atonement and Personality*, p. 130.

57. Thomas à Kempis, *The Imitation of Christ*, bk. 2, chap. 12.

58. Ibid., bk. 4, chap. 8.

59. Abelard, "Epistle to the Romans," pp. 280f.; Anselm, *Why God Became Man*, chap. 18.

60. Abelard, "Epistle to the Romans," p. 283.

61. Ibid., p. 284.

62. Martin Luther, quoted from Roland Bainton, *Here I Stand: A Life of Martin Luther*, p. 65.

63. Ibid.

64. Martin Luther, "A Treatise on Christian Liberty," *Works of Martin Luther*, vol. 2, p. 317.

65. Ibid., p. 338.

66. Roland Bainton, *Life of Martin Luther*, p. 65.

Chapter V. The Fall and Original Sin

1. Tertullian, *On the Soul*, chap. 41.

2. Macquarrie, *Christian Theology*, p. 242; Stephen Langton, "A Question on Original Sin," *A Scholastic Miscellany*, p. 352.

3. Anselm, *On the Virginal Conception*, chap. 38.

4. Calvin, *Institutes*, bk. 2, chap. 1, sec. 8.

5. Immanuel Kant, *Religion within the Limits of Reason Alone*, p. 35.

6. F. R. Tennant, *The Origin and Propagation of Sin*, pp. 167f.

7. Aristotle, *Metaphysics*, bk. 4, chap. 2.

8. Macquarrie, *Christian Theology*, pp. 237f.; Charles Gore, ed., *Lux Mundi*, p. 230.

9. Mary Douglas, *Purity and Danger*, pp. 55–72.

10. Gerhard Kittel, *Theological Dictionary of the New Testament*, vol. 1, p. 279.

11. Mircea Eliade, *Patterns in Comparative Religion*, secs. 105–108.

12. Clement of Alexandria, *Miscellanies*, bk. 2, chap. 18.

13. 2 Esdras 3:7, quoted from F. R. Tennant, *The Sources of the Doctrines of the Fall and Original Sin*, p. 224.

14. 2 Esdras, 4:30f., quoted from Tennant, *Doctrines of the Fall*, pp. 225f.

15. Wisdom of Solomon 2:23 KJV; cf. 1:13.

16. Sirach (Ecclesiasticus) 15:14f., trans. and quoted from N. P. Williams, *The Ideas of the Fall and of Original Sin*, p. 62.

17. Talmud, Kiddushin, sec. 30b.

18. Reinhold Niebuhr, *The Nature and Destiny of Man*, vol. 1, p. 164.

19. Justin Martyr, *Dialogue with Trypho*, chaps. 95, 98.

20. Justin Martyr, *First Apology*, chap. 10.

21. Justin Martyr, *Dialogue with Trypho*, chaps. 88, 124.

22. Justin Martyr, *First Apology*, chap. 61.

23. Justin Martyr, *Second Apology*, chap. 5; *First Apology*, chap. 61.

24. Tennant, *Doctrines of the Fall*, pp. 149f.

25. Irenaeus, *The Proof*, chap. 12; *Against Heresies*, bk. 4, chap. 38, sec. 1.

26. Irenaeus, *The Proof*, chap. 12.

27. Irenaeus, *Against Heresies*, bk. 5, chap. 6, sec. 1.

28. Origen, *First Principles*, bk. 1, chap. 8, sec. 1, quoted from Kelly, *Early Christian Doctrines*, p. 180.

29. Origen, *Against Celsus*, chap. 3, sec. 66.

30. Origen, *First Principles*, bk. 1, chap. 8, sec. 1.

31. Athanasius, *The Incarnation of the Word of God*, chap. 1, sec. 3; sec. 3; sec. 5; sec. 4.

32. Augustine, *The Free Choice of the Will*, bk. 3, chap. 24.

33. Augustine, *The Incomplete Work Against Julian*, chap. 5, sec. 1.

34. Ibid., chap. 5, sec. 64; chap. 6, sec. 27; chap. 6, sec. 14.

35. Augustine, *On the Merits and Remission of Sins*, bk. 2, chap. 41.

36. Augustine, *On Marriage and Concupiscence*, bk. 2. chap. 15.

37. F. R. Tennant, *The Origin and Propagation of Sin*, pp. 177ff; Paul Ricoeur, *The Conflict of Interpretations*, pp. 279f.

38. Augustine, *On Marriage and Concupiscence*, bk. 1, chap. 7.

39. For a summary of the three most plausible interpretations see Gunther W. Plaut, ed., *The Torah: A Modern Commentary*, pp. 38–40.

40. Schleiermacher, *Christian Faith*, pp. 295f.

41. John Hick, *Evil and the God of Love*, pp. 68ff.

42. Anselm, *Anselm of Canterbury; Trinity, Incarnation and Redemption: Theological Treatises*, p. 42.

43. Augustine, *The Free Choice of the Will*, bk. 3, chap. 24.

44. Schleiermacher, *Christian Faith*, p. 293.

45. Samuel McCauley Jackson, ed., *The New Schaff–Hertzog Encyclopedia of Religious Knowledge*, vol. 10, p. 436.

46. B. O. McDermott, S.J., "Original Sin: Recent Developments," *Theological Studies*, vol. 38, p. 486.

47. Thomas Aquinas, *Summa Theologica*, pt. 1, pt. 2, q. 82, a. 2 in c.

48. McDermott, "Original Sin," p. 486.

49. Jackson, *New Schaff–Hertzog Encyclopedia*, vol. 10, p. 436.

50. Tennant, *Origin of Sin*, pp. 155f.

51. P. T. Geach, *Providence and Evil*, p. 84.

52. Thomas Aquinas, *Summa Theologica*, pt. 1, q. 44, a. 4 in c.

53. Geach, *Providence and Evil*, p. 96; Niebuhr, *Nature and Destiny*, vol. 1, p. 246.

54. Quoted from Niebuhr, *Nature and Destiny*, vol. 1, p. 246.

55. Williams, *Ideas of the Fall*, pp. 380f.

56. J. S. Whale, *Christian Doctrine*, p. 49.

57. Niebuhr, *Nature and Destiny*, vol. 1, p. 263.

58. Reinhold Niebuhr, *Discerning the Signs of the Times*, p. 43.

59. Niebuhr, *Nature and Destiny*, vol. 1, pp. 255–260.

60. Ibid., chaps. 7–8.

61. Ibid., p. 186.

62. Ibid., p. 233.

63. Reinhold Niebuhr, *Faith and History: A Comparison of Christian and Modern Views of History*, p. 94.

64. Niebuhr, *Nature and Destiny*, vol. 1, p. 261n.

65. Calvin, *Institutes*, bk. 2, chap. 5, sec. 1.

66. Helmut Thielicke, *The Evangelical Faith*, vol. 1, p. 145.

67. Ricoeur, *Conflict of Interpretations*, p. 286.

68. Niebuhr, *Nature and Destiny*, vol. 1, p. 252.

69. J. L. Connor, "Original Sin: Contemporary Approaches," *Theological Studies*, vol. 29, p. 226.

70. McDermott, "Original Sin," p. 507.

71. Karl Rahner, *Theological Investigations*, vol. 11, pp. 251f.

72. Ibid., pp. 255, 262.

73. Ibid., pp. 253f.; cf. McDermott, "Original Sin," p. 480.

74. McDermott, "Orginal Sin," p. 512.

75. Cf. Niebuhr, *Nature and Destiny*, vol. 1, p. 252.

76. Schleiermacher, *Christian Faith*, pp. 290f.
77. Macquarrie, *Christian Theology*, p. 240.
78. Thomas Aquinas, *Summa Theologica*, pt. 1, pt. 2, q. 77, a. 4 in c.
79. Ibid., a. 4 ad 4.
80. Niebuhr, *Nature and Destiny*, vol. 1, p. 287.
81. Ibid., p. 257.
82. Valerie Saiving Goldstein, "The Human Situation: A Feminine View," *Journal of Religion*, vol. 40, p. 108.
83. Bernard of Clairvaux, *The Love of God*, chaps. 8–15.
84. Bernard of Clairvaux, *Letters*, no. 417.
85. Paul Tillich, *The Shaking of the Foundations*, p. 158.

Chapter VI. The Age of Natural Theology

1. J. L. Mackie, *The Miracle of Theism*, p. 253.
2. Immanuel Kant, *Critique of Pure Reason*, Transcendental Dialectic, bk. 2, chap. 3, sec. 7.
3. Augustine, *Confessions*, bk. 1, chap. 1.
4. Augustine, *Epistles*, no. 120.
5. Augustine, *Exposition on the Psalms*, Ps. 44.
6. Augustine, *Concerning Order*, bk. 2, chap. 9, sec. 26.
7. Augustine, *Commentary on the Gospel of John*, Tract 40, no. 9.
8. Anselm, *Proslogion*, chap. 2.
9. Gaunilo, *Reply to Anselm*, chap. 6.
10. Alvin Plantinga, *God, Freedom, and Evil*, p. 108.
11. Hartshorne, cited in Alvin Plantinga, *The Ontological Argument*, p. 127.
12. Augustine, *On Christian Doctrine*, bk. 1, chap. 7.
13. Plantinga, *Ontological Argument*, p. 61.
14. Ibid., pp. 61–62.
15. Ibid., pp. 95f.
16. Plantinga, *God, Freedom, and Evil*, p. 112.
17. Ibid.
18. Thomas Aquinas, *Summa Theologica*, pt. 1, q. 2, a. 3.
19. Ibid., pt. 1, q. 46, a. 1–2.
20. Ibid., a. 2 in c.
21. Thomas Aquinas, *Summa Contra Gentes*, bk. 1, chap. 13, sec. 30.
22. F. C. Copleston, *Aquinas*, p. 122.
23. G. E. M. Anscombe and P. T. Geach, *Three Philosophers*, p. 115.
24. Thomas Aquinas, *Summa Theologica*, pt. 1, q. 2, a. 3 in c.
25. David Hume, *Treatise of Human Nature*, bk. 1, pt. 3, sec. 3.
26. Mackie, *Miracle of Theism*, p. 89.

27. Moses Maimonides (Moses ben Maimon), *The Guide of the Perplexed*, pt. 2, chap. 1. It is well known that St. Thomas drew heavily on earlier forms of the cosmological argument in the writings of the Arab philosopher, Avicenna (980–1037), and the Jewish philosopher, Moses Maimonides (1135–1204). Maimonides' form of the argument is of particular interest since its first section is presented in terms of the contrast between temporal and eternal beings, the form of the argument that makes for the most satisfactory interpretation of St. Thomas' Third Way.

28. David Hume, *Dialogues Concerning Natural Religion*, pt. 9.

29. Mackie, *Miracle of Theism*, p. 86.

30. William L. Rowe, *The Cosmological Argument*, pp. 22–38.

31. G. W. Leibniz, *The Monadology*, para. 37.

32. Ibid., para. 38.

33. Mackie, *Miracle of Theism*, pp. 84f.

34. Ibid., p. 85.

35. Thomas Aquinas, *Truth*, q. 3, a. 2; *Summa Theologica*, pt. 1, q. 2, a. 3 in c.

36. Hume, *Dialogues Concerning Natural Religion*, pt. 2.

37. William Paley, *Natural Theology*, vol. 2, p. 47n.

38. Stephen Jay Gould, *The Panda's Thumb*, p. 20.

39. Immanuel Kant, *The Critique of Judgement*, pt. 2, chap. 4, sec. 2, para. 86; Joseph Butler, *The Analogy of Religion*, pt. 1, passim.

40. Peter A. Bertocci, *Introduction to the Philosophy of Religion*, p. 355.

41. Ibid., p. 372.

42. Quoted from A. R. Peacocke, *Creation and the World of Science*, p. 77.

43. Bertocci, *Philosophy of Religion*, p. 386.

44. Carl G. Hempel, *Aspects of Scientific Explanation*, pp. 185f.

45. Julian S. Huxley, *Evolutionary Ethics*, p. 35.

46. Ibid., p. 42.

47. Thomas Aquinas, *Summa Theologica*, pt. 1, q. 2, a. 3 in c.

48. Hume, *Dialogues Concerning Natural Religion*, pt. 4.

49. Mackie, *Miracle of Theism*, pp. 142f.

50. Moses Maimonides, *Guide of the Perplexed*, bk. 2, chap. 20.

51. Terence Penelhum, *Problems of Religious Knowledge*, pp. 147f.

52. Aristotle, *On Interpretation*, chap. 9.

53. Augustine, *The Free Choice of the Will*, bk. 3, chap. 21.

54. Ibid., chap. 28.

55. Ibid., chap. 29.

56. Augustine, *Confessions*, bk. 8, chap. 12.

57. Ibid.

58. Augustine, *The Spirit and the Letter,* chap. 52.

59. Augustine, *The Predestination of Saints,* chap. 5.

60. Thomas Aquinas, *On Evil,* q. 16, a. 7 in c.

61. Thomas Aquinas, *Truth,* q. 2, a. 12 in c.

62. Thomas Aquinas, *Summa Contra Gentes,* bk. 1, chap. 66, sec. 7.

63. Anthony Kenny, *The God of the Philosophers,* p. 45; Nelson Pike, *God and Timelessness,* p. 88.

64. N. Pike, ibid., pp. 77ff.

65. John Duns Scotus, *Lectures on the First Book of the Sentences,* d. 39, q. 3.

66. Duns Scotus, *Oxford Commentary,* bk. 1, d. 38; d. 39, no. 23.

67. William of Ockham, *Predestination, God's Foreknowledge, and Future Contingents,* assump. 6.

68. Ibid., q. 2, sec. L.

69. Ockham, *Quodlibeta Septem,* q. 1, a. 1.

70. Ockham, *Predestination,* assump. 6.

71. Plantinga, *God, Freedom, and Evil,* pp. 34–36.

72. In this way of looking at God's omniscience, there are many issues that are not well understood. For example, can God determine which chance outcome will take place? If so, then from a theistic point of view there will be no chance, but only apparent chance. However, the proposal that God could determine chance outcomes may simply be contradictory. Anthony Kenny suspects that the notion of possible worlds is incoherent, as does Peter Geach when he describes "future-land" as "a region of fairytale" (Kenny, *God of the Philosophers,* p. 67; Geach, *Providence and Evil,* pp. 52f).

73. Geach, *Providence and Evil,* p. 53.

74. Charles Hartshorne, *Omnipotence and Other Theological Mistakes,* p. 39.

75. Thomas Aquinas, *Summa Contra Gentes,* bk. 1, chap. 57, sec. 7.

76. Ibid., bk. 1, chap. 55, sec. 7.

77. Thomas Aquinas, *Summa Theologica,* pt. 1, q. 14, a. 7 in c.

78. N. Pike, *God and Timelessness,* p. 175.

79. Charles Hartshorne, *A Natural Theology for Our Time,* p. 75.

80. N. Pike, *God and Timelessness,* pp. 177f.

81. J. S. Whale, *The Christian Answer to the Problem of Evil,* p. 16.

82. Hume, *Dialogues Concerning Natural Religion,* pt. 10.

83. Nelson Pike, *God and Evil,* pp. 88f.

84. Thomas Aquinas, *Summa Theologica,* pt. 1, q. 25, a. 4 in c.

85. Thomas Aquinas, *Summa Contra Gentes,* bk. 2, chap. 25.

86. L. Urban and W. Walton, *The Power of God,* pp. 131ff.

87. Mackie, *Miracle of Theism,* p. 162.

Swinburne?

88. L. Urban and W. Walton, *The Power of God*, pp. 206f.
89. Hartshorne, *Natural Theology*, p. 119.
90. Augustine, *Commentary on the Gospel of John*, Tract 26, no. 2.
91. John Hick, *Faith and Knowledge*, p. 135.
92. Mackie, *Miracle of Theism*, p. 93.

Chapter VII. Authority and Revelation

1. Augustine, *Epistles*, no. 137; Thomas Aquinas, *Summa Theologica*, pt. 3, q. 43, a. 4.
2. Butler, *Analogy of Religion*, pt. 2, chap. 2, sec. 3.
3. Ninian Smart, *Philosophers and Religious Truth*, p. 26.
4. David Hume, *Enquiry Concerning Human Understanding*, sec. 10, pt. 1.
5. Ibid.
6. Ibid., sec. 2.
7. Schleiermacher, *Christian Faith*, p. 72.
8. Hume, *Enquiry*, sec. 2; Van A. Harvey, *The Historian and the Believer*, p. 71.
9. Robert Boyle, *Selected Philosophical Papers of Robert Boyle*, pp. 160, 174.
10. Ibid., p. 205.
11. Baron d'Holbach, "Système de la nature," vol. 1, chap. 4, quoted from Ernst Cassirer, *The Philosophy of the Enlightenment*, p. 69.
12. John Henry Newman, *Apologia pro Vita Sua*, p. 189.
13. Thomas Aquinas, *The Power of God*, q. 4, a. 1.
14. Westminster Confession, chap. 1, sec. 10.
15. J. I. Packer, *"Fundamentalism" and the Word of God*, p. 48.
16. Ibid., pp. 96ff.
17. John Henry Newman, *A Newman Reader*, pp. 241f.
18. Charles Hodge, *Systematic Theology*, vol. 1, p. 165.
19. Henry M. Morris, *Scientific Creationism*, pp. 171ff.
20. Packer, *"Fundamentalism,"* pp. 97f.
21. Newman, *Apologia*, p. 190.
22. Augustine, *The Morals of the Catholic Church*, chap. 2, sec. 3.
23. Newman, *Apologia*, p. 187.
24. Søren Kierkegaard, *Kierkegaard's Concluding Unscientific Postscript*, p. 189; p. 188.
25. Both quotations from ibid., p. 195.
26. H. L. Mansel, *Letters, Lectures, and Reviews*, p. 115.
27. A. A. Hodge, quoted from Hick, *Faith and Knowledge*, p. 30.

28. H. L. Mansel, *The Limits of Religious Thought,* lec. 8.

29. Søren Kierkegaard, *On Authority and Revelation,* p. 92; p. 114; pp. 115f.

30. Packer, *"Fundamentalism,"* p. 59.

31. Ibid., pp. 54–58.

32. Hodge, *Systematic Theology,* vol. 1, p. 500; p. 168; p. 170.

33. Newman, *Apologia,* p. 188; p. 189.

34. Ibid., p. 196.

35. Quoted from Patrick Henry, *New Directions in New Testament Study,* p. 143.

36. Schleiermacher, quoted from H. R. Mackintosh, *Types of Modern Theology,* p. 62.

37. Schleiermacher, *Christian Faith,* pp. 14f.

38. Ibid., p. 17.

39. Schleiermacher, quoted from Richard B. Brandt, *The Philosophy of Schleiermacher,* p. 110.

40. Schleiermacher, *Christian Faith,* pp. 26ff; p. 385; p. 388.

41. Ibid., p. 368.

42. Ibid., p. 377.

43. Albrecht Ritschl, *Three Essays,* pp. 188, 198.

44. Ibid., pp. 221–223.

45. Ibid., p. 19.

46. Ritschl, quoted from Otto Pfleiderer, *The Development of Theology in Germany and Great Britain,* pp. 184f.

47. Adolf Harnack, *What Is Christianity?,* p. 128; pp. 70ff; pp. 144ff.

48. Ibid., p. 6; p. 35.

49. Albert Schweitzer, *The Quest of the Historical Jesus,* p. 335.

50. Ibid., p. 339.

51. Rudolf Otto, *The Idea of the Holy,* p. 10.

52. Ibid., p. 173.

53. Rudolf Bultmann, "New Testament and Mythology," *Kerygma and Myth,* vol. 1, p. 41.

54. Karl Barth, *Church Dogmatics,* vol. 1, pt. 2, chap. 2.

55. Bultmann, *Kerygma and Myth,* vol. 1, p. 41.

56. Ibid.

57. Ibid., p. 16.

58. Norman Perrin, *The Promise of Bultmann,* p. 55.

59. Bultmann, *Kerygma and Myth,* vol. 1, p. 41.

60. Ibid.

61. James M. Robinson, *A New Quest of the Historical Jesus,* p. 31n.

62. Perrin, *Promise of Bultmann,* p. 63.

63. Robinson, *New Quest*, p. 94.

64. H. C. Kee, F. W. Young, and K. Froelich, *Understanding the New Testament*, pp. 105ff.

65. Norman Perrin, *The New Testament: An Introduction*, p. 290.

66. Kee, *Jesus in History*, p. 80.

67. H. C. Kee, F. W. Young, and K. Froelich, *Understanding the New Testament*, pp. 95, 106.

68. Norman Perrin, *A Modern Pilgrimage in New Testament Christology*, pp. 10ff.

69. Ibid., p. 58.

70. Ibid., pp. 70f.

Chapter VIII. Discovering the Foundations

1. Søren Kierkegaard, *Philosophical Fragments*, p. 69.

2. Thomas Aquinas, *Summa Theologica*, pt. 2, pt. 2, q. 2, a. 9 ad 2.

3. Ibid., a. 9 ad 3.

4. Alasdair MacIntyre, "The Logical Status of Religious Belief," *Metaphysical Beliefs*, p. 209.

5. John Hick, *The Center of Christianity*, pp. 47f.

6. Otto, *Idea of the Holy*, p. 11n.

7. William James, *The Varieties of Religious Experience*, p. 58, quoted from Otto, *Idea of the Holy*, p. 10n.

8. Julian of Norwich, *Fourteenth Revelation*, quoted from Steven T. Katz, ed., *Mysticism and Religious Traditions*, p. 155.

9. Meister Eckhart, Sermon 6, quoted from Colledge and McGinn, *Meister Eckhart: The Essential Sermons*, p. 188.

10. W. T. Stace, *The Teachings of the Mystics*, p. 20.

11. *Milindapañha*, bk. 4, chap. 8, par. 76.

12. James, *Varieties of Religious Experience*, p. 68.

13. Jan van Ruysbroeck, *Supreme Truth*, chap. 11.

14. Meister Eckhart, *Tractate*, no. 2.

15. Martin Buber, *Eclipse of God*, p. 128; *I and Thou*, p. 75; p. 110; p. 112.

16. Martin Buber, *Between Man and Man*, p. 24; p. 30.

17. Buber, *I and Thou*, p. 82.

18. Buber, *Eclipse of God*, p. 98.

19. Karl Barth, *Church Dogmatics*, vol. 1, part 1, pp. 98–140.

20. Ibid., pp. 150ff.

21. Barth, *Dogmatics in Outline*, pp. 23f.

22. Barth, *The Knowledge of God and the Service of God*, p. 26;

Church Dogmatics, vol. 1, pt. 1, p. 278; p. 214; *Dogmatics in Outline,* p. 24.

23. Buber, *Between Man and Man,* pp. 13f, 24.

24. Stace, *Teachings of the Mystics,* pp. 126–130.

25. James, *Varieties of Religious Experience,* pp. 422f.

26. Keith Lehrer, *Knowledge,* pp. 76ff.

27. Bertrand Russell, *The Problems of Philosophy,* pp. 151f.

28. Nicholas Rescher, *The Coherence Theory of Truth,* p. 318.

29. Ibid., p. 40.

30. William James, *Selected Papers on Philosophy,* p. 215.

31. James, *Varieties of Religious Experience,* pp. 66f.

32. Ibid., p. 422.

33. Martin Heidegger, quoted from Walter Kaufmann, *Existentialism from Dostoevsky to Sartre,* pp. 207–221.

34. Tillich, *Systematic Theology,* vol. 1, p. 237.

35. Karl Rahner, *A Rahner Reader,* p. 5.

36. Tillich, *Systematic Theology,* vol. 1, p. 237.

37. Ibid., p. 189.

38. Paul Tillich, *Theology of Culture,* pp. 23f; *My Search for Absolutes,* p. 125.

39. Karl Rahner, quoted from Karl-Heinz Weger, *Karl Rahner: An Introduction to His Theology,* p. 47.

40. Tillich, *Systematic Theology,* vol. 1, pp. 215f.

41. Paul Tillich, *Biblical Religion and the Search for Ultimate Reality,* p. 25.

42. Ibid., p. 31.

43. Ibid., p. 65.

44. Ibid., p. 83.

45. Tillich is notorious for remarks like "It is as atheistic to affirm the existence of God as it is to deny it" (*Systematic Theology,* vol. 1, p. 237), which seem to imply that God or being-itself is without reality. However, this is not Tillich's intent. His concept that God is being-itself, or the power of being, permits one to say, "God *is*" (ibid., vol. 2, p. 11). It is thus to be inferred that Tillich uses "existence" in a very restricted sense. Its use is confined to finite and contingent realities, to "some*thing* or some*one* who might or might not exist" (ibid., vol. 1, p. 205). Since "to be something is to be finite" (ibid., vol. 1, p. 190), to say that "God is being-itself, not *a* being," (ibid., vol. 1, p. 237) is to remove existence—the kind of contingent reality that finite beings have— from the possible properties of the power of being in everything that has being. Thus, "being" is the wider term, applicable to the infinite and to

finite realities. "Existence" is the narrower term, applicable only to finite, contingent realities.

46. Rahner, *Rahner Reader*, pp. 7f.
47. Karl Rahner, *Theological Investigations*, vol. 3, p. 280.
48. Ibid., vol. 13, pp. 122ff.
49. Karl Rahner, quoted from Weger, *Karl Rahner: Introduction*, p. 95.
50. Karl Rahner, *Christian at the Crossroads*, pp. 11-14.
51. Rahner, *Theological Investigations*, vol. 11, p. 159.
52. Rahner, *Christian at the Crossroads*, p. 17.
53. Ibid., p. 16.
54. Evelyn Underhill, *Concerning the Inner Life*, p. 4.
55. Friedrich Heiler, *Prayer*, p. 358.
56. Evelyn Underhill, *Concerning the Inner Life*, p. xi.
57. Ibid.

Chapter IX. Sacraments

For all Popes, the dates in parentheses refer to the pontificate.

1. See Mircea Eliade, *Cosmos and History*, pp. 55–58.
2. See Bernhard W. Anderson, *Understanding the Old Testament*, esp. pp. 522–525.
3. Royden Keith Yerkes, *Sacrifice in Greek and Roman Religions and Early Judaism*, pp. 122–124.
4. See above, p. 9.
5. Homer, *The Iliad*, bk. 1, line 444.
6. Jean-Jaques Olier, *Introduction to The Christian Life and Virtues*, quoted from Hugh B. Urban, Jr., *Manasoyajña/Logike Thusia* (The Reasonable Sacrifice), unpublished.
7. Flavius Josephus, *The Jewish War*, bk. 2, chap. 14.
8. Genesis Rabba, chap. 42, sec. 8.
9. See above, p. 130.
10. Talmud, Yebamoth, 46a.
11. Flavius Josephus, *Jewish Antiquities*, bk. 18, chap. 19.
12. J. Delorme, "The Practice of Baptism in Judaism at the Beginning of the Christian Era," *Baptism in the New Testament: A Symposium*, pp. 36f.
13. Josephus, *Jewish War*, bk. 2, chap. 8, sec. 5. In these matters the Qumran *Manual of Discipline* confirms Josephus' account.
14. Delorme, "The Practice of Baptism in Judaism," p. 37.
15. Leonel L. Mitchell, *The Meaning of Ritual*, p. 88.
16. Ibid., pp. 51–56, 70.
17. Ibid., pp. 88–90.

18. Ibid., pp. 90–92; Hippolytus, *The Apostolic Tradition,* chaps. 21–23.
19. Shepherd of Hermas, Similitude 8, chap. 2, secs. 2f.
20. Epistle of Barnabas, chap. 11, sec. 11; chap. 16, secs. 7f.
21. Clement of Rome, *First Letter,* chap. 46, sec. 6.
22. Justin Martyr, *First Apology,* chap. 61.
23. Irenaeus, *Proof of the Apostolic Preaching,* chaps. 41f; *Against Heresies,* bk. 5, chap. 11, sec. 2; quoted from Kelly, *Early Christian Doctrines,* p. 195.
24. Tertullian, *Against Marcion,* bk. 1, chap. 28, sec. 2.
25. Mitchell, *Meaning of Ritual,* p. 75.
26. Didache, chap. 9, sec. 5; chap. 10, sec. 3.
27. Ignatius of Antioch, *Epistle to the Smyrneans,* chap. 7.
28. Kelly, *Early Christian Doctrines,* pp. 214f.
29. Justin Martyr, *First Apology,* chaps. 65–67.
30. Cyprian, *Letters,* no. 17, quoted from Kelly, *Early Christian Doctrines,* p. 215.
31. Shepherd of Hermas, Mandate 4, chap. 3, sec. 1.
32. *Epistle to the Philadelphians,* chap. 3, sec. 2; chap. 8, sec. 1; *Epistle to the Philippians,* chap. 11, sec. 4.
33. Clement of Rome, *Second Letter,* chap. 8, secs. 1–3.
34. Apostolic Constitutions, bk. 2, chaps. 10–16.
35. Kelly, *Early Christian Doctrines,* p. 437.
36. Ibid., p. 209.
37. Hippolytus, *Apostolic Tradition,* chap. 21, sec. 4.
38. Tertullian, *On Baptism,* chap. 18.
39. See above, chap. 6.
40. Augustine, *On the Merits and Remission of Sins,* bk. 1, chap. 55. See also *On the Grace of Christ and Original Sin,* bk. 2, esp. chaps. 3–6. See also *The Baptism of Infants against Marcellinus,* esp. bk. 1.
41. Ambrose, *On Repentance,* bk. 2, chap. 95, quoted from Kelly, *Early Christian Doctrines,* p. 438.
42. Kelly, *Early Christian Doctrines,* p. 439.
43. P. Palmer, "The Sacrament of Penance," *The New Catholic Encyclopedia,* vol. 11, p. 75.
44. Tertullian, *On Baptism,* chap. 6.
45. J. D. C. Fisher, *Confirmation: Then and Now,* pp. 132–136.
46. *Gallican Homily,* quoted from Darwell Stone, *Holy Baptism,* p. 82.
47. Peter Lombard, *The Fourth Book of the Sentences,* dist. 7, quoted from Stone, *Holy Baptism,* p. 82.
48. Augustine, *Sermons,* no. 174, sec. 7.
49. Thomas Aquinas, *Summa Theologica,* pt. 3, q. 80, a. 9 ad 3.
50. Ambrose, *On Mysteries,* sec. 54.

51. Ambrose, *On the Sacraments*, bk. 4, chap. 21.

52. Darwell Stone, *A History of the Doctrine of the Holy Eucharist*, vol. 1, p. 29.

53. Ibid., p. 34.

54. Augustine, *Tractates on the Gospel of John*, no. 26, chap. 11, sec. 2.

55. Augustine, *Sermons*, no. 272, quoted from Kelly, *Early Christian Doctrines*, pp. 422f.

56. Ambrose, *On Faith to Gratian*, bk. 4, sec. 124, quoted from Stone, *Holy Eucharist*, vol. 1, p. 105.

57. Gregory of Nyssa, *Catechetical Oration*, chap. 37.

58. Justin Martyr, *First Apology*, chap. 66.

59. Stanislaus J. Grabowski, *The Church: An Introduction to the Theology of St. Augustine*, pp. 183ff.

60. Augustine, *Sermons*, no. 134, sec. 2, quoted from Stone, *Holy Eucharist*, vol. 1, p. 83.

61. Augustine, *Sermons*, no. 272, quoted from Grabowski, *The Church*, p. 186.

62. A. J. Macdonald, *Berengar and the Reform of Sacramental Doctrine*, p. 359.

63. Augustine, *Sermons*, no. 272, quoted from Berengar of Tours, *Reply to Lanfranc*, p. 196.

64. Augustine, *Epistles*, no. 98, sec. 9.

65. Kelly, *Early Christian Doctrines*, pp. 447–449.

66. Ambrose, *Narrations on the Psalms*, no. 38, sec. 25, quoted from Kelly, *Early Christian Doctrines*, p. 453.

67. Kelly, *Early Christian Doctrines*, p. 454. See Augustine, *Epistles*, no. 98, sec. 9.

68. Augustine, *City of God*, bk. 10, chap. 6.

69. Augustine, *Sermons*, no. 229.

70. Radbertus, *On the Lord's Body and Blood*, chap. 1, sec. 2.

71. Ibid., chap. 1, sec. 6.

72. Ratramnus, *Christ's Body and Blood*, sec. 54.

73. Ibid., sec. 69.

74. Ibid., sec. 16.

75. Macdonald, *Berengar and the Reform of Sacramental Doctrine*, pp. 210f.

76. Peter Lombard, *Fourth Book of the Sentences*, dist. 11, and *First Book*, dist. 4; see Stone, *Holy Eucharist*, vol. 1, p. 305.

77. Thomas Aquinas, *Summa Theologica*, pt. 3, qq. 75–77.

78. William of Ockham, *The Body of Christ*, chap. 5.

79. Thomas Aquinas, *Summa Theologica*, pt. 3, q. 75, a. 2 in c.

80. Ibid., q. 77, a. 1 in c.; see also William of Ockham, *Body of Christ*, chap. 7.

81. Thomas Aquinas, *Summa Theologica*, pt. 3, q. 76, a. 5 in c.

82. Ibid., pt. 3, q. 83, a. 1 ad 1.

83. Ibid., pt. 3, q. 79, a. 7 ad 3.

84. See above, pp. 117–119.

85. See Francis Clark, *Eucharistic Sacrifice and the Reformation*, pp. 93–95, for a convenient summary of late medieval doctrine concerning the Eucharist. *Not all agree with Li—*

86. Thomas Aquinas, *Summa Theologica*, pt. 3, q. 83, a. 1 ad 1.

87. Gabriel Biel, *Exposition on the Sacred Canon of the Mass*, lecture 20, sec. K, quoted from Clark, *Eucharistic Sacrifice*, p. 85.

88. Thomas à Kempis, *The Imitation of Christ*, bk. 4, chap. 8.

89. See above, p. 153.

90. See, for example, Martin Luther, *Luther's Works*, Jaroslav Pelikan and Helmut T. Lehmann, eds., vol. 38, p. 228.

91. Francis Clark in his *Eucharistic Sacrifice and the Reformation* holds a somewhat different view on this issue.

92. See pp. 122–123 above.

93. Luther, "Treatise on Christian Liberty," in *Works of Martin Luther*, vol. 2, p. 338.

94. Luther, *Luther's Works*, vol. 36, pp. 28–29.

95. William of Ockham, *Body of Christ*, chap. 5.

96. Luther, *Luther's Works*, vol. 37, p. 306.

97. Ibid., vol. 37, pp. 290–292.

98. Oliver Chase Quick, *The Christian Sacraments*, p. 206. Quick gives a somewhat different account of Virtualism.

99. Calvin, *Institutes*, bk. 4, chap. 17, sec. 31.

100. John Calvin, *The Best Method of Obtaining Concord*, reprinted in *Calvin: Theological Treatises*, J. K. S. Reid, trans., p. 329.

101. Ibid.

102. Ibid., p. 328.

103. Thomas Cranmer, *A Defence of the True and Catholic Doctrine of the Sacrament of the Body and Blood of Our Savior Christ*, bk. 1, chap. 7. Although there are passages in Cranmer's works that reflect a Zwinglian and subjectivist interpretation of Christ's presence in the Eucharist (ibid., bk. 1, chap. 16), nonetheless on the crucial issue as to whether Christ's presence is the result of Christ's contemporaneous activity, as is the case in Calvin, or whether Christ is present only though our human agency, as is the case with Zwingli, Cranmer sides with Calvin. See, for example, *An Answer unto a Crafty and Sophisticall Cavillation devised by Stephen Gardiner*,

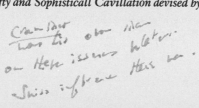

sec. 4, where Cranmer clearly states that in the Supper Christ is present as an active cause, acting along with the material components.

104. John Calvin, *Opera omnia quae supersunt*, vol. 1, p. 119, quoted from François Wendel, *Calvin: The Origin and Development of His Religious Thought*, p. 332. See also Calvin, *Institutes*, bk. 4, chap. 17, sec. 10.

105. *The Book of Common Prayer*, Protestant Episcopal Church in the USA, 1928 ed.

106. Ulrich Zwingli, "The Sixty-Seven Articles," reprinted in *The Protestant Reformation*, Lewis W. Spitz, ed., art. 18.

107. Quoted from Massey H. Shepherd, Jr., comp., *Holy Communion: An Anthology of Christian Devotion*, p. 134.

108. Ulrich Zwingli, *An Exposition of the Faith*, in *Zwingli and Bullinger*, G. W. Bromiley, ed., p. 258.

109. Zwingli, *On the Lord's Supper*, in *Zwingli and Bullinger*, p. 198.

110. Conrad Grebel, "Letters to Thomas Müntzer by Conrad Grebel and Friends," reprinted in *Protestant Reformation*, Spitz, ed., p. 76.

111. Thomas Cranmer, *Defense of the True and Catholic Doctrine*, bk. 1, chap. 7.

112. Philip Schaff, ed., *The Creeds of Christendom*, vol. 3, p. 741.

113. George Fox, *An Autobiography*, pp. 101–104.

114. Ibid., p. 105.

115. Ibid., p. 115.

116. Calvin, *Institutes*, bk. 4, chap. 15, sec. 10. See Luther, *The Babylonian Captivity of the Church*, in *Luther's Works*, vol. 36, pp. 66–68; Zwingli, *On Baptism*, in *Zwingli and Bullinger*, p. 154.

117. Luther, *Babylonian Captivity*, in *Luther's Works*, vol. 36, pp. 58f.

118. Zwingli, *On Baptism*, in *Zwingli and Bullinger*, pp. 134ff; Calvin, *Institutes*, bk. 4, chap. 15, secs. 1–12, and chap. 16, sec. 2.

119. Zwingli, *On Baptism*, in *Zwingli and Bullinger*, p. 148; Calvin, *Institutes*, bk. 4, chap. 15, sec. 13.

120. Michael Sattler, *The Schleitheim Confession of Faith*, reprinted in *Protestant Reformation*, Spitz, ed., p. 91.

121. Ibid., p. 149.

122. Luther, *Babylonian Captivity*, in *Luther's Works*, vol. 36, p. 73.

123. Zwingli, *On Baptism*, p. 148; and Calvin, *Institutes*, bk. 4, chaps. 16 and 18.

124. Calvin, *Institutes*, bk. 4, chap. 16, sec. 7.

125. J. D. C. Fisher, *Christian Initiation: The Reformation Period*, p. 260.

126. Calvin, *Institutes*, 1536 ed., quoted from Fisher, *Christian Initiation*, p. 258.

127. Fisher, *Christian Initiation*, pp. 165–167.

128. *Canons and Decrees of the Council of Trent*, sess. 22, canon 1; in Schaff, ed., *Creeds of Christendom*, vol. 2, p. 184.

129. Joseph Pohle, "The Sacrifice of the Mass," *The Catholic Encyclopedia*, vol. 10, p. 7.

130. *Canons and Decrees*, sess. 22, chap. 11; in Schaff, ed., *Creeds of Christendom*, vol. 2, p. 179.

131. Thomas Aquinas, *Summa Theologica*, pt. 3, q. 83, a. 5.

132. David N. Power, *The Sacrifice We Offer: The Tridentine Dogma and Its Reinterpretation*, p. 108.

133. Pohle, "Sacrifice of the Mass," p. 7.

134. Ibid., p. 8.

135. *Canons and Decrees*, sess. 22, chap. 1; in Schaff, ed., *Creeds of Christendom*, vol. 2, pp. 176–177.

136. Pohle, "Sacrifice of the Mass," p. 8.

137. Ibid., pp. 14ff.

138. Ibid., p. 15.

139. Friedrich Schleiermacher, *The Christian Faith*, p. 654.

140. Ibid., p. 638.

141. Ibid., p. 639.

142. Ibid., p. 640.

143. Ibid., p. 641.

144. Ibid., p. 649.

145. Ibid., p. 653.

146. Charles Davis, *Liturgy and Doctrine*, pp. 14ff.

147. See pp. 252–254 above.

148. Faith and Order Commission, *Baptism, Eucharist and Ministry*, paras. 11, 20, 15.

149. See John Reumann, *The Supper of the Lord: The New Testament, Ecumenical Dialogues, and Faith and Order on Eucharist*, p. 144.

150. Ibid., pp. 192f.

151. See Schleiermacher, *Christian Faith*, pp. 633–638.

152. See Daniel B. Stevick, *Baptismal Moments; Baptismal Meanings*, pp. 75f., and Liam G. Walsh, *The Sacraments of Initiation: Baptism, Confirmation, Eucharist*, pp. 149–158, for discussions of this issue.

153. See pp. 145–151 above.

154. "Agreed Statement on Eucharistic Doctrine," *Documents on Anglican Roman Catholic Relations II*, compiled by the Bishops' Committee on Ecumenical and Interreligious Affairs and the Joint Commission on Ecumenical Relations, sec. 6; also Karl Rahner, *Theological Investigations*, vol. 4, pp. 302f.

155. USA National Committee for Lutheran World Federation and The Bishop's Committee for Ecumenical and Interreligious Affairs, "The Eu-

charist as Sacrifice," *Lutherans and Catholics in Dialogue III*, p. 196.

156. Edward Schillebeeckx, *The Eucharist*, pp. 94ff.

157. Edward Schillebeeckx, *Christ the Sacrament of the Encounter with God*, esp. pp. 43ff.

158. Davis, *Liturgy and Doctrine*, pp. 78 and 88.

159. Louis Bouyer, *Eucharist*, p. 467.

160. Schillebeeckx, *Eucharist*, pp. 108f.

161. Reumann, *Supper of the Lord*, p. 75; Walsh, *Sacraments of Initiation*, pp. 259f.

162. Quick, *Christian Sacraments*, p. 207.

163. Pohle, "Sacrifice of the Mass," pp. 6 and 11.

164. Calvin, *Institutes*, bk. 4, chap. 17, sec. 10.

165. Ibid., bk. 4, chap. 17, sec. 18.

166. Thomas Aquinas, *Summa Theologica*, pt. 3, q. 77, a. 1 in c.

167. Many of these points have been made in Quick, *Christian Sacraments*, pp. 207–209.

168. Theodore G. Tappert, ed., *The Book of Concord*, p. 256.

169. *Anglican–Lutheran International Conversations: The Report of the Conversations 1970–1972 authorized by the Lambeth Conference and the Lutheran World Federation*, sec. 64, quoted from Reumann, *Supper of the Lord*, p. 119.

170. "Agreed Statement on Eucharistic Doctrine," *Documents on Anglican Roman Catholic Relations II*, p. 25.

171. Anglican–Lutheran International Conversations, sec. 64.

172. Lutheran/Roman Catholic Joint Commission, *The Eucharist*, p. 21, n. 59.

173. H. Meyer and L. Vischer, eds., *Growth in Agreement: Reports and Agreed Statements of Ecumenical Conversations on a World Level*, p. 354, n. 66.

174. See Power, *Sacrifice We Offer*, p. 23.

175. Ibid., pp. 21 and 23. For views even more conservative than those of John Paul II, see Rama P. Coomaraswamy, *The Problem of the New Mass*.

Chapter X. The Church and the Ministry

For all Popes, the dates in parentheses refer to the pontificate.

1. Paul Minear in *Images of the Church in the New Testament* lists ninety-six such metaphors.

2. No mention is made of Christ as head of the Church or of the Spirit as its soul in Rom. 12 and 1 Cor. 10 and 12. However, in Colossians and

Ephesians the emphasis is on Christ's headship and the Church's subordination to him.

3. Irenaeus, *Against Heresies,* bk. 3, chap. 24, sec. 1.

4. See Kelly, *Early Christian Doctrines,* pp. 206f.

5. See Howard Clark Kee, *Understanding the New Testament,* 4th ed., p. 304.

6. Kee, *Understanding the New Testament,* 4th ed., p. 300.

7. Bernard Cooke, *Ministry to Word and Sacraments: History and Theology,* pp. 60ff.

8. See, for example, Kee, *Understanding the New Testament,* 4th ed., p. 400.

9. Didache, chap. 15.

10. Didache, chap. 11, sec. 3, and chap. 13, sec. 2.

11. Shepherd of Hermas, Similitude 9, chap. 16, sec. 5.

12. Shepherd of Hermas, Vision 2, chap. 4.

13. Shepherd of Hermas, Similitude 9, chap. 27, sec. 2; Vision 3, chap. 5, sec. 1.

14. Clement of Rome, *First Letter,* chap. 44.

15. Ibid., chap. 24.

16. Ibid., chaps. 42 and 44.

17. Ignatius of Antioch, *Epistle to the Magnisians,* chap. 3, secs. 1–2, and chap. 6, sec. 1; *Epistle to the Trallians,* chap. 3, sec. 1.

18. Ignatius of Antioch, *Epistle to the Ephesians,* chap. 6.

19. Ignatius of Antioch, *Epistle to the Philippians,* chap. 7.

20. Hippolytus, *Apostolic Tradition,* chaps. 2–4 and 7–8.

21. See Cooke, *Ministry to Word and Sacraments,* pp. 61f.

22. Ibid., p. 65.

23. Didache, chap. 15; Jerome, *Letter 146* [*to Evangelus*].

24. See above, p. 79.

25. See the letter of Irenaeus to Florinus contained in Eusebius, *Ecclesiastical History,* bk. 5, chap. 20, secs. 5–7; and Irenaeus, *Against Heresies,* bk. 3, chap. 3, sec. 1.

26. See Cyprian, *Letters,* no. 33, sec. 1.

27. Ibid., no. 66, sec. 8.

28. See above, pp. 62–66.

29. The Martyrdom of Polycarp, chap. 8, sec. 1.

30. Vincent of Lérins, *Commonitory,* chap. 2.

31. Ibid.

32. Augustine, *The Utility of Belief,* chap. 14, sec. 31.

33. Boethius, *On the Catholic Faith,* lns. 257–261.

34. Jerome, *Against Vigilantius,* chap. 5, quoted from Pelikan, *Christian Tradition,* vol. 1, p. 333.

35. Athanasius, *Apology against the Arians*, chap. 30, sec. 1.

36. Augustine, *Against the Epistle of the Parmesians*, bk. 3, chap. 4, sec. 24, quoted from Pelikan, *Christian Tradition*, vol. 1, p. 334.

37. John Cassian, *On the Incarnation of the Lord against Nestorius*, bk. 1, chap. 6.

38. Macrobius, *Commentary on the Dream of Scipio*, bk. 1, chap. 14, sec. 15. See *On the Divine Names*, chap. 4, for Pseudo-Dionysius' account of the same progression.

39. Thomas Aquinas, *Summa Theologica*, pt. 1, q. 108, a. 1 in c.

40. Bonaventure, *Commentary on the Sentences*, bk. 2, dist. 9, quoted from Pelikan, *Christian Tradition*, vol. 3, p. 293.

41. Thomas Aquinas, *Summa Theologica*, pt. 1, q. 108, a. 4 ad 3.

42. Pseudo-Dionysius, *The Ecclesiastical Hierarchy*, chap. 5.

43. Bernard of Clairvaux, *On Consideration*, bk. 3, chap. 4, sec. 18.

44. Giles of Rome, *On Ecclesiastical Power*, chap. 9, in Evart Lewis, *Medieval Political Ideas*, vol. 2, p. 384.

45. Giles of Rome, *On Ecclesiastical Power*, chap. 2, quoted from Frederick Copleston, *A History of Philosophy*, vol. 2, p. 465.

46. Augustine, *Epistles*, no. 34, sec. 3; *Sermons*, no. 22, sec. 9.

47. Augustine, *Of the Good of Marriage*, chaps. 11 and 8; *Holy Virginity*, chaps. 13 and 27.

48. Augustine, *On Marriage and Concupiscence*, chap. 1, sec. 24.

49. P. Delhaye, "History of Celibacy," *The New Catholic Encyclopedia*, vol. 3, p. 370.

50. Clement of Alexandria, *Miscellanies*, bk. 1, chap. 3.

51. Cooke, *Ministry to Word and Sacraments*, p. 558.

52. Ibid.

53. Delhaye, "History of Celibacy," p. 371.

54. Ibid., p. 372.

55. Eusebius, *Ecclesiastical History*, bk. 6, sec. 43.

56. Grabowski, *The Church*, pp. 102–109.

57. See Augustine, *The Free Choice of the Will*, bk. 2, chaps. 20 and 54; *The True Religion*, bk. 7, chap. 13; *On Music*, bk. 6, chaps. 56–57; *The Literal Interpretation of Genesis*, bk. 4, chaps. 3–4, 7–9.

58. Augustine, *On Genesis against the Manichians*, bk. 1, chap. 16, in Vernon J. Bourke, *Augustine's View of Reality*, p. 49.

59. Augustine, *The Literal Interpretation of Genesis*, bk. 4, chap. 2; *The Trinity*, bk. 4, chaps. 4 and 6.

60. Pseudo-Dionysius, *The Celestial Hierarchy*, chaps. 6–10.

61. *The Fathers According to Rabbi Nathan*, chap. 37.

62. Venerable Bede, *On Genesis*, *Patrologia Latina*, vol. 91, col. 192.

63. Bernard McGinn, *The Calabrian Abbot: Joachim of Fiore in the History of Western Thought*, pp. 145–161, 180.

64. John of Salisbury, *The Seven Divisions of Seven*, Patrologia Latina, vol. 199, cols. 945–964.

65. See Otto Georg von Simson, *The Gothic Cathedral.*

66. Thomas Aquinas, *Summa Theologica*, pt. 3 (supplement), q. 37, a. 2 in c.

67. Ibid., pt. 3, q. 65, a. 1 in c.

68. Ibid., pt. 1, q. 108, a. 4 ad 3.

69. Augustine, *Sermons*, no. 295, sec. 4, quoted from Grabowski, *The Church*, p. 135, and Kelly, *Early Christian Doctrines*, p. 419.

70. Augustine, *Epistles*, no. 43, sec. 7.

71. Kelly, *Early Christian Doctrines*, pp. 417–419.

72. See Augustine, *Retractions*, bk. 1, chap. 21, sec. 1.

73. Leo I, *Epistles*, no. 14, sec. 11.

74. Council of Chalcedon, quoted from Cooke, *Ministry to Word and Sacraments*, p. 439.

75. Williston Walker, *A History of the Christian Church*, p. 135.

76. Boniface VIII, *Unum Sanctum*, quoted from ibid., p. 291.

77. Augustinus Triumphus, *Summa on Ecclesiastical Power*, q. 6, a. 8, in Lewis, *Medieval Political Ideas*, vol. 2, p. 391.

78. Giles of Rome, *On Ecclesiastical Power*, quoted from Lewis, *Medieval Political Ideas*, vol. 2, p. 363.

79. Nicholas of Cusa, *The Catholic Concordance*, bk. 1, chaps. 2, 9 and 10.

80. Donation of Constantine, quoted from Walker, *History of the Christian Church*, p. 204.

81. See Lewis, *Medieval Political Ideas*, vol. 2, pp. 358f.

82. Nicholas of Cusa, *Conjecture about the Last Days*, quoted from Pelikan, *Christian Tradition*, vol. 4, p. 11.

83. Jean De Gerson, *On the Doctrine of Ramond Lull*, quoted from Pelikan, *Christian Tradition*, vol. 4, p. 12.

84. Jean De Gerson, *The Unity of the Church*, quoted from Pelikan, *Christian Tradition*, vol. 4, p. 73.

85. Walker, *History of the Christian Church*, p. 318.

86. Marsilius of Padua, *Defender of the Peace*, discourse 2, chap. 24, sec. 11.

87. Ubertino of Casale, *The Tree of the Crucified Life of Jesus*, bk. 4, chap. 5, quoted from Pelikan, *Christian Tradition*, vol. 4, p. 93.

88. Desiderius Erasmus, *The Praise of Folly*, secs. 28–31.

89. Luther, *Babylonian Captivity*, *Luther's Works*, vol. 36, p. 113.

90. Luther, *The Misuse of the Mass*, *Luther's Works*, vol. 36, p. 139.

91. Ibid.

92. Luther, *Treatise on the New Testament, Luther's Works*, vol. 35, p. 101.

93. Luther also drew a distinction between the visible and the invisible Church. The visible Church was the assembly of Christians here on earth. In the visible Church the separation of saints and sinners had not yet taken place. The invisible Church, which might be called the real Church, was made up of the elect, both those in heaven and on earth. Of course many of the latter's members were known only to God.

94. "Augsburg Confession," Article VII, in Schaff, ed., *Creeds of Christendom*, vol. 3, pp. 11f.

95. Calvin, *Institutes*, bk. 2, chap. 15, sec. 6.

96. Ibid., bk. 4, chap. 1, sec. 9.

97. Ibid., bk. 4, chap. 10, sec. 30.

98. See Elsie Ann McKee, *Elders and the Plural Ministry*, chaps. 5 and 8, for a study of the origins of Calvin's ideas on lay ministry.

99. Spitz, ed., *Protestant Reformation*, p. 91.

100. Fox, *An Autobiography*, p. 105.

101. *Canons and Decrees*, sess. 13, chap. 3, in Schaff, ed., *Creeds of Christendom*, vol. 2, pp. 129f.

102. Ibid., sess. 23, chap. 2.

103. "Tridentine Profession of Faith," Article X, in Schaff, ed., *Creeds of Christendom*, vol. 2, p. 209.

104. Robert Bellarmine, *On Controversies*, vol. 2, bk. 3, chap. 2, quoted from Avery Dulles, *Models of the Church*, p. 14.

105. Dulles, *Models of the Church*, p. 31.

106. Philip Melancthon, *Apology of the Augsburg Confession*, art. 7, sec. 23.

107. *Canons and Decrees*, sess. 23, chap. 1, in Schaff, ed., *Creeds of Christendom*, vol. 2, pp. 186f.

108. Richard Hooker, *The Laws of Ecclesiastical Polity*, bk. 5, chap. 73, sec. 2.

109. Ibid., bk. 3, chap. 1, sec. 2.

110. Ibid., bk. 7, chap. 4, secs. 1 and 2.

111. Ibid., bk. 5, chap. 8, sec. 2.

112. Ibid., chap. 8, sec. 1.

113. William Laud, *The Works of William Laud*, vol. 6, p. 173.

114. Dulles, *Models of the Church*. A different but analogous analysis is provided in Cooke, *Ministry to Word and Sacraments*.

115. "The Westminster Shorter Catechism," in Schaff, ed., *Creeds of Christendom*, vol. 3, p. 676.

116. Underhill, *Worship*, p. 5.

117. St. John of the Cross, quoted from ibid.

118. "Düsseldorf Theses of 1933," quoted from Pelikan, *Christian Tradition*, vol. 5, p. 290.

119. Jürgen Moltmann, *The Church in the Power of the Spirit*: A Contribution to Messianic Ecclesiology, pp. 207ff.

120. Søren Kierkegaard, A *Kierkegaard Anthology*, p. 446.

121. Ibid., p. 447.

122. See Søren Kierkegaard, *Fear and Trembling*, Problem I.

123. Both quotations are from Schleiermacher, *Christian Faith*, p. 525.

124. Ibid., p. 565.

125. Ibid., p. 651.

126. Ibid., p. 641.

127. Ibid.

128. Ibid., p. 681.

129. Moltmann, *Church in the Power of the Spirit*, p. 33.

130. Ibid., p. 65.

131. Ibid., pp. 96ff.

132. Ibid., pp. 252f.

133. Ibid., p. 253.

134. Robert N. Bellah et al., *Habits of the Heart: Individualism and Commitment in American Life*, pp. 240ff.

135. Alasdair MacIntyre, *After Virtue: A Study in Moral Theory*, pp. 244f.

136. Jürgen Moltmann, *The Gospel of Liberation*, p. 68.

137. José Comblin, *The Church and the National Security State*, p. 106.

138. Kant, *Religion within the Limits of Reason Alone*, pp. 90–92.

139. Albrecht Ritschl, *The Christian Doctrine of Justification and Reconciliation*, vol. 3, p. 29, and *Instruction in the Christian Religion*, secs. 29–33; quoted from Pelikan, *Christian Tradition*, vol. 5, p. 221.

140. Ritschl, *Christian Doctrine of Justification and Reconciliation*, p. 284, quoted from John Kenneth Mozley, *Ritschlianism: An Essay*, p. 234.

141. Harnack, *What Is Christianity?*, p. 101.

142. Ibid., p. 112.

143. Walter Rauschenbusch, A *Theology of the Social Gospel*, p. 131.

144. Walter Rauschenbusch, *Christianity and the Social Crisis*, p. 349.

145. Ibid., p. 185.

146. Martin Luther King, Jr., *Strength to Love*, p. 169.

147. Martin Luther King, Jr., *Stride toward Freedom*, p. 187.

148. Gustavo Gutierrez, A *Theology of Liberation*, p. 261.

149. Ibid., pp. 291, 295.

150. Ibid., p. 302.

151. Jose Miguez-Bonino in *Doing Theology in a Revolutionary Situation* gives a good introductory survey, as does Philip Berryman in *Liberation Theology*.

152. See Miguez-Bonino, *Doing Theology*, pp. 95–97.

153. Wilfrid Ward, *William George Ward and the Catholic Revival*, quoted from Alec R. Vidler, *The Church in an Age of Revolution*, p. 153.

154. Pius IX, *The Syllabus of Errors*, in Anne Fremantle, ed., *The Papal Encyclicals in Their Historical Context*, p. 27.

155. Ibid., p. 152.

156. Note: "Fundamentalism" is here used in its broad sense to refer to a belief in Biblical inerrancy.

157. J. Gresham Machen, *Christianity and Liberalism*, p. 160.

158. George M. Marsden, *Fundamentalism and American Culture: The Shaping of Twentieth-Century Evangelicalism: 1870–1925*, p. 132.

159. Bellah et al., *Habits of the Heart*, p. 264.

160. Robert Hofstadter, quoted from Marsden, *Fundamentalism and American Culture*, p. 211.

161. Marsden, *Fundamentalism and American Culture*, p. 194.

162. Rule of Taizé, quoted from George H. Tavard, *Two Centuries of Ecumenism*, p. 211.

163. *Draft for Sections*, p. 13, para. 6, quoted from Harold E. Fey, ed., *A History of the Ecumenical Movement: 1948–1968*, vol. 2, p. 421.

164. Book of Common Prayer, The Episcopal Church, 1978 ed., pp. 877f.

165. Fey, *History of the Ecumenical Movement*, vol. 2, p. 162.

166. Leo XIII, quoted from Tavard, *Two Centuries of Ecumenism*, p. 82.

167. Vatican II, *Decree on Ecumenism*, sec. 3.

168. Vatican II, *Decree on Ecumenism*, sec. 1; Hans Küng, *The Church*, p. 283.

169. Vatican II, *Decree on the Church's Missionary Activity*, sec. 15. See also *Decree on Ecumenism*, sec. 3.

170. Vatican II, *Decree on Ecumenism*, sec. 1.

171. Faith and Order Commission, *Baptism, Eucharist and Ministry*, p. 24, para. 19.

172. Ibid., p. 26, com. 26.

173. Moltmann, *Church in the Power of the Spirit*, p. 73.

174. Küng, *The Church*, p. 240.

175. Ibid., pp. 234–241; Moltmann, *Church in the Power of the Spirit*, pp. 72f.

176. Küng, *The Church*, pp. 235f.

177. Paul Tillich, *The Protestant Era*, p. 226. He would have found

equally problematic an idea voiced by several Fundamentalists. Instead of regarding the Church as Christ's continuing incarnation, they describe the Scriptures in a similar fashion. They speak of Christ's presence today as "Inscripturation."

178. Hans Küng, *Infallible? An Inquiry*, pp. 181f.

179. Ibid., p. 183.

180. Ibid., pp. 31–33.

181. Ibid., pp. 58–63. See J. P. Toner, "Infallibility," *The Catholic Encyclopedia*, vol. 7, p. 796, and Küng, *Infallible? An Inquiry*, p. 100, for treatments of the formal requirements of infallible pronouncements.

182. John J. Kirvan, *The Infallibility Debate*, p. 80.

183. Brian W. Harrison, "The Ex Cathedra Status of the Encyclical *Humanae Vitae*," *Faith and Reason*, vol. 19, pp. 25–78.

Chapter XI. Epilogue

Author's dates are omitted in the Epilogue because they are almost all contemporary.

1. Thomas Aquinas, *Summa Theologica*, pt. 2, pt. 2, q. 2, a. 7.

2. See T. C. O'Brien's "A Commentary on 1a2ae. 89, 6," in *Thomas Aquinas: Summa Theologiae*, vol. 27, p. 129.

3. Rahner, *Theological Investigations*, vol. 5, pp. 118–132. Rahner has referred to adherents of other religions as in varying degrees "anonymous Christians" (ibid., p. 132), as if to say that somehow they are Christians without knowing it; what he means by this is that Christianity implies that non-Christians are also being led into truth by the God in whom Christians have their faith.

4. C. S. Lewis, *Letters to an American Lady*, p. 11.

5. Antony Fernando, *Buddhism and Christianity: Their Inner Affinity*.

6. See the documents in *More Stepping Stones to Jewish-Christian Relations*, compiled by Helga Croner.

7. Martin Buber, *Two Types of Faith*, p. 174.

8. See, for example, the documents cited at pp. 74 and 202 in *More Stepping Stones*.

9. Elizabeth Dodson Gray, *Green Paradise Lost*, p. ix.

10. "Condorcet's Pleas for the Citizenship of Women," *Journal de la Société de 1789*, 3 July 1790. English trans.: *The Fortnightly Review*, June 1870, pp. 719–720, quoted from Rosemary Radford Ruether, *Sexism and God-Talk*, p. 103.

11. Elizabeth A. Johnson, *She Who Is*, p. 157.

12. Søren Kierkegaard, "That Individual," in Walter Kaufmann, ed., *Existentialism from Dostoevsky to Sartre*, p. 97.

13. Paul Tillich, *My Search for Absolutes*, pp. 94f; *Systematic Theology*, vol. 3, pp. 8of.

14. Paul Tillich, *Morality and Beyond*, p. 39.

15. C. S. Lewis, "Priestesses in the Church?", in *God in the Dock*, p. 236.

16. Cited in the Vatican Declaration "Inter Signiores," quoted by Paul K. Jewett, *The Ordination of Women*, p. 82.

17. Reumann, *Ministries Examined*, p. 87.

18. The pervasive subordinationism of the culture is discussed by Wayne A. Meeks in *The Origins of Christian Morality*, pp. 38–41.

19. See Reumann, *Ministries Examined*, pp. 80–97, for a careful examination of the relevant New Testament passages.

20. Tillich, *Systematic Theology*, vol. 1, pp. 240f.

21. Ruether, *Sexism and God-Talk*, p. 23.

22. Naomi Goldenberg, *Changing of the Gods*, p. 22. See also Mary Daly, "After the Death of God the Father," in *Womanspirit Rising*, C. Christ and J. Plascow, eds., p. 29.

23. Goldenberg, *Changing of the Gods*, p. 90.

24. Christine Downing, *The Goddess: Mythological Images of the Feminine*, p. 6.

25. Anne Carr, *Transforming Grace: Women's Experience and Christian Tradition*; Sallie McFague, *Models of God*; Ruether, *Sexism and God-Talk*; Elisabeth Schüssler Fiorenza, *In Memory of Her*; Johnson, *She Who Is*.

26. Johnson, *She Who Is*, chap. 3.

27. Ibid., p. 101. See also Caroline Walker Bynum, *Jesus as Mother*, p. 125.

28. Anselm, "Prayer to St. Paul," quoted from Johnson, *She Who Is*, p. 150.

29. Julian of Norwich, *Showings*, quoted from Johnson, *She Who Is*, p. 34.

30. Letter 322, *Patrologia Latina*, vol. 182, col. 527, quoted from Bynum, *Jesus as Mother*, p. 117.

31. See Bynum, *Jesus as Mother*, pp. 120–125.

32. Johnson, *She Who Is*, p. 55.

33. See also McFague, *Models of God*, pp. 84–87.

34. See pp. 40–52 above.

35. Johnson, *She Who Is*, p. 166.

36. As indicated above (p. 50), Philo used "Son" as a title for the Logos.

His usage may have influenced Paul and John. However, several of Philo's titles for the Logos have fallen into disuse. Why not this one?

37. Johnson, *She Who Is*, p. 35.

38. See p. 65 above.

39. Johnson, *She Who Is*, p. 81.

40. Bernard Häring, *Free and Faithful in Christ*, p. 139; quoted from Johnson, *She Who Is*, p. 161.

41. Augustine, *Confessions*, bk. 9, chap. 10.

Bibliography

Unless otherwise noted, quotations from the Scriptures are taken from the Revised Standard Version of the Bible, with Apocrypha, copyrighted 1946, 1952, 1965, © 1971, 1973, 1977. Used with permission. Occasionally I have used a variant reading of the Hebrew or Greek text. KJV is an abbreviation for the King James Version and BCP for the Book of Common Prayer. Because ancient, medieval, and classic texts appear in many editions, they are cited by author and title only, except for a few texts that are hard to find. Quotations from these sources are taken from one of the standard translations.

Ancient and Medieval Writings

Abelard, Peter. "Exposition of the Epistle to the Romans (An Excerpt from the Second Book)." In *A Scholastic Miscellany: Anselm to Ockham*, edited and translated by E. R. Fairweather. Philadelphia: Westminster Press, 1956.

Ambrose. *Narrations on the Psalms.*

——. *On Faith to Gratian.*

——. *On Mysteries.*

——. *On Repentance.*

——. *On the Sacraments.*

Anselm. *Anselm of Canterbury: Trinity, Incarnation and Redemption: Theological Treatises.* Edited and translated by J. Hopkins and H. W. Richardson. New York: Harper & Row, 1970.

——. *The Incarnation of the Word of God.*

——. *Proslogion.*

——. *The Virginal Conception.*

——. *Why God Became Man.*

Apocrypha.
   2 Esdras.
   Wisdom of Jesus Son of Sirach (Ecclesiasticus).
   Wisdom of Solomon.
Apollinarius. *Epistle to the Bishops of Diocaesarea*.
———. *Epistle to Dionysius*.
———. *Fragments*.
The Apostolic Constitutions.
Aristotle. *On Interpretation*.
———. *The Metaphysics*.
Athanasius. *The Apology against the Arians*.
———. *The Defense of the Decrees of the Council of Nicea*.
———. *The Incarnation of the Word of God*.
———. *Orations against the Arians*.
Augustine. *Against the Epistle of the Parmesians*.
———. *Against Maximus*.
———. *The Baptism of Infants against Marcellinus*.
———. *Christian Doctrine*.
———. *The City of God*.
———. *Concerning Order*.
———. *The Confessions*.
———. *Diverse Questions*.
———. *Epistles*.
———. *Exposition on the Psalms*.
———. *The Free Choice of the Will*.
———. *Holy Virginity*.
———. *The Incomplete Work against Julian*.
———. *The Literal Interpretation of Genesis*.
———. *The Morals of the Catholic Church*.
———. *Narrations on the Psalms*.
———. *Of the Good of Marriage*.
———. *On Genesis against the Manichians*.
———. *On the Grace of Christ and Original Sin*.
———. *On Marriage and Concupiscence*.
———. *On the Merits and Remission of Sins*.
———. *On Music*.
———. *The Predestination of Saints*.
———. *Retractions*.
———. *Sermons*.
———. *The Spirit and the Letter*.
———. *Tractates on the Gospel of John*.
———. *The Trinity*.

———. *The True Religion.*

———. *The Utility of Belief.*

Augustinus Triumphus. *Summa on Ecclesiastical Power.*

Basil of Caesarea. *Epistles.*

———. *Homily on the Psalms.*

Berengar of Tours. *Reply to Lanfranc.* In *Corpus Christianorum, Continuatio Mediaevalis*, vol. 84. Turnholt, Belgium, 1988.

Bernard of Clairvaux. *Letters.*

———. *The Love of God.*

———. *On Consideration.*

Biel, Gabriel. *Exposition of the Canon of the Mass.* Edited by H. A. Oberman and W. J. Courtney. Wiesbaden: Franz Steiner Verlag GMBH, 1963–67.

Boethius. *On the Catholic Faith.*

Bonaventure. *Commentary on the Sentences.*

Book of Enoch.

Clement of Alexandria. *The Exhortation to the Heathen.*

———. *The Miscellanies.*

Clement of Rome. *First Letter.*

———. *Second Letter.*

Cyprian. *Letters.*

Dead Sea Scrolls. Manual of Discipline.

Denzinger, H., and A. Schönmetzer, eds. *Enchiridion Symbolorum.* 32d ed.

The Didache.

Duns Scotus, John. *Commentary on the Sentences (Ordinatio).*

———. *Lectures on the First Book of the Sentences.*

———. *The Oxford Commentary.*

Eckhart, Meister. *Meister Eckhart: The Essential Sermons, Commentaries, Treatises and Defense.* Edited by E. Colledge and B. McGinn. New York: Paulist Press, 1981.

Epistle of Barnabas.

Eusebius. *Ecclesiastical History.*

Gallican Homily.

Gaunilo. *Reply to Anselm.*

Genesis Rabbah.

Giles of Rome (Aegidius Romanus). *On Ecclesiastical Power.*

Gospel of Thomas.

Gregory of Nyssa. *Against Eunomius.*

———. *Catechetical Oration.*

Hippolytus. *Against the Noetian Heresy.*

———. *The Apostolic Tradition.*

Homer. *The Iliad.*

Ignatius of Antioch. *Epistle to the Ephesians.*
———. *Epistle to the Magnisians.*
———. *Epistle to the Philadelphians.*
———. *Epistle to the Philippians.*
———. *Epistle to the Smyrneans.*
———. *Epistle to the Trallians.*
Irenaeus. *Against Heresies.*
———. *Proof of the Apostolic Preaching.*
James of Viterbo. *The Christian Government.*
Jean de Gerson. *On the Doctrine of Ramond Lull.*
———. *The Unity of the Church.*
Jerome. *Against Vigilantius.*
———. *Letters.*
John Cassian. *On the Incarnation of the Lord against Nestorius.*
John of Damascus. *The Orthodox Faith.*
John of Salisbury. *The Seven Divisions of Seven.*
Josephus, Flavius. *Jewish Antiquities.*
———. *The Jewish War.*
Julian of Norwich. *Showings.*
Justin Martyr. *The Dialogue against Trypho.*
———. *The First and Second Apologies.*
Langton, Stephen. "A Question on Original Sin." In *A Scholastic Miscellany*, edited and translated by E. R. Fairweather. Philadelphia: Westminster Press, 1956.
Leo I. *Epistles.*
———. *Tome of Leo.*
Macrobius. *Commentary on the Dream of Scipio.*
Marsilius of Padua. *Defender of the Peace.*
The Martyrdom of Polycarp.
Mishna. Ketuboth.
Moses Maimonides (Moses ben Maimon). *The Guide of the Perplexed.*
Nestorius. *The Bazaar of Heracleides of Damascus.*
Nicholas of Cusa. *The Catholic Concordance.*
———. *Conjecture about the Last Days.*
Origen. *Against Celsus.*
———. *The Commentary on the Gospel of Matthew.*
———. *First Principles.*
Peter Lombard. *The Four Books of the Sentences.*
Philo of Alexandria. *Abraham.*
———. *The Allegorical Interpretations.*
———. *The Change of Names.*
———. *The Cherubim.*

————. *The Creation of the World.*

————. *Husbandry.*

————. *The Posterity and Exile of Cain.*

————. *The Special Laws.*

————. *The Virtues.*

————. *Who Is the Heir?*

————. *The Worse Attacks the Better.*

Plato. *Timaeus.*

Pseudo-Athanasius. *Against Apollinarius.*

Pseudo-Dionysius. *The Celestial Hierarchy.*

————. *The Ecclesiastical Hierarchy.*

————. *On the Divine Names.*

Rabbi Nathan. *The Fathers According to Rabbi Nathan.*

Radbertus. *On the Lord's Body and Blood.*

Ratramnus. *Christ's Body and Blood.*

Richard of St. Victor. *The Trinity.*

Ruysbroeck, Jan van. *The Book of Supreme Truth.*

The Shepherd of Hermas.

Talmud. Kiddushin.

————. Pesahim.

————. Yebamoth.

Tertullian. *Against Marcion.*

————. *Against Praxeas.*

————. *The Answer to the Jews.*

————. *The Antidote for the Scorpion's Sting.*

————. *The Flesh of Christ.*

————. *On Baptism.*

————. *The Soul.*

Theodore of Mopsuestia. *Against Eunomius.*

Thomas Aquinas. *Commentary on the Sentences.*

————. *On Evil.*

————. *The Power of God.*

————. *Summa Contra Gentes.*

————. *Summa Theologica.*

Thomas à Kempis. *The Imitation of Christ.* London: J. M. Dent & Sons, 1960.

Tosefta. Sanhedrin.

————. Yebamot.

Ubertino of Casale. *The Tree of the Crucified Life of Jesus.*

Venerable Bede. *On Genesis.*

Vincent of Lérins. *Commonitory.*

William of Ockham. *The Body of Christ.* In *De Sacramento Altaris,* edited by T. Bruce Birch. Burlington, Iowa: Lutheran Literary Board, 1930.

———. *Predestination, God's Foreknowledge, and Future Contingents.*

———. *Quodlibeta Septem.*

Reformation and Later

"Agreed Statement on Eucharistic Doctrine." In *Documents on Anglican Roman Catholic Relations II*, compiled by the Bishops' Committee on Ecumenical and Interreligious Affairs and the Joint Commission on Ecumenical Relations. Washington, DC: United States Catholic Conference, 1973.

Anderson, Bernhard W. *Understanding the Old Testament.* 3d ed. Englewood Cliffs, NJ: Prentice-Hall, 1975.

Anglican–Lutheran International Conversations: The Report of the Conversations 1970–1972 authorized by the Lambeth Conference and the Lutheran World Federation. London: Society for the Promotion of Christian Knowledge, 1973.

Anscombe, G. E. M., and P. T. Geach. *Three Philosophers.* Ithaca: Cornell University Press, 1961.

Audet, Jean Paul. "Affinités litteraires et doctrinales du *Manuel de Discipline.*" *Revue Biblique,* vol. 59 (1952), pp. 219–238.

Aulén, Gustav. *Christus Victor.* London: Society for the Promotion of Christian Knowledge, 1945.

Baeck, Leo. *Judaism and Christianity.* New York: Athenaeum, 1970.

Baillie, D. M. *God Was in Christ.* New York: Charles Scribner's Sons, 1948.

Bainton, Roland. *Here I Stand: A Life of Martin Luther.* New York: Abingdon Press, 1950.

Baptism, Eucharist and Ministry. Faith and Order Commission Paper No. 111. Geneva: World Council of Churches, 1982.

Barbour, Ian G. *Issues in Science and Religion.* Englewood Cliffs, NJ: Prentice-Hall, 1966.

Barnard, L. W. *Justin Martyr: His Life and Thought.* Cambridge: Cambridge University Press, 1967.

Barth, Karl. *Church Dogmatics.* Edinburgh: T. and T. Clark, 1955–1969.

———. *Dogmatics in Outline.* New York: Harper & Row, 1959.

———. *The Knowledge of God and the Service of God.* New York: Charles Scribner's Sons, 1939.

Battenhouse, Roy W., ed. *A Companion to the Study of St. Augustine.* New York: Oxford University Press, 1955.

Bellah, Robert N., et al. *Habits of the Heart: Individualism and Commitment in American Life*. Berkeley: University of California Press, 1985.

Bellarmine, Robert. *On Controversies*. Vols. 1–4 of *Opera Omnia*. Neapoli: C. Pedone Lauries, 1872.

Berryman, Philip. *Liberation Theology*. New York: Pantheon Books, 1987.

Bertocci, Peter A. *Introduction to the Philosophy of Religion*. New York: Prentice-Hall, 1951.

Bourke, Vernon J. *Augustine's View of Reality*. Villanova, PA: Villanova Press, 1964.

Bouyer, Louis. *Eucharist: Theology and Spirituality of the Eucharistic Prayer*. Translated by Charles Underhill Quin. Notre Dame: University of Notre Dame Press, 1968.

Bowker, John W. *The Targums and Rabbinic Literature*. London: Cambridge University Press, 1969.

Boyle, Robert. *Selected Philosophical Papers of Robert Boyle*. Edited by M. A. Stewart. Manchester: Manchester University Press, 1979.

Brandt, Richard. *The Philosophy of Schleiermacher*. New York: Harper and Brothers, 1941.

Buber, Martin. *Between Man and Man*. New York: Macmillan, 1965.

———. *Eclipse of God*. New York: Harper and Brothers, 1952.

———. *I and Thou*. 2d ed. New York: Charles Scribner's Sons, 1958.

———. *Moses: The Revelation and the Covenant*. New York: Harper & Row, 1958.

———. *Two Types of Faith*. New York: Harper & Row, 1961.

Buescher, Gabriel N. *The Eucharistic Teaching of William Ockham*. Washington, DC: Catholic University of America Press, 1950.

Bultmann, Rudolf. *Existence and Faith*. Cleveland: World Publishing Co., 1960.

———. *New Testament and Mythology*. Vol. 1 of *Kerygma and Myth*, edited by H. W. Bartsch. New York: Macmillan, 1953.

Butler, Joseph. *The Analogy of Religion*. London: G. Bell and Sons, 1902.

Bynum, Caroline Walker. *Jesus as Mother: Studies in the Spirituality of the High Middle Ages*. Berkeley: University of California Press, 1982.

Calvin, John. *Calvin: Institutes of the Christian Religion*. Edited by John T. McNeill. Philadelphia: Westminster Press, 1960.

———. *Calvin: Theological Treatises*. Translated by J. K. S. Reid. London: SCM Press, 1944.

———. *Ecclesiastical Ordinances*. 1541.

———. *Opera omnia quae supersunt (Corpus Reformatoren)*. Brunswick: Berolini, 1863–1900.

Canons and Decrees of the Council of Trent. Vol. 2 of *Creeds of Christendom*, edited by Philip Schaff. 6th ed. New York: Harper and Brothers, 1919.

Carr, Anne. *Transforming Grace: Women's Experience and Christian Tradition*. San Francisco: Harper & Row, 1988.

Cassirer, Ernst. *The Philosophy of the Enlightenment*. Boston: Beacon Press, 1955.

Catholic Theological Society of America. "The Bilateral Consultations between the Roman Catholic Church in the United States and Other Christian Communions (1972–1979)." *Proceedings*, vol. 34 (1979), Appendix C, pp. 253–285.

Clark, Francis. *Eucharistic Sacrifice and the Reformation*. 2d ed. Devon: Augustine Publishing Co., 1980.

Cobb, John B., Jr. *Beyond Dialogue: Toward a Mutual Transformation of Christianity and Buddhism*. Philadelphia: Fortress Press, 1982.

Comblin, José. *The Church and the National Security State*. Maryknoll, NY: Orbis Books, 1979.

Cone, James H. *A Black Theology of Liberation*. Philadelphia: Lippincott Co., 1970.

Connor, J. L. "Original Sin: Contemporary Approaches." *Theological Studies*, vol. 29 (1968), pp. 215–240.

Cooke, Bernard. *Ministry to Word and Sacraments: History and Theology*. Philadelphia: Fortress Press, 1976.

Coomaraswamy, Rama P. *The Problem of the New Mass*. London, Ont.: Canadian Chess Consultants Press, 1989.

Copleston, Frederick C. *Aquinas*. Baltimore: Penguin Books, 1961.

———. *A History of Philosophy*. 7 vols. Westminster, MD: Newman Press, 1955–1963.

Cranmer, Thomas. *An Answer unto a Crafty and Sophisticall Cavillation devised by Stephen Gardiner*. 1551.

———. *A Defence of the True and Catholic Doctrine of the Sacrament of the Body and Blood of Our Savior Christ*. 1550.

Croner, Helga. *More Stepping Stones to Jewish-Christian Relations*. New York: Paulist Press, 1985.

Daly, Mary. "After the Death of God the Father." In *Womanspirit Rising*, edited by C. Christ and J. Plascow. San Francisco: Harper & Row, 1979.

Davis, Charles. *Liturgy and Doctrine: The Doctrinal Basis of the Liturgical Movement*. New York: Sheed and Ward, 1960.

Decrees of the Second Vatican Council:
Declaration on the Relation of the Church to the Non-Christian Religions.
Decree on Ecumenism.

Decree on the Church's Missionary Activity.

Decree on the Eastern Catholic Churches.

Delhaye, P. "History of Celibacy." *The New Catholic Encylopedia*, vol. 3, pp. 369–374. New York: McGraw-Hill, 1967.

Delorme, J. "The Practice of Baptism in Judaism at the Beginning of the Christian Era." In *Baptism in the New Testament: A Symposium*, translated by David Askew, pp. 25–60. Baltimore: Helicon Press, 1964.

——, et al. *The Eucharist in the New Testament.* Baltimore: Helicon Press, 1964.

Dodd, C. H. *The Epistle of Paul to the Romans.* New York: Harper and Brothers, 1932.

Douglas, Mary. *Purity and Danger.* Harmondworth: Penguin Books, 1970.

Downing, Christine. *The Goddess: Mythological Images of the Feminine.* New York: Crossroad, 1981.

Dulles, Avery. *Models of the Church.* Garden City, NY: Doubleday, 1974.

Dunn, James D. G. *Christology in the Making: A New Testament Inquiry into the Origins of the Doctrine of the Incarnation.* Philadelphia: Westminster Press, 1980.

Eckhart, A. Roy. *Elder and Younger Brothers: The Meeting of Jews and Christians.* New York: Schocken Books, 1973.

Eliade, Mircea. *Cosmos and History: The Myth of the Eternal Return.* New York: Harper & Row, 1959.

——. *Patterns in Comparative Religion.* Cleveland: World Publishing Co., 1963.

Erasmus, Desiderius. *The Praise of Folly.* Princeton: Princeton University Press, 1941.

Fernando, Antony. *Buddhism and Christianity: Their Inner Affinity.* Kelaniya, Sri Lanka: Empire Press, 1981.

Fey, Harold E., ed. *A History of the Ecumenical Movement: 1948–1968*, vol. 2. Philadelphia: Westminster Press, 1970.

Fiorenza, Elisabeth Schüssler. *In Memory of Her.* New York: Crossroad, 1983.

Fisher, J. D. C. *Christian Initiation: The Reformation Period.* London: Society for the Promotion of Christian Knowledge, 1970.

——. *Confirmation: Then and Now.* London: Alcuin Club/SPCK, 1978.

Fox, George. *An Autobiography.* Edited by Rufus M. Jones. Philadelphia: Friend's Book Store, 1919.

——. *The Autobiography of George Fox.* London: S. W. Partridge and Co., 1886.

Fremantle, Anne, ed. *The Papal Encyclicals in Their Historical Context.* New York: G. P. Putnam's Sons, 1956.

Geach, P. T. *Providence and Evil*. Cambridge: Cambridge University Press, 1977.

Georg von Simson, Otto. *The Gothic Cathedral: Origins of Gothic Architecture and the Medieval Concept of Order*. New York: Pantheon Books, 1956.

Goldenberg, Naomi R. *Changing of the Gods*. Boston: Beacon Press, 1979.

Goldstein, Valerie Saiving. "The Human Situation: A Feminine View." *Journal of Religion*, vol. 40 (1960), pp. 100–112.

Gonzalez, Justo L. *A History of Christian Thought*. 3 vols. Nashville: Abingdon Press, 1970–1975.

Goodenough, Erwin R. *An Introduction to Philo Judaeus*. New Haven: Yale University Press, 1940.

Gore, Charles. *The Church and the Ministry*. 5th ed. London: Longmans, Green and Co., 1902.

———, ed. *Lux Mundi*. 5th ed. New York: John W. Lovell Co., n. d.

Gould, Stephen Jay. *The Panda's Thumb*. New York: W. W. Norton, 1980.

Goulder, Michael, ed. *Incarnation and Myth: The Debate Continued*. London: SCM Press, 1979.

Grabowski, Stanislaus J. *The Church: An Introduction to the Theology of St. Augustine*. St. Louis and London: B. Herder Book Co., 1957.

Grant, Robert M. *The Early Christian Doctrine of God*. Charlottesville: University Press of Virginia, 1966.

Gray, Elizabeth Dodson. *Green Paradise Lost*. Wellesley: Roundtable Press, 1981.

Grebel, Conrad. "Letters to Thomas Müntzer by Conrad Grebel and Friends." In *Spiritual and Anabaptist Writers*, edited by G. H. Williams. Philadelphia: Westminster Press, 1957.

Gregg, R. C., and D. E. Groh. *Early Arianism: A View of Salvation*. Philadelphia: Fortress Press, 1981.

Grillmeier, Aloys. *Christ in Christian Tradition*, vol. 1. 2d, rev. ed. Atlanta: John Knox Press, 1975.

Gutierrez, Gustavo. *A Theology of Liberation*. Maryknoll, NY: Orbis Books, 1973.

Guttmann, Alexander. *Rabbinic Judaism in the Making: A Chapter in the History of the Halakhah from Ezra to Judah 1*. Detroit: Wayne State University Press, 1970.

Häring, Bernard. *Free and Faithful in Christ*. New York: Crossroad, 1984.

Harnack, Adolf. *What Is Christianity?* New York: Harper and Brothers, 1957.

Harrison, Brian W. "The Ex Cathedra Status of the Encyclical *Humanae Vitae*." *Faith and Reason*, vol. 19 (1993), pp. 25–78.

Hartshorne, Charles. *A Natural Theology for Our Time*. LaSalle: Open Court Publishing Co., 1967.

————. *Omnipotence and Other Theological Mistakes*. Albany: State University of New York, 1984.

Harvey, Van A. *The Historian and the Believer*. New York: Macmillan, 1966.

Hebert, A. G. *Liturgy and Society: The Function of the Church in the Modern World*. London: Faber and Faber, 1935.

Heiler, Friedrich. *Prayer: A Study in the History and Psychology of Religion*. New York: Oxford University Press, 1958.

Hempel, Carl G. *Aspects of Scientific Explanation, and Other Essays in the Philosophy of Science*. New York: Free Press, 1965.

Henry, Patrick. *New Directions in New Testament Study*. Philadelphia: Westminster Press, 1979.

Herford, R. Travers. *The Pharisees*. Boston: Beacon Press, 1962.

Hick, John. *The Center of Christianity*. San Francisco: Harper & Row, 1978.

————. *Evil and the God of Love*. New York: Harper & Row, 1966.

————. *Faith and Knowledge*. 2d ed. Ithaca: Cornell University Press, 1966.

————. *God and the Universe of Faiths*. London: Macmillan Press, 1973.

————, ed. *The Existence of God*. New York: Macmillan, 1964.

————. *The Myth of God Incarnate*. Philadelphia: Westminster Press, 1977.

Hodge, Charles. *Systematic Theology*. 3 vols. Grand Rapids, MI: Wm. B. Eerdmans Publishing Co., 1970.

Hodges, H. A. *The Pattern of Atonement*. London: SCM Press, 1955.

Hodgson, Leonard. *The Doctrine of the Atonement*. New York: Charles Scribner's Sons, 1951.

Hooker, Richard. *The Laws of Ecclesiastical Polity*. Edited by John Keble. 3d ed. Oxford: The University Press, 1845.

Hordern, William. *A Layman's Guide to Protestant Theology*. New York: Macmillan, 1956.

Hubert, H. and M. Mauss. *Sacrifice: Its Nature and Function*. Chicago: The University of Chicago Press, 1964.

Hume, David. *The Dialogues Concerning Natural Religion*.

————. *An Enquiry Concerning Human Understanding*.

————. *Treatise of Human Nature*.

Huxley, Julian S. *Evolutionary Ethics*. London: Oxford University Press, 1943.

Jackson, Samuel McCauley, ed. *The New Schaff-Herzog Encyclopedia of*

Religious Knowledge. 13 vols. Grand Rapids, MI: Baker Book House, 1949.

James, William. *Selected Papers on Philosophy.* London: J. M. Dent and Sons, 1917.

———. *The Varieties of Religious Experience.* New York: Longmans, Green and Co., 1902.

Jeremias, Joachim. *New Testament Theology,* vol. 1. London: SCM Press, 1971.

Jewett, Paul K. *The Ordination of Women: An Essay on the Office of Christian Ministry.* Grand Rapids, MI: Wm. B. Eerdmans Publishing Co., 1980.

John Paul II. "Dominicae Cenae: Epistula de SS Eucharistiae Mysterio et Cultu." *Notitiae,* vol. 16 (1980).

Johnson, Elizabeth A. *She Who Is: The Mystery of God in Feminist Theological Discourse.* New York: Crossroad, 1992.

Kant, Immanuel. *The Critique of Judgment.*

———. *The Critique of Pure Reason.*

———. *Religion within the Limits of Reason Alone.* Translated by T. M. Greene, H. H. Hudson, and J. R. Silber. New York: Harper and Brothers, 1960.

Kässemann, Ernst. *Commentary on Romans.* Translated and edited by Geoffrey W. Bromiley. Grand Rapids, MI: Wm. B. Eerdmans Publishing Co., 1980.

Katz, Steven T., ed. *Mysticism and Religious Traditions.* Oxford: Oxford University Press, 1983.

Kaufmann, Walter, ed. *Existentialism from Dostoevsky to Sartre.* Cleveland: World Publishing Co., 1957.

Kaufmann, Yehezkel. *The Religion of Israel: From Its Beginnings to the Babylonian Exile.* Translated and abridged by Moshe Greenberg. Chicago: The University of Chicago Press, 1960.

Keck, Leander E. *A Future for the Historical Jesus.* Nashville: Abingdon Press, 1971.

Kee, Howard Clark. *Jesus in History.* 2d ed. New York: Harcourt Brace Jovanovich, 1977.

———. *Understanding the New Testament.* 4th ed. Englewood Cliffs, NJ: Prentice-Hall, 1983.

Kee, H. C., F. W. Young, and K. Froelich. *Understanding the New Testament.* 3d ed. Englewood Cliffs, NJ: Prentice-Hall, 1973.

Kelly, J. N. D. *Early Christian Doctrines.* New York: Harper & Row, 1958.

Kenny, Anthony. *The God of the Philosophers.* Oxford: Oxford University Press, 1979.

BIBLIOGRAPHY / 435

Kierkegaard, Søren. *Christian Discourses*. New York: Oxford University Press, 1961.

———. *Fear and Trembling, and The Sickness unto Death*. Princeton: Princeton University Press, 1954.

———. *A Kierkegaard Anthology*. Edited by Robert Bretall. New York: Random House, 1948.

———. *Kierkegaard's Concluding Unscientific Postscript*. Princeton: Princeton University Press, 1944.

———. *On Authority and Revelation*. New York: Harper & Row, 1966.

———. *Philosophical Fragments*. Princeton: Princeton University Press, 1936.

———. "That Individual." In *Existentialism from Dostoevsky to Sartre*, Walter Kaufmann, ed., pp. 92–99. Cleveland: World Publishing Co., 1957.

King, M. L., Jr. *Strength to Love*. New York: Pocket Books, 1964.

———. *Stride toward Freedom*. New York: Harper & Row, 1964.

———. *Why We Can't Wait*. New York: Harper & Row, 1964.

Kirk, Kenneth. *The Epistle to the Romans*. Oxford: Clarendon Press, 1937.

Kirvan, John J. *The Infallibility Debate*. New York: Paulist Press, 1971.

Kittel, Gerhard. *Theological Dictionary of the New Testament*. Grand Rapids, MI: Wm. B. Eerdmans Publishing Co., 1964–1976.

Klausner, Joseph. *The Messianic Idea in Israel*. New York: Macmillan, 1955.

Koenig, John. *Jews and Christians in Dialogue*. Philadelphia: Westminster Press, 1979.

Kohler, Ludwig H. *Old Testament Theology*. Philadelphia: Westminster Press, 1957.

Küng, Hans. *The Church*. London: Burns & Oates, 1968.

———. *Infallible? An Inquiry*. Garden City, NY: Doubleday, 1971.

———. *On Being a Christian*. Garden City, NY: Doubleday, 1976.

Lampe, G. W. H. *God as Spirit*. Oxford: Oxford University Press, 1977.

Laud, William. *The Works of William Laud*. 7 vols. Oxford: John Henry Parker, 1857.

Lehrer, Keith. *Knowledge*. Oxford: Clarendon Press, 1974.

Leibniz, Gottfried Wilhelm. *The Monadology*. Pittsburgh: University of Pittsburgh Press, 1991.

Lewis, C. S. *The Case for Christianity*. New York: Macmillan, 1950.

———. *Letters to an American Lady*. Grand Rapids, MI: Wm. B. Eerdmans Publishing Co., 1967.

———. "Priestesses in the Church?" In *God in the Dock: Essays on Theology and Ethics*, pp. 234–239. Grand Rapids, MI: Wm. B. Eerdmans Publishing Co., 1970.

Lewis, Evart. *Medieval Political Ideas*. 2 vols. New York: Alfred A. Knopf, 1954.

Lonergan, Bernard. *The Way to Nicea*. Philadelphia: Westminster Press, 1976.

Lovejoy, Arthur O. *The Great Chain of Being: A Study of the History of an Idea*. Cambridge: Harvard University Press, 1982.

Luther, Martin. *Luther's Works*. 55 vols. Edited by Jaroslav Pelikan and Helmut T. Lehmann. St. Louis and Philadelphia: Concordia Publishing House and Fortress Press, 1959–1986.

————. *The Works of Martin Luther*. 6 vols. Philadelphia: A. J. Holman Co., 1915.

Lutheran/Roman Catholic Joint Commission. *The Eucharist*. Geneva: The Lutheran World Federation, 1980.

Macdonald, A. J. *Berengar and the Reform of Sacramental Doctrine*. Merrick, NY: Richwood Publishing Co., 1977.

Machen, J. Gresham. *Christianity and Liberalism*. New York: Macmillan, 1923.

MacIntyre, Alasdair. *After Virtue: A Study in Moral Theory*. Notre Dame: University of Notre Dame Press, 1981.

————. "The Logical Status of Religious Belief." In *Metaphysical Beliefs*, edited by A. MacIntyre. London: SCM Press, 1957.

Mackie, J. L. *The Miracle of Theism*. Oxford: Oxford University Press, 1982.

Mackintosh, H. R. *Types of Modern Theology*. New York: Charles Scribner's Sons, 1937.

Macquarrie, John. *Principles of Christian Theology*. New York: Charles Scribner's Sons, 1966.

Mansel, H. L. *Letters, Lectures, and Reviews*. London: John Murray, 1873.

————. *The Limits of Religious Thought*. London: John Murray, 1859.

Manson, T. W. *The Teaching of Jesus*. Cambridge: Cambridge University Press, 1943.

Marsden, George M. *Fundamentalism and American Culture: The Shaping of Twentieth-Century Evangelicalism: 1870–1925*. New York: Oxford University Press, 1980.

Mascall, E. L. *Via Media*. Greenwich, CT: Seabury Press, 1957.

Maurice, Frederick D. *The Kingdom of Christ*. 3d ed. 2 vols. London: SCM Press, 1958.

McAdoo, Henry R. *The Spirit of Anglicanism: A Survey of Anglican Theological Method in the Seventeenth Century*. London: Adam & Charles Black, 1965.

McDermott, B. O. "Original Sin. Recent Developments." *Theological Studies*, vol. 38 (1977), pp. 478–512.

McFague, Sallie. *Models of God: Theology for an Ecological Nuclear Age.* Philadelphia: Fortress Press, 1987.

McGiffert, Arthur C. *A History of Christian Thought.* 2 vols. New York: Charles Scribner's Sons, 1932–1933.

McGinn, Bernard. *The Calabrian Abbot: Joachim of Fiore in the History of Western Thought.* New York: Macmillan, 1985.

McKee, Elsie Anne. *Elders and the Plural Ministry: The Role of Exegetical History in Illuminating John Calvin's Theology.* Geneva: Librairie Droz S. A., 1988.

Meeks, Wayne A. *The Origins of Christian Morality: The First Two Centuries.* New Haven: Yale University Press, 1993.

———, comp. *The Writings of St. Paul.* New York: W. W. Norton, 1972.

Melancthon, Philip. *Apology of the Augsburg Confession.*

Meyer, H., and L. Vischer, eds. *Growth in Agreement: Reports and Agreed Statements of Ecumenical Conversations on a World Level.* New York: Paulist Press, and Geneva: World Council of Churches, 1984.

Miguez-Bonino, Jose. *Doing Theology in a Revolutionary Situation.* Philadelphia: Fortress Press, 1975.

Minear, Paul. *Images of the Church in the New Testament.* Philadelphia: Westminster Press, 1960.

Mitchell, Leonel L. *The Meaning of Ritual.* Harrisburg, PA: Morehouse, 1977.

Moberly, R. C. *Atonement and Personality.* New York: Longmans, Green and Co., 1916.

Moltmann, Jürgen. *The Church in the Power of the Spirit: A Contribution to Messianic Ecclesiology.* HarperSanFrancisco, 1991.

———. *The Gospel of Liberation.* Waco, TX: Word Books, 1973.

———. *The Trinity and the Kingdom.* San Francisco: Harper & Row, 1981.

More, P. E., and F. L. Cross, comps. and eds. *Anglicanism.* London: SPCK, 1935.

Mowinckel, Sigmund. *He That Cometh.* Oxford: Oxford University Press, 1959.

Mozley, John Kenneth. *Ritschlianism: An Essay.* London: James Nisbet & Co., 1909.

Neill, Stephen. *Jesus through Many Eyes: Introduction to the Theology of the New Testament.* Philadelphia: Fortress Press, 1976.

Neusner, Jacob. *From Politics to Piety: The Emergence of Pharisaic Judaism.* Englewood Cliffs, NJ: Prentice-Hall, 1973.

———. *The Rabbinic Traditions about the Pharisees before 70.* 3 vols. Leiden: E. J. Brill, 1971.

Newman, John Henry. *Apologia pro Vita Sua.* New York: W. W. Norton, 1968.

————. *A Newman Reader*. Edited by Francis X. Connolly. Garden City, NY: Doubleday, 1964.

Niebuhr, Reinhold. *Discerning the Signs of the Times*. New York: Charles Scribner's Sons, 1946.

————. *Faith and History: A Comparison of Christian and Modern Views of History*. New York: Charles Scribner's Sons, 1949.

————. *An Interpretation of Christian Ethics*. New York: Harper and Brothers, 1935.

————. *Moral Man and Immoral Society*. New York: Charles Scribner's Sons, 1932.

————. *The Nature and Destiny of Man*. 2 vols. New York: Charles Scribner's Sons, 1943.

Nock, Arthur Darby. *Early Gentile Christianity and Its Hellenistic Background*. New York: Harper & Row, 1964.

————. *St. Paul*. New York: Harper & Row, 1963.

Norris, R. A., Jr. *The Christological Controversy*. Philadelphia: Fortress Press, 1980.

————. *God and World in Early Christian Theology*. New York: Seabury Press, 1965.

O'Brien, T. C. "A Commentary on 1a2ae. 89, 6." In *Thomas Aquinas: Summa Theologiae*, vol. 27, pp. 125–133. New York: McGraw-Hill, 1974.

Ogden, Schubert M. *The Point of Christology*. San Francisco: Harper & Row, 1982.

Otto, Rudolf. *The Idea of the Holy*. New York: Oxford University Press, 1958.

Packer, J. I. *"Fundamentalism" and the Word of God*. Grand Rapids, MI: Wm. B. Eerdmans Publishing Co., 1958.

Paley, William. *Natural Theology*. 2 vols. New York: Harper and Brothers, 1840.

Palmer, P. "The Sacrament of Penance." In *The New Catholic Encyclopedia*, vol. 11, pp. 73–78. New York: McGraw-Hill, 1976.

Pannenberg, Wolfhart. *Jesus, God and Man*. Philadelphia: Westminster Press, 1968.

Patrologia Cursus Completus, Series Graeca. Edited by J. P. Migne. 1800–75.

Patrologia Cursus Completus, Series Latina. Edited by J. P. Migne. 1845–85.

Peacocke, A. R. *Creation and the World of Science*. Oxford: Clarendon Press, 1979.

Pelikan, Jaroslav. *The Christian Tradition: A History of the Development of Doctrine*. 5 vols. Chicago: The University of Chicago Press, 1971–1989.

Penelhum, Terence. *Problems of Religious Knowledge*. New York: Herder and Herder, 1971.

Perrin, Norman. *A Modern Pilgrimage in New Testament Christology*. Philadelphia: Fortress Press, 1974.

———. *The New Testament: An Introduction*. New York: Harcourt Brace Jovanovich, 1974.

———. *The Promise of Bultmann*. Philadelphia: Fortress Press, 1979.

Pfleiderer, Otto. *The Development of Theology in Germany and Great Britain*. London: Swan Sonnenschein and Co., 1890.

Pike, James A. *A Time for Christian Candor*. New York: Harper & Row, 1964.

Pike, Nelson. *God and Evil*. Englewood Cliffs, NJ: Prentice-Hall, 1964.

———. *God and Timelessness*. New York: Schocken Books, 1970.

Pittenger, W. Norman. *His Body the Church*. New York: Morehouse-Gorham, 1945.

———. *The Word Incarnate*. New York: Harper and Brothers, 1959.

Plantinga, Alvin. *God, Freedom, and Evil*. San Francisco: Harper & Row, 1974.

———, ed. *The Ontological Argument: From St. Anselm to Contemporary Philosophers*. Garden City, NY: Doubleday, 1965.

Plaut, Gunther W., ed. *The Torah: A Modern Commentary*. New York: University of American Hebrew Congregations, 1981.

Pohle, Joseph. "The Sacrifice of the Mass." In *The Catholic Encylopedia*, vol. 10, pp. 6–24. Edited by Charles G. Habermann. New York: Robert Appleton Company, 1907–14.

Power, David N. *The Sacrifice We Offer: The Tridentine Dogma and Its Reinterpretation*. New York: Crossroad, 1987.

Prestige, G. L. *God in Patristic Thought*. London: Society for the Promotion of Christian Knowledge, 1964.

Quick, Oliver Chase. *The Christian Sacraments*. London: Nisbet & Co., 1955.

Rahner, K., and W. Thüsing. *A New Christology*. New York: Seabury Press, 1980.

Rahner, Karl. *Christian at the Crossroads*. New York: Seabury Press, 1975.

———. *A Rahner Reader*. Edited by G. A. McCool. New York: Seabury Press, 1975.

———. *Theological Investigations*. 13 vols. New York: Seabury Press, 1974.

———. *The Trinity*. New York: Herder and Herder, 1970.

Rashdall, Hastings. *The Idea of Atonement in Christian Theology*. London: Macmillan, 1919.

Rauschenbusch, Walter. *Christianity and the Social Crisis*. New York: Harper & Row, 1964.

———. *A Theology of the Social Gospel*. New York: Charles Scribner's Sons, 1917.

Rees, Thomas, trans. *The Racovian Catechism*. Lexington, KY: American Theological Library Assoc., 1962.

Rescher, Nicholas. *The Coherence Theory of Truth*. London: Oxford University Press, 1973.

Reumann, John H. P. *Ministries Examined: Laity, Clergy, Women, and Bishops in a Time of Change*. Minneapolis: Augsburg, 1987.

———. *The Supper of the Lord: The New Testament, Ecumenical Dialogues, and Faith and Order on Eucharist*. Philadelphia: Fortress Press, 1985.

Richardson, Cyril C. *The Doctrine of the Trinity*. New York: Abingdon Press, 1958.

Ricoeur, Paul. *The Conflict of Interpretations*. Evanston: Northwestern University Press, 1974.

Ritschl, Albrecht. *Die Chrisliche Lehr von Rechtfertigung* (The Christian Doctrine of Justification and Reconciliation). 3 vols. Bonn: A. Marcus, 1882–83.

———. *Three Essays*. Philadelphia: Fortress Press, 1972.

———. *Unterrich in der Christliche Religion* (Instruction in the Christian Religion). Bonn: A. Marcus, 1875.

Robinson, James M. *A New Quest of the Historical Jesus*. London: SCM Press, 1959.

Rouse, R., and S. C. Neill, eds. *A History of the Ecumenical Movement: 1517–1948*. 2d ed. Philadelphia: Westminster Press, 1967.

Rowe, William L. *The Cosmological Argument*. Princeton: Princeton University Press, 1975.

Ruether, Rosemary Radford. *Sexism and God-Talk: Toward a Feminist Theology*. Boston: Beacon Press, 1983.

Rusch, William G. *The Trinitarian Controversy*. Philadelphia: Fortress Press, 1980.

Russell, Bertrand. *The Problems of Philosophy*. London: Oxford University Press, 1954.

Sanders, E. P. *Paul and Palestinian Judaism*. Philadelphia: Fortress Press, 1977.

Sandmel, Samuel. *The First Christian Century in Judaism and Christianity: Certainties and Uncertainties*. New York: Oxford University Press, 1969.

———. *The Hebrew Scriptures: An Introduction to Their Literature and Religious Ideas*. New York: Oxford University Press, 1978.

————. *Judaism and Christian Beginnings*. New York: Oxford University Press, 1978.

————. *Philo of Alexandria: An Introduction*. New York: Oxford University Press, 1979.

Sattler, Michael. *The Schleitheim Confession of Faith*. In *The Protestant Reformation*, edited by Lewis W. Spitz. Englewood Cliffs, NJ: Prentice-Hall, 1966.

Sayers, Dorothy L. *The Mind of the Maker*. New York: Harcourt, Brace and Co., 1941.

Schaff, Philip, ed. *The Creeds of Christendom*. 6th ed. 3 vols. New York: Harper and Brothers, 1919.

Schillebeeckx, Edward. *Christ the Sacrament of the Encounter with God*. New York: Sheed and Ward, 1963.

————. *The Eucharist*. New York: Sheed and Ward, 1968.

————. *Jesus: An Experiment in Christology*. New York: Seabury Press, 1979.

Schleiermacher, Friedrich. *The Christian Faith*. Edinburgh: T. and T. Clark, 1956.

————. *On Religion: Speeches to Its Cultured Despisers*. New York: Harper and Brothers, 1958.

Scholem, Gershom. *The Messianic Idea in Judaism and Other Essays on Jewish Spirituality*. New York: Schocken Books, 1971.

Schweitzer, Albert. *The Quest of the Historical Jesus*. New York: Macmillan, 1922.

Scott, Nathan A., Jr., ed. *The Legacy of Reinhold Niebuhr*. Chicago: The University of Chicago Press, 1975.

Shepherd, Massey H., Jr., comp. *Holy Communion: An Anthology of Christian Devotion*. Greenwich, CT: Seabury Press, 1959.

Sigal, Phillip. "Aspects of Dual Covenant Theology: Salvation." *Horizons in Biblical Theology*, vol. 5 (1983), pp. 1–48.

Smart, Ninian. *A Dialogue of Religions*. London: SCM Press, 1960.

————. *Philosophers and Religious Truth*. London: SCM Press, 1964.

Spitz, Lewis W., ed. *The Protestant Reformation*. Englewood Cliffs, NJ: Prentice-Hall, 1966.

Stace, W. T. *The Teachings of the Mystics*. New York: New American Library of World Literature, 1960.

Stendahl, Krister. "The Apostle Paul and the Introspective Conscience of the West." In *The Writings of St. Paul*, Wayne Meeks, comp., pp. 422–434. New York: W. W. Norton, 1972.

Stevick, Daniel B. *Baptismal Moments; Baptismal Meanings*. New York: Church Hymnal Corporation, 1987.

———. "Types of Baptismal Spirituality," *Worship*, vol. 47 (1973), pp. 11–26.

Stone, Darwell. *A History of the Doctrine of the Holy Eucharist*. 2 vols. London: Longmans, Green and Co., 1909.

———. *Holy Baptism*. 4th ed. London: Longmans, Green and Co., 1905.

Stone, Merlin. *When God Was a Woman*. New York: Harcourt Brace Jovanovich, 1978.

Swinburne, Richard. *The Existence of God*. New York: Oxford University Press, 1979.

Tappert, Theodore G., trans. and ed. *The Book of Concord: The Confessions of the Evangelical Lutheran Church*. Philadelphia: Fortress Press, 1959.

Tavard, George H. *Two Centuries of Ecumenism*. Notre Dame: Fides, 1961.

Taylor, Vincent. *The Cross of Christ*. London: Macmillan, 1956.

Tennant, F. R. *The Origin and Propagation of Sin*. Cambridge: Cambridge University Press, 1908.

———. *Philosophical Theology*. 2 vols. Cambridge: Cambridge University Press, 1956.

———. *The Sources of the Doctrines of the Fall and Original Sin*. Cambridge: Cambridge University Press, 1903.

Thielicke, Helmut. *The Evangelical Faith*. 3 vols. Grand Rapids, MI: Wm. B. Eerdmans Publishing Co., 1974–1982.

Tillich, Paul. *Biblical Religion and the Search for Ultimate Reality*. Chicago: The University of Chicago Press, 1955.

———. *The Courage to Be*. New Haven: Yale University Press, 1952.

———. *Morality and Beyond*. New York: Harper & Row, 1963.

———. *My Search for Absolutes*. New York: Simon and Schuster, 1967.

———. *The Protestant Era*. Chicago: The University of Chicago Press, 1948.

———. *The Shaking of the Foundations*. New York: Charles Scribner's Sons, 1948.

———. *Systematic Theology*. 3 vols. Chicago: The University of Chicago Press, 1951–1963.

———. *Theology of Culture*. New York: Oxford University Press, 1964.

Toner, J. P. "Infallibility." In *The Catholic Encyclopedia*, vol. 7, pp. 790–800. New York: Appleton, 1907–1912.

Townsend, J. T. "1 Corinthians 3:15 and the School of Shammai." *Harvard Theological Review*, vol. 61 (1968), pp. 500–504.

Troeltsch, Ernst. *The Social Teaching of the Christian Churches*. 2 vols. London: George Allen & Unwin, 1949.

Underhill, Evelyn. *Concerning the Inner Life*. New York: E. P. Dutton and Co., 1926.

―――. *Worship*. New York: Harper and Brothers, 1937.

Urban, Hugh B., Jr. *Manasoyajña/Logike Thusia* (The Reasonable Sacrifice). Bachelors Thesis, American University, n. d.

Urban, Linwood. "Was Luther a Throughgoing Determinist?" *Journal of Theological Studies*, vol. 22 (1971), pp. 113–139.

Urban, L., and W. Walton. *The Power of God*. New York: Oxford University Press, 1978.

Urban, Linwood, and Patrick Henry. " 'Before Abraham Was I Am': Does Philo Explain John 8:56–58?" *Studia Philonica*, vol. 6 (1979–1980), pp. 157–195.

U.S.A. National Committee for Lutheran World Federation and The Bishops' Committee for Ecumenical and Interreligious Affairs. "The Eucharist as Sacrifice." In *Lutherans and Catholics in Dialogue III*. New York and Washington, DC, 1967.

Van Buren, Paul. *Christ in Context*. San Francisco: Harper & Row, 1988.

―――. *A Christian Theology of the People of Israel*. New York: Seabury Press, 1983.

―――. *Discerning the Way*. New York: Seabury Press, 1980.

Vidler, Alec R. *The Church in an Age of Revolution: 1789 to the Present Day*. Baltimore: Penguin Books, 1961.

von Hügel, Baron Friederich Freoherr. *Selected Letters (1896–1924)*. London: J. M. Dent, 1928.

Vriezen, Theodorus Christiaan. *An Outline of Old Testament Theology*. Wageningen: H. Veenman, 1958.

Walker, Williston. *A History of the Christian Church*. New York: Charles Scribner's Sons, 1945.

Walsh, Liam G. *The Sacraments of Initiation: Baptism, Confirmation, Eucharist*. London: Geoffrey Chapman, 1988.

Ward, Wilfrid. *William George Ward and the Catholic Revival*. London: Macmillan, 1893.

Weger, Karl-Heinz. *Karl Rahner: An Introduction to His Theology*. New York: Seabury Press, 1980.

Welch, Claude. *In This Name: The Doctrine of the Trinity in Contemporary Theology*. New York: Charles Scribner's Sons, 1952.

Wendel, François. *Calvin: The Origin and Development of His Religious Thought*. Translated by Philip Mairet. New York and Evanston: Harper & Row, 1950.

Whale, J. S. *The Christian Answer to the Problem of Evil*. London: SCM Press, 1936.

————. *Christian Doctrine*. Cambridge: Cambridge University Press, 1950.

Whitehead, Alfred North. *Religion in the Making*. Cambridge: Cambridge University Press, 1926.

Wiles, Maurice. *The Making of Christian Doctrine*. Cambridge: Cambridge University Press, 1967.

Williams, George Huntston, and Angel M. Mergal, eds. *Spiritual and Anabaptist Writers*. Philadelphia: Westminster Press, 1957.

Williams, N. P. *The Ideas of the Fall and of Original Sin*. London: Longmans, Green and Co., 1927.

Wilmore, Gayraud S., and James H. Cone, eds. *Black Theology: A Documentary History, 1966–1979*. Maryknoll, NY: Orbis Books, 1979.

Wolfson, Harry A. *Philo: Foundations of Religious Philosophy in Judaism, Christianity, and Islam*. 2 vols. Cambridge: Harvard University Press, 1947.

————. *The Philosophy of the Church Fathers*, vol. 1. Cambridge: Harvard University Press, 1956.

Yerkes, Royden Keith. *Sacrifice in Greek and Roman Religions and Early Judaism*. New York: Charles Scribner's Sons, 1952.

Zwingli and Bullinger. Edited by G. W. Bromiley. Philadelphia: Westminster Press, 1953.

Zwingli, Ulrich. "The Sixty-Seven Articles." Reprinted in *The Protestant Reformation*, edited by Lewis W. Spitz. Englewood Cliffs, NJ: Prentice-Hall, 1966.

Index

Abelard, Peter
  on the Atonement, 109, 111, 118
  Moral Influence Theory of, 112,
    121–24
Absurd. *See* Paradox
Acts of the Apostles, The, 25, 34, 103
  baptism, confirmation in, 268, 271,
    273, 302
  Church in, 315–16
  circumcision in, 265
  kerygma in, 217
  Luke and, 29–30
  Messiahs in, 21
  ministry in, 318–20, 376
  Q and, 227
  salvation by Christ alone, 366
  Suffering Servant in, 31
Adam and Eve
  childlike, 138, 145–46
  knowledge of good and evil, 141–42
  perfection of, 126, 138, 140, 142–43
Adam's sin. *See* the Fall
Adoptionism, 6, 63, 75–76, 81–82, 85,
    97
Aelred of Rievaulx, 381
Afro-American church, 352, 374
Albert the Great, 330
Alexander VI, Pope, 336
Alexandrian Christianity, 79, 83, 86
Alienation (estrangement, separation)
  Atonement and, 101, 114, 118
  sin and, 103–4, 126, 129, 130–31, 136–
    37, 150
Alston, William, 161
Ambrose, 272, 328, 346

  on Eucharistic presence, 274, 276, 278
  on Eucharistic sacrifice, 277, 312
Americans, native, 379
Amish, 293, 340
Amman, Jacob, 340
Amos, Book of, 17–18, 259
Anabaptists
  on the Eucharist, 290
  on infant baptism, 292, 293, 340
  as sect, 324, 339–40
Anglican Church, Anglicanism, 254,
    300, 304, 311–13, 342–43, 344, 356–
    57, 361–62
Anselm of Canterbury
  on the Atonement, 109, 111, 116, 117–
    19, 120, 124, 281
  on faith and reason, 158
  on maternal imagery of God, 380
  on natural theology, 156
  on the ontological argument, 158–61
  on Original Righteousness, 129
  on Original Sin, 126, 128
Antiochean Christianity, 84–85
Anti-Semitism, 370, 371, 394 n. 13
Anti-slavery movement, 351, 373–74
Anxiety, 105, 148
Apocalyptic literature, 19, 27. *See also*
    Daniel; Enoch; Esdras; Second
Apocalyptists, 10
Apocrypha. *See* Scripture, canon of
Apollinarius, Apollinarianism, 83–84,
    87, 88, 90, 95
Apostles, Apostolic tradition, 25, 34, 79,
    200, 203, 227, 318, 321
Apostolic succession. *See* Ministry

445